Blockbuster History in the New Russia

Blockbuster History in the New Russia

Movies, Memory, and Patriotism

STEPHEN M. NORRIS

INDIANA UNIVERSITY PRESS

Bloomington & Indianapolis

This book is a publication of

Indiana University Press
601 North Morton Street
Bloomington, IN 47404-3797 USA

www.iupress.indiana.edu

Telephone orders 800-842-6796
Fax orders 812-855-7931

♾ The paper used in this publication meets the minimum requirements of the American National Standard for Information Sciences—Permanence of Paper for Printed Library Materials, ANSI Z39.48-1992.

Manufactured in the United States of America

Library of Congress Cataloging-in-Publication Data

Norris, Stephen M.
Blockbuster history in the new Russia : movies, memory, and patriotism / Stephen M. Norris.
p. cm.
Includes bibliographical references and index.
ISBN 978-0-253-00679-0 (cloth : alk. paper) — ISBN 978-0-253-00680-6 (pbk. : alk. paper) — ISBN 978-0-253-00708-7 (electronic book) 1. Motion pictures—Russia (Federation)—History—21st century. 2. Russia (Federation)—In motion pictures. 3. Patriotism in motion pictures. I. Title.
PN1993.5.R9N68 2012
791.430947—dc23

2012018524

1 2 3 4 5 18 17 16 15 14 13

To Melissa

CONTENTS

PREFACE

On July 13, 2008, I was fortunate enough to meet Grigorii Chkhartishvili. Better known by his pseudonym, Boris Akunin, he suggested that we meet at a coffee shop in Moscow's Chistie prudy neighborhood. After I interviewed him about his work on the film *The Turkish Gambit* (he wrote the screenplay), our conversation turned to politics. He joked that Russia's two greatest problems in 2008 were traffic and Putin—in that order. When I pressed him about Putin, who had recently returned to the office of prime minister, Chkhartishvili turned more serious, telling me that Putin's seemingly extraordinary popularity did not have as much to do with what he did—his particular policies—as what he did not do. The state, he suggested, had mostly left people alone for the last eight years. As a result, Russians had learned how to be individuals: they cared about the cost of a car, the cost of food and apartments, the cost of their children's education, and the traffic. Eventually, Chkhartishvili concluded, Russians will become more and more individualistic, more and more secure in their lives, and will care more about the specific policies of the state.

Over the next three years, as I finished research on this book, wrote a draft, received feedback on it, and then went through the process of submission, peer review, editing, and publication, I came to realize just how much Grigorii Chkhartishvili had articulated something significant on that Sunday in July. This project originated from my general interests in visual culture, Russian national identity, and the study of memory. Frequent trips to Russia throughout the 2000s, to work on previous projects and take part in summer workshops, made me aware of just how much Russian popular and consumer culture had changed since 1991. Fast-food places such as Elki Palki (I am a sucker for their pelmeni), coffee shops such as Shokoladnitsa (I am a sucker for their mochas, iced or hot), bookstores such as Biblio-Globus (I am a sucker for virtually everything there), and movie stores such as Soiuz (I have spent far too much money at them) had sprung up throughout Moscow and St. Petersburg during that decade. At the same time, while I was on research trips, I went to the movies a lot and watched a lot of television at night. It was hard not to realize that historical epics began to dominate big and small screens alike by 2005. *Blockbuster History in the New Russia* emerged out of these observations, and these new films seemed like the perfect source for analysis of how history in the present worked, how Russian remembrance developed after communism, and how Russian nationhood evolved since 1991. I initially connected these developments and my own experiences to the person who served as Russia's president in those years, Vladimir Putin. In an early draft, I even used the term "Putin era" in the subtitle of the book.

Over the last three years, Chkhartishvili's words have forced me to rethink its use (Serguei Oushakine also deserves thanks for making me reconceptualize this part of the project). The historical processes that helped me understand cinema, remembrance, and nationhood in the new Russia did not all come about because of Vladimir Putin. Instead, as the chapters that follow attempt to demonstrate, the patriotic culture that dominated Russia's movie screens stemmed from sources other than the state in general and Putin in particular. Certainly the Kremlin played a role in promoting this brand of Russianness (and not just through the State Agency for Cinema) and certainly capitalized on aspects of this cinematic patriotism, but it did not play the only role. My training as a historian of Russian culture led me to historical films. While researching and writing this book I read articles, newspaper pieces, reviews, blogs, and other sources that featured a cacophony of voices. Directors, producers, actors, critics, scholars, and audiences liked to argue about the meanings of the past as presented onscreen. I was struck by these arguments and by how much they differed from the usual picture of Russian politics and society as depicted in newspapers and other journals—depictions that tended to cover the state and its leaders. I decided to write about other topics and largely left Putin out.

Then, after I had submitted my final revisions of this book, Putin announced he would run for president again in 2012. Putin also named film director Stanislav Govorukhin his campaign manager. Putin's opponents began to criticize the "PR show" that would certainly drive the campaign. Russian blogs and other sites began to chatter about these decisions and what they meant. The December 4, 2011, Duma elections and all the protests that followed also channeled this discontent. In addition to blogger Aleksei Navalny (who famously dubbed Putin's United Russia "the party of crooks and thieves"), one of the most important voices of protest to gain prominence was that of Grigorii Chkhartishvili. When we met in July 2008 he told me his observations were tentative ideas. They have turned out to be prescient ideas—regardless of what happens in March 2012, when Russians return to the polls to vote for president.

This book is ultimately a history of Russia in the 2000s as told through its movies. It is mostly about memory, history, and nationhood after communism. But perhaps it will help to explain in part why the events of late 2011 and early 2012 happened—for the people involved in my story, as well as the sites I visited, all played roles in this drama.

ACKNOWLEDGMENTS

This book could not have been written without the support of a number of institutions and individuals. It is a pleasure to thank them.

Blockbuster History in the New Russia is very much a product of my association with the Havighurst Center for Russian and Post-Soviet Studies at Miami University. The intellectual atmosphere and interdisciplinary spirit fostered by the Center inspired the book and gave me a place to test out ideas. Karen Dawisha, the Center's director, has created a special place and I am grateful to be a part of it. My colleagues Venelin Ganev, Scott Kenworthy, Neringa Klumbyte, Dan Prior, and Gulnaz Sharafutdinova have offered insightful critiques at various stages of the project. Vitaly Chernetsky and Ben Sutcliffe have done the same and also fielded numerous questions about translations. I was also fortunate to have Doug Rodgers, Michael Rouland, Brigid O'Keeffe, and Josh First as colleagues when they all held postdocs at the Center. Doug provided early comments on this project, Michael introduced me to Kazakh cinema, Brigid gave useful suggestions in our works-in-progress series, and Josh read an entire draft of this book.

Writing about Russian film gave me an entryway into another remarkable community of scholars. Denise Youngblood, the preeminent historian of Russian and Soviet cinema, has been a great inspiration and a great supporter of this project, reading various parts of this book and a rough draft of the manuscript. Vladimir Padunov invited me to write reviews for *KinoKultura* and allowed me to test out for the first time many of the ideas that appear in this book. He also invited me to speak at the 2008 Pittsburgh Russian Film Symposium, where I met a number of Russian film scholars. Among the Pittsburgh crowd, I particularly want to thank Nancy Condee, Greg Dolgopolov, Sasha Prokhorov, Lena Prokhorova, and Dawn Seckler (if I could thank everyone by name at the 2008 symposium and get away with it, I would).

Although she was unable to attend the Pittsburgh party, Birgit Beumers has been a valuable resource for this project ever since I met her at the 2006 Central Asian Film Festival in Almaty, Kazakhstan. Birgit has supplied a great deal of information since that time, invited me to test out ideas at various conferences, and, after she became editor of *KinoKultura,* continued to invite me to write reviews for that journal. Anyone working on contemporary Russian film knows how invaluable Birgit's expertise is; I am fortunate that she has shared it with me so often.

Others have shared their expertise as well. A Dolibois Grant from Miami's Farmer School of Business allowed me to travel to Moscow in July 2008 and conduct interviews with a number of people involved in the film industry. I thank Natal′ia Markova at the Foundation for the Support of Patriotic Cinema, Leonid Baglai and Sergei Gurevich at Studio Tri-te, Karen Shakhnazarov at Mosfil′m, Grigorii Chkhartishvili, and Father Vladimir Vigilianskii for enlightening conversations. A meeting with Aleksei Balabanov in July 2007 still ranks as one of my most memorable experiences in the last decade (and I am sure the rest of the Miami people with me on that day would agree). And a special thank-you goes to Andrei Riabovichev and Dmitrii Puchkov for answering a number of e-mail queries (and again to Andrei for agreeing to let me reproduce his work for *Prince Vladimir*).

Various parts of the chapters that follow were presented at Miami University; the University of Cincinnati (which hosted the 2005 IAMHST conference); the Eurasian Film Festival in Almaty, Kazakhstan; several AAASS (and then ASEEES) annual conferences; the University of Pennsylvania; the Pittsburgh Russian Film Symposium; the American Philosophical Society (as part of the APS / Humboldt Foundation annual humanities symposium); the Eighth World Congress of ICCEES in Stockholm, Sweden; and the University of Montana. I thank all the people responsible for invitations and acceptances to these venues and particularly to all the receptive audiences. Earlier versions of these chapters first appeared in *The Historical Journal of Film, Radio, and Television; KinoKultura;* and *Studies in Russian and Soviet Cinema.* I thank the journal editors for allowing me to reprint portions of these articles. Lara McCoy Roslof has also allowed me to publish pieces about recent Russian cinema for *Russia Beyond the Headlines,* and I thank her for the opportunity to write for a broader audience.

The history department at Miami University continues to be the most collegial place I have ever encountered. All of my colleagues have at one time or another heard me go on and on about film; I thank them for humoring me. Drew Cayton, Erik Jensen, and Amanda McVety have humored me more than anyone else and deserve particular gratitude.

Serguei Oushakine deserves an entire paragraph of thanks. I first met Serguei at a Havighurst Center conference in October 2005, and discovered we had many shared intellectual interests. From that time on, Serguei has provided a steady stream of information, invited me to take part in conferences, and read several versions of chapters. He also read the first draft of this book and then revealed himself to be one of the anonymous reviewers for Indiana University Press. Serguei's critiques have made this book far better.

After working with Indiana on two edited volumes, Janet Rabinowitch, director of the Press, asked me what my next book would be about. She expressed early interest in my answer and has remained a firm supporter of this project from its inception. Peter Froehlich, Angela Burton, and June Silay also deserve a great deal of thanks for this latest project. And Dawn Ollila has been the perfect copyeditor for two of my books with the Press.

Finally, my sons, Jack and Sam, had to watch far too many Russian films in their young lives. Most of these viewings came in the middle of the night while I held them and gave them bottles, so I'll call it even. Melissa Cox Norris has not had to endure any late-night screenings, but has had to endure much, much more. Dedicating this book to her once again seems like not enough, but I hope it will do.

Blockbuster History
in the New Russia

Karo's October Theater, New Arbat Street, 2008. Soviet symbols compete with Hollywood blockbusters.

INTRODUCTION

Multiplexing Russia

The renovated October Theater on Moscow's New Arbat Street is a nice place to watch a film. Owned and operated by the Karo Group, Russia's largest multiplexer, October houses eleven state-of-the-art cinema halls, Karo's offices, a video store, restaurants, and other commercial outlets. You can sit and have gelato or grab a cocktail before you watch your movie.

The theater is also a battleground. October has clearly made the transition from a Soviet-era movie house into a post-Soviet multiplex, but in making this change, October and its fellow Karo multiplexes have become sites of contestation. These theaters are not just entertainment centers: they are the foci of heated debates about Russian national cinema, post-Soviet politics, and the state of patriotism.

Founded in 1997, Karo Film first renovated the crown jewel of Russian cinema halls, the Rossiia [Russia] Theater on Moscow's Pushkin Square. In 2000 it opened the first-ever Russian multiplex at Moscow's first Ramstore (the Turkish-based mega supermarket chain). A year later, Karo unveiled its first multiplexes in St. Petersburg and Nizhnii Novgorod. By 2008, the company had built in Samara, Kazan′, and Kaliningrad, as well as in Moscow suburbs such as Podolsk and Mytishchi. The company boasts that it runs 34 modern multiplexes with 165 cinema halls, serving a capacity of 38,000. In total, 1.55 million Russians watch films on Karo screens each month.[1]

These statistics are impressive, all the more so given the state of Russian cinema in 2000. The Soviet film industry was once one of the world's largest, putting out 150 films per year. Soviet citizens once went to the movies more than any other people on earth—twenty times per annum per capita in the 1960s and 1970s.[2] By 1996, average cinema attendance in the former Soviet Union had fallen thirty- to fortyfold: only one in four Russians went to the movies once per year. By then, American and European films made up 75 percent of the movies shown on Russian screens. The state of Russian film, therefore, reflected the state of Russia itself: dilapidated, chaotic, and wistfully recalling its glory days.

In 1996, however, the situation changed. Paul Heth of Eastman Kodak opened the first state-of-the-art cinema in Moscow. Heth named the cinema—located in an old movie hall near Pushkin Square—Kodak KinoMir, or Kodak Cinema World. The Cinema World model suggested that multiplexes could get Russians back to the movies: the theater sold out for nearly two years straight and the first film screened there, the Nicolas Cage blockbuster *The Rock,* brought lines of cinemagoers.[3] It was right after Kodak's success that Leonid Ogorodnikov founded Karo and funded the renovation of the Rossiia, which was renamed Pushkin Theater.

"In the early nineties," Ogorodnikov states, "no one believed that the cinema industry could recover: all the cinemas were empty. Some were furniture parlors, others were car shops."[4] Buoyed by Heth's success, Ogorodnikov got into the cinema business and plunged into the Rossiia project. The renovated Pushkin opened for the Moscow International Film Festival in 1997. Said Ogorodnikov, "[W]e analyzed the financial results [of Pushkin's renovation] and came to the conclusion that [it] could be interesting and lucrative. So we decided to focus on theaters." He admitted, "[W]e didn't study this business: no one in the country held such knowledge."[5] By 2000, the Pushkin Theater had been visited by four million people, making it the most popular site to watch a film in Russia.

The multiplex alone could not get Russians back to the theaters. Nice halls with Dolby surround sound represented steps in the right direction, but what appeared on screen had to meet the spectators' expectations. "While choosing the repertoire for our Company," Ogorodnikov stated, "we first look at the commercial expediency and commercial potential of the movie." Karo Film held the Russian premieres of Hollywood blockbusters such as *Titanic* and *Pearl Harbor.* In September 1999, the company signed an agreement with Warner Brothers to distribute their films, which included the *Matrix* series, the *Harry Potter* series, and *The Lord of the Rings* trilogy.[6] The initial success of Karo and the return of the Russian spectator to theaters came through screening Hollywood blockbusters in American-style multiplexes. Even popcorn and cola—quintessential American movie treats, but unavailable in Soviet movie houses—"became an indispensable feature of a modern Russian cinema visit."[7]

Hollywood blockbusters may have brought people back, but they also served as the impetus for patriotic renewal. The perceived threat that American cinema posed for Russian culture loomed large in the minds of filmmakers and government officials. Some in the film industry pushed for quotas on the number of American films to be screened. Ogorodnikov and others opposed the idea, stating categorically, "you cannot improve the Russian cinema industry by implementing any quotas."[8] Improvement instead came through adapting Hollywood techniques to Russian themes. Karo Film got into this game and set up a production company that makes the corporation not just the largest multiplexer in Russia, but also a significant financial backer of Russian movies.

Their formula has worked. In 2000 the country had just 78 modern screens housed in fifty-five theaters. In 2008, the number of state-of-the-art screens in Russia surpassed 1,500.[9] That year, the head of the Federal Agency for Culture and Cinematography declared that 2,500 new screens would open each year thereafter.[10] Russian cinema enjoyed a much-discussed revival in the early 2000s, largely because of the appearance of "Russian" blockbusters such as Timur Bekmambetov's *Night Watch,* which debuted at the Pushkin Theater and smashed box-office records in 2004. Other blockbusters followed, beginning a debate about the relationship between the new Russian cinema of Karo and its competitors and whether or not this cinema was really "Russian" at all. Critics argued that the Karo formula essentially replaced "Russian cinema" with Hollywood-style blockbusters.

The new blockbuster, as Oleg Sul′kin has argued, combined American styles with Russian content: "Russian filmmakers realized they couldn't make a pure genre picture. Their films continue to be guided by the notion that a film must have an idea, a message, convey the national spirit somehow."[11] Success—and by 2008 Russian films made up nearly 40 percent of the market—came by merging the past with contemporary patriotism. Mikhail Shvydkoi, who in 2000–2004 served as the minister of culture, and afterward as director of the Federal Agency for Culture and Cinematography, promised that his agencies would fund "films of a patriotic and historical nature" and "films for children." These films, he stated, would "send a particular message to the Russian people: that Russia is once again in the ascendant, and that family values and hard work can conquer all."[12] The key for Shvydkoi, in other words, was to create blockbuster history.

After the success of *Night Watch,* a fantasy epic based on a popular series of novels set in 1990s Moscow, Russian cinema increasingly looked to the past. In 2005, the action-detective epic *The Turkish Gambit,* which was set during the Russo-Turkish War of 1877–78, broke the record for the highest-grossing film in Russian history. Just a few months later, the Afghan War picture *Ninth Company* shattered its records. When Vladimir Putin watched the film at a private screening, he declared the Russian film industry "reborn."[13] This rebirth came about because enough Russian filmmakers and film producers wanted to develop "audience-friendly films" for Russian consumers. At the same time, the leading lights of the Russian film world wanted to make movies with a "Russian" content. They found that Hollywood blockbusters, in order to appeal to a worldwide market, tended to ignore the past. The days of the American historical epic exemplified by *Gone with the Wind* had long since vanished—when Hollywood made blockbuster history, it tended to be with epics such as *Troy* or romantic dramas such as *Titanic.* The Hollywood blockbuster that dominates worldwide box offices does not attempt to ask questions or provide meaningful answers about history.[14] In the view of many Russian critics and filmmakers, "Hollywood blockbuster" means fancy special effects, a sophisticated marketing campaign, and an empty plot. Blockbusters by nature do not educate, they entertain, and in doing so establish American cultural hegemony. At the same time,

Hollywood blockbusters are popular worldwide, a fact that everyone in the Russian industry acknowledged and many envied. To combat Hollywood's influence, critics believed, Russian film had to become more like Hollywood blockbusters. It had to become a business that could also appeal to domestic consumers.[15] The key lay in the past.

Blockbuster History in the New Russia examines the links between economics, politics, history, memory, patriotism, and cinema in the New Russia. The birth of blockbuster history—or the way American cultural practices could be adapted to make Russian historical epics—parallels the rise of Putin and the resurgence of Russian political nationalism. These links and processes, as this book argues, are far from coincidental but not always connected, for what Leonid Ogorodnikov discovered in his 1997 business plan was precisely what Vladimir Putin discovered to be useful in his presidential administration: patriotism and the past sell.

RUSSIAN THEATERS OF MEMORY

Karo's multiplexes and the blockbuster histories screened inside function as theaters of memory. Films serve as a powerful medium that shape individual and group memories of the past. This memory work is complex and sometimes contradictory—films are read in multiple ways by different audiences and groups. Historical films in particular subvert pre-existing narratives as often as they reinforce them.[16] In this significant role, movies offer a performance of the past and past memories. Like all performances, they require behind-the-scenes production beforehand, they offer certain stories about the past when they appear, they receive reviews after this occasion, and then become the subject of water cooler, online, and other forms of discussions. This process of remembrance begins with the people who produce cinematic memories and ends with the people who make sense of the memories they see onscreen. In the case of post-Soviet cinematic remembrance, the behind-the-scenes production developed out of a host of particular perceptions that shaped the 1990s. Remembering the past was not about getting it right; in the zero years (as Russians frequently refer to the 2000s) Russian remembrance used the past as a means of projecting present-day pride.

This process of historical remembrance has not taken place within a vacuum. All over the former Soviet empire national cinema traditions reasserted themselves by making historical blockbusters. Most of these cinematic acts of remembrance explored pasts that communist governments had censored. Most also used the past to illustrate how Soviet control had harmed the "real history" of the country in question. Post-Soviet cinematic narratives directly responded to the Soviet memory project: the Bolsheviks took power in 1917 believing that they were following the laws of history. Because of this ideological stance, officials began to oversee the creation of new historical narratives in a process one historian has called "the rapid 'Bolshevizing' of revolutionary memory."[17] Soviet historians had to follow certain scripts when writing about the past—and so, too, did filmmakers, authors, and artists. By the Stalin era, cinema had become the medium of history itself and, more than any other media form, created historical myths and provided the "right" historical interpretations to the past.[18] The result of this state memory project was, as Aleksandr Solzhenitsyn argued rather forcefully, that "what we remember is not what actually happened, not history, but merely that hackneyed dotted line they have chosen to drive into our memories by incessant hammering."[19] History over the course of the Soviet period became an evolving state memory project.

Across the former Second World, filmmakers and film audiences attempted to overturn the Soviet memory project, to unmake and remake historical memories, transforming socialist-era narratives about the past into postsocialist plots.[20] Filmmakers frequently mined the past to create new national narratives that in part blamed the ills of the twentieth century on Russia. In the Czech Republic, for example, Jan Svěrák's 2001 *Dark Blue World* told the story of Czech pilots who had fought for the British Air Force during World War II and who had later been imprisoned by communist authorities for this service. Coming on the heels of Svěrák's Academy Award–winning *Kolya, Dark Blue World* had the largest budget in Czech film history and earned $2 million at the domestic box office.[21] Andrzej Wajda reinterpreted the past for present-day audiences in several postcommunist films, most notably his 1999 adaptation of the Polish epic *Pan Tadeusz* and his 2007 *Katyń,* which focused upon the 1940 murder of Polish officers by Soviet NKVD agents (Wajda's father was among those murdered). The massacre had long been the source of antagonistic relations between Poland and the Soviet Union. Wajda's film debuted on September 17, the anniversary of the Soviet invasion of Poland in 1939. "I think my film shows how the lie about Katyn was brought to Poland with the Red Army and the communist administration," he commented, "and how this lie—that the Polish officers were murdered by the Germans—lingered for so many years." The Polish president, Lech Kaczynski, attempted to use the film's debut to score domestic political points at the expense of relations with Russia.[22] The film made $13.5 million in Poland, making it the highest-grossing domestic film of all time.[23] The Czech and Polish pattern was replicated across the former Soviet space: films that revised World War II narratives enjoyed particular popularity and frequently cast nationalities as double victims of both Nazi and Soviet systems.[24]

In the new Russia, the process of remembrance began from the same point but took a different path. Several specific contexts shaped the work of memory that got screened in cinema halls. None was more significant than the ways the 1990s—Boris Yeltsin's decade—shaped Russian attitudes. The Yeltsin years quickly came to be seen by most Russians as a distinct epoch in history. In part this view emerged when Yeltsin resigned on New Year's Eve 1999. Most Russians believed they had lived in a permanent state of crisis during the decade, transforming the extraordinary into the routine as the economy experienced a downturn far worse than the Great Depression.[25] By the time Russian cinema had recovered, and in part because of the messages Russian blockbuster history offered, the feeling of a permanent state of crisis had ended.

History, or more precisely historical memory, proved to be central to this end of an era and birth of a new one. Vladimir Sorokin, the outspoken and controversial writer, claimed that "the ordeal of the free market turned out to be more frightening than the Gulag, and more burdensome than the bloody war years, because it forced people to part with the oneiric space of collective slumber, forced them to leave the ideally balanced Stalinist cosmos behind."[26] Hyperbolic though he may be, Sorokin had a point: the introduction of a market-based economy in the 1990s, in other words, forced Russians to leave Soviet ways of life behind. Its extreme hardships meant that the Soviet era became history; that is, something from the past that could no longer be conceived of as belonging to the present. Russian filmmakers could begin to revise the historical productions of Soviet cinema; Russian filmgoers could do the same. What Leonid Ogorodnikov began to discover in 1997 was that Russians wanted to find a way out of the chaos that was the 1990s. They wanted to begin to feel proud of themselves and proud of their history again. They wanted, in part, to follow the path of Danila Bagrov.

DANILA'S WORLD: FROM OVERKILL CULTURE TO PATRIOTIC CULTURE

The paradigmatic hero of the 1990s was Danila Bagrov, the protagonist in Aleksei Balabanov's extraordinarily popular films *Brother* (*Brat,* 1997) and *Brother 2* (*Brat 2,* 2000). The first film became an instant cult classic, making the director and the star (Sergei Bodrov, Jr.) into celebrities. Danila (Bodrov) is a recently demobilized soldier who heads to St. Petersburg to find his brother. He, like his fellow Russians, is searching for a meaning to his life. His mother tells him to head to St. Petersburg and to work for his brother. Danila obeys. The city he encounters is very much a Dostoevskian force of evil, controlled by bandits. Danila's brother is a professional hit man and soon employs his little brother in this work. Danila operates in a world without order and rules; he kills people who deserve it and feels no remorse. His world, while stylized and exaggerated, is the Russia of the 1990s.

Throughout the film, Danila searches for the new CD by Nautilius Pompilius. Although he owns a Sony Discman and shops in the new kiosks and stores that have sprung up after communism, Danila wants *Russian* rock. Danila metes out justice against "black-asses" from the Caucasus and against the non-Russian gangsters who seem to control the city. He provides order in a landscape that lacks it. In the face of the "chasm of unbelief" that opened up after 1991, Danila offered viewers something to believe in again, even if it was a patriotism of despair.[27] No wonder the oligarch Boris Berezovskii declared that "if you want to understand the 1990s in Russia, watch *Brother.*"

The sequel initially finds Danila in Moscow, where he learns that the brother of one of his army buddies is a hockey player for the Chicago Blackhawks who is being blackmailed by an American businessman. Danila heads to Chicago, where he shoots his way through a maze of African American pimps and gangsters to rescue both a Russian prostitute and the hockey player. In the final scene, as Danila confronts the businessman, he says, "Tell me, American, does power come from money? I think the person who has the truth [*pravda*] is the more powerful one." *Brother 2* was a sensation in the summer of 2000. It featured a host of lines that became popular slang: "'Are you gangsters?' 'No, we are Russians'"; "We Russians have to stick together"; "Russians never give up on their own." Nautilius Pompilius's perestroika-era song "Goodbye, America" plays throughout the film and, as Anthony Anemone argues, "punctuate[s] the end of the 'utopian dream' of America for Balabanov's audience."[28]

Brother 2 represented the apotheosis of what Eliot Borenstein has termed "overkill culture"; that is, the violent and nihilistic excess that saturated Russian popular culture throughout the 1990s. Balabanov's film also gave birth to the culture of the early zero years, a new nationalistic form of patriotism that centered on rejecting Americanization and proclaiming Russian strength. The film appeared May 11, 2000, just two months after Vladimir Putin won the presidential elections. *Brother 2*'s popularity can be explained in part because audiences viewed Danila as a new hero to emulate.[29] Danila's vigilante justice meted out to African American pimps resembled a first-person shooter game and tapped into the rage of many Russians, who were fed up with the culture of *bespredel* (literally, "without limits") and dissatisfied with the state of the market economy. The video game based on the movie provided some Russians with the opportunity to say "goodbye to America" by shooting American pimps, while the catchphrases and messages of the film gave audiences a chance to rebel against the 1990s and believe that a strong, patriotic Russia had reappeared.

The reaction among young people was particularly significant. *Iskusstvo kino* commissioned Evgenii Gusiatinskii, an eighteen-year-old student at VGIK, the state film school, to write about *Brother 2*'s importance. He wrote,

> How we lived earlier without the brother is completely incomprehensible. It seems as if he had always existed. It is just *we* who had gone astray, set off down the wrong path. But with our brother it is possible no longer to be afraid; he will always point out exactly the right road. The brother lived, lives, and will live. . . . *Brother 2* is quite possibly the most important picture in the history of post-perestroika cinema. . . . The lead character is not Danila Bagrov, but each person sitting in the hall. . . . It is completely obvious to me that the *Brother 2* phenomenon is first of all social and ideological and secondly artistic and cinematic.[30]

Gusiatinskii argues that post-Soviet culture had been based on negatives. What had previously been impermissible became possible. The result of this freedom, as he sees it, was destruction, a "complete negation of the past." "This process of destruction," he argues, "has to have an end." It came with *Brother 2,* which "overturns the entire process of post-perestroika cinema" by returning to the past, for the film is "the first post-Soviet film that completely resuscitates our Soviet past with all its components."[31] What Gusiatinskii meant is that Balabanov's brothers do not attempt to hide the fact that they were born in the Soviet Union and have had to deal with its loss. At the same time, Gusiatinskii notes that *Brother 2* captures "two parallel realities, without which it is difficult to imagine life today—television and video games."[32] The movie was shot as an extended music video of sorts and the plot begins at Ostankino, the tower of Russia's largest station. The narrative structure of the film, as noted above, also follows that of popular video games. Gusiatinskii argued that the film successfully captured the emerging popular media and popular culture in postsocialist Russia while also articulating a Soviet-era desire to "catch up and overtake America."[33]

Brother and *Brother 2* established the contours of blockbuster history in the zero years. Balabanov embraced Western genres while using the gangster film and the film sequel—two genres he borrowed from Hollywood—to reject perceived American cultural intrusion. Danila Bagrov lives in a world that is far removed from the Soviet one. He remains "Russian," though, and specifically seeks Russian consumer products and helps his Russian brothers along the way. Bagrov's post-Soviet world is one that reveals the "creative destruction" that capitalism brought—in this instance, the influx of Western goods that forced Russians to adapt, to think about the market, and to develop products that borrowed from American styles but simultaneously appealed to Russian consumers.[34] What concerned Danila and Russians like him was that American products threatened to destroy "traditional Russian culture." The solution for so many Russians, as the following chapters argue, was to create something new that could appeal to patriotism.[35] Because of these circumstances, consumption had become a potent cultural symbol by the end of the 1990s: whereas the terms "ours" and "native" had referred to Soviet products before 1992, increasingly they became ethnic and political terms that excluded "alien" groups.[36]

This patriotic process in turn shaped the way Russian filmmakers represented the past on screen and how audiences made sense of the meanings of cinematic remembrance. Danila's world captured the turn toward "Russian products" while also focusing cinemagoers and filmmakers alike on the need to adapt Western genres to Russian circumstances. Danila became a representation of the move from a patriotism of despair, one that centered on loss and a nihilistic outlook on post-Soviet life, to a patriotism of pride, one in which Russians could reassert themselves and view their history differently. Danila's decisions signified a new way of thinking about what was "patriotic" in post-Soviet Russia.

Patriotism had served as one of the primary values binding Soviet citizens together. As Stephen Lovell has argued, "the sense that the USSR was a great world power, that it had achieved great things (whatever crimes its leaders had perpetrated in the process), that it had saved Europe from the catastrophe of Nazism . . . may well have kept Soviet socialism in business as a belief system for longer than it would otherwise have warranted."[37] Balabanov's films perfectly illustrated the search for a new meaning in Russia that communism's collapse precipitated. *Brother* illuminates a Russia without values. By the time *Brother 2* appeared, Russian political parties and political actors had begun to appeal to a "patriotism" that could mobilize the population. Balabanov's sequel also was of a new genre, the "Russian blockbuster," which belonged to this mobilization. *Brother 2*—and Danila's behavior within it—thus initiated what can be called blockbuster history.

WHAT IS THE RUSSIAN BLOCKBUSTER?

The debates about the state of Russian cinema took place as part of the general process of unmaking Soviet life. The development of homegrown blockbusters, as Karo's story indicates, took place largely after the August 1998 collapse of the ruble. With the economy in shambles again, Russian movie producers and television producers needed cheaper, native products marketed as audience friendly. They needed *Russian* blockbusters. The term "blockbuster" (*blokbaster*) itself became part of the Russian language, and whether "Russian blockbusters" represented a rebirth or a death of national cinema became a hotly contested issue.

The year 1998 emerged as a year of preconditions for the birth of blockbuster history. In December 1997 Nikita Mikhalkov was elected president of the Russian Filmmakers Union: five months later, he delivered a speech that called for "new heroes" in Russian cinema who would build a new Russian patriotism. In April 1998 Karen Shakhnazarov became the head of Mosfil′m and openly called for "audience-friendly cinema" as a means of reviving the Russian cinema industry. That year Konstantin Ernst, the general producer at ORT, produced his first feature-length film and decided that cinema, particularly television serials, could be a catalyst for a new Russia. In 1998, four books written by an unknown author named Boris Akunin appeared: *Azazel′, Turkish Gambit, The Leviathan,* and *The Death of Achilles.* Akunin became a sensation, introducing Russians to a new literary hero and a new way of viewing the tsarist past. And in that year the newly renamed and refurbished Pushkin Theater sold more movie tickets than the rest of the Russian movie theaters combined. Blockbuster history was conceived out of these developments.

By the zero years in Russia, the most widely felt desire was for patriotism. Homegrown products increasingly were sold by appealing to patriotism as a brand. The impetus for this "brand Russia" came with the 1998 ruble collapse and with it the need for cheaper products for Russian consumers. New "national" advertising found that patriotism sold best when packaged as part of Russian history.[38] The most successful emotional brand, and one that film followed, was one packaged around "our" history, "our" cinema, and "our" heroes.

The Russian blockbuster emerged out of these trends. In September 2005, the St. Petersburg film journal *Seans* (*Performance*) devoted a special issue to defining it. In Lidiia Maslova's view, the "Russian blockbuster" developed from Aleksei Balabanov's *Brother* films, which "inherited American traditions" but made them more "cynical" by "breaking down the boundaries between good and evil." American blockbusters, in other words, have good guys who win; Russian blockbusters are more likely to have the bad guys win.[39] Both Denis Gorelov and Evgenii Maizel′ believed that the Russian blockbuster emerged from Boris Akunin's popularity and the "retro-history" he created. Maizel′ dismissed the history onscreen in Akunin adaptations such as *Turkish Gambit* and instead declared the film to be "representative of the breed of Russian blockbusters" because it was "predominately made with the yeast of *kvas* patriotism." The film, and others such as *Night Watch*, goes down well with Russians who want a "nostalgic, retrograde idea" about Russianness. Maizel′ connects the rise of kvas patriotism onscreen to political events: it produced Putin's enthusiasm for "a united and indivisible" Russia that would also taste like a patriotic drink.[40] Larisa Iusipova, echoing other writers in the special issue, believed that the Russian blockbuster could be defined through its attempts "to compete with Hollywood at the box office" by employing Hollywood-style advertising. The central site of this battle, she argues, is Karo's Pushkin Cinema and its policy of "showing our films." The main "ideologue" of this battle, Iusipova posits, is Konstantin Ernst, who employs "patriotic rhetoric" in order to promote films he produces. Ernst's formula is the same as Karo's: "to make big blockbusters, to put them out in a maximum number of copies, to screen them in as many cinemas as possible, and to use an aggressive, expensive advertising campaign" that brands them as "Russian."[41]

Seans also asked a host of important people associated with the film industry "what is the Russian blockbuster?" The responses demonstrated just how contested an issue the "audience-friendly" film formula developed by Karo Film was. Shakhnazarov, the head of Mosfil′m, declared that the Russian blockbuster was "a necessary segment of our film market" while also warning that some films could be "too Americanized." Russian directors, he stated, have to "not only borrow forms, to master technologies, and to develop new habits, they also have to introduce something of our national culture."[42] Pavel Chukhrai, the director of some art-house hits that explored the Soviet past, stated that blockbusters nevertheless are "a necessary and important development in our cinematography, but they must be made to draw the spectator, to make them get a taste for Russian cinema, for the Russian language, for Russian heroes, and for the history of our country."[43] For those who responded positively, most agreed that blockbusters could be good as long as they contained something "Russian," something patriotic. On the other side of the debate, the actress Renata Litvinova called blockbusters "not very interesting" and "a tomb for our directors and authors." Vadim Abdrashitov, art-house director, declared, "[T]he Russian blockbuster is our contribution to the worldwide process of cinema-hamburgerization [*kinogamburgerov*]."[44] Resistance to such blockbusters was also seen as a patriotic act. For opponents of this "hamburger culture," art-house cinema could be the way to preserve "Russian" film.[45]

The journal's debates highlight an important point: while everyone surveyed agreed there was such a thing as the "Russian blockbuster," no one agreed upon a central definition of what one was and what it meant for the Russian national film tradition. Most agreed that it had something to do with special effects, big budgets, and big PR campaigns (all hallmarks of the American blockbuster). Yet beyond these basics, people disagreed about what the Russian blockbuster was—it might make money at the box office, but many also suggested that the hallmark of the *Russian* blockbuster was the use of a big budget to make the past appeal to the present. The multiplex and the domestic blockbusters screened in them became the focus for sustained debates. They also served as the focus for a wide-ranging discussion on the state of Russian history and the state of Russian patriotism.

NATIONHOOD IN THE ZERO YEARS: A SHORT COURSE ON BLOCKBUSTER HISTORY

The advent of the market era in Russia produced disillusionment combined with resignation that the new economy was here to stay. The imaginary West that had developed under socialism—an invented dream land created in the minds of Soviet citizens who could not travel abroad—

eroded during the 1990s in the encounter with market capitalism.[46] At the same time, Russia experienced the dilemma of Americanization in a fashion similar to—although more rapidly than—European countries, who had all been seduced by and simultaneously resisted the irresistible empire that American consumer culture represented.[47] The postsocialist Russian response to this new culture of consumption was a patriotic one. On the one hand, more and more Russian companies urged consumers to purchase "Russian" goods. On the other hand, new companies made these appeals in the language and forms of the consumer culture they allegedly resisted.

Blockbuster History in the New Russia follows this story by focusing on film, one of the most significant loci for debates about the Americanization of Russia after communism. Film became a central site for the acceptance of American styles and simultaneously for articulating resistance to American market forces. Russian history and historical remembrance provided the scripts for this process and moviemakers found fertile historical territory to explore. Because of the way television came to dominate Russian cinema in the zero years—the largest producers of feature films are television stations—blockbuster history played out on both large and small screens.[48] The people behind this production of the past and its subsequent screening of memory were not just film directors—television producers, businessmen, and even popular authors all played a role in the behind-the-scenes development of the historical blockbuster. Films explicitly billed as "blockbusters"—using Ernst's formula—dominated the revival of Russian cinema at the multiplexes that sprouted up. At the same time, several films became cultural phenomena because of the attention they received (Pavel Lungin's *The Island,* for example): they, too, deserve to be understood as blockbusters.

What got screened took place because of the work done by composers, animators, video game entrepreneurs, critics, and spectators. The following chapters examine films that appeared after 1999. All were set in the past yet all used history for present-day patriotic purposes. All attempted to answer Shvydkoi's call for "films of a patriotic and historical nature." The chapters that explore these movies also explore the stories behind their production and the public discourses they generated. Each focuses on a particular film and a particular person associated with the film's production. Their stories collectively tell us how historical memory work developed and how Russian patriotism has been redefined after communism. *Blockbuster History in the New Russia* is organized like a Karo multiplex. The chapters—while arranged thematically and chronologically—can be read individually or out of order in a fashion similar to checking out what played at the local Karo multiplex.

This book tells the story of the zero years and the cultural obsessions with patriotism and the past. It differs from the conclusions reached by Nancy Condee in her absorbing study of recent Russian cinema, *The Imperial Trace*. Condee examines the films of six directors and how they indicate "Russia's cultural environment and its distinct difference from the national cultures of Western Europe."[49] This difference largely is the result, Condee posits, of the absence of a robust national identity in Russia. Building on the work of a number of scholars and theorists,[50] Condee concludes that Russian cinema today reflects the historic lack of nationhood and the loss felt by the imperial collapse of 1991. Their films indicate the country's "imperial cascade" and "respond with impulses, manifestly diverse but sharing a common engagement with that process, whether that engagement is expressed as a move toward nostalgic conservation, apocalyptic acceleration, undoing what has been done, transcoding it into a different symbolic register with different valences, or other forms of serotine play."[51] Post-Soviet cinema, in other words, carries in it the traces of loss; it contains the vestiges of a vanished imperial culture.

Blockbuster History in the New Russia reaches a different conclusion to the same story by arguing that historical blockbusters generated widespread discussions about patriotism and belonging in the new Russia. Filmmakers, producers, screenwriters, composers, and other people involved in the cinema industry all attempted to articulate their vision of a "patriotic" film. They did so by traveling to the past. At the same time, the "patriotism" articulated onscreen led to widespread debates about what "Russian patriotism" meant in the post-Soviet period. For some, it conveyed nationalistic connotations: "our" films ultimately helped to perpetuate an ethnically Russian bond. Others interpreted the cinematic pasts offered onscreen as a chance to feel individual pride in their country and its history. *Blockbuster History,* therefore, analyzes the ways in which historical films encoded ideas about patriotism as well as the ways in which audiences decoded these appeals to Russianness. What got recreated on screen in the 2000s served as a primary battleground for the redefinition of the Russian nation after communism. Historical films not only attempted to wrestle with contentious pasts; they also offered visual and aural menus of Russianness that audiences could consume.[52] As the following chapters reveal, blockbuster history films contained familiar symbols, scenes, and sounds that provided an à la carte menu of Russianness for audiences to select from and to reinterpret as the basis for a new nationhood.[53] Contemporary Russian films certainly carried traces of empire within them; they also contained elements of nationhood.[54]

Patriotic journeys to the past also charted the paths that cinematic remembrance took in the zero years, beginning with blockbusters about the late tsarist era. This "Russia that we lost" (to invoke Stanislav Govorukhin's influential 1992 documentary of that name) became the source of a renewed sense of Russianness that stretched beyond the Soviet era. Movies such as Mikhalkov's *The Barber of Siberia* and Shakhnazarov's *The Rider Named Death* reminded viewers of a past that had vanished after 1917. Beginning in 2002, and exploding onscreen in 2004, films about the Great Patriotic War explored the one Soviet event about which most contemporary Russians could feel pride. These cinematic explorations reinforced the war's importance and also shattered Soviet myths. Interest in the Great Patriotic War fueled interest in the Brezhnev era. Several mid-decade polls suggested that Russians considered the era of developed socialism to be a Golden Age.[55] Filmmakers served as guides to this remembrance, exploring Orthodoxy under communism and even nostalgia for Brezhnev-era cinema. As the zero years ended, fantasy history replaced these explorations. Blockbusters invented alternative historical realities, whether set in the Soviet period, the pre-Kyivan past, or a mythic seventeenth century. These paths are charted in four sections that follow. Russian blockbuster history offered a chance for audiences to escape into alternative histories: the tsarist era to the Russia we lost, Great Patriotic War films to the patriotism displayed by their parents' generation, late socialism to the values of stable socialism and a lost childhood, and fantasy history to an invented past with clear values.

It is clear that Leonid Ogorodnikov, the founder of Karo Film, did not just develop multiplexes. He took part in the renovation of Russian cinema, Russian history, Russian memory, Russian values, and the Russian nation. Soon after Karo renovated the Pushkin Theater and launched its plans to multiplex Russia, Nikita Mikhalkov launched his epic film *The Barber of Siberia.* Mikhalkov successfully branded himself and his film as examples of the "new Russian patriotism." *The Barber of Siberia* had its premiere at the Kremlin and produced a great deal of fireworks after its release. His reimagining of the "Russia that we lost" also defined the dominant culture of the zero years.

PART ONE

The Russia That We Lost

If a film's success can be measured by how well it defines an era and enters public discourse, then Stanislav Govorukhin's documentary *The Russia That We Lost* (*Rossiia, kotoruiu my poteriali,* 1992) may be the most significant movie of the 1990s. Aired on television as the Soviet Union was disintegrating around the viewers who tuned in, Govorukhin's film visualizes a prerevolutionary Russia where peasants were healthy and happy, workers earned a living wage, projects such as the Trans-Siberian Railroad made Russia powerful, and vibrant aristocratic and intellectual cultures flourished. Based on S. S. Ol′denburg's 1939 émigré history *The Reign of Nicholas II,* Govorukhin's film creates a dream world. The nightmare began in 1917, when Lenin's Bolsheviks destroyed the tsarist dream and with it Russian traditions (Govorukhin at one point ominously notes that Lenin "had Jewish grandparents"). Worse, the Bolsheviks conducted a forced memory project that erased memories of the "real Russia" that had existed in 1913.[1] "The history of Russia," Govorukhin declares in the film, "has been written by her murderers. We must know Russia, we must know who our fathers were, in order to be able to build our future."[2]

The Russia That We Lost aired on the heels of Govorukhin's 1990 glasnost exposé *We Cannot Live Like This* (*Tak zhit′ nel′zia*), which presented socialism as a miserable, degraded system that had completely failed its citizens. That film won the Nika (Russia's equivalent to the

Academy Award) for best director and best screenplay, the only documentary ever to capture these prizes. Taken together, Govorukhin's two documentaries present a clear historical narrative: the Russian nation lost its identity between 1917 and 1991. To recover it, Govorukhin declared, meant resuscitating a lost past and exercising the demons of communism.

The Russia That We Lost became an active site of memory by deliberately unmaking Soviet-era historical narratives and replacing them with alternatives. When the Bolsheviks took power in 1917, they immediately set out to reshape historical narratives and to create new ones that could serve as foundational myths. Bolshevik memory makers attempted to do away with tsarist historical memory and replace it with a new, revolutionary one. To do so, the Bolsheviks created a new chronology and new interpretations of the past for the populace.[3] Cinema played an important role in this process, particularly in the 1927 anniversary films dedicated to narrating the new, revolutionary past: Sergei Eisenstein's *October,* Vsevolod Pudovkin's *The End of St. Petersburg,* and Esfir Shub's *The Fall of the Romanovs* all provided a neat, dramatic tale to the inevitable events of October 1917.[4] All three films helped to remake previous historical memories, replacing them with a new narrative that turned pre-1917 Russia into a dirty, oppressive, disgusting place.

The Civil War became the event that the new regime held up as the defining experience of making socialism. Once again films played a starring role in this process. The first Soviet "hit" was Ivan Perestiani's 1923 *Little Red Devils,* a story of Reds fighting Nestor Makhno's "Greens" in the Civil War.[5] After the 1927 anniversary films established the cinematic narrative of the Revolution, directors began to turn to the meanings of the Civil War. The biggest success in this effort was Georgii Vasiliev's and Sergei Vasiliev's 1934 *Chapaev,* which told the story of Vasilii Chapaev, an uneducated peasant who became a Civil War hero before his death in 1919. It became the canonical film of the Stalin era—Stalin himself watched it sixteen times in the six weeks after its release—and enjoyed a long afterlife, remaining popular long after the dictator died.[6] Films such as *Chapaev* established the dominant historical memory of the Civil War and its meanings: the experience served as the necessary process of political education, while watching a Civil War film helped viewers go through the same process, identifying the good guys and the bad guys and learning that the people and the Party worked together to build the socialist state.

To create the new way of life (*novyi byt*), Bolshevik activists also targeted specific elements of what they identified as the old way of life (*staryi byt*). The attack on all aspects of religion, particularly Orthodoxy, served as an important front in this cultural battle. Bolsheviks, often working for the League of Militant Godless, traveled to Russian villages and cities to expose the relics of saints, tear down church bells, and attack other symbols of Orthodoxy.[7] These anti-religious policies waxed and waned over the course of the Soviet period, but certainly, as Andrei Tarkovsky found out while working on his *Andrei Rublev* in the mid-1960s, making a film that featured religious imagery and religious music would alert the Soviet authorities.

Govorukhin's film attempted to reverse these Bolshevik memory projects. His title quickly became a sort of shorthand for remembering Romanov Russia and for interpreting the Soviet experiment. It also provided an interpretive phrase for any number of other "lost" ideals in need of recovery.[8] By 2003, the newspaper *Novaia gazeta* declared that the cinema of the previous decade had been "The Cinema that We Lost." A host of prominent critics weighed in on this view over the next three years in the paper. Because no one went to the movies in the 1990s, the critics decided to highlight some of the best films from the "lost" decade and remind readers that Russian cinema had managed to survive.[9]

The idea of a "lost cinema" captured two trends that had become prevalent by 2003. The first was just how much Govorukhin's concept had generated a framework for understanding the past as a series of things lost. "The Russia That We Lost" became a powerful means through which Russians could express a myth of national decline. The "real Russia" and its values, in other words, had disappeared after 1917. The second —and the impetus behind the *Novaia gazeta* series—was the emergence of the Russian blockbuster and particularly historical films that explored Govorukhin's "lost Russia" for similar purposes. By 2004, Russian filmgoers no longer had a lost cinema and they no longer had to rely solely on Govorukhin for a "history lesson" about late tsarist Russia. Russian audiences could travel back to a pristine Siberia and old Moscow. They could also hear the sounds of loss, particularly the Orthodox requiem, at the movies. They could watch movies that presented radically different interpretations of the tsarist era from the Soviet films they had watched. To recover these symbols of Russianness, they could turn to Nikita Mikhalkov, Karen Shakhnazarov, Boris Akunin, or Eduard Artem′ev, who all offered cinematic visions and sounds of national renewal.[10]

Ground zero for blockbuster history: Studio Tri-te, Moscow.

TWO

The First Blockbuster of the New Nation

Nikita Mikhalkov's Studio Tri-te understandably exudes confidence. The studio's offices and location mirror the centrality of its creator, the Oscar-winning director of 1994's *Burnt by the Sun*. Located between Pushkin Square and Patriarch's Ponds in central Moscow, Studio Tri-te inhabits an entire Soviet-era apartment building. It is one of the Russian film industry's hubs and ground zero for the turn to "audience-friendly blockbusters" that dominated the zero years.

Studio Tri-te is a perfect representation of the connections between post-Soviet commercial concerns, patriotism, and personalities. Founded in 1988 and named for "three-Ts: creativity [*tvorchestvo*], comradeship [*tovarishchestvo*], and labor [*trud*]," the studio's symbol has a Russian bear gripping three Ts in its paws. As a combination of Russian and Soviet patriotic culture, Studio Tri-te's symbols would be hard to top. Clear to anyone who visits the premises, though, this studio is a center for promoting the persona of its founder, Nikita Mikhalkov. On its website, Studio Tri-te describes him as "an elegant man, a conqueror of women's hearts, a nobleman of the new Russia, a famous film director, a distinguished politician, and an ardent apologist for the Russian national idea."[1]

Leaving aside whether Mikhalkov is both a man's man and a ladies' man, the other descriptions of the director turned producer turned politician turned nationalist are apt. They are present in his 1999 post-Soviet blockbuster, *The Barber of Siberia*. Moreover, *Barber* proved that selling an image of a strong Russian state led by a masculine Russian man could not just make money; it could also revive patriotic culture. *Barber* was a cultural eruption and the first explosion that made Putin's use of patriotism possible.

NEW HEROES NEEDED: APPLY ONSCREEN

By May 1998, Russian cinema had sunk to a new low. Successful films drew three hundred thousand people at best (by contrast, late Soviet films such as 1988's *Little Vera* or 1989's *Intergirl* sold between forty to fifty million tickets).[2] Decrepit cinema halls had fallen victim to thieves and neglect. American films—some good, but many poor B movies that found no audience in the United States—made up the vast majority of the offerings. Ticket prices at one of the few theaters with Dolby sound ranged between five and thirty dollars, or a week's wages for an average Russian. Video piracy ensured that Russians who had access to VCRs could watch films more cheaply at home. The dark films that dominated Russian screens kept people away in droves and were part of the phenomenon Russians referred to as *chernukha*. Derived from the adjective "dark [*chernyi*]," chernukha culture depicted late Soviet and early post-Soviet life as deeply pessimistic, violent, and broken.[3] Mosfil′m, once the largest studio in Russia, could afford to put out only five to seven films per year. Lenfil′m rented out some of its space to a car wash.[4] Life, as the film producer Sergei Sel′ianov claimed, had become more important than art, whereas once art offered an escape from Soviet life.[5]

The state of Russian cinema by 1998 produced a lot of hand wringing. Daniil Dondurei, the venerable Russian critic and editor of *Iskusstvo kino* (*The Art of Cinema*), admitted in late December 1997 that the cinema of the 1990s had failed its audience. Speaking at the Filmmakers' Union Congress, Dondurei commented that chernukha films had a negative effect on viewers. "We all know perfectly well," he stated, "that the heroes of a commercially successful cinema cannot be cynics, defeatists, failures, or unmotivated killers. A national inferiority complex cannot be cultivated in cinema."[6] Worse, Russian audiences had turned to America for their heroes. Calling Hollywood "the most important myth-maker" in the world, Dondurei stated that "after ten years of exposure, our Russian spectators are proud of American heroes, American detectives, American dogs and, especially, the American government."[7] Clearly something was needed and Dondurei had an answer: "make films that appeal to mass audiences."[8]

Enter Nikita Mikhalkov. At the end of the December 1997 Congress, the members elected him president of the Russian Filmmakers Union. The editors of *Soviet Screen* explained the reasons behind the choice: "The filmmakers found themselves sitting on the ruins of their disintegrating Union. Blaming the current secretariat for all their miseries, they felt a craving for the 'iron fist' and entrusted the reins of government to Nikita Mikhalkov, the strong and pragmatic leader."[9]

Mikhalkov responded,

> I want to know why you're calling on me today, and I'm not sure I will accept because what I see here is horrifying. . . . In seven years, starting from scratch, *we* have established a studio with *our* labor, without producing a single sex or violent flick or a commercial spot. And *our* studio, Tri-te, was rated by *Variety* ahead of Mosfil′m. Talent is a gift from God, money can be made by gambling, esteem and respect are acquired through labor. Labor.[10]

He accepted the position.

Just five months later, the new president called an Extraordinary Congress. Using his connections, Mikhalkov held it at the Kremlin's Palace of Congresses. He prepared a montage film made up of clips from chernukha films to show to the 4,400 invited members. And then the fireworks began.

That Mikhalkov had achieved the position is not surprising. He is the son of Sergei Mikhalkov, a children's writer who also penned the lyrics to the Soviet anthem; and Natal′ia Konchalovskaia, a poet and the daughter of the painter Petr Konchalovsky and granddaughter of the painter Vasilii Surikov. Mikhalkov's aristocratic roots have no rival in Russia, nor does he have many who can rival him in sheer star power. As an actor, Mikhalkov first turned heads in 1963, when he starred in Georgii Daneliia's *I Am Walking around Moscow*. As a director, Mikhalkov first made his name with his 1974 Civil War adventure film, *At Home among Strangers, a Stranger at Home*. Since these appearances, Mikhalkov's movies have consistently evoked nostalgia for the past. His films present the countryside as more "Russian" than "artificial" cities such as St. Petersburg, Russian art as a "natural" expression of the soul in contrast to the decadence of Western art, and history as something to be resurrected because the past contains values that need to be reclaimed. In Birgit Beumers's apt encapsulation, his films "perform a shift from a nostalgia that is openly constructed as a myth to a nostalgia for a past that pretends to be authentic."[11] Mikhalkov himself has swiveled "between officialdom and the intelligentsia's dissidence, between popular and auteur cinema, between patriotism and nationalism, artist and prophet, storyteller and moralist, director and public figure, aesthete and politician."[12] Few Russians are as recognizable as Nikita Mikhalkov. His name is virtually synonymous with Russian cinema.

Mikhalkov took advantage of the new possibilities afforded first by perestroika and then by the transition from a socialist economy. Studio Tri-te, founded in 1988 after he had broken from Mosfil′m, became the most successful film studio in the 1990s because it carried the name of Mikhalkov. Having successfully branded his name abroad as a "Russian" director, Mikhalkov also enjoyed both the money and the connections necessary to buy the apartment block that still serves as his personal studio. He then cannily negotiated deals with the French company Camera One and allowed Tri-te to be used by American film companies, charging foreign companies local rates with no markup. Sergei Gurevich, one of the studio's producers, worked as the Moscow-based producer on Philip Noyce's *The Saint* (1997) and admitted that "we learned everything about how to market movies, produce movies, and shoot movies in the new conditions" from this experience.[13] In addition to his shrewd business techniques, Mikhalkov kept his company together by the sheer force of his persona. George Faraday, who conducted interviews with Mikhalkov's staff in the 1990s, quoted one Tri-te employee who said of the boss, "[H]e's so powerful. When you're with his organization you feel like there's a wall around you and you're free of the government and the mafia. . . . He'll be famous forever because of his work. He's a genius. . . . And his father was the famous Sergei Mikhalkov. He was never with the government. All the women of Russia love him and he's a model to many of the men of Tri-te. He's clean. He's a moral authority." Faraday characterizes his management style as that of a feudal squire, or *barin*.[14]

Mikhalkov's stature only grew when his 1994 meditation on Stalinism, *Burnt by the Sun,* captured the Academy Award for best foreign language film. The film, coproduced by Studio Tri-te and France's Channel One, presents history as a pastoral family drama. Alternating between Moscow and the Kostroma landscapes seen in several of Mikhalkov's other films, *Burnt by the Sun* transfers Chekhov's prerevolutionary world into the Soviet era. Mikhalkov plays the Civil War veteran General Kotov, who is a committed Bolshevik out of love for his country and his family, not love for socialism. Kotov's nemesis is Mitia, a Silver Age intellectual who fought for the Whites in the Civil War and who now works for the NKVD. He has arrived back to the same house in which he grew up—the house of Kotov's wife—to take Kotov into custody. The film introduces the idea that the Mitias and the Kotovs of the world both acted out of nostalgic patriotism. Both loved the same land and same landscapes and both loved the same woman. Mikhalkov suggests that Soviet history is best viewed as a long civil war fought between family members who acted out of deep love for their motherland. The film's success in Russia, as many critics suggested, sprang from this redemptive message. Dedicated "to those burnt by the sun of revolution," the film was intended as a means to forgive both the Mitias and the Kotovs by blaming only Stalin for the horrors of the 1930s.[15] Mikhalkov himself stated, "Bolshevism did not bring happiness to our country," but questioned whether "it is morally correct on the basis of this indisputable fact to pass judgment on the life of entire generations only on the grounds that people happened to be born not in the best of times."[16] The film made Mikhalkov into a superstar, the most popular filmmaker in post-Soviet Russia by far: it led video sales for forty-eight straight weeks after it appeared.

It was this popularity, combined with Mikhalkov's business savvy that got him elected to helm the filmmakers' union. When he took the stage to deliver his keynote address in May 1998, he did so to outline what Russian cinema needed. First, he reminded his audience of cinema's place in Soviet culture: it was, he said, the "most important of the arts" because it "was capable of shaping the masses." Although Mikhalkov referred to the way Soviet ideology "manipulated this most powerful weapon," he still saw cinema as a way "of facilitating the creation of a model for a new society, and for a hero which the state and the authorities needed at a particular time." Russian cinema in 1998, Mikhalkov made clear, was in need of a new model and new heroes, particularly because "America has forced the world to perceive it through cinema." Mikhalkov wondered "what should be going on in his soul when [a cinemagoer] leaves the cinema, having bought a ticket from a salary he received four months late?" Russians, Mikhalkov concluded, "know who Stallone and Schwarzenegger are," but do not have "a model, a symbol" of their own. And, as Mikhalkov claimed, "man cannot exist without a hero."[17]

Yet Russian cinema, as Mikhalkov saw it, did not just lack heroes. Russian directors in the 1990s offered up anti-heroes, prostitutes, and killers who defined Russian values in negative ways. After he commented that American cinema had produced positive heroes with positive values, Mikhalkov asked, "What do we have?" He then pressed play and let his audience watch scenes from chernukha films. Afterwards, Mikhalkov asked a series of rhetorical questions:

> What will become of our children? What will they know about their own country? Why should they love their country? What should keep them in this land? What can help them survive in such harsh conditions?

Clearly the films of the 1990s, which "are directed toward evil and destruction," could not accomplish these lofty tasks. "Cinema is the most powerful weapon," Mikhalkov declared, and "if we let go of this weapon, it may be seized by our enemies and work against us." The result could be catastrophic: "if our present situation does not change then in fifteen years' time we shall have a government and people who know nothing about their own country."[18]

Mikhalkov listed several practical ideas for resurrecting the Russian film industry. State support topped the list. Better regulation of cinema and television was also needed. So, too, were tighter laws against piracy and for licensing domestic cinema. Russia needed the construction and reconstruction of film theaters. But above all, Mikhalkov noted, "the industry can be reborn only by the spectator, who will, however, pay only for a cinema in which he recognizes himself."[19] Russian cinema, as Mikhalkov saw it, needed blockbuster history. Not coincidentally, Mikhalkov had finished filming a three-hour historical epic that would attract audiences, offer new heroes, and beat Hollywood at its own game. *The Barber of Siberia* would debut at the very same Kremlin Palace at which Mikhalkov delivered his speech, this time decked out with state-of-the-art Dolby sound. In its subject material and its reception, Mikhalkov's *Barber* helped to give birth to a new nation.

"HE'S RUSSIAN: THAT EXPLAINS A LOT"

Mikhalkov's film ranks as one of the most expensive films ever made outside of Hollywood—at $49 million, it was the third-most expensive in European history when it debuted. It also is a nostalgic take on Russian values; ultimately, though, Mikhalkov looks to the future in his reassessment of the past. Because of its romantic view of Russia's past, as Birgit Beumers argues in her perceptive reading of the film, it deserves to be compared to *Gone with the Wind.*[20] Given its use of history to articulate contemporary concerns, *Barber* also deserves to be compared to *Birth of a Nation.*

Mikhalkov's blockbuster explicitly used history for present-day purposes, just as David O. Selznick and D. W. Griffith had. In this sense, *Barber* should be viewed, as Pierre Sorlin has argued, "as a document of social history that . . . aims primarily at illuminating the way in which individuals and groups of people understand their own time."[21] Sorlin states that we should not "neglect the political or economic base" of historical films either. The most significant historical films for historians to study, Sorlin posits, fulfill four criteria: they are original, they relate to current events, they are received positively by the public, and they are produced and distributed in a time of crisis.[22] According to Sorlin, "every historical film is an indicator of a country's basic historical culture, its historical capital."[23] What can be important in evaluating a historical film is "the underlying logic of history"; that is, the characters, scenes, and symbols that the director need not even introduce because audiences will recognize them as part of their historical heritage. Although "historical films are all fictional," "the essential thing [about them] is the history—in other words, the way the film has been marked by the political variations of its time."[24]

In the way Sorlin has outlined the historical film, *Barber* serves as an ideal test case: conceived as the Soviet Union collapsed, the film remained in utero for most of the 1990s as Mikhalkov gathered the necessary funds. Birthed in 1999, in the midst of the economic and political crises that had gripped post-Soviet Russia, *Barber* became the focus of numerous discussions about not just the state of Russian cinema, but the state of the Russian nation.

The film took a long time to make, and had been much talked about for over a decade. The script was written in 1987–88, as the Soviet Union collapsed; it was published in Russia in 1992–93, amid widespread economic, political, and social dislocation. Mikhalkov filmed it between 1995 and 1997, a period of relative stability and one when Moscow itself was undergoing a revival along the lines of that Mikhalkov depicted. Mayor Iurii Luzhkov embarked on a series of renovations that saw tsarist-era churches rebuilt and streets renamed, among other projects. Mayor Luzhkov's ambitious renovation plans coincided with Mikhalkov's desire to show old Moscow in other ways: the Iverian Gate, recently rebuilt in its original location, was featured in the film, as was the Christ the Savior Cathedral.[25]

Ultimately, *The Barber of Siberia* represented Mikhalkov's attempt to answer his own questions posed in his 1998 speech. He tells a mythical story about Russia's past in order to shape the future values of Russia. He suggests that the traditions of the east, and not the west, are more truly "Russian," thus engaging in the centuries-old debate about whether Russia is European, Asian, both, or neither. In the ad campaign, Oleg Menshikov, the star, was introduced with the line "he is Russian; that explains a lot." This line also was used in the film by an American sergeant to denote the strangeness and irrationalness that is Russia—Mikhalkov celebrates this feature of Russian identity throughout his film and, indeed, throughout his entire series of historical pictures dating back to the 1970s.[26] He tells a love story without a happy ending, one that runs counter to Hollywood films, but he tells it in the most Hollywood-like film ever made in Russian history. Finally, Mikhalkov presents a more positive look at Russia and its values, morals, and heritage than other films of the 1990s. The director himself stated: "we've had enough of Hollywood depicting Russians as mobsters, hit men, and

"He's Russian: That Explains A Lot." Poster for *The Barber of Siberia.*

prostitutes."[27] Released right after the ruble collapse but also after the calls for cinema to create new heroes, *The Barber of Siberia* became one of the most important cultural moments of post-Soviet life.

Barber tells the story of Jane Callaghan (played by Julia Ormond), an American woman who travels to Russia in 1885 to assist the Irish-American inventor, Douglas McCracken (played by Richard Harris). Jane is there to help McCracken secure funding for his "business," a machine known as the "Barber of Siberia" that will chop down the Siberian forests with ruthless efficiency. The parallel here, of course, is with Russia in the 1990s, when foreign capitalists tried to establish various "business schemes," many of them out to capitalize on Russia's rich natural resources. Mikhalkov, therefore, set a contemporary talking point and hot issue back in Alexander III's Russia, when the country first engaged in serious industrialization (albeit one funded by French backers).[28]

McCracken has run out of money and he hires Jane to play his daughter, specifically to charm General Radlov (Aleksei Petrenko), the head of a Moscow Military Academy. Jane and McCracken hope to use Radlov in order to gain access to the Grand Duke. Jane represents on one level a ruthless business approach to life, symbolized above all by her apparent willingness to even sell her body. But Jane's character is not quite this simple, and takes on more meaning when she encounters Mikhalkov's "positive hero," the young cadet Andrei Tolstoy, played by Oleg Menshikov. Tolstoy is the moral hero Mikhalkov sought to create, one that could serve as a model for Russians living in the 1990s and into the twenty-first century. Andrei's heroism is personified in his honor and in his "Russian spirit," an ephemeral yet vital component to understanding Russian nationhood.[29] Once Tolstoy has announced his love for Jane, he is prepared to give up everything for her, including his life. He fights in a duel, where he strikes Radlov and subsequently is sent to Siberia. Andrei's actions, which stem entirely from his sense of honor, stand in marked contrast to Jane's behavior. That he is Russian and she is American is particularly important in this context, and again has contemporary overtones—Russians act out of sincere belief, whereas Americans act solely for economic gain.

Jane's relationship with Tolstoy, however, causes her to think about her morals and the country in which she finds herself. We learn that she lacked a happy family life, was abused, and thus was forced into the life she leads. Because of these experiences, all of which took place in the West, she has not experienced love, has nothing to believe in, and no sense of moral purpose. Her experiences with Andrei and in Russia lead Jane to think about her values. Ultimately, she never truly grasps these matters, because in a way, as Mikhalkov is telling us in the film, Russia cannot be grasped by reason.

Despite Jane's problems understanding Russianness, *Barber* depicts many concrete ideas about it for his audience—its history, culture, and traditions all are discussed during the course of the film. Mikhalkov pays a great deal of attention in his film to "Russian traditions" in an effort to rekindle tsarist-era values in contemporary society. Andrei's life and devotion to family, honor, and his country, as well as his place in a Russian military school, are all invoked as traditions of Russian history worth rediscovering in the present era. *Barber* attempted to revive the honor of the Russian army, which had been the subject of countless press reports in the 1990s that focused on low pay, hazing, and incompetence (particularly in Chechnya). Mikhalkov dedicated his film to "Russian officers, the pride of the nation" while Alexander III (played by Mikhalkov) praises the "courage, steadfastness, and endurance" of the Russian soldier. The "Russian traditions" embodied in Andrei and his fellow cadets represent a package of timeless ideals about Russianness above all represented by the honorable, patriotic soldier.

Mikhalkov's decision to play Alexander III, tsar of Russia, led many observers to conclude that the director was making a play at becoming the leader of Russia. He had commented several times before 1999 that he might be interested in a run at the presidency and stated at the premiere: "if the people really need and want me as President, then I would have to think seriously about it."[30] Perhaps more significantly, Mikhalkov used himself as an embodiment of the Russian nation and as a means to suggest to viewers that the patriarchal family represents a "Russian tradition."[31] Typically, Mikhalkov casts members of his own family in the film: his elder daughter, Anna (subject of one of his earlier films) plays Dunia, the "authentic" love of Andrei; and his younger daughter, Nadia, who starred in *Burnt by the Sun,* appears in the memorable Shrovetide carnival scene. His son Artem plays one of Andrei's fellow cadets. Many critics interpreted this casting as a sign that Mikhalkov intended to promote an ideal of family life in the new Russia, one headed by a powerful, tsar-like patriarch, and thus a return to the "family model" of Russian identity during the nineteenth century.[32]

When Alexander III officially commissions the cadets on screen, the scene's stress is on the ceremony, the setting, and on the tsar's words to his officers. The order, pageantry, and ceremony of the affair catch the eye, along with its location in Cathedral Square, in Moscow. This setting is significant, for it takes place in Moscow, heart of the old Russia and its traditions, not the home of the tsar, St. Petersburg—the restored Christ the Savior Cathedral that appears digitally enhanced in the film also adds to this characterization.[33] *Barber* therefore offers a specific visual menu of Russianness. Mikhalkov's "lost Russia" is in old Moscow and in the pristine Siberian forests. It can be recovered through old traditions such as Maslenitsa or the values of the imperial officer corps. The stetting and ceremony of this scene also reflects changes that took place in Alexander III's Russia. Alexander passed laws that changed the appearance of the Russian army in an effort to make them look more "Russian." To achieve this aim, the tsar ordered that uniforms should resemble the Russian caftan, guards had to wear Russian boots, and all soldiers should wear Russian caps. Alexander himself, in the words of Richard Wortman, "took on the aspect of the *bogatyr′*." Interestingly, Alexander also grew a beard and expected his officers to do the same—these physical changes were directed at Peter the Great and his attempts to make Russians look like Europeans.[34] In order to be European, Russians must look like Europeans, which in Peter's mind meant shaving off the beards that defined an Orthodox Russian. Alexander's Russia, by contrast, was an attempt by the tsar to reinvent the monarchy and the army by turning to the past and to Muscovy. For Alexander III, Moscow, the Kremlin, and Red Square symbolized the "real Russia," one that demonstrated Russian traditions in their finest manifestations. Alexander, in other words, was "inventing a tradition," and Mikhalkov reinvented it.[35]

Finally, Mikhalkov also reinvents Maslenitsa, the Russian Shrovetide celebration, as a timeless national tradition. Mikhalkov intended his memorable Maslenitsa scene to be a showcase for Russian traditions and all that is incomprehensible yet compelling about Russia itself. We see a fireworks display, all kinds of booths and spectacles, and those most Russian of traditions, drinking vodka and eating *bubliki*. The Maslenitsa scene also contains factory workers engaging in fistfights on the ice, after which they ask for forgiveness from each other in the spirit of the holiday. Overall, the effect is one seen through the eyes of Jane, who is amazed yet uncomprehending—she cannot grasp the power of these "Russian traditions."[36]

Mikhalkov's movie, then, explains a lot about Tolstoy's Russianness while attempting to explain a lot about the "Russian soul" and what makes it work. The roots of the Russian soul that *Barber* presents are located in the Russian landscape. Mikhalkov's patriotic message is that Russians should feel proud of their past and of their homeland. It's a message that he has captured in many of his films: *Barber* represented the ninth time Pavel Lebeshev had shot Russian landscapes for Mikhalkov as director of photography and the twelfth time Eduard Artem′ev had composed soulful scores to match the scenes onscreen. The day before the big premiere, Mikhalkov stated at a press conference,

> In this film there is one aim—I want people to feel their dignity and respect their history. It's impossible to live without the past. If you live without the past, you have no future. Once our dignity awakens, we can set to work on the economy. Then we will start to make something, instead of waiting for Snickers bars or the next gift from the West.[37]

Mikhalkov's 1998 speech certainly raised eyebrows within the film world. His cinematic gift to the Russian people produced fireworks of another kind.

AN OINTMENT FOR THE SOUL: *BARBER* IN THE EYES OF VIEWERS

Mikhalkov made the film into a cultural event. For a week before its premiere, he appeared on countless television shows, promoting his patriotic product, while some channels screened retrospectives of his work and biographies of Mikhalkov. He also hired the computer firm Comstar to set up the first-ever website accompaniment to a Russian film.[38] Because of the economic crisis of August 1998, *Barber* was not launched in ten Siberian cities as planned. Instead, the film officially opened at a lavish reception held in the Kremlin Palace of Congresses, on February 20, 1999. It was the first film to be premiered there in over twenty years, and the palace had been specially fitted with a Dolby stereo surround system for the event.[39] Scalpers outside the theater sold tickets for as high as $700.[40]

Only at an event like this premiere could one see Evgenii Primakov and Boris Berezovskii in attendance. Both praised the film and its director. That they were involved in a major political battle at the time seemed irrelevant to the patriotism of the night. In fact, the premiere itself attracted politicians of all types, and for one night all were united in praise of the director and the ideals of his film. Former prime minister Viktor Chernomyrdrin, Mikhail Gorbachev, Communist Party leader Gennadii Ziuganov, and Yabloko leader Grigory Yavlinsky all attended the gala, and all gave positive reviews of the appeal to Russian national identity, despite the fact that this identity centered on tsarist Russia. In a bizarre twist to this tale of government praise, months later members of the Russian Duma launched an inquiry into whether the Russian government should have paid the $11 million it did for the film and its premiere, a scandal that was directed primarily at Chernomyrdrin, who had approved of the grant when he was prime minister.[41] Just as surreal was the egg-throwing incident of National Bolshevik Party members soon after the premiere. Several present-day Bolsheviks entered a roundtable talk given in Moscow by Mikhalkov about his film and threw eggs at him as a sign of protest against the nationalism depicted in it.[42] In a very real way, therefore, Mikhalkov's film had important political overtones and provoked responses from a wide range of political groups, all of them reacting to the nationalism of *Barber.*

The film attracted 42,000 spectators at the Cinema World theater alone in its first week (by contrast, *Titanic* sold 31,000 tickets).[43] In his publicity leaflet produced for the film, Mikhalkov wrote, "I hope that our film will help the spectator to feel pride again in the genuine merit of his Fatherland."[44] For Mikhalkov, Russian "traditions" such as honor and love for the fatherland are sources for a renewed Russian patriotism in the 1990s. Given the context of the times, it should not be surprising that Mikhalkov launched a brand of vodka called "Russian Standard" and two new colognes, "Cadet #1" and "Cadet #2," and also initiated a competition among the students at the Russian Film Institute to make short films on the five components of the Russian spirit: creation, trust, perfection, experience, and patriotism.[45]

Barber's significance, however, lay not just with the lavish Kremlin premiere and the commercial tie-ins; it became a cultural event because of the discussions it unleashed. In this way, Pierre Sorlin's views about what a historical film represents serve as a useful means to evaluate Mikhalkov's movie. For Sorlin, too many critics read films as articulating a single message, usually that of the director. Sorlin counters, "[A] film *has* no meaning, and we should not be concerned with the purpose of the filmmaker."[46] Given Mikhalkov's significance and the way he stood at the center of several cultural debates, Sorlin's views do not quite fit in *Barber's* case. However, as Sorlin elaborates, "[O]n the question of meaning, I would say that a film does not *necessarily* demonstrate anything. If it does make a point, it does so in such an obvious way that it is simply not very interesting."[47] Instead, we should pay attention to the multiple meanings given to the film by critics and particularly by spectators for understanding how it uses history to make present-day political statements.

Critics savaged the film. Lidiia Maslova commented in the paper *Kommersant* that the film itself is a commercial for the "product Russia," an astute observation given the film's goals of linking the past to the present.[48] Writing in *Itogi,* Nikita Sokolov declared that although one normally shouldn't waste time commenting about historical inaccuracies in art, *Barber* was "a special case." "All aspects of Mikhalkov's Russia," he concluded, "are mounted according to the law of dreams, as free associations outside of time and space."[49] Tat′iana Moskvina, a leading film critic writing in *Iskusstvo kino,* criticized Mikhalkov's attempt to use culture to shape public perceptions of the past, and concluded, "Nikita Mikhalkov has carried out the treasured dream of the Russian symbolists and has destroyed the border between art and life." Moskvina also addressed the film's focus on Moscow as the more "authentic" Russia, thus placing Mikhalkov's art in the debate over Moscow and Petersburg as the more important locus for Russianness. To her mind, Mikhalkov demonstrates a dislike for St. Petersburg, the capital of Imperial Russia, by excluding it altogether from his film. "This Russia consists of Moscow and Siberia, precisely corresponding to the mythical geography of our fatherland in the West's perception."[50] For Moskvina and other critics, Mikhalkov has—in their minds, unfairly—reinforced a Western stereotype of Russia as a mystical, almost oriental society that defies Western understanding. She concluded her review by stating that Mikhalkov's film was ultimately about Russian patriotism, even if it was "aroused with the help of sugary and well-dressed lies." She dismisses the film as a "Russian souvenir," but concludes that "Mikhalkov's Russia" does not bother her, because she "lives in a different Russia."[51]

Other reactions responded to Mikhalkov's attempt to use art to create a revived national idea—the director had stated that the film "must be viewed as it is, as a work of art," and not as "a political act."[52] Lev Anninskii claimed, "It seems Mikhalkov was able to do what Govorukhin had tried to do before: bring back 'the Russia we lost.' Virtually—like they say nowadays. . . . And this is filmed in such a way that we all moan from nostalgia."[53] Igor Zolotusskii, also writing in *Iskusstvo kino,* compares the reaction to Mikhalkov's film to that of the famous showing of A. A. Ivanov's 1858 painting "Christ Appearing to the People" in St. Petersburg. According to Zolotusskii, Ivanov's painting, which had been officially commissioned by Tsar Nicholas I, became a "work of art that became history" because of the multi-layered response to his painting, the government support for it, and the help of foreign financiers.[54] Zolotusskii believes that *The Barber of Siberia* also represents an important artistic moment in Russian history, but doubts that it will be a positive one. Mikhalkov, he writes, "wants us to look again at Russian cinema and he has achieved this." The film was screened for Russians and will be to foreigners, but this "show," as Zolotusskii calls *Barber,* will not produce a "Russian revelation," as Ivanov's painting did. He also questions the mixing of national identity in Mikhalkov's film and its meanings in a very interesting way: in the film, "Mozart soars in the skies, but on the ground Maslenitsa causes a sensation, Russian drunkenness hums, bears dance, trotters skip, bubliki shake on their cords, and Kustodiev meddles with Surikov, Shishkin with Repin, and Iaroshenko with Perov [a list of great Russian artists of the later Imperial period]." Interspersed with this blend of Russianness is a scene of Alexander III on Cathedral Square reviewing his troops. In the crowd, as Zolotusskii notes, is the current prefect of Moscow, A. Muzykantskii. What bothers the author, however, is the meaning of this cultural mix of past and present: is it a presentation for "continuity of authority," for the "union of the nineteenth century with the twentieth," or a "direct course from the post-Soviet pyramid to autocracy?"[55]

Many reviewers such as Zolotusskii expressed concern about the way in which the film would be received by the public. Many believed that Mikhalkov was attempting to sell an outdated patriotism that glossed over the tsarist past and overly criticized the West. Every reviewer in the major artistic journals expressed this fear, and all worried about the "product Russia" presented to Russians and foreigners alike in the *Barber of Siberia* (ironically, the film never found an American distributor after it provoked such a negative response at the Cannes Film Festival). Few critics echoed Natal′ia Sirivlia's response: "Mikhalkov's movie is an ointment on the wounds of national pride and has a very therapeutic function. For that, many thanks."[56]

Critics who worried about reception did so because the film became a box-office smash, earning $2.6 million and setting records for video sales a year later. *Barber* became the highest-grossing Russian film of all time and it set attendance records across the country (that the film did not earn back its budget had to do with the economic collapse that occurred after most of the filming had ended and before its premiere). Newspapers and television programs widely reported the responses of viewers and journals such as *Itogi* and *Iskusstvo kino* devoted entire issues to the film and its reception. Although we should be careful of the responses printed in these sources, at the same time they represent a glimpse into the reception of a given film, and again clarify the importance of this film as an event in post-Soviet life.

Most viewers talked about the film's intentions to build a sense of national identity and suggested that it did act as a "national ointment." A young woman interviewed by *Itogi* commented that the film presented the "Russian spirit [*dukh*]," and "felt patriotism" while viewing the film. A student who saw the film in Moscow commented to reporters that Mikhalkov "speculates on the people's feelings [about nationalism]" and commented that the film was a political campaign commercial. A group of students stated that they "sobbed" at this "extremely interesting film," which was "staggering and historical." A male student exclaimed after seeing the film, "I am proud that I am Russian." An elderly woman in the capital only commented that "Mikhalkov spent millions of dollars filming when miners are starving in Russia," while a second woman thanked Mikhalkov for the portrayal of Russian valor and claimed she did not want to leave the hall after the film ended. Similar responses were recorded throughout the country in the months after the film appeared.[57] "This is the film of a patriot. We are patriots too," commented one woman after leaving the theater. "I liked the film a lot. I've watched a lot of good films and somehow never considered myself a patriot. I am ashamed to talk about that, but I don't think I love my country [right now]. But I felt how it needs to be loved—with the eyes of Mikhalkov," opined another.[58] In a poll conducted by *Itogi,* 420 people were asked whether they liked the film; 95 percent said yes, a response that led the journalists to dub Mikhalkov "the people's favorite."[59] Andrei Eshpai of *Iskusstvo kino* argued in July 1999 that Mikhalkov had created a "new spectator" in Russia and even acknowledged that after Soviet culture and chernukha culture that the emotional ties created between director and audience over a patriotic melodrama might be "necessary for our society."[60] Ten years after the film appeared, internet users continued to post responses to the film and how it "revealed our strange Russian soul" and "strange Russian traditions."[61]

It was this sort of public reaction that fed critic's concerns.[62] Iurii Gladil′shchikov, writing as part of *Itogi*'s unprecedented coverage of the film, saw some interesting signs for the future in Mikhalkov's epic and the response to it. He entitled his review "The First Blockbuster of the Russian Empire" and commented that Mikhalkov's *Barber* had given birth to a new Russian film genre, the "patriotic melodrama."[63] The film, as Gladil′shchikov saw it, revealed a Russia that Mikhalkov wants to see, complete with a new "father of the nation." Moreover, this father has provided a new means to discuss national cinema, one that is aimed not at critics but spectators. *Barber* is, at its essence, an attempt to unite the masses around certain Russian symbols and to leave the intelligentsia out of the national equation.[64] Mikhalkov creates a film where a spectator can see a beautiful Russia where "love for a woman is equal in importance to love for the tsar," not so much "mass culture for intellectuals" as "intellectual culture for the masses."[65] But for Gladil′shchikov, Mikhalkov has also introduced a new way of thinking about the post-Soviet polity, one where the leader is not a head of state but the head of a nation.[66] Gladil′shchikov views the film's ideology as "neo-conservative" and "patriotic," and one that contains elements of Russophilia and Russophobia. Russia, as the film articulates, is not like the West. Business, democracy, and freedom do not work in Russia; instead, mysticism, national peculiarities, Orthodoxy, and one's soul guide Russia.[67] Ultimately, Gladil′shchikov sees in "Mikhalkov's system" one of "classical authoritarianism," for he wants to "impose an entirely new Russian cinema" of "Mikhalkov Hollywoodism." Moreover, Mikhalkov wants his "system" to tie the masses to "single emotions" and "ideologies" without giving them "a freedom of choice."[68] At the Pushkin Cinema premiere held three days after the Kremlin festivities, Mikhalkov staked out this territory, responding to critical scorn aimed at his product Russia, by referring to the press as "dogs" and insinuating that their attacks were nothing less than an attack on the new Russian nation. As Gladil′shchikov posited, if Mikhalkov were to become president, "then film critics will have to become the first political emigrants and political prisoners."[69]

Whether or not Gladil′shchikov's diagnosis fits *Barber* and its creator, it does sound awfully familiar, particularly to Russian political observers. A patriotic melodrama with a new father of the nation who unites a nation and not a state around emotional appeals to patriotism while labeling critics anti-Russians: this is Putin's Russia. Mikhalkov just provided the brand.

BRANDING RUSSIANNESS

By June 1999, even the writers in *Iskusstvo kino* had to admit in their lead comments devoted to the *Barber* phenomenon that "Mikhalkov conducted an unprecedented experiment" and "this experiment was successful." After the doldrums of the 1990s, the magazine acknowledged, "Mikhalkov dared to make large Hollywood-style cinema in our country."[70] What Mikhalkov had accomplished, according to the journal editors, was a fusion of classical culture, mass culture, Soviet culture, and professional filmmaking that in turn produced a popular historical epic that spoke to the mythic "Russian soul." Although the journal remained critical in its reviews of the product onscreen, *Iskusstvo kino* admitted that Mikhalkov had successfully launched a new era in Russian film.

The way Mikhalkov articulated a sense of patriotism proved to be the focus of the film's reception. In repeated interviews he spoke about the need for Russian audiences to feel pride in their country, their national traditions, and their national history. As Mikhalkov claimed,

> I did not put Russian history on the screen and I did not want to teach anything to anyone. I only wanted the rhythm and pulse of the film to convey the measured and grand rumbling of the earth. . . . A mighty, powerful energy fuels the picture.[71]

That energy is patriotism, branded by Mikhalkov.

In a 1996 newspaper interview Mikhalkov claimed that "fraternal service, the union of faith, honor, and self-sacrifice on the part of the citizens and the president—this is the ancient tradition of Russian statehood."[72] Mikhalkov held up his own family as exemplars of "personality in its collective symphonic incarnation" and therefore "not a naked individuum, but a complex, hierarchical unity of man, family, society, and state."[73] In other words, according to Mikhalkov, the Russian nation and Russian patriotism may best be understood as an extension of the Mikhalkov family and their service.

After *Barber,* Mikhalkov began to take part in a series of state services. He became the president of the Moscow International Film Festival in 2000 and aimed to turn it into an audience-friendly stage for Russian and world cinema that would rival Cannes and Venice. In 2002, he established the Golden Eagle film awards as a counterweight to the Nikas, or the Russian Oscars. Held each year at Mosfil′m, the Golden Eagles act as Russia's Golden Globes, but also serve as a means for Mikhalkov to put one over on the critics who had blasted his *Barber.*[74] He also has produced, through Studio Tri-te, a number of television films, mostly with Konstantin Ernst of Pervyi kanal. The Studio Tri-te/Pervyi kanal production of *Azazel′,* based on Boris Akunin's first Fandorin novel, was a bust, but the studio and Ernst followed up with historical hits such as Vladimir Khotinenko's *Death of the Empire* (2005). Mikhalkov and his studio also funded historical blockbusters, including Khotinenko's *72 Meters*, which was set in the Soviet era but loosely based on the 2000 Kursk disaster; and Khotinenko's *1612*, a blockbuster fantasy set during the Time of Troubles. Studio Tri-te also produced two other adaptations of Akunin works: *The Turkish Gambit* and *The State Counsellor*. When not engaged with these productions, Mikhalkov also worked on his massive epic, *Burnt by the Sun 2*, which premiered in time for Victory Day 2010.

Mikhalkov also engaged in other cinematic service to the Russian nation. He directed and screened two documentaries devoted to his famous family, *Father* and *Mama*, which both aired on television in 2003 and which celebrated the service his family had performed for the state over the centuries. He also produced and narrated Elena Chavchavadze's 2003 television series *Russians without Russia* [*Russkie bez Rossii*, also titled *Russkii vybor*, or *The Russian Choice*]. The series rehabilitated former Soviet enemies such as Aleksandr Kolchak and Anton Denikin, White Generals who, like Mitia in *Burnt by the Sun*, fought for a different Russia but who could now be seen as patriots. His experiences in visiting these pasts led Mikhalkov to campaign for Denikin's remains to be brought back to Russia. The campaign worked, for in October 2005 Denikin was reburied at the Donskoi Monastery along with the exiled philosopher Ivan Il′in, in a ceremony that included Moscow Mayor Iurii Luzhkov and Patriarch Aleksei II. Mikhalkov used the event as a chance to appeal for Rachmaninov's remains to be repatriated next. After all, in *Oblomov* he had cast the Russian composer as an embodiment of Russian art and Russia itself.[75] Mikhalkov uses the celebrity status of other figures to promote his own, acting as the primary guardian of all things Russian. He believed that his work in returning these patriots was a spiritual service to the entire nation. After the ceremony, he declared, "This [reburial] is the beginning of the end of the Civil War and a spiritual gathering together for the country."[76] He added, "The Civil War was fought over truths, but there is only one higher truth. The higher truth is in not surrendering."[77] The ceremony, which was held exactly twelve years after the day Yeltsin ordered Russian troops to storm the Russian White House during the 1993 constitutional crisis, served as a means to bury the past and past patriots.

He has been rewarded for this state patriotism. A People's Artist of Russia since 1985, Mikhalkov has also received the Presidential Order "for service to the fatherland, III degree" in 1995, the Order of St. Sergius from Patriarch Aleksei II in 1995, the order "for service to the fatherland in the II degree" in 2005, and the Order of Alexander Nevsky, the highest public award in Russia, on 23 November 2005.[78] Mikhalkov has been president of the Russian Cultural Fund since 1993 and a UNESCO spokesman since 1995. He sees his role in all of these activities, embodied in all of these awards, as patriotic service.

In one interview, Mikhalkov defined "patriotism" as "when I say I love this and propose that you love it, too." He calls this "enlightened patriotism [*prosveshchennyi patriotizm*]."[79] Mikhalkov's films, and *Barber* most prominently, feature a conservative political order, a strong state, the patriarchal family as the center of society, and Orthodoxy as the source for national unity. *Barber* also includes Mikhalkov's visual markers of Russianness: sweeping landscapes, Russian traditions such as Maslenitsa, and Moscow and its environs. As for the "roots of a [patriotic] system," Mikhalkov believes that they consist of "your mom, your family, your grandfather."[80] In other words, Russian patriotic culture is essentially the Mikhalkov family tree.

Mikhalkov's *Barber* presented a masculine hero who could be read by audiences as "Russian." At the same time, Mikhalkov and his studio openly used Hollywood techniques to revive the Russian cinema industry. *Barber* came packaged as "Russia's first blockbuster." It proved that audiences would return to cinema halls if the product was right. It also proved that history could be mined as a means to revive Russian patriotism. Mikhalkov commented when the film debuted at Cannes, "This film is like a dose of oxygen to the Russian people. It shows Russia as it should be. Russia should be strong enough to stand alone and not have to beg for a living."[81]

Leonid Vereshchagin, the producer of *The Barber of Siberia* and the main producer for Studio Tri-te, stated in 2005 that the film was the first blockbuster in Russian history but remained special because it did not just revive domestic cinema, it also contained "spirituality [*dukhovnost′*]." "In the final analysis," he concluded, "the basic themes upon which we build our blockbusters are themes that our society badly missed: a sense of self-respect and a feeling of healthy patriotism."[82] In short, *Barber* provided the script for the patriotic culture of the zero years.

Shakhnazarov's set: The recreated Moscow of 1905.

THREE

Terrorism Then and Now

Director of Mosfil′m, Europe's largest film studio, since 1998, Karen Shakhnazarov has personally overseen his studio's cinematic renaissance, a stunning about turn that he considers to be his greatest achievement. At the time he became the studio's head, the Russian film industry had shrunk to its lowest-ever point, producing just twenty-eight features in 1996 compared to the three hundred made in 1990.[1] Shakhnazarov lamented this state when he compared the relative freedom artists found with the economic deprivations of the Yeltsin years, stating in 1995, "now there's no censorship. But then again, we don't have any films to censor."[2] Taking over as the studio's head in the year of the 1998 ruble collapse, Shakhnazarov knew his work was cut out for him. He jokingly claimed that his immediate goal was to finance just one film. His long-term goals, though, were far bolder, for he wanted Mosfil′m to rid itself of its Soviet relics and to produce "audience-friendly cinema [*zritel′skoe kino*]." Shakhnazarov realized that audience-friendly films required funds, which were sorely lacking after the ruble collapse. "Cinema blooms if there is free money that appears in the economy or if films become an important part of state policy," Shakhnazarov mused. "Right now in Russia, cinematography is not a component of the state's ideology."[3]

By the time he made his first postsocialist blockbuster, billed as "an historical thriller," *A Rider Named Death* (*Vsadnik po imeni smert′*) in 2004, Shakhnazarov the director was working in a completely revitalized film industry created in part by Shakhnazarov the producer. The key to the revival, as the director readily admitted, was history, or at least the uses of history. "All films about the past are essentially about the present—its politics, concerns, and so on," he has stated.[4] In making blockbuster history, Shakhnazarov had seen his wish for Russian cinema realized, for the Russian government did begin to see film as an important part of state ideology and to use it as a weapon to revive Russian patriotism. For the first time since the end of communism, Russian producers and directors had money available to make "audience-friendly movies" that could combat Hollywood epics.

A Rider Named Death, which Shakhnazarov adapted from Boris Savinkov's 1909 novel about political terrorism before the 1917 revolutions, attempts to interpret Russia's twentieth century while simultaneously recreating the past (literally) to engage in debates about the meanings of terrorism. The film appeared on screens eighteen months after the October 2002 attack that left at least 130 audience members in Moscow's Dubrovka Theater dead; critics, audiences, government leaders, and Shakhnazarov all claimed that it offered some sort of commentary on the meanings of violence in the contemporary world. The expensive outdoor set created just for *Rider* not only represented a site meant to capture the "atmosphere" of Moscow in 1904, it also became a parallel site to the Dubrovka Theater, a malleable movie set that other films exploring the contemporary meanings of political terror could use. *Rider*'s set serves as an important site for understanding the political, economic, and cultural uses of history in the zero years—built sparing no expense and trumpeted by Shakhnazarov as being "second to no set in the world," the recreated Moscow of 1904 was visited by Putin himself and continues to be a part of all Mosfil′m tours.

"BLOOD BEGETS BLOOD": TERRORISM THEN

A century-old novel by a former Socialist Revolutionary terrorist may not seem like the most likely key to reviving the Russian film industry, but to Shakhnazarov, Savinkov's *The Pale Horse* (*Kon′ blednyi*) not only is the work of "a gifted writer," it also captures the essence of Russia's twentieth century, "an era of destruction."[5] Writing under the pen name

"V. Ropshin," Savinkov wrote two novels that explored the rise of terrorism in early-twentieth-century Russia. As Shakhnazarov has stated, "Savinkov wrote about what he knew," for his career as a novelist started only after his career as a terrorist had seemingly petered out. Although not well known today, Savinkov was something of a terrorist celebrity in 1909 (Shakhnazarov claimed, "[I]t would be like Bin Laden writing a novel about terrorism today").[6] As the head of the combat organization for the Socialist Revolution Party between 1903 and 1908, Savinkov oversaw and participated in the assassinations of Viacheslav von Plehve, the Minister of the Interior, and Grand Duke Sergei Aleksandrovich, Moscow's Governor General and Nicholas II's brother. Hailed by Vera Figner as "the most brilliant person I have ever met,"[7] and befriended by Silver Age luminaries such as Maksimilian Voloshin and Dmitrii Merezhkovskii, Savinkov was truly a man of his time—when he was not throwing bombs at tsarist officials, he was charming ladies with his urbane wit, composing poems (perhaps as a means to charm more ladies), experimenting with opium and occultism, and grappling with the meanings of Dostoevsky and Nietzsche. It is tempting to dub Savinkov the quintessential Silver Age man; at the very least, he embodies all the fashions, emotions, and aspirations of that early-twentieth-century "age of anxiety," when "politics in Russia became a creative endeavor."[8]

The Pale Horse traces the tense time when a group of terrorists attempt to kill the governor general of "N," ultimately succeeding after several failed tries. Given the history behind "V. Ropshin," the novel is best seen as an autobiographical account of Savinkov's cell and their assassination of Moscow's governor general (after years of lame denials, Savinkov would eventually admit as much).[9] The leader of the group, George, is a ladykilling killer whose obsession with murdering the grand duke is equaled only by his obsession with a young noblewoman named Elena. As his group of conspirators makes their assassination attempts, they also debate the meaning of their actions, carrying on conversations that encompass Dostoevsky (no one wants to be "a Smerdiakov," the villain of *The Brothers Karamazov*), the apocalyptic overtones of the Silver Age, and Nietzsche's calls for the strong individual to act above accepted morality. George is almost impenetrable in his reasoning, a characterization that clearly matches that of his real-life doppelgänger,

Savinkov, whom many believed possessed no underlying motive for his revolutionary activities. By contrast, he is surrounded by believers of all types: Heinrich, the idealistic young student radical who blanches before violence; Fedor, a peasant who hates the wealth of the reactionary classes; and, most intriguingly, Vania, a fictionalized Ivan Kaliaev who manages to rationalize his Orthodox faith with his political activities.[10] Ultimately, though, *The Pale Horse* is George's/Savinkov's story, one in which we slowly see the success of the political murder overshadowed by his realization that terror equals "blood beget[ting] blood [*krov′ rodit krov′*]."[11] Over the course of the novel, George claims that he is a total stranger to himself and everyone else, for he has let his two obsessions—murder and jealousy of Elena's husband—overwhelm him.[12] The grand duke's murder is accomplished outside of the narrative (George hears an explosion caused by Vania's bomb and reads about the death in the papers), but a duel with Elena's husband that results in his death is described in vivid detail. Afterward, George admits, "Now I have killed for my own sake," and asks, "Why is it good to kill for an ideal, necessary to kill for one's country, but impossible for one's own sake?"[13] The message, Savinkov tells us, is that "we all live by deceit and blood [*my vse zhivem obmanom i krov′iu*]."[14] George cannot distinguish between the ideals of murdering reactionary tsarist ministers and his personal desire to eliminate Elena's husband—both are driven by hatred and both are simply murder.

Savinkov's actions and his willingness to dissect them led to a furious and fractious debate among his peers about the meanings of political violence. As publicist A. S. Izgoev exclaimed in a 1913 *Russkaia mysl′* article, "[T]he history of our generation is entrusted with the task of coming to terms with terror."[15] Savinkov threw himself into this task, combining his Nietzschean philosophic flirtations with the style of his friend Merezhkovskii to produce novels that both captured the essence of terrorism and criticized its immorality. His works, as no less a figure than Georgii Plekhanov would claim, were "a major literary event that struck at the very heart of the revolutionary movement."[16] Others, such as Elena Koltonovskaia, praised their examination of "the psychological nature of terror" and particularly Savinkov's admission that the sources for this violence were rarely because of noble desires, but "dominant feelings of animosity and bitterness."[17] Critics such as Aleksandr Amfiteatrov cried foul and claimed instead that political assassins "are conscious and convinced individuals in the name of a clearly understood political aim: *pro bono publico*."[18] Viktor Chernov, the Party's chairman, believed that Savinkov had offered at least some justification for the use of terror by depicting characters who struggled with the moral ramifications of killing, concluding that "the permissibility of the violation of the ultimate norm is measured by the degree of one's revulsion at its violation."[19] At a time when political terrorism counted victims in the thousands (3,611 government officials killed or wounded in 1905 alone),[20] Savinkov the figure and Ropshin/Savinkov the writer were hot topics of café and newspaper debates. *The Pale Horse* appeared in the midst of this wave of violence and it served as an important impetus to discuss the meaning of it all. Merezhkovskii, ever ready to supply a blurb for his friend Savinkov, called *The Pale Horse* "the most Russian book of the period."[21] Izgoev, in other words, hit the nail on the head when he declared that his generation's task was to come to terms with all the terror around him.

These central questions from Savinkov's blockbuster novel figure prominently in Shakhnazarov's blockbuster film. *Rider* follows the plot and dialogue of *Pale Horse* closely, although it makes two significant departures—the first for dramatic effect and the second for reasons that will become clearer later. Aleksandr Borodianskii's and Karen Shakhnazarov's script lifts entire passages from Savinkov's novel and follows the tight plot centered on the attempts to assassinate the Grand Duke Sergei Aleksandrovich. Even the actor who plays the grand duke is a dead ringer for the real one. Shakhnazarov used the film as a vehicle for promoting Mosfil′m's revival and therefore the revival of the Russian film industry. History, and "our history" in particular, was central to these triumphs, and *Rider* received a lavish promotional campaign with ads on the radio and television as well as posters plastered in city streets announcing the film as a new masterpiece.[22] Given its topic, its setting, and its use of past figures, Shakhnazarov intended *A Rider Named Death* to be a statement about Russia's history and its ability to shed light on contemporary issues.

In this respect, Shakhnazarov's film is a useful test case for exploring one important aspect of the relationship between history and cinema.

Robert Rosenstone has recently argued that historians should abandon long-standing prejudices about historical films needing to be accurate in their details and instead evaluate historical films for what they are—a visual medium that "can render an important past [and] do a kind of history that is complex enough so that we must learn how to read it."[23] Historical films, Rosenstone argues, can interrogate the past just as well as monographs can. They do it, however, in their own way, not by providing literal truths about the past, but metaphoric ones.[24] In short, films about the past can convey serious history in part "by coming to grips with the issues from the past that trouble and challenge us in the present."[25] In this conceptualization *Rider Named Death* certainly accomplishes something. Much was made in the Russian media about the extensive and expensive set that Shakhnazarov built on the Mosfil′m lot in order to lend his film the "look" of old Moscow. According to the director, the "old Moscow" before 1917 does not physically exist anymore ("Moscow is not really . . . Moscow anymore"),[26] and therefore, "it was important to create the atmosphere of early twentieth-century Moscow streets, to fill the camera with the life of that time."[27] Technical consultants for the film scoured old picture books for photos of the fin de siècle and used them to build a set that adds a "realistic" look to the film.

A Rider Named Death certainly has the look of Moscow's turn-of-the-century commercial mosaic that lent the city "both the fragrance of the past and the fresh air of modernity," for *bulochnaias* butt up against banks on set.[28] *Rider* fulfills the views of Hayden White that "imagistic (and especially photographic and cinematic) evidence provides a basis for a reproduction of the scenes and atmosphere of past events much more accurate than any derived from verbal testimony alone."[29] In its visual depiction of history, therefore, *Rider* is a more meaningful account than any monograph about political terrorism in early-twentieth-century Russia and certainly more so than Savinkov's novel, which is largely devoid of scenery. Shakhnazarov's recreated Moscow is also more historically minded than the actual Moscow Nikita Mikhalkov used in *The Barber of Siberia*. From the red stars on the Kremlin to the open spaces around St. Basil's that did not exist in 1885 but did in 1997, Mikhalkov's "old Moscow" looks a lot more like Iurii Luzhkov's new one (which, given the good mayor's proclivities, can be viewed as a rebuilt nostalgic site meant to evoke a feeling of the past if not the actual look of it).[30] The set for *Rider,* by contrast, succeeds in filling the camera with the look of 1904 Moscow.

Yet it is not just the lavish set that lends itself to the history on screen. It is also the relationship between word and image that makes the atmosphere of Savinkov and his associates emerge more clearly. Not only does Andrei Panin mouth the words of George/Savinkov (both as dialogue and as voice-over), he also *looks* like Savinkov and *acts* like him. Anna Geifman, the leading contemporary Western historian of terrorism then, describes Savinkov as

> [a] handsome man, [who] had an animated and nervous face marked by gentility, with eyes that sometimes seemed sad and sometimes cold, almost cruel. He was slender to the point of appearing impulsive, yet graceful in his movements. His elegant clothes, his urbane, amusing, and slightly ironic conversation, his refined, uninhibited manners all contributed to his image as a veritable dandy, a European gentleman, and an intellectual. Moreover, . . . Savinkov had a rare talent that enabled him to charm people and to evoke their sympathy and interest, impressing and attracting many with his intelligence, his vivacious and sardonic flair, and especially with his enthusiasm and determination.[31]

Panin's performance brings this description to life, giving it flesh but also meaning. When we see George confess his love for Elena and his disdain for Erna on screen, it fills out the character in a way *The Pale Horse* cannot. Similarly, when Panin kills Elena's husband and his voice reads Savinkov's words that "this time I killed for myself," Panin's cold yet angry look conveys the essential dilemma at the heart of Savinkov's analysis of Russian terrorism. *Rider* no more fictionalizes the past and the history of political terrorism than any other work of history. In many respects, particularly visually, it is better.

By contrast, Elena Monastireva-Ansdell's analysis of the film's historical accuracy argues that the Moscow set is "too pristine" and contains action "in what seems almost like an historical vacuum." In her reading, the film excludes references to the social strife and anxieties that "plagued Russian society at the time of the Empire's humiliating defeat in the bloody Russo-Japanese War." Without some sort of depiction of government repression, Nicholas II's incompetence, and bloodshed from tsarist agents, in other words (a list of "necessary" contexts that would really make for a miniseries), we get the impression "that the terrorists are involved in terror for terror's sake, rather than as a response to the gross injustices of Russia's autocratic regime."[32]

As the reactions to Savinkov's novel suggest, many critics believed similarly—for Chernov and Amfiteatrov, Savinkov's chilling admission that he killed because he wanted to and not because of some great ideal was nothing short of slanderous. Both *A Rider Named Death* and *Pale Horse,* however, suggest a more nuanced view of history than these criticisms allow for. George may kill because, as he tells Vania, "I can," but the film and novel present a hodgepodge of underlying societal problems: Heinrich is a radical student, Vania a believer in redemptive violence, Fedor an angry killer out for vengeance because tsarist police killed his wife, and Erna a Jewish radical who makes bombs out of misplaced love for George. Moreover, Ropshin's "characters" adopted by Shakhnazarov are hardly fictional, for Savinkov admitted that they are based on his comrades in combat, particularly Kaliaev/Vania. By presenting various motivations for political murder, *Rider* accomplishes exactly what Monastireva-Ansdell claims it does not—scripted into these biographies are past histories that, when uncovered, do tell us much about repression, emotions, and the historical contexts for the assassination. The angry operagoer who nearly exposes George's cover because he is posing as an Englishman—and therefore someone who "helped Japan"—is a nice reference to the seething anger left over from Tsushima.

The one actual alteration from Savinkov and from the history he describes is harder to explain, but still very suggestive. The murder of the grand duke came at the hands of Ivan Kaliaev on February 4, 1905, when "the poet" (as Kaliaev was known, no doubt for such verbiage as "a Soviet Revolutionary without a bomb is not a Soviet Revolutionary") threw a homemade explosive at the royal carriage. The resulting blast could be heard all over Moscow—George hears it clearly in *The Pale Horse*—and at the site "there lay a shapeless heap . . . of small parts of the carriage, of clothes, and of a mutilated body . . . [with] no head."[33] *A Rider Named Death* alters this event, however, for dramatic purposes: Vania/Kaliaev hurls his bomb and kills the driver and two bystanders. In the novel and real life, he is injured, captured, and hanged. The novel has Vania write a final letter to George, an act also accomplished by Kaliaev. In the film, however, Vania is killed by his own bomb and the grand duke survives.

Seeing history: George shoots the grand duke. Still from Karen Shakhnazarov, *The Rider Named Death* (2004).

Enraged that his plans have once again gone awry, George vows to kill the tsarist official by himself, stalks him, and shoots him at the Bolshoi Theater during a performance of Verdi's *Un ballo in maschera,* which follows a group of masked conspirators and their efforts to assassinate a popular king. Verdi's opera takes the side of the king, and as George flees from the scene and lies in bed contemplating his actions, the chorus's words about the assassin ("Death and infamy to the traitor! Let the sword of justice cut him down") continue to play.[34]

The change certainly tends to be the sort of alteration that leads some historians to cry foul about how films distort history, yet the dramatic effect is one that conforms to Savinkov's musings and therefore can be interpreted along the lines Rosenstone drew. We see George's face onscreen as he shoots the grand duke moments before we see the very same face and the very same facial expression as he shoots Elena's husband. Once again the visuals say everything that Savinkov would want us to take from his writings—killing a grand duke for an idea and

"This time I killed for myself": George shoots Elena's husband. Still from Karen Shakhnazarov, *The Rider Named Death* (2004).

killing an officer out of jealousy are both murders. In this short visual encapsulation of Savinkov's message, we see how blood begets blood, just as we get the atmosphere of early-twentieth-century Moscow's streets that Shakhnazarov desired. The director admitted that "the story was elaborated [in this way] in order to strengthen the key points of Savinkov himself, so we decided to do it this way."[35] As an historical representation about terrorism, then, *A Rider Named Death* successfully captures the "destructive epoch" it recreates.

"THE PROBLEM WILL BE ON OUR AGENDA FOR A LONG TIME": TERRORISM NOW

Shakhnazarov sees his role as an historian in terms of what his films can say about the connection between the past and present. He claims that only an artist can take facts and "infuse them with intuition"; an artist can interpret them in a way that historians and politicians cannot. As he asks rhetorically, "for instance, wasn't 1812 best interpreted by Tolstoy?"[36] Whether we want to see Shakhnazarov's film as the Tolstoy of terrorism, his view of his primary role as historian is equally provocative. For him, "all films about the past are essentially about the present—its politics, concerns, and so on."[37] Historical films, in Shakhnazarov's reading, need to use the past to be successful in the present.

A Rider Named Death uses the history it narrates in two significant ways. First, the film provides historical context and interpretations. *Rider* is a cinematic articulation of the argument many Russian scholars have made about the Soviet Century's essence. Alexander Yakovlev, one of Mikhail Gorbachev's influential ministers and the person placed in charge of the post-Soviet Commission on the Rehabilitation of Victims of Political Repression, described the legacy of the Soviet system in terms of its violence: "[F]rom horizon to horizon Russia is sown with crosses and with the nameless graves of its citizens, felled in wars, killed by famine, or shot at the whim of the Leninist-Stalinist regime."[38] Yakolev offered both a damning critique of communism and a historical explanation for its unprecedented violence. When he asked, "What did Bolshevism give to the world, to its peoples, to the individual?" he answered, "To the world: revolts, destruction, violent revolutions, civil wars, violence toward the individual. To its peoples: poverty, destitution, lawlessness, slavery both material and spiritual. To humankind: endless suffering." The roots of this "demonic frenzy," as Yakolev termed it, can be found in Russia's history of violence before Bolshevism, its cults of "might, violence, despotic power, and lawlessness" that "became part of the Russian people's way of life."[39]

Yakolev's views correspond to those articulated by several prominent historians: Vladimir Buldakov, in *Krasnaia smuta* [*Red Time of Troubles*], argues that pre-1917 imperial structures produced a society that embraced violence;[40] Oleg Budnitskii sees political violence and the widespread sympathy for it among educated Russians as defining features of the nineteenth and twentieth centuries. In his view, the "morality of the bomb" resulted from the "moral impasse" that emerged by 1904, a situation where violence made sense as the only method capable of resisting the tsarist regime.[41] One could also add Stanislav Govorukhin's 1992 "history lesson," *The Russia that We Lost,* to this list. In it, the director declares that Lenin unleashed "a war against his own people" that would wage for seventy-five years and kill sixty-six million people.[42]

Western scholars have also begun to historicize the violence unleashed in Russia during the early parts of the twentieth century. Most pertinently, Anna Geifman and Budnitskii have engaged in heated debates about the Socialist-Revolutionary (hereafter SR) terrorists and their actions. In Geifman's view, those who engaged in violence either did it for violence's sake (such as Savinkov) or because of psychological abnormalities (or both).[43] Her attempt to "demystify and deromanticize the Russian revolutionary movement" led Budnitskii to charge that she "looked at events from the Police Department's window."[44] In response, Geifman has claimed that Budnitskii romanticizes violence and its practitioners by taking their ideology more seriously than their bloodlust,[45] thereby ensuring that the same circular debate that waged when Ropshin first published *A Pale Horse* continues today.

Peter Holquist has historicized this wave of violence best by situating it within the wider European "epoch of violence" that encompassed wars, famines, revolutions, and pogroms between 1905 and 1925. The Bolshevik regime that emerged within this European epoch embodied "a society steeped in a worldview of 'catastrophic historicism,' a worldview that both conditioned state policy and informed individual identity."[46] In short, the historical study of Russian violence and its meanings has produced a wide body of recent scholarship, all of it attempting to study "the causes and mechanisms of some of the most controversial episodes in the modern period."[47]

Shakhnazarov has explicitly situated his blockbuster within these debates, for he has claimed that his film traces the transition from the nineteenth century to the twentieth in Russia, or a change from "the last era of accord" to "an epoch of destruction."[48] Moreover, in Shakhnazarov's view, Savinkov himself "suffered as a person," for "he lived from the end of the nineteenth century—a humanitarian, cultural, and harmonious era—into the twentieth—an era of mass culture, totalitarianism, and destruction."[49] To convey this history beyond Savinkov's pages, Shakhnazarov added an ending to his film that wrestled with the historical ramifications of violence. The end is based not on Ropshin's novel, but on Savinkov's actual fate and is narrated by George/Panin (apparently speaking from beyond the grave). After George walks away from his role as a terrorist as the novel ends, we learn what happens to the characters who survive the assassination plots, tracing some of their histories into the Soviet period. Erna, we are told, died when a bomb she made exploded in her apartment and could be identified only by her hands. Heinrich, whose name was Tadeusz Sikorsky, successfully killed an official in Warsaw before being arrested and executed. The head of the Central Committee of the SR Party, Valentin Kuzmich, turned out to be a tsarist agent (thus, a fictional Azev) and died in a World War I displaced persons camp. George/Savinkov himself, he says, left the combat organization and "when the Bolsheviks took over, I fought against them," eventually "organizing terror within the USSR." In 1925, he was arrested and "threw [him]self from a Lubianka window."

While debate continues about whether Savinkov committed suicide or was thrown from the window by police agents,[50] Shakhnazarov inserts this history into his film to further Savinkov's claim that "blood begets blood." The end accomplishes two functions: first, it gives a sense for the "epoch of destruction's" costs in a fashion similar to that evoked by Yakovlev's crosses; and second, it provides a visual account of the Silver Age embrace of apocalyptic violence in the form of Maksimilian Voloshin (a friend of Savinkov's), who reads a poem about impending doom and how "the iron century has beaten you with impassioned flames and feverish delirium" as we look at George's bleeding corpse. It is this emotion evoked by the Silver Age poet, Shakhnazarov suggests, that produced the even greater waves of violence that followed. The effect is to offer a meaning to the violence depicted on screen and its ultimate costs for Russia, a point driven home by the last lines of the film, a reading of Revelation about the pale horse of death appearing and "hell followed with him." The hell of twentieth-century violence, in other words, is Shakhnazarov's attempt "to use some facts from Savinkov's biography in order to intensify the artistic impact" of what Savinkov's life meant for Russian history.[51]

If one reading of *Rider* involves a contemporary comment on the meanings of twentieth-century Russian violence, a second revolves around what the film had to say about terrorism in the present. According to Shakhnazarov, *Rider* obviously had something to say about Russia in 2004 just as it did about Russia in 1904 and no shortage of people weighed in on this subject. As for the director himself, aside from his views on the "epoch of destruction" unleashed around the time of Savinkov, Shakhnazarov stated that he simply hoped that the film would awaken interest among the audience, for "the problem of terrorism will be on our agenda for a long time. . . . And not just in Russia, but everywhere. Governments everywhere grow more vulnerable to the contemporary methods of terror, but the readiness to compromise power produces new waves of violence."[52] If he saw part of the film as a means to get people thinking about the meanings of terrorism, so too did Shakhnazarov intend for *Rider* to provide a commentary on past and present motivations for terror. What interested him, he claimed, was the intelligence of the Russian terrorists; he concluded that "the intellectual level of Russian terror at the beginning of the past century was incomparably higher than that of the present."[53] Reading Nietzsche and Dostoevsky, it seems, makes the terrorist.

As far as the contemporary terrorists, Shakhnazarov had even more interesting comments to share. His film was not one meant to incite fear, but to secure life. Shakhnazarov believes his film should not be viewed as one sympathetic to terrorism and its practitioners, but he also does not believe that it presents them solely as manifestations of evil, stating that to "fight with them [terrorists] only saying 'it is bad, it is evil,' is useless."[54] In order to win the fight, Shakhnazarov states, "we must first understand the ideological basis of their convictions. . . . You can never defeat them with repressions or with strength, because it's impossible to defeat someone with repressive measures if they've already decided to die."[55] In his view, *Rider,* like *Pale Horse,* is ultimately "anti-terrorism," revealing the complex lives and fates of those who turn to violence. According to Shakhnazarov, because Savinkov represents the only prominent terrorist who became a good writer, he should be read by governments today: "[I]f I were in the place of the world's security services, the first thing I would do is read this book."[56]

Shakhnazarov's statements and his view about his film also focus on the spectator. According to the director, his film is meant to suggest meanings, get people talking, and get viewers to think about the ways past events reflect current realities. In short, his version of "audience-friendly cinema" is meant to minister, not preach. Jay Winter's views about the relationship between film and historical memory, published as part of a 2001 *American Historical Review* symposium on the subject, captures this idea: "[L]ike poetry, film—film at the highest level—does not instruct or indicate or preach. It ministers, it challenges conventional categories of thought, it moves the viewer. Other films do so to a lesser degree, but no film is strictly didactic, since images have a power to convey messages of many kinds, some intentional, some not."[57] For Winter, "film is never the same as text, and the ways in which cinema presents past events are never direct or unmediated," for they involve the use of memories that are themselves "a set of signifying practices linking authorial encoding with audience decoding" about the messages.[58]

Given the buzz about *Rider,* its recreated set, its marketing campaign, and its literary tie-ins (it was possible to buy new editions of Savinkov's work renamed *Vsadnik po imeni smert´* and emblazoned with the film's ubiquitous poster on the cover), the film produced no shortage of reactions that attempted to decode what Shakhnazarov had presented to them. *Rider* opened in April 2004 with respectable box office returns, placing second behind *Starsky and Hutch* but beating *Passion of the Christ,* eventually earning $1.34 million—in early 2004, before the explosion of *Night Watch,* these were respectable box office numbers.[59]

For many Russian film critics, Shakhnazarov's open admission that the film was meant to offer deep commentary, combined with its blockbuster label and appearance, did not sow the seeds for positive reviews. In one of the few, Irina Kozel sees *Rider*'s achievement less in historical terms than in contemporary economic ones, a refrain that would grow louder and louder in the years afterwards: for her, the film certainly offers a view of "the horrors of the consequences of terrorist acts," but mostly offers proof that "Russian cinema did not die and did not lose face in its pursuit of commercial success. This is cinema that preserved its strength and its craftsmanship . . . more pictures of this kind, and our cinematography would not only be great in the past and future, but also have a great present."[60]

Lev Anninskii, veteran writer for *Iskusstvo kino,* was less concerned with economic triumphs and rosy futures than the uses of the past in 2004. Calling Savinkov "a second-rate though scandalous prose writer,"

Anninskii claims that "Savinkov would hardly be of interest . . . if not for the fact that today, seven decades after its liquidation, terror had not revived—to the confusion of sociologists, political scientists, culturologists, and psychologists—as the outstanding feature of planetary existence." Thus, the only significance of the film is its contemporary uses of the past and its commentary on the meanings of terror. Anninskii believes that this relationship falls flat. When he saw it at the Pushkin Theater in the afternoon, "the hall was half-empty." The underperforming matinee, Anninskii concludes, means that contemporary viewers, having seen the images of 9/11, "look indifferently at the dynamic jelly [*dinamitnyi studen'*] of Azev's time [because they are] already accustomed to them." Moreover, the answers provided to the question of why the killers kill are hazy at best, for we don't see the suffering *narod,* we don't understand Vania's Christian faith that leads him to kill (Anninskii believes Vania perhaps stands for contemporary terrorists who kill in the name of Allah), nor do we understand George's motives for assassinating the grand duke. Shakhnazarov's take on terror, as Anninskii sees it, is "that it always was and is" and that "we do not know why and cannot know why."[61]

Although Anninskii couldn't find the artistic encoding at the core of the film in a half-empty hall, Valerii Kichin found too much encoding at a packed screening in the very same Pushkin Theater—attending the evening one certainly made a difference. After analyzing the pros and cons of Shakhnazarov's picture (Panin is a pro, all the women of the film cons), Kichin concludes that the film is both "an attraction and a warning." The attraction is Moscow, or at least the city recreated by set designer Liudmila Kusakova, who used old photographs and other sources to make "a museum panorama." At the same time, Kichin claims, "the secret of creativity is not in constructing, but in rendering [this Moscow] habitable." In this regard, Kichin sees the film's use of history as a warning, for the depiction of terrorism on the recreated streets of Moscow in 1904 and the motives of the actors who walk them "is insufficient for understanding contemporary terrorism."[62] Making a movie about terrorism in the past and claiming it has something to say about terrorism in the present, in other words, does not make this claim correct, just as making a representation of 1904 Moscow does not make it habitable in 2004.

This sense of the contemporary political overtones of the film provoked a comment from Mikhail Shvydkoi, the head of the Russian Cultural and Film Agency and the figure responsible for opening government coffers to fund the Moscow set. Shvydkoi claimed that *Rider* "is a serious attempt to analyze the emergence of terrorism," and "the message is that in the long run a terrorist comes to a complete moral crisis by taking the path of murder."[63] These sorts of comments are what Ekaterina Barabash had in mind when she reviewed the film for *Nezavisimaia gazeta*. The film, at least as Barabash sees it, is Shakhnazarov's attempt "to rummage through the gloomy, ideological souls of murderers" and transfer them onto contemporary screens. The result has a clear political message: "that terrorism is doomed at the start of the last century" and implicitly at the start of this one. However, Barabash echoes Kichin in her view that "today's rider named death could not be envisioned by Savinkov and his associates," for "George/Savinkov's repentance, his Dostoevskian doubts, whether he had the right to dispose of another's life, would not be shared by his colleagues in bombing one hundred years later." For Barabash, then, "history, contrary to popular opinion, repeats itself not always as a farce, but more often as trebled, even tenfold tragedy."[64]

Elena Monastireva-Ansdell takes this criticism even further, arguing that *Rider* "paints an overall biased image of terrorism." Shakhnazarov's film "successfully de-romanticizes the heroic freedom-fighter" but in doing so "romanticizes the Russian state in the form of a benevolent ruler." In this sense, she argues, *Rider* "upholds the political values of Vladimir Putin's presidency with the latter's influence on centralized strong-hand ruler as a guarantor of national (or imperial?) order and stability." Because the grand duke looks like Nicholas II, in Monastireva-Ansdell's reading, and because he has "visual markers" of a "benevolent aristocratic ruler," the film has to be an endorsement of Putin.[65]

All of these critical takes on *Rider* implicitly (and sometime explicitly) placed the spectator at the center of their readings. For some, the film marked a positive change in Russian cinema and its audiences, who could now see "their history" packaged as well as Hollywood's. For others, *Rider*'s uses of history were manipulative, meant to invoke not the past but respect for the present political stability in the form of Putin.

As for the spectators themselves, the explosion of internet chat rooms in the 1990s and in the early 2000s gives us at least a sense of what some cinemagoers thought about *Rider*'s messages. For example, after a few posts on the kino.ru website comparing the film to the war in Iraq, one viewer wrote, "The essential difference between the situation in Iraq from the situation in Russia and connected with this film is in the fact that the *Rider Named Death* shows our PAST, which completely and actually existed, but NOT THE FUTURE." One respondent wondered "what REAL PAST did Shakhnazarov show? Have you studied the history that this film shows?" A viewer named "Nikolai" admitted he went to see *Rider* because of its marketing blitz ("the radio and television proclaimed it as a new masterpiece, just as the posters everywhere did") but found it disappointing because he thought the film presented George as a hero and a view that "terror in Russia was as necessary as air is to man." For Nikolai, the depiction of terrorism did not do enough to reveal Lenin's terror and that of "the Bolsheviks and their entire ugly regime."[66]

These reactions indicate that *Rider* accomplished what Rosenstone has seen as the essence of film's ability to render history: it "can successfully meditate upon, interrogate, and analyze the past."[67] The history film "creates rich images, sequences, and visual metaphors that help us to see and think about what has been."[68] *Rider* allowed filmmakers, critics, and audiences to engage in interpretation (some quite nuanced, and some quite frightening) and attempt to draw conclusions about the past presented to them on screen and its meanings for the present. The fact that no one viewer or reviewer reached the same conclusion about the film's message speaks to its ability to minister.

Perhaps the most important commentator of all said no words about the film in public. Still, when Vladimir Putin visited the outdoor set for *Rider* in November 2003, it helped to put the picture into the mainstream media and news reports. Shakhnazarov himself took the president for a stroll through the early-twentieth-century historical recreation, a walk widely captured on the news and in papers. When Andrei Bandenko of *Itogi* asked if the two men talked terrorism, Shakhnazarov bristled: "No, more about cinema. Vladimir Vladimirovich confirmed that Mosfil′m will preserve its status as a federal unitary enterprise. . . .

But what did you see that [made you think] we must have discussed the theme of terror?" When Bandenko suggested that Shakhnazarov had not brought up the subject because he might not have supported Putin's anti-terrorist operations, the director shot back, "That's the problem of the special forces, not film directors."[69] Putin, at least according to Shakhnazarov, did not talk terrorism but did talk cinema, staying on the set longer than scheduled. "There was even a moment when I wanted to say, 'Maybe we should go?'" Shakhnazarov recalled, "But he kept looking and asking questions."[70]

This event marked an important moment for Mosfil′m and its director. The atmosphere of the old Moscow created in the middle of the new one proved to be seductive for Putin as well as Shakhnazarov. Putin's stroll and promise to continue to support Russian cinema ensured that discussions about "terrorism today" took a backseat to discussion about Russian culture and its ability to make good on Shakhnazarov's promise to make Mosfil′m into a true competitor to Hollywood. Putin's assurances to Shakhnazarov meant that the director got his 1998 wish: the government now saw film as an important part in its ideology. *Rider*'s most significant contemporary achievement, therefore, was more about economics and patriotic culture than the meanings of terror. The past, it turned out, could be used profitably.

BATTLES TO BE WON: TOURS THROUGH TERRORISM AND OLD MOSCOW

In retrospect, 2004 was a breakthrough year for the terrorist blockbuster. While *Rider* galloped onto streets and screens as an "historical epic," Evgenii Lavren′tev's *Countdown* [*Lichnyi nomer*] blasted its way into discussions as "Russia's first action movie." The film followed the fortunes of Agent Aleksei Smolin's attempts to save first Rome and then Moscow from dirty bombs made by Islamic radicals, Chechen terrorist actions, and a London-based oligarch named Pokrovskii (obviously meant to be Boris Berezovskii); or, as the film's producer stated, "against both external and internal terrorists." *Countdown* did not explore the deep roots of terrorism, choosing instead to play to more contemporary perceptions and prejudices: the main villain, just in case one did not get the all-too-obvious message, is a dead ringer for Osama bin Laden. It did clean up at the box office, placing first for two weeks in a row and eventually earning nearly $5 million.[71]

Countdown also carried with it the blessing of President Putin, who did not have to visit its set but did get a private screening along with Nikolai Patrushev, the head of the FSB—both men gave it the thumbs up. Like *Rider, Countdown* received state support amounting to 10 percent of its $7 million budget. Unlike *Rider, Countdown* did not attempt to provide serious debates or discussions about violence in Russian history. After the final scene, we are told that the film "is based on true events: the life of Russian SAS officer Aleksei Galkin. After being imprisoned by Chechens, he continued his army service and was awarded the medal 'Hero of Russia.' Today, together with Galkin, each and every one of us continues the battle with terrorism. A battle we must win!"[72] No descent into hell caused by Russian terrorists out to end an oppressive regime, nor are there any attempts to understand why human beings engage in political violence. *Countdown* counteracts *Rider* by taking the past out and by suggesting that terrorists are always evil and those that fight them are always good. Smolin, therefore, is the complete opposite of Savinkov. As a model for a new Russian hero *Countdown* suggests that Russia needs, well, a Putin.

Yet Shakhnzarov's film resonated long after *Countdown* had its run, though not so much for its popularity as a film but as a film site. The recreated set of Moscow in 1904 became more than just a place to film deep thoughts about terrorism and a site to take President Putin for a stroll. In creating the atmosphere of old Moscow and packaging it around an historical blockbuster, Shakhnazarov offered a ready-made site for other directors to take their turns around the block. By the end of the following year (2005), the set had already been used for two more big-budget productions: Vladimir Khotinenko filmed his ten-part television series *Death of the Empire* [*Gibel′ imperii*] on it, while Filipp Iankovskii used it for his Boris Akunin blockbuster, *The State Counsellor* [*Statskii sovetnik*]. Both the television series and the film were produced by Russia's First Channel and by Nikita Mikhalkov's Studio Tri-te and therefore had A-list actors, big budgets, and slick advertising. Both, intriguingly enough, dealt with political violence, the first set around the time of World War

I and the second with terrorism in the early years of Alexander III. Both used the past in a fashion similar to *Rider* and both did well commercially, though (much like *Rider*) critics and audiences divided over their meanings and significance.[73]

The State Counsellor, even more than *Rider,* represented a victory over Hollywood in the coveted box-office battle, placing first in its opening weekend in April 2005 over *The Pacifier* and *Sahara*—Russian historical blockbusters, it turned out, could beat even Vin Diesel.[74] Iankovskii's adaptation of the Boris Akunin novel also bears the closest resemblance to *Rider* in its use of history and its look of the past. In it, the tsarist policeman (and hero of the Akunin series) Erast Fandorin combats a group of terrorists who assassinated a government minister. Yet the real villains are not the terrorists, who are acting out of misplaced but noble ideas, but the conniving careerists in the Moscow gendarmes and the Petersburg policeman Prince Pozharsky (played by Nikita Mikhalkov). In its take on terrorism and the tsarist efforts to combat it, *State Counsellor* suggests that the violence used by the police and that of the terrorists are no different. Grigorii Chkhartishvili, who writes as Akunin and who wrote the screenplay based on his novel, has claimed that the film and novel are both "histories of terrorism" and posit that "Russia's eternal misfortune" is that "good is defended by fools and scoundrels, while evil is served by martyrs and heroes."[75] Inevitably *The State Counsellor* was compared to *Rider* by critics, audiences, and even by Shakhnazarov himself, who, when asked by the film journal *Seans* (*Performance*) what he thought of Akunin, stated, "I didn't see *State Counsellor*. . . . The television series *Azazel′* [based on Akunin's first novel and also dealing with terrorists] was somehow unconvincing. It seems to me that within Akunin's texts a sense of self-irony is hidden. . . . But in the films this element is missing entirely—they are too serious. . . . The films cannot be played as if they are Tolstoy. Or not even like Savinkov's *Rider Named Death*. It has drama, clean drama. Akunin does not. And even his terrorists are not frightening and terrible. They are alien [*chuzhoi*]."[76] That Shakhnazarov should feel like it was necessary to defend his version of history in the face of Akunin's is not that surprising, given the immense popularity of the latter's novels, scripts, and even plays. But then again, that is a story worthy of its own chapter.

The most talked-about production that used Shakhnazarov's outdoor set was Aleksandr Proshkin's 2006 miniseries *Doctor Zhivago,* starring Oleg Menshikov in the title role. Billed as "our Zhivago returning home," the series attempted to move beyond the American 1965 film and the 2002 British series—no balalaikas strummed in its 500 minutes and Lara was a brunette, not a Julie Christie blonde. In a way, this use of history and use of the set best sums up the ways in which the historical film has developed in the zero years. As an act of cultural recall in the present, all four films that used the set tapped into cultural memories of the past built around historical phenomena, in this case, the meanings of the fin de siècle, its politics and culture, and the descent into Bolshevism. *Rider, Death of the Empire, State Counsellor,* and *Doctor Zhivago* all turned cultural memories into cultural memorization, for they consistently reminded Russians of the importance of terrorism then and now and in doing so made sure that the past was "continuously modified and redescribed" and even performed as a means to "mediate and modify difficult or tabooed moments of the past."[77] All four used American-style marketing techniques and the blockbuster format to revisit this past. All four used a recreated old Moscow as a visual marker of Russianness—elegant terrorists, imperial doctors, and Russian soldiers all walked the same streets of this "lost Russia." Shakhnazarov has conceded that the "blockbuster is a necessary part of the film market" and that while "our blockbusters are done under the strong influence of Hollywood," they can still "not only borrow from them, but introduce something of our national culture."[78] Not only did *Rider* fulfill this task, so too did *Death of the Empire, State Counsellor,* and *Doctor Zhivago.* All four helped to produce debates about the meanings of violence, the collapse of the tsarist system, the romance with the pre-1917 past, and the usefulness of this history for contemporary concerns ranging from economics to politics. Finally, all four appeared with proclamations that "our history" has returned and even vanquished Hollywood versions of the past. At the same time, the history Shakhnazarov offers on screen perhaps makes these rewards worthwhile, for it does, as the director argues, "show that terrorism has had an important role in Russian history. Unfortunately."[79]

Taken together, these four films and their uses of history represent the fulfillment of Shakhnazarov's dreams about Mosfil′m and its role in post-Soviet Russia. In his 2003 *Itogi* interview, Shakhnazarov stated that "we recreated a corner of old Moscow," a historic set built with money from the Ministry of Culture and its funds to rebuild Russian patriotism.[80] Old Moscow in the heart of Mosfil′m could be used again and again to package "our history" in blockbuster format.[81] Shakhnazarov's set therefore found the lost Russia of pre-tsarist times. Shakhnazarov has trumpeted this triumph, stating that he not only recreated the past, but an entire contemporary film industry: "in five years, we created a studio that from the technological point of view is inferior to none in Europe and even the world."[82] Apparently European and American directors heard this message, for Mosfil′m could now be used for their blockbusters—Shakhnazarov, it turns out, has not just overseen the revival of Russian film, he has also allowed Hollywood blockbusters to use the studios, sets, and technicians as well.[83]

According to critics like Iurii Gladil′shchikov, the state patriotism built on cinema has a simple formula, one worked out best by Shakhnazarov: "give us money for these necessary films and we shall provide you with patriotism."[84] Blockbuster history, therefore, paid in the zero years, and Karen Shakhnazarov's Mosfil′m Studios reaped the rewards.

Турецкий гамбит

Борис Акунин

FOUR

Wars and Gambits

Dzhanik Faiziev's film *The Turkish Gambit,* a mystery set amidst the Russo-Turkish War of 1877–78, debuted in February 2005. It went on to earn $18.5 million—more than any other film in Russian history—besting the previous year's blockbuster, *Night Watch.* Produced by Konstantin Ernst, the head of Pervyi kanal, and Leonid Vereshchagin, Nikita Mikhalkov's producer at Studio Tri-te, *The Turkish Gambit* was both hailed and reviled as a sign that Russian cinema had either refound its footing or lost the battle with Hollywood altogether. To supporters, the fact that the film topped the Russian box office for three weeks straight (eventually another Russian film, *Shadow Boxing,* bested it), was a sign of Russian cinematic strength. Russian films led the box office for the entire month of March 2005, the first time this feat had been achieved since communism's collapse. For detractors, however, this "victory" meant nothing, for it represented a triumph of Hollywood style over Russian substance. "Russian" cinema, for some critics, had ceased to exist, replaced by action films that deliberately used American conventions to dumb down the masses.

Faiziev figured very little in this debate. Instead, the film's scriptwriter, Boris Akunin, served as the central subject of heated conversation. For the most part, the film revived an ongoing debate about the

Facing. Akunin's gambit: Cover of the movie tie-in edition of *Turkish Gambit,* published by the Moscow publisher Zakharov and First Channel in 2004.

merits of Akunin, who by the time the film premiered had emerged as Russia's most popular postcommunist author. The St. Petersburg journal *Seans* (*Performance*) included an entire section on Akunin in its September 2005 issue, which appeared after the film's box office success. Titled "What Do You Think about Boris Akunin?" the journal asked various luminaries to weigh in with their answers.[1] Television personality Leonid Parfenov stated that "it's necessary to be grateful" to him for killing off the sacred myth of Russian literature and for creating new genres that audiences love. Aleksei Slapovskii, a writer and scriptwriter, stated, "Akunin is characteristic of this era's super-brands such as Nescafé and Lipton." He called Akunin his "class enemy. A joke. Not really." For Slapovskii, "there is culture and there is mass culture" and although detective novelists can be good, "a good, average writer is always better than a great detective writer." Given that Slapovskii had authored the scripts for the television serials *Ostanovka po trebovaniiu* (2000–2001) and would write the script for *Irony of Fate 2* in 2008, this dismissal might seem a little hypocritical.

Others mostly followed these two respondents. Aleksandr Prokhanov called Akunin "an undoubted cultural strategist" and left it up to readers to judge whether it was good or bad he was a symbol of "the market era." Pavel Lungin provided a similar backhanded compliment, calling Akunin "clever entertainment." El′dar Riazanov likes Akunin. Aleksei German and Aleksandr Rogozhkin do not. Eduard Limonov, the National Bolshevik leader and subject of the film *Russkoe* (which also came out in 2005), unsurprisingly, does not like Akunin, claiming he represents a cultural nostalgia for the imperial period and the "lost Russia" that could be found before 1917. The harshest criticism came from Aleksandr Ivanov, who dismissed Akunin as "a state writer" and offered as "proof" that the answer to the question "Who is your favorite writer?" "has to be 'Boris Akunin,'" just as the answer to the question "Who is your favorite director?" "has to be 'Nikita Mikhalkov.'" For Ivanov, "Akunin clearly personifies several state directives of Putin's Russia." First and foremost, "Akunin is completely competitive," a "successful manager" who puts profit first and art second. Secondly, Akunin personifies the ideological nostalgia that Ivanov believes rests at the heart of Putin's country, "the Russia we lost" of the nineteenth century "that must now become our future." Finally, in Fandorin, Akunin's main literary and cinematic hero, is "the prototype, the heavenly grandson," of the Federal Security Service (FSB) agent. Although no "state decree" created Akunin and his hero, the writer nonetheless recognized that a tsarist police agent who solved murders in the last years of the Romanov empire would help fuel Putin's success.[2] No one, it should be added, debated what they thought about Dzhanik Faiziev.

Who is this Akunin and why did a film adapted from his novel provoke such a debate? Akunin is really two people. The first Akunin is his creator, for Akunin is a pseudonym used by a Georgian literary scholar of Japan named Grigorii Chkhartishvili. The second Akunin is the creator of an alternate past, a place described by the author as "a country resembling Russia," where the forces that sustained and ultimately dissolved the Romanov Empire are turned into playful points of debate and the basis for a good detective story. The first Akunin is a product of the specific milieu of late socialism, and the second is a product of the post-Soviet cultural desire to understand the Russia that may have been lost in 1917. As a writer, Akunin's tremendous popularity is second to none.[3] Fans and critics alike are right to speak about the "Akuninization" of Russia: in his own way, Akunin made "the Russia that we lost" into a site of patriotic renewal.

THE LIFE AND WORK OF GRIGORII CHKHARTISHVILI

Born in May 1956 in Tbilisi, Grigorii Chkhartishvili grew up in Moscow. He did so amidst the cultural relaxation of the Thaw, nuclear brinksmanship with the United States, the Soviet conquest of space, and the stagnant stability of the Brezhnev era. As a child in this environment, Grigorii turned inward, first to the safety and excitement of books, devouring virtually everything he could find. He also developed an interest in Japan after attending a Moscow kabuki theater. This introverted aspect of his Soviet childhood informed his decision to major in Japanese history and languages at the Institute of Asia and Africa at Moscow State University, which he entered in 1973. The interest in Japan, as Chkhartishvili later claimed, came because it "seemed so exotic and so unlike the Soviet Union."[4] In this sense, he followed the course of many young

Soviet citizens of the 1970s—not fully dissidents, not Party enthusiasts, but citizens who simply carved out space where they could pursue their own interests. As a product of the late Soviet empire and therefore late socialism itself, Chkhartishvili by the 1970s was also typically untypical, representing a strange embodiment of the way the Soviet empire worked and shaped its citizens: Georgian by ethnicity and on his passport, a Muscovite by inclination and upbringing, a devotee of Russian literary classics and world literature, an enthusiast of Japanese culture and history, and a Soviet citizen who had no strong political views but a general sense of "slight discontent." This strange mix of selfhood may only be explained by simply stating that the person who united these seemingly disparate elements lived in Brezhnev-era Moscow, a sentiment later articulated by Chkhartishvili: "It's Moscow and everyone has different roots. My life and education was typically Muscovite and typically Soviet." As a child in the 1960s, Chkhartishvili mused, "I was a happy kid in the happiest country in the world. Then in the 1970s, when I got older, I started to think, to compare things in the Soviet Union with what I read and heard about other places, and to see the lies all around. I was not as happy and neither was my country."[5]

After graduation, Chkhartishvili worked as an academic and literary expert. He published articles on Japanese literature and translated works from Japanese and English (including Yukio Mishima and Malcolm Bradbury), though some of these translations could not be published until the Gorbachev era. For the most part, Chkhartishvili remembers the era of Brezhnev as being "boring."[6] And then, as is the case with many of the last Soviet generation, Gorbachev arrived, and everything changed. During the 1990s, Chkhartishvili, like many of his compatriots, experienced an existential crisis. To deal with it, he researched and wrote *The Writer and Suicide* (*Pisatel′ i samoubiistvo*), which appeared in 1999 with Novoe literaturnoe obozrenie, a well-respected Moscow publisher. Aimed at a broad audience, the book examines literary suicides in a number of works, showcasing Chkhartishvili's longstanding habit of reading voraciously and broadly. He admitted that the research for his work on suicide took a toll on him mentally. For kicks, and as a much-needed break, he decided to indulge his love for detective stories and his increasing interest in genre-bending works by writing a series of detective scripts and novels. This therapy, it turned out, provided the cure for his ailments, for Chkhartishvili decided to keep his writing a secret and to assume another persona, that of Boris Akunin.

Chkhartishvili chose the name for two reasons: first, as homage to Mikhail Bakunin, the founder of modern anarchism (B. Akunin). Second, *akunin* means "bad person" (or "villain") in Japanese. Thus, Chkhartishvili draws on several strands of Russian national and imperial memories in order to play with the past, to cause chaos and anarchy in the accumulated memories about the nineteenth century in particular and the baggage of the Russian imperial project over the centuries. In the chaotic 1990s where bad guys could do good and vice versa, Chkhartishvili's choice of Akunin for a pseudonym worked perfectly.

Akunin is best known for his detective series starring Erast Fandorin, a Moscow member of the tsarist police force. He began the series in 1998 and has since published thirteen books in the series, which became a sensation by the time the fifth book, *Special Assignments,* appeared in 1999. In just one year, Akunin went from a complete unknown who had never written a novel before to a literary and cultural sensation. Since 1998, the Fandorin series has sold millions of copies (the first in the series, *Azazel′,* has sold about fifteen million alone), with individual titles selling two hundred thousand copies in the first week—in a country where the entire novels can be found legally for free on the internet and illegally everywhere. Akunin himself maintains a website where all his works can be found in their entirety. Boris Akunin, it is fair to say, is a celebrity. His books are best sellers, his film scripts are blockbusters, and his rewriting of Chekhov's *The Seagull* (*Chaika*) even sold out the Moscow Arts Theater when it appeared in 2000.

Akunin's works play with Russia's past, particularly the Romanov and Soviet Empires. Much as his name has two meanings, his works deliberately distort the history of Russia's empire in order to challenge widely held views about this entity. For the most part, he tells these histories in a genre that Russia traditionally lacked: the detective story.

Akunin's reworking of war in the Fandorin novel *The Turkish Gambit* (the second in the series), which he later adapted into the 2005 blockbuster film, captures his writing well. The plot of this "spy detective" novel revolves around the Russo-Turkish War of 1877–78, when Pan-

Slavist sentiment raged through Russia and, after a bloody siege of the Turkish fortress at Plevna, when Russian forces nearly captured Constantinople. The spectacular Russian successes in the war and the subsequent Treaty of San Stefano shook European leaders enough that Otto von Bismarck called a special Congress of Berlin and brought all the major heads of state to the Prussian capital in order to revise Russian gains. For a few months in 1878, however, Russian imperialists rejoiced, seemingly reaching a new zenith in imperial expansion. The Pan-Slavist dream of making Constantinople into Tsargrad seemed a near reality for the first and only time of the nineteenth century.

Set in this complex and often heady period, Akunin's mystery has Fandorin at the Turkish front attempting to uncover the machinations of a shadowy mole named Anwar Effendi, an urbane enemy who seemingly slips unseen in and out of both Russian and Turkish headquarters. Effendi's gambit is to draw Russian forces further and further into the war and into Turkey, in the end by playing on General Mikhail Sobelev (modeled on the popular hero of the war, the "White General" Mikhail Skobelev) and his dreams of becoming a new national hero.[7] As Sobelev confesses to Varvara, the feminist volunteer who helps Fandorin, "my true passion is my ambition, and everything else comes second. That's just the way I am. But ambition is no sin if it is directed to an exalted goal."[8] Anwar Effendi sees this view for what it is—a puffed-up desire to be worshipped—and lures Sobelev into Constantinople to provoke a general European war and the end of Russian power on the continent. Sobelev follows, and in the end thwarts Effendi's gambit.

At novel's end, however, we are not certain who has played their pieces better, for Effendi—who turns out to be Charles Paladin, a French reporter—tells Varvara that he plays chess for the white pieces while Russia is the black. In the Turkish spy's words,

> [Y]our immensely powerful state constitutes the main danger to civilization. With its vast expanses, its multitudinous, ignorant population, its cumbersome and aggressive state apparatus.... The mission of the Russian people is to take Constantinople and unite the Slavs? To what end? So that the Romanovs might once again impose their will on Europe? A nightmarish prospect indeed! It is not pleasant to hear this, *Mademoiselle Barbara,* but lurking within Russia is a terrible threat to civilization. There are savage, destructive forces fermenting within her, forces that will break out sooner or later, and then the world will be

> in a bad way. It is an unstable, ridiculous country that has absorbed all the worse features of the West and the East. Russia has to be put back in its place; its reach has to be shortened.[9]

The novel closes with Anwar Effendi dead but seemingly proven correct, for the announcement of the Congress of Berlin is printed in the press. Is Akunin's reimagined empire, then, a romantic setting in which spies and detectives played elegant games and in which Fandorin, a committed monarchist, is a true hero and nostalgic reminder of the "Russia we have lost"?[10] Or are Effendi's/Paladin's words a reminder that the Romanov Empire was a dangerous creation that in turn produced "destructive forces" in the form of the Bolsheviks and therefore a reminder that the Russia of 1998 continued to harbor "aggressive and cumbersome" ideas? The reader is left to wonder these questions, for Akunin provides no clear answers.

In his film script, Akunin plays with these pasts and inconclusive conclusions even more, claiming, "It's boring to make the same borscht."[11] He introduces a new villain, Ismail-Bei (played by Gosha Kutsenko), who controls the mole. Although all the novel's characters remain, the spy turns out to be Perepelkin, a military attaché assigned to Sobelev. Anwar Effendi is not motivated by ideology in this version, but by sheer greed. While Akunin plays with imperial history in the novel, he plays with contemporary history in his film script. In their review for *KinoKultura,* Elena Prokhorova and Alexander Prokhorov argue, "as long as Russia is fighting Muslim separatists in Chechnya *now,* no Russian viewer needs an explanation about why Russians fought treacherous Turks in Bulgaria *then*"—a history lesson they characterize as a "computer-age patriotic woodcut."[12] Then again, at the end Fandorin, when asked by Varvara who won, states, "Anwar played his gambit well." Russian expansion has been stymied, and Fandorin is disillusioned with military intrigues, so he decides to head to Japan.

Akunin openly admits the connections between the past and present in his works in his response to an Italian interviewer:

> [T]he problems that Russia faced at the end of the nineteenth century are essentially the same problems we have in Russia today. I don't want to go on at great length about the political and economic aspects of these problems. That's not really the point. Right now there is an ongoing debate in my country about

> which values deserve the highest priority: whether individual values need to be emphasized, or whether we should return to social and collective interests. Last century, Russia chose an answer to this question that led to the tragedies of the twentieth century. Now we find ourselves at a similar crossroads, but we don't know yet which road will be taken this time.[13]

As for Fandorin's being great-grandfather to a certain KGB agent turned Russian president, Akunin told his interviewer, "I don't believe that Fandorin would have taken part in Putin's military campaign against Chechnya. Yes, Fandorin is a detective in the czar's police force, but he is above all a man of solid moral principles. The war against Chechnya is taking place in an atmosphere of immorality."[14]

Not surprisingly, because of his popularity, his provocative suggestions on Russian history, and his use of genre, Akunin has received a lot of critical attention. When the Fandorin series became a phenomenon, some critics believed that Akunin romanticized tsarist Russia, creating a positive hero out of a policeman and an elegant empire that gave way to a brutal dictatorship. Fandorin and Akunin might even be seen as conservative xenophobes, a charge leveled by Roman Arbitman.[15] Other critics see another Akunin, one that created a "self-indulgent individual who scorns everything Russian."[16] Because of his repeated critiques of Russian power in the past, some critics claim that Akunin is a Russophobe and that he hates his homeland.[17]

Lev Pirogov praises Akunin for popularizing Russian history[18] and Elena Diakova writes that Akunin's nineteenth century empire is a fascinatingly complex place.[19] Akunin embraces this latter view, referring to himself as a "belletrist" and not an "author [*pisatel′*]," thereby publicly scorning the mantle of prophet that has often accompanied important Russian writers of the past.[20] Although Akunin does not want to be read and championed in the tradition of Gogol, Dostoevsky, Tolstoy, or Bulgakov (to just name a few), many of his readers want to see him as the latest incarnation of the artistic genius who lays bare all the essential meanings of life. Russian academics such as Georgii Tsiplakov see Akunin—because of Chkhartishvili's interest in Eastern culture and his preference for postmodern literary games with the reader—as a "cunning and masterful Taoist who demonstrates to the heroes of his books the inexorability of the Tao. . . . He [Akunin] has fun with his villains, but he himself is the principal villain. It is he, not his criminals, who is the master of the chess gambit."[21] Ultimately, Akunin's recreated empire is a space where the author can "set Taoism against romanticism, East against West, inaction against the desire to act and create" and where Fandorin—like Akunin—is a passive mediator, a perfect blend of the age-old belief that Russia is both East and West.[22] Western academics have tended to view Akunin as an embodiment of the supposedly widespread nostalgia for the Romanovs in post-Soviet Russia (albeit a remarkably gifted nostalgic),[23] or even as a writer who articulates "homosexual panic" by writing about the "perverted leanings" of characters in novels such as *Turkish Gambit.*[24] What unites these views is the tendency to understand Akunin's popularity in terms of the author's ability to recreate a "Russia that we lost" on the page.

Well before he entered the film world, writing adaptations for Russian television (*Azazel´*, First Channel, prod. Ernst, 2002) and his two novels, *The Turkish Gambit* and *The State Counsellor,* Akunin had become a cultural phenomenon. Akunin became a lightning rod for criticism about the state of Russian literature and the state of Russian culture after communism. And then his film topped the box office.

THE VICTORY OF THE MARKET OVER ART?

Gambit's success, which followed on that of Timur Bekmambetov's *Night Watch,* reignited the debate about Russian blockbusters. It often replicated the earlier debates about Akunin's novels. For supporters, the Hollywood-style effects and action format transferred to a Russian plot signaled a new era—Russian films could learn from the West, adapt their cultural forms, but still produce a "Russian" success that beat Hollywood at its game. For critics, the film marked a new era as well, but one that meant the end to "artistic Russian cinema" in favor of market-driven blockbusters. *Gambit* appeared after an intense marketing blitz, which some critics saw as the source of its success. One Russian research firm calculated that the *Turkish Gambit* trailer aired for a total of 435 minutes between January 5 and March 12 on Pervyi kanal alone.[25] The advertising campaign led the Duma's State Auditing Chamber to launch an investigation about the film's financing and its profits (Konstantin

Ernst, the film's producer, is also head of the state-run channel).[26] Faiziev responded to critics that charged this campaign was solely responsible for the film's financial success by pointing out that the usual drop in attendance from one week to the second in Russia is 40 to 70 percent, while *Gambit* experienced only a 20 percent drop. In his words, "it means the spectator is satisfied" with the product and not just turned on by the ads.[27] The interpretive lines had been drawn, however—the film succeeded either because of its slick advertisements or because of its slick use of history and special effects.

The most engaged debate took place on the pages of *Rossisskaia gazeta*. Initiated by the film director Andrei Konchalovsky-Mikhalkov, the discussion involved art-house directors, film critics, cultural critics, and even poets. At issue was whether or not films such as *Turkish Gambit* represented "Russian" cinema or whether *Gambit*'s success, as Konchalovsky eventually defined it, meant that the market had triumphed over Russian art. The film director wrote an "urgent letter" to the newspaper that called on other cultural figures and readers to debate whether "marketology [*marketologi*]" had won out over "creativity [*tvorchestvo,* one of the three Ts in his brother's Studio Tri-te]."[28] Konchalovsky lamented that "armchair producers" had turned to "amateurs and MTV" for directors in the new Russian commercial cinema, a decision that meant a "decline in craftsmanship." Furthermore, cinema today no longer engaged with deep philosophical questions, but with corporate gain, leading to a situation in which "marketing has become the most significant driving force in civilization's development, for marketing's strength is in the fact that the quality of goods is less important that the quality of its advertisement [*Marketing stal glavnoi dvizhushchei siloi razvitiia tsivilizatsii, ibo sila marketinga v tom, chto kachestvo tovara menee vazhno, chem, kachestvo ego reklamy*]."[29] He fears that young people see all artistic creation as "kitsch" because postmodernism has taught that everything is relative. The result is that classics are no longer in demand; instead, Russians run to the kiosk and purchase Tarantino or "whoever else is in fashion." Konchalovsky sets the stakes very high—the death of artistic culture is nothing less than the death of Western civilization. The internet and advertising have dealt the potential fatal blow. As Konchalovsky claims, "the internet changed the history of mankind, . . . [but] the greater the information we possess, the less we know." To avoid another decline of the West, he concludes, Russians must rediscover skill in all the arts, cinema most of all.[30]

Konchalovsky's article appeared thirteen days before Akunin's cinematic version of *Turkish Gambit* hit Russian theaters. A month after the first article appeared, the newspaper printed a roundtable that included, among others, Konchalovsky, Kirill Razlogov (director of the Institute of Culturology), and Daniil Dondurei (editor of *Iskusstvo kino*). Titled "Flight from the Black Square: How to Create a Market without Sacrificing Culture," the exchange took place after Faiziev's film had dominated the Russian box office. This success formed the backdrop of the conversation, which featured Dondurei challenging what he called Konchalovsky's "super-conservative view" that "the market kills quality and kills skill." In Dondurei's view, Russia has witnessed "a democratization of artistic production," which in turn means both good and bad products sell.[31] Dondurei also asserted that one should evaluate the relationship between the market and art through two temporal lenses: the immediate and the long term. As he views it, immediate success is proof of the market's democratizing trends, whereas long-term success affirms artistic success. In cinematic terms, he argues, "*Turkish Gambit* is the absolute champion [of immediate, democratic success]" but "Tarkovsky's *The Mirror* became a success over the course of ten years."[32] Konchalovsky, naturally, disagreed, and argued that the success of *Turkish Gambit* and *Night Watch* rested less on democratizing markets than on a "new Politburo" made up of television producers who want to sell mass products over educational culture. The problem, Konchalovsky (quoting Mikhail Epstein) states, is that this market creates "post-information trauma and a shortening of memory."[33] Watching, listening to, or reading blockbuster culture, in other words, creates a society that lacks knowledge and cultural depth.

A further salvo in the discussion about *Gambit* and blockbusters concerned the issue of history. Fired at the end of March by Aleksandr Tolkachev, a St. Petersburg–based writer and critic, "Cinematic Lokhotron" took issue with *Gambit*'s market appeal and with its exploration of the past. In the former critique, Tolkachev sees films such as *Gambit* as a sort of sophisticated pyramid scheme—the 1990s scandals no longer will dupe the masses, so now new capitalists and television producers have turned to pop culture. As proof of *Gambit*'s nefarious game, he cites Marx's famous footnote to *Kapital,* in which the author states that for a 300 percent profit, capital will commit any crime.[34] *Turkish Gambit,* Tolkachev pointed out, had made $16 million on its $5 million budget. Its "crime" is that it serves as an "imaginary winning ticket" that cinemagoers will use again and again for similarly light fare.[35] The crimes against history committed by the film are equally grave. "The hero," Tolkachev writes, "is primitive," "defeats the villain and saves the empire" single-handedly. He concludes, "*Turkish Gambit* is to historical authenticity what a cabin is to a palace. It is understandable that its authors made a detective film, not an historical one. But why then does Boris Akunin, in the First Channel advertising trailer, travel through the Russo-Turkish War's war locales? It seems only for an increase in box office profit. By the way, the trailer came out more interesting than the film itself." The light history on display, Tolkachev opines, will fool unknowledgeable spectators into believing that the past presented on screen is an "objective" view of the Muslim enemy and the war itself.[36]

Two months later in the same paper, art-house director Vadim Abdrashitov picked up on Tolkachev's points. By May the film's victory over American blockbusters had become clear and Konchalovsky's lamentations now could be applied to a specific Russian blockbuster. In his piece, "In Place of Casino Cinema in the National Scale," Abdrashitov first faced a question about *Turkish Gambit.* Abdrashitov, although generally in agreement with Konchalovsky, put a more positive spin on *Gambit*'s meanings. He answered that the film's triumph "pleased him," because "people who left the cinema halls now are returning." Furthermore, "in this success *Turkish Gambit* differs, let us say, from *Night Watch*'s success. For the first time in years there is a positive hero in the simplest, most editorial sense in *Gambit.* And he prevails over the forces of evil." The result is that *Gambit* "encourages optimism."[37] Valerii Kichin, who conducted the interview, interjected, "But *Watch, Gambit,* and *Shadow Boxing* are artistically primitive and not made for a thinking person." Abdrashitov agreed, although he still preferred *Gambit,* but also argued that culture has always involved consumption. What was needed to combat casino culture, violence, and popcorn ideology, according to Abdrashitov, was simply good art. More specifically, Abdrashitov believed that *Gambit*'s success would help to bring spectators back to art-house cinema. The key, he identified, was the past: "Almost everything that has appeared [in art house films] is in dialogue with the past: *Driver for Vera, Svoi, The Long Goodbye, Moscow Saga, Children of the Arbat, Brezhnev* . . . All dashed there. Because man cannot live without foundations."[38] As he sees it, "everything now must be adapted for mass consumption, even Russian history itself. And here on TV and in the cinema blockbusters appear, easily grasped by the wide public, and even for foreign viewers." The return to the past, in other words, provides a necessary means of dealing with the present.[39]

As this debate and others like it—both *Iskusstvo kino* and *Seans* carried special sections about the meanings of historical blockbusters in the wake of *Gambit*'s victory—captured dynamic contradictions about the state of Russian cinema and the state of historical memory in 2005.[40] Kichin, writing later as Akunin's next adaptation was about to appear, reflected on the sudden appearance of historical blockbusters:

> The touchstone was *The Barber of Siberia*. All the attractive marks of the blockbuster were made in it: the impressive views, a breathtaking subject, an abundance of stars, luxurious balls and operatic effects, the large-scale Maslenitsa scene, which ate up a huge part of the budget. With the appearance of *Night Watch* the business was delivered as if on a production line. We were not forced to wait for results: in our box office figures *Night Watch* approached that of an American hit, *Turkish Gambit* passed it, while *State Counsellor*, will, I think overtake this record. [It did not.][41]

As to the reason for this success, Kichin wrote, "*Turkish Gambit* was made dashingly and beautifully, but historically it is more than inaccurate. The conveyor belt production is seen in it to the highest degree: many special-effects are copied as if from *Night Watch*." Ultimately, all three movies "are made by the same hand," the production line of a Russian historical blockbuster. For Evgenii Maizel′, historical inaccuracies aside, *Turkish Gambit* had become "representative of the 'Russian blockbuster' breed," which "feeds the yeast of kvas patriotism."[42] The nostalgic-retro detective story that had seemed daring in the Yeltsin years, Maizel′ writes, had become part of the Putin government's calls for unity. For most critics, *Turkish Gambit*'s use of the past had become the key to a new, pop-culture brand of Russian patriotism. Many critics interpreted *Gambit* as an attempt to restore a lost Russia on screen. In performing this role, the film ensured that contemporary Russianness and its artistic heritage would be sacrificed.

AKUNIN'S HISTORY AND PATRIOTISM

The debates amused Grigorii Chkhartishvili. The person better known as Boris Akunin likes to play with critics and consumers as much as he plays with the past. "I feel absolutely free to deal with history as I like," he has stated. "My aim is not to reproduce the facts but to know them in order to create an historical atmosphere."[43] Although he conducts extensive historical research and reads only nonfiction, he does not believe that anyone should see his works as strictly historical. "The reader must believe in the atmosphere, in the little details I note," he argues, "but people shouldn't learn history from novels." Instead, the past can serve as a means to comment on the present, for "the problems we are facing today are more or less the same problems Fandorin faced." Far more important, however, is that Akunin's products are entertaining—"my novels focus on law and order, which are present-day concerns, but I don't want to put words into peoples' mouths about what their present-day implications are. My primary goal is to entertain."[44]

And entertain he has. One secret to Akunin's success is his embrace of new genres and new market strategies. He engages in marketing and successfully sells himself and his products, one reason for his success and the same reason so many intellectual critics loathe him. He has stated, "I like to experiment with mass culture, mass literature, and the book trade. It's still possible in Russia. The market mechanism is a new and unexplored thing for us. Mass culture in Russia is also terra incognita."[45] His original aim was to launch a series of ten films that in turn would lead to ten television series that would in turn lead to ten books. All would follow the same loose structure but the endings would change in each. "All would reinforce the marketing of the other," Akunin stated. Viewers would see a movie, hear about a television series that expanded on it, and finally watch a commercial during the series that would advertise the book. Akunin wrote the scripts and got the first film project funded.

Then came the August 1998 ruble collapse and, with it, any chance to make a movie or a TV series that relied on historical details. Instead, Akunin started the Fandorin project. By 2004, with the economy improving, Akunin used his original plan for the film and television versions of *Turkish Gambit.* His original novel, he claims, was an attempt to make a war novel popular with women as well as men (his test audience was his wife's book club). For the film, "with less time to bring out a sophisticated enemy, I had to make a cruder one." His four-part television miniseries, which aired in 2006, restored the French journalist as the enemy. The goal all along was to tease audiences, both those who had read the novel and those who had not.

His use of genres expanded for *Gambit* when he filmed a documentary for Pervyi kanal with Leonid Parfenov, whose 2002 *Russian Empire* series had drawn massive ratings. Parfenov had been fired in June 2004 from NTV for airing an interview with the widow of a Chechen rebel. Akunin jumped at the chance to work with him: "Leonid is a true professional, the best documentary filmmaker in Russia. Although he had been forced out of television, I wanted to work with someone who knew what he was doing."[46] The pair traveled to the locales where the war was fought, at one point even rowing across the Danube together, framing the series around the solitary monument to the Russo-Turkish War that stands in Moscow's Ilinskii Gardens. It aired just before the film premiered, and for Akunin "should be seen as a kind of ad for the feature film. . . . Many people will become acquainted with the Russo-Turkish War of the nineteenth century from Parfenov's TV version, not from the feature film."[47] Parfenov agreed with Akunin's reasons: for him the film could serve as a useful history lesson. "You ask anyone about the Russo-Turkish War," Parfenov declares, "and they will answer: 'This is when Kutuzov had his eye knocked out?' No. 'It was the time of Izmail?' No. 'It is when Peter very nearly was captured?' No. 'Admiral Nakhimov and the Cat?' No. All of these involve Russo-Turkish Wars, but not Akunin's war."[48] The series was also a smash, garnering the highest ratings of the week and serving as a means to provide further historical background to the film's events.[49]

Akunin also agreed to work with Studio Tri-te and with Nikita Mikhalkov for similar reasons. "I don't like Mikhalkov's views or his politics very much," he states, "but you realize when you meet him that he is a true professional, the best director and the best actor that we have in Russia." Moreover, Mikhalkov played Prince Pozharsky in *The State Counsellor*, a St. Petersburg chief of police who comes to Moscow in order to deal with terrorists. At the end of the book and the film, we learn that Pozharsky has deliberately used the terrorists as a means to assume almost dictatorial powers. "Pozharsky is an archetypical figure in Russian history and culture," Akunin states. "He is a larger-than-life figure who thinks he can remake society and who thinks the ends justifies the means. . . . I wrote the novel during the 1999 apartment bombings in Moscow. They had nothing to do with the Chechens, even though Chechens were blamed for them—someone like a Pozharsky, or later a Putin, was behind them."[50] In the film, Pozharsky stands in for Putin, and in Akunin's script, Russia's biggest Putin supporter plays him.

Akunin's take on contemporary patriotism in Russia and his role in building it is an interesting one. "Patriotism in Russia today is a compromised word because it is typically used by dumb xenophobes," he claims. "I am a patriot but don't like to make this claim. . . . Patriotism isn't just about saying everything is good, it's also about investigating bad things to make them better, it's often about loving your country while not liking it." For Akunin, Putin and his supporters have hijacked the term "patriotism" in an effort to equate love for country with love for the state. Yet this effort has been unsuccessful: "Putin's popularity is a myth, or at least misunderstood. People are now more concerned with providing for themselves and for their families, not with politics. Putin is liked because he doesn't interfere with this revolutionary process."[51] When asked what the two biggest problems facing Russia today were, Akunin mused, "Traffic first, then Putin."

Viewers that reviewed the film on kinopoisk.ru (3,874 in all) scored it a 7.4/10 on average.[52] Many responded to the visual and aural representations of a lost Russia that the film evoked. "Kino-Maniac" wrote, "There are some films that are enjoyable independent of their realism and authenticity within them because they contain an interesting plot, remarkable acting, beautiful landscapes, nice music, they are beautifully made and wonderfully produced. *Turkish Gambit* is such a film." Moreover, questions of strict historical accuracy are immaterial, for the film contains "a grain of historical truth" and "the history captured in this film is interesting, captivating, and entertaining." "Kent Light" disagreed about the historical accuracy (he wanted more), but still concluded that the film was a milestone in Russian cinema, was beautiful entertainment to watch, and enjoined readers "to support native cinema." "This new film," he posted, "is a new page in our cinema's history." Many wrote that they hadn't yet read Akunin but would after seeing the film. Others wondered "where Akunin was" in an otherwise "beautiful" but "historically superficial" film. Few agreed with "Auja's" rant that the film presents Russian officers as homosexuals that "converted our glorious war into a cheap comic."[53] For the most part, viewers who posted on this and other forums thought the past could be useful entertainment and that *Turkish Gambit* represented the beating out of Hollywood fare by "Russian topics."

One sign that Akunin had impacted historical understanding (again, depending on your position, either negatively or positively) came in a report about Russia's new educational testing system for high school students, EGE (Unified State Exam). This new set of standards, which the government introduced in 2009, was mostly criticized by educators and students alike. One student that took the exams in history argued that she did not learn a great deal about history preparing for the exam, but passed the history exam with a perfect score. She guided *Izvestiia* journalists through her thought process concerning the toughest questions. One question, number 17, asked students to name the young, heroic general of Plevna. The options were Ermolev, Kutuzov, Skobelev, or Bagration. As she recounted, "Boris Akunin came to my aid, for I remembered the military adventures of Erast Fandorin and I checked 'Skobelev.'"[54] Parfenov's prediction had come true.

One offshoot of the debate about *Gambit*'s blockbuster appeal was that the film did not delve into the "right kind" of history. On Victory Day 2005, the sixtieth anniversary, many Russian critics lamented what they saw as a lack of cinema space for veterans. Although the Russian government celebrated the holiday, the most popular television series was the Konstantin Ernst–produced and Vladimir Khotinenko–directed *The Death of the Empire* [*Gibel′ imperii*], a historical spy thriller set during World War I. Anna Kachkaeva of Radio Freedom lamented that the Akunin-style *Gibel′ imperii* and the insipid TV drama *Star of the Epoch* (about a 1930s actress modeled on Liubov′ Orlova who lives through the war) meant that no serious cinematic reflections of the war appeared on the big or small screens to commemorate the anniversary. Instead, as she argued, "the stylistics of semiofficial nostalgia overpowered the holiday."[55] Natal′ia Rostova of *Novaia gazeta* lamented the "banality" of television coverage of the holiday and historical events and wondered whether Russian cinema could come up with new examinations of the war. Elena Afanas′eva of *Echo Moscow* called the celebrations a reaffirmation of the Russian Empire, an announcement to the world that Russia was a superpower again. She regretted, however, that First Channel's coverage of Victory Day meant that they did not learn the lessons from their own series *Death of the Empire,* which had been presaged in films such as *The Turkish Gambit.* The message, in other words, was that Russian blockbusters—for both television and big screen—had not done enough memory work. Excellent series such as *Death of an Empire* and entertaining films such as *Turkish Gambit* had presented visions of imperial overstretch, providing historical background both for what happened in 1917 and what occurred in 1991. Instead of learning lessons from these cinematic visions, Russian television channels such as Pervyi kanal (which had produced both the series and the film) covered Victory Day 2005 as if Russia needed a new empire. What Russian media needed, a host of critics argued, were more explosive examinations about the Great Patriotic War.

Apparently the authors of these critiques had not tuned into other channels, for the critical view of Victory Day 2005 was misguided. At the end of 2004, a host of television series and blockbuster films about World War II had fired bombs at the existing mythologies about the conflict—the very myths that Putin tapped into. By the end of 2005, not only had these myths been confronted, but the Duma would also investigate whether or not a blockbuster film about the war was "unpatriotic." While these explosions took place, Russians could also tune into another important exploration of "the Russia that we lost": *Zhivago*'s Russia.

Artem´ev's soundscape: Soundtrack for *Doctor Zhivago*.

FIVE

A Requiem for Communism

One of the most memorable aspects of David Lean's 1965 adaptation of Boris Pasternak's novel *Doctor Zhivago* is its soundtrack. Love it or hate it, Maurice Jarre's "Lara's Theme" strums throughout the film with the help of balalaikas and burns itself into your brain. Anyone who watches the film cannot help but whistle or hum the tune afterward, an effect that no doubt contributed to the American Film Academy's decision to award Jarre an Oscar for best musical score.

"Lara's Theme" in many ways acts as audio shorthand for how many Russians view "their" *Zhivago*'s having gone wrong. The sweeping sound of balalaikas tends to be viewed as one of many ways that Hollywood turns Russian culture into kitsch. "Lara's Theme" sounds like Russian music to Western audiences because it conforms to preconceived ideas, images, and sounds of a romantic Russia, as do Robert Bolt's screenplay, Freddie Young's cinematography, and Lean's directing (and only Lean failed to win the Oscar for this Western imagining of Russia). This *Zhivago* is mostly a sad love story, a tale of a man who must choose between two women while history swirls around him. Jarre's score reinforces this theme, impressing upon Western audiences the romance and exoticness of old Russia in a fashion similar to Max Steiner's mock Arabic music for *Casablanca*.

When Aleksandr Proshkin decided to film a television series based on Pasternak's novel, clearly the result would be a blockbuster, for a Russian adaptation of *Doctor Zhivago* would be the first of its kind. Produced by Central Partnership and Karen Shakhnazarov's Courier Studio and airing on NTV in May 2006, Proshkin's film not only attempted to capture the essence of Pasternak's prose and its present-day applications, it also attempted to wrest the look and sounds of the Russian Revolution and Civil War away from its previous versions—by the time Proshkin's project appeared, the BBC had aired its own three-part series starring Keira Knightley. The challenge, as Proshkin saw it, was to make his *Zhivago* the reverse of the others, a story about history and how the Russian intelligentsia dealt with the twentieth century. The love story, as Proshkin viewed matters, was secondary to capturing the mood of an era.

Enter Eduard Artem′ev. The Russian John Williams, Artem′ev has worked with Andrei Tarkovsky, Andrei Konchalovsky-Mikhalkov, Karen Shakhnazarov, and Nikita Mikhalkov on their films, adding sounds to a host of canonical movies such as *Mirror, Slave of Love, Siberiade,* and *Zero City.* Chances are, if you ever hummed a tune from a Soviet-era historical film, you were humming the music of Eduard Artem′ev. The composer's work only continued after the collapse, for he was responsible for the soundtracks of films such as *Burnt by the Sun, The Barber of Siberia, A Driver for Vera,* and *House of Fools.* Who better to counter the influence of "Lara's Theme" with a more "Russian" sound for "our *Zhivago*"?

Artem′ev's score for the television series was anything but mere accompaniment, for it added an essential component to the way "our" *Zhivago* returned home. Not one episode featured strumming balalaikas. Instead, the core of Artem′ev's music for the series was the Orthodox requiem, a perfect musical match for the main message of this "Russian" *Zhivago.* If Lean's movie had offered up romantic melodrama with a Russian backdrop, Proshkin's series, authored by Iurii Arabov, presented a new *Zhivago* that provided a requiem for communism. Artem′ev's music fulfilled this task to the fullest, surrounding viewers of the show with the musical sounds of a funeral hymn.[1]

PATRIOTIC SOUNDSCAPES: EDUARD ARTEM′EV'S MUSIC

Born in 1938 in Novosibirsk, Eduard Artem′ev possessed musical talents that led him all the way to the Moscow Conservatory, from which he graduated in 1960. A meeting with Evgenii Murzin that year proved to be the most significant encounter of his life, for Murzin was one of the inventers of the electronic synthesizer. Thereafter Artem′ev devoted himself to exploring the sonic range allowed by the instrument and in many ways his name is synonymous with both electronic music and the soundtrack in Russia. He has composed for over 150 films, making him by far the most prolific musical artist in the history of Russian cinema. And the sounds he has created are equally recognizable. Working with Andrei Tarkovsky, Artem′ev claims, gave him a chance to experiment with music and how one could translate sensations into sounds for film. Working with Andrei Konchalovsky during his Hollywood years gave him the chance to meet and discuss film music with Maurice Jarre himself.[2]

The very specific sounds of Soviet and Russian cinema are frequently those created by Artem′ev. The frightening noise of Tarkovsky's *Solaris* or the creepy sounds of *Stalker* are his. The disconcerting music in Mikhalkov's *Oblomov* or the sweeping sounds of Siberia in *Barber* sprang from his imagination. None of these films can really be imagined without Artem′ev's compositions. His "Household of the Fatherland [*Dym otechestvo*]" from Nikita Mikhalkov's *Unfinished Piece for Mechanical Piano* (1977), to list just one example, uses a synthesizer to evoke the emotions of homeland. Appearing in the film when the Chekhovian house comes into view, Artem′ev's piece conveys the essence of home despite using an instrument not present in the era the film depicts. The textured sound offered by the synthesizer and accompanying vocals evokes both the future and a sense of timelessness, transporting the audience member beyond Chekhov's world to their own contemporary landscape. Twenty years later Artem′ev also blurred the distance between the past and the present when he wrote the music for Mikhalkov's *The Barber of Siberia* (1999). His song "Love" uses the Moscow Chamber Orchestra, not a synthesizer, to express the feelings between Jane and Andrei, but also the love for Siberia and for Russia itself. Artem′ev's soundtracks do not just locate the cinematic scenes in terms of time and place; they convey important auditory representations of landscape and nationhood.[3]

Although it is difficult to prove in the way most historians look for it, Artem′ev's soundscapes may be the best case for understanding the ways musicologists have moved beyond the soundtrack as it usually is conceived. The soundtrack is frequently relegated to secondary status as mere accompaniment to a film's more visual significance. Yet recent music scholarship has called this subordinate status into question. Film music may not just be diegetic (a part of the film narrative) or extradiegetic (a layer of commentary to the visual narrative); it may have agency, providing important meaning to the film itself.[4] Film music, as Caryl Flinn has noted in her study of German films of the 1970s and 1980s, can also demonstrate a commitment to historical memory.[5] The music in a film, as Flinn argues, often provokes serious memory work on the part of the spectator, forcing them to think about the past in personal ways. The use of Beethoven's Ninth Symphony in Hans-Jürgen Syberberg's *Hitler: Ein Film aus Deutschland* (1977), Alexander Kluge's *Die Patriotin* (1979), and Rainer Werner Fassbinder's *Die Ehe der Maria Braun* (1979), Flinn suggests, offer multiple ways for audience members to work through the trauma of the Nazi era. Far from being mere accompaniment to a scene, these musical moments capture important meanings embedded within the film and its take on German culture—Syberberg attempts to redeem it, Kluge reworks it, and Fassbinder assails it.[6]

Moreover, recent research by cognitive psychologists into the soundtrack has suggested that film music is also not subordinate to the visuals, but shapes the way a certain scene is understood and remembered by viewers. "Without music," Annabel Cohen writes, "the images seem prosaic, mundane, even lifeless; with music, however, the world of film comes alive." It is through music, in other words, that audience members come to participate in the meanings of the film. The music we hear affects the way we understand, remember, and contemplate the film itself.[7]

Artem′ev's music has accomplished all of the above, inscribing a Russian soundscape to the visual landscapes created by the directors with whom he has worked. The emotional responses audience members had when seeing Mikhalkov's *The Barber of Siberia* (see chapter 2) may be proof that Artem′ev's sweeping, affective score scored with consumers. As "Love" plays for the last time when we see the shot of the Siberian forest, viewers are provided with an important auditory clue into how they should think of the film, an homage to lost values and lost histories that need to be reclaimed. When we process this music and that from most Russian cinematic scores, what we are doing is imagining Russia through sounds created by Eduard Artem′ev.

At a 2006 concert in Iaroslavl′ listeners commented that they felt a healing effect when they heard Artem′ev's familiar music. Some attendees claimed that they came with headaches and left without.[8] Artem′ev has frequently argued that his music is an expression of emotion, particularly emotions that can resonate with listeners and therefore clarify the latent feelings the visual components of a film attempt to convey. As he states, "music has energy in it, the rest is up to you to understand it."[9] For most audience members who have listened to his film music, there is something familiar to it, a very Russian expression of landscape, nationhood, and history. His work, in short, has created a patriotic soundscape. And in 2006 he added a requiem to it.

PASTERNAK WITHOUT PASTERNAK: THE LANDSCAPES AND SOUNDSCAPES OF A RUSSIAN *ZHIVAGO*

Ekaterina Barabash entitled her review of Proshkin's series "Pasternak Without Pasternak," a perfect summary of the contradictions on display. Iurii Arabov, a poet and scriptwriter for art-house darling Aleksandr Sokurov, adopted Pasternak's prose. Artem′ev's compositions ensured a dream team of sorts. The team only grew stronger with the addition of Oleg Menshikov, fresh from playing Fandorin in *The State Counsellor,* as Zhivago. Chulpan Khamatova played Lara, not long after her performance as Lara in *Goodbye, Lenin!* Khamatova had become something of a serial historical actress, having played Olga Nesterovskaia in *Gibel′ imperii,* Tania Kukotskaia in *Kazus Kukotskogo,* and Varia Ivanova in *Deti Arbata.* The scene-stealing legend Oleg Iankovskii as Komarovskii rounded out the main cast. Throw in Proshkin, the director of 1987's *The Cold Summer of '53* and 1999's blockbuster *Russkii bunt* (based on Pushkin's *Captain's Daughter*), and you indeed have the dream team for remaking history on television.

And yet, as Barabash alludes to, the series departs significantly from Pasternak's novel, both in its script and its sound. Proshkin and Arabov decided to employ a very Russian adaptation (*ekranizatsiia*) that first developed in the 1960s, one that used the original text as the basis for a new version billed as "based on the themes of" a particular author (*po motivam . . .*).[10] Paradoxically, the look, sound, and feel of this *Zhivago* are all closer to Pasternak's historical prose than the two previous adaptations because of this approach.[11] As Arabov, the scriptwriter, commented, the problem with the American movie rested with its literal approach to Pasternak—the uncertainty of Zhivago's persona, which Arabov believes to be at the heart of the novel, was conveyed simply by "having Omar Sharif look at a birch tree and roll his eyes as the music of Maurice Jarre played."[12] For Arabov and Proshkin, to convey the tragedy of Zhivago, to make sense of how he was swept up in the whirlwinds of history; in other words, to make Pasternak appropriately for the screen, required a departure from Pasternak's prose. To make sense of this conundrum, perhaps a short tour through the tumultuous history of Pasternak's novel and its reception is necessary.

The story of Pasternak's summer of 1956 is well known: his initial attempts to publish his only novel; its rejection at the hands of the editors of *Novyi mir* (*New World*) for its "non-acceptance of the spirit of the socialist revolution"; the subsequent smuggling of *Doctor Zhivago* out of the USSR and its publication first in Italy and then throughout the world; the Nobel Prize Committee awarding the 1958 award to Pasternak for his novel; Pasternak's decision not to accept the award after considerable political pressure placed on him; Pasternak's banishment from the Writer's Union and subsequent smear campaign in Soviet papers for "slandering the socialist regime and people"; and Pasternak's death in 1960 at the age of seventy.[13] If this plot sounds like a Cold War spy thriller, that's how it got reported in the U.S. media at the time, with details of the smuggling, the letters of denunciation signed by prominent Soviet writers, and the diplomatic furor the "Pasternak affair" caused splashed across headlines throughout the country. In fact, the publication story often tended to dominate the actual story Pasternak wrote. While the novel was greeted with silence in the Soviet Union, it received mostly favorable reviews in the West, though some critics such as Vladimir Nabokov dismissed its artistic value. Few scholars wrote about the novel and its meanings. For most of its history, *Doctor Zhivago* was a novel interpreted as a diplomatic event, a work by an author who was a better poet than novelist, and a love story made into an epic film. While most believed that the publication story was both a monumental and tragic affair, many scholars and critics thought the Cold War backdrop was far more significant than the tale of Iurii Zhivago.

Glasnost′ and perestroika put Pasternak and his work back in the minds of Soviet citizens, who could only read it in samizdat form before. Up until the late 1980s, Pasternak's novel and its interpretations had remained a Western matter—Zhivago, as a literary and cinematic character, did not truly "belong" to Russian culture. *Novyi mir,* as an act of atonement, began publishing the novel in its January 1988 issue and printed one million copies to accommodate demand. As readers snapped up copies, their acts of reading and discussing the novel began the process of returning the literary Zhivago "home" to Russia.

The journal's editors asked Dmitrii Likhachev, who, along with Andrei Sakharov, had acquired the label of "national conscience," to write the introduction to the novel's reissue. Likhachev created a powerful literary welcoming mat, writing an eloquent account of how much *Doctor Zhivago* meant to him personally and to the country as a whole. He believed that Zhivago is an "inner Pasternak," an intellectual everyman whose "hesitations and doubts" allow him to observe important events and accommodate himself to them without ultimately affecting their outcome. He is, in other words, an individual who manages to live through history and observe it while preserving his inner feelings—a real Soviet person, Likhachev suggests, not a new Soviet man. In his doubts, Zhivago also does what many Soviet citizens did—ponder historical events, wrestle with their meanings, but also accept his own powerlessness, "tak[ing] life and history as they are." Ultimately, Likhachev argues, Pasternak's novel and its view of history represents a worthy successor to Tolstoy's national epic, *War and Peace* (which *Zhivago* references more than once), for while Pasternak's "lyric intensity" in *Zhivago* reveals a "tremendous modesty" on the part of the author, it also reveals his "full awareness of his role as a portrayer of events."[14]

What Likhachev recognized at the heart of *Doctor Zhivago* is precisely what the *Novyi mir* reviewers recognized: Pasternak's story mattered because it offered a quietly explosive view of Soviet history, an unvarnished account of one ordinary individual who lived through extraordinary changes. The appearance of the novel in 1988 produced a host of reactions, perhaps none more interesting and important than the two roundtables held in two venerable Soviet journals, *Voprosy istorii* (*Questions of history*) and *Voprosy literatury* (*Questions of literature*). Contributors to both discussions viewed *Doctor Zhivago* more as a historical interpretation than a literary one. While the appearance of the novel came at a time when previously banned books such as Andrei Platonov's *Foundation Pit* (first published in 1987) were suddenly on the scene and the subject of frenzied reading and frenzied arguments, *Zhivago* was different for its explosive take on the foundational events of Soviet history. To capture this paradox, *Voprosy istorii* entitled its June 1988 forum "History and Literature: From One Cradle." As S. P. Zalygin, the editor of the journal, opened his account of *Zhivago*'s importance, "there are no closer regions of human activity than history and literature," for if literary work is truly great, then it is historic and eventually becomes part of history itself. For him, *Doctor Zhivago*'s significance is greater because of the history it covers, the foundations of the Bolshevik state, when the relationship between the past and literature had deliberately been altered by Soviet authorities. Pasternak's achievement, according to Zalygin, is not in the facts about the past, particularly the Civil War (which in his mind was still covered better by Mikhail Sholokhov's *Quiet Flows the Don*), but in how his narrator thinks about the past and its events, for these critical faculties were absent from Soviet approaches to history.[15] G. A. Belaia's response in the journal drew an even more important conclusion, "It becomes increasingly clearer that Russia's history is the history of the moral and spiritual stoicism of its artists. By acquiring knowledge of this history, people strengthen their spirit and their faith in mankind's possibility."[16] As the two authors here and the three who contributed to the *Voprosy literatury* roundtable all acknowledged (and all took their cue from Likhachev), what mattered about Pasternak's work of art was how it interpreted the past.[17] It was the past and the way Zhivago/Pasternak experienced it and critiqued it that made *Doctor Zhivago* an explosive account of early Soviet rule, of the Thaw, and even of the 1980s, for the novel reaffirmed what is at the heart of historical investigation—the ability of an individual to come to his own conclusions about the past—and how Soviet officials had attempted to suppress it.

David Lean's adaptation did not just have the hokey (to Russian ears) "Lara's Theme," it also took a lot of this history out, turning Pasternak's novel into a love story set against an historical backdrop while remaining true to the novel's plot (a *Gone with the Wind* for Soviet history, a comparison many Russian critics have made). By contrast, Proshkin's adaptation took great liberties with Pasternak's prose, its plot, and its characters, choosing instead to remain true to the essence of Pasternak's history. Much of what made the novel so controversial and later so beloved was Pasternak's attempt to wrestle with the meaning of early-twentieth-century Russian history. For Pasternak in the 1950s and for Soviet readers in the 1980s, *Zhivago*'s take on the past was a contemporary one—writing *Zhivago* proved to be a means for Pasternak to come to terms with his own participation in Soviet history, while Zhivago's story provided a means for glasnost′-era readers to understand their own roles in the Soviet drama. Iurii Arabov's script captures this feature of the novel and takes it to the small screen. Major differences exist between the two Russian versions, too numerous to mention (perhaps the most glaring is the complete absence of Zhivago's half-brother Evgraf, played by Alec Guinness in Lean's version).[18] Arabov, however, remembered his feelings when he first read the novel in samizdat form over the course of 1978. For him, Pasternak's work was not about plot and narrative, but "mood and philosophy and the musical construction of a phrase."[19] For most reviewers and viewers, however, Proshkin, Arabov, and Artem′ev's evocation of *Zhivago*'s musical moods meant that they got Pasternak right, updating Zhivago's turmoil for those who lived through the 1990s.[20]

The mood evoked by Pasternak appears most powerfully in the ninth episode, when Iurii Zhivago lives with Red partisans and sees the Civil War's brutality. In this episode, we can get a sense for how the television blockbuster adapted Pasternak's novel for present-day consumption. The episode takes chapters 11 and 12 from Pasternak and darkens their tone, capturing the devastation caused by the Civil War in eastern Russia. Forcibly conscripted by partisans at the end of episode 8, Zhivago then wrestles with his helplessness and his faith. During a skirmish between the Reds and Whites, Zhivago maintains his morality by firing his rifle into the air. In the process, he accidentally shoots one of his opponents. When he examines the body afterwards, he finds the man has carried a piece of paper that reads "God help the living." As a partisan starts to loot the body, Zhivago pulls him off and drags the man away. At this moment, we return to Lara's apartment in Yuriatin. She enters briskly and finds her daughter, Katya, eating kasha. Worried that some marauder might have entered while she was away and upset that her daughter has eaten food when it would have been better to save it, Lara lashes out at her. The episode closes with Lara asking for Katya's forgiveness.

The ninth episode takes up the theme of forgiveness and makes it the centerpiece of the entire series's examination of the past. It begins after Zhivago has spent a year with the partisans. It is winter and Zhivago and his comrades are freezing, enduring not just hardships of weather and war but also their own brutal nature. They inhabit a wintry apocalypse surrounded by wolves that seem to understand that it is only a matter of time before they can have their way (apparently the Mosfil′m set used wild wolves that frightened Oleg Menshikov, helping him express his fear on film).[21] Zhivago forages for berries, fights with his comrades over mundane items, and barely speaks a word in the entire episode. His life in Moscow as a member of the liberal intelligentsia is long gone; instead, he has lived through years of unending apocalypse, captured presciently in the print he keeps from the outset of the film, Albrecht Dürer's 1510 *Christ Taken Captive* (the image does not appear in the novel). The leader of the partisans, Liberius Mikulitsyn, tells Zhivago to weave baskets to ward off frostbite and to play chess to keep his mind warm. Mikulitsyn has become a wolf-like predator, issuing violent orders, sniffing cocaine, and even howling at times. His beastliness and that of his men have specific, historic roots. We learn about them through Pasha's—another partisan's—story. Pasha learned his violent ways first in the Imperial Army, where he killed for the tsar and then for the Bolsheviks, where he killed opponents in the bloody Civil War. The camp encounters between Zhivago and his fellow men visually depict how violence has dehumanized both the Bolsheviks and the doctor—in a sense one could read the episode as an epilogue to Shakhnazarov's *Rider Called Death.*

When asked by Pasha how he came to be a Bolshevik, Zhivago answers that he did not, for he was taken. This cinematic Zhivago serves the role Likhachev identified as central to the character's importance, that of an everyman swept up by history but not responsible for it. As Zhivago stumbles through the cold hell, we see how Reds and Whites torture each other, how families caught in the struggle starve, and even how Pasha's wife sacrifices her newborn to the wolves to save the rest of her family. The doctor struggles with his changed self and his inability to extricate himself from this camp. He fails to leave even after Mikulitsyn gives him permission to do so. Zhivago, for his part, believes he has to atone for his sins and for the sinful conditions around him, doing so by nursing back to health the former White soldier he shot. When White soldiers approach the encampment because Zhivago lit a nighttime fire, the formerly wounded soldier tries to escape. Zhivago fires and kills him, making his transition from a principled humanist to a murderer complete. He has also become a Bolshevik in the eyes of the Whites.

Up to this point, the episode's stark depictions were paralleled by the lack of sound. At the moment when Zhivago's transformation is complete, however, a solitary female voice sings a heartrending song. Titled "Zaiushka," it is sung by a partisan in the novel; the words are Pasternak's. In the television sequence, Artem′ev takes it, one the novelist described as a folk song that makes "an insane attempt to stop time by means of its words," and places it in the mouth of Pasha's wife. She is singing the folk song about a hare running through the woods past a rowan tree, one infused with memory and loss, to her children. Moments later, fearful of the tortures the Whites will mete out to them, Pasha kills his entire family with an axe. The song ends and Mikulitsyn shoots Pasha. He then tells Zhivago to leave.

Artem′ev's changes reflect many of the differences between the novel and the film. This is not Pasternak's plot and yet it is very much Pasternak's theme. The author entitled the chapter in which Pasha murders his family "The Rowan Tree" and describes the tune around which it is built by writing that "a Russian folk song is like water held back by a dam." Slowly it breaks through and "suddenly reveals itself and astounds us. This is how the song's sorrowing spirit comes to expression."[22] For Pasternak, the song is about a rabbit hounded by beasts and worried that the beauty of a rowan tree will be destroyed too. Pasternak uses it to evoke Zhivago's tragedy and the tragedies of his encircled comrades; Artem′ev does the same, turning it into a sorrowful lament for the needless deaths of not just one family, but thousands of families caught up in the forces of history. As Zhivago and the partisans leave, Artem′ev provides the solemn music for their exit and for Zhivago's decision to stay with the Reds. The entire sequence is unthinkable without the sound, without a soundscape to match the visual snow-covered landscape. It is a song Artem′ev uses several times in the series, one he entitled "Send Off to the Front [*Provody na front*]." Its recurrence audibly conveys the way Pasternak depicts his hero, constantly moving against his will.

The music also makes the transition from this scene to the next, where we learn it is 1921 and where we see Lara trying to get news about Zhivago's fate. She hears from a friend that Iurii may be back in town, frequenting the church. When Lara states that she thought the priest had been shot, her friend retorts, "People still gather there." The Yuriatin church indeed reveals the damage done to Orthodoxy and its buildings, yet people still gather in its sacred space. Lara goes and learns that Zhivago has indeed been spotted. When she returns to her apartment, her journey to God's house has been rewarded—a shattered, grey-haired Zhivago is within. As Lara begins to feed him, to return him to the world of the living and to its love, Artem′ev's music again provides the sounds to convey what words cannot, slow yet slowly sweeping emotions of return and repentance that Zhivago will undergo. It is the process described by Pasternak in his novel; on screen it is rendered as the close of the episode about man's inhumanity and return to humanity. Artem′ev called this soundscape "Encounter in the Church [*Vstrecha v tserkvi*]."

This episode captures how the series can be interpreted as "Pasternak without Pasternak." While the basic plot comes from the novel, much of its language and its details diverge from Pasternak. At the same time, the novel's depiction of Zhivago among the partisans is one that precisely conveys the larger characterization of this everyman: how he is caught up in forces larger than him, how he is at times powerless to resist them, how he tries to maintain his humanity, and how he loses it in the midst of the violence and cold hell all around him. Arabov's script and Proshkin's scenes still convey this very Pasternakian vision, but it is Artem′ev's music that conveys the feelings and emotions at the heart of Zhivago's world as Pasternak imagined it.

Script changes notwithstanding, Proshkin's *Zhivago* triumphed as a more "authentic" one because it *looked* more like revolutionary Russia and particularly because it *sounded* more like Russia. The look was accomplished by filming in Kostroma and on Mosfil′m's "Old Moscow" set (the site of Shakhnazarov's *Rider Called Death*) rather than in Granada or Helsinki, where Lean had shot his epic. Artem′ev's compositions for these landscapes are not just subordinate to this adaptation, they are central to the series and its messages. Without the music, the film would not be the same. Without Artem′ev's piece at the end of episode 10, for example, the entire meaning of this "authentic" *Zhivago* would be lost. In it, Zhivago and Antipov (Lara's husband) both inhabit Lara's apartment after she has fled from Russia. The liberal doctor and former ardent revolutionary discuss the violence that has descended upon them and discuss who is responsible for it. Antipov realizes that he bears some responsibility and wanders off into a snow-covered landscape with his pistol. The camera pans across the land and focuses upon a nearby monastery. Antipov gazes at this most Russian of sites and shoots himself. Just then a crescendo of solemn voices accompanies his exit. The overall effect—both visually and aurally—is one of a prayer for those who have been swept up in the violence of 1917 such as Zhivago. In the case of Pasternak's character, Zhivago has lost both his family and his lover to the forces unleashed by the Revolution. He has discussed with Lara earlier in episode 10 that it will take four generations before the sins of 1917 have been paid. While this discussion never takes place in the novel, Pasternak does write about the outrages Russians inflicted on each other, a "social evil of immorality." For readers and viewers, one of Pasternak's primary messages is that of atonement. The scene at the end of this episode, which concludes the exploration of Zhivago's Civil War, is therefore a liturgy for the dead, one offered for both Antipov and his victims. Artem′ev entitled his piece for it "Requiem."

In the Orthodox faith, like that of other Christian denominations such as Catholicism, the requiem serves as the formal service for departed souls. It is both a liturgy—the words of the priest praying for the departed and offering comfort for the living—and a hymn—particularly the sounds of "*vechnaia pamiat′* [memory eternal]" that end a requiem. The Orthodox requiem stresses the brevity of life and penitence.

Artem′ev's "Requiem" performs this task too, offering Zhivago's observations and sufferings as a requiem for communism itself. Life is short, it suggests, while many have died in the apocalyptic times of the Civil War. The duty of the living, like Zhivago, is to observe these events and preserve their memories while offering prayers to those who have passed. The scene at the end of episode 10—this requiem for communism—appears nowhere in Pasternak's novel. Yet just as Likhachev and others viewed Pasternak's novel as an act of cultural recall that allowed readers to remember forever, so too does the scene in the series capture the same feature of Pasternak's work. Artem′ev's requiem is the blockbuster version of "Memory Eternal." Above all, though, it is *Russian,* for it sounds like an Orthodox service—an aural connection with the heavenly that makes an attempt to make good on Artem′ev's overall view of his music, which he calls "a tool given to mortals to make contact with God."[23]

THE CONTINUED RETURN OF THE REPRESSED: *ZHIVAGO* AS PATRIOTIC RECLAMATION

Analyzing glasnost from below, Geoffrey Hosking wrote in 1990 that the confrontation with Soviet history generated by reading Solzhenitsyn and Pasternak was nothing less than a "return of the repressed" that helped average citizens cope with the traumas of the past. This confrontation also served as the basis for a civil society in the making.[24] The appearance of *Doctor Zhivago* in print form as a result of Gorbachev's policies played a significant part in the ways many Soviet citizens dealt with their past, consumed its meanings, and ultimately decided to disbelieve in the system itself.[25] *Zhivago*'s first homecoming was truly revolutionary and Pasternak's protagonist became a guide for exploring the entire meanings of the socialist experiment, truly becoming the everyman imagined by Likhachev when the novel first appeared in print.[26]

When the Russian *Zhivago* came home again, many Russians initially tuned out. Ratings were not as strong as hoped for by NTV, although the reasons behind the disappointment are almost as interesting as the smuggling of Pasternak's manuscript in 1956. The series wrapped up filming and post-production in December 2005, when Proshkin delivered it to the channel. Rather than broadcast immediately, given the buzz the series had already generated, NTV's television producers decided to wait until after the May holidays. While the finished series sat on a shelf, someone at NTV or Mosfil′m "acquired" it and sold it to video pirates. *Doctor Zhivago* the series began to appear illegally in February. By March 2006 the entire series could be bought in any kiosk, underground pass, internet store, or video store in Russia. It sold well, as even Proshkin lamented in interviews.

Worse was yet to come. When the series did debut on May 10, 2006, NTV included twenty-six minutes of commercials with the forty-four-minute first episode. Proshkin understandably raged in the press. The fact that the series garnered 17 percent of viewers is therefore remarkable.[27] The entire scandal sums up the way pirating affects the Russian film market these days—one article about the 2006 Pasternak Affair had the headline, "This Is Your Motherland, *Doctor Zhivago*!" It did surprisingly well in other parts of the former Soviet world: in Belarus, 30 percent of the population (and 45 percent of urban residents) tuned into the series—perhaps because Lukashenko's system made the meanings of the series more resonant, although it is more likely the government battled video pirates a little more effectively.[28]

Proshkin's *Zhivago* was also far from the only television adaptation of a banned book to hit the small screen in the new Russia. The literary adaptation, which had seemed dead just a few years before, revived in 2003 with Vladimir Bortko's commercially successful version of Dostoevsky's *Idiot*.[29] Just two years later, viewers could watch a host of controversial subjects lifted from the page to the screen, including lavish adaptations of Solzhenitsyn's *First Circle* and Bulgakov's *Master and Margarita* (both of which garnered high ratings in 2005). The year before, Dmitrii Barshchevskii's *Moscow Saga* (based on Vasily Aksyenov's novel of the same name and produced by Konstantin Ernst for the First Channel) and Andrei Eshpai's *Children of the Arbat*, which starred Chulpan Khamatova, aired in October and November, respectively. Eshpai, when discussing his version of Anatolii Rybakov's glasnost′ blockbuster novel, stated that he made his film so that younger Russians would come to know "the tragic absurdity and the horror of the Soviet system's crimes," concluding that his series would act as "a spiritual" retelling of sorts.[30] Writing in *Iskusstvo kino*, Slava Taroshchina argued that these serials about the Stalin era represented a continuation of the Gorbachev-era obsession with the forgotten past. Ultimately, the success of the serials helped to provide some answers to "our continually uncertain past."[31] In an era where many politicians rehabilitated the Stalinist era and with it the entire communist past, these television series, according to Taroshina, acted as an important counterpoint to politically charged historical amnesia. For her, the series were a "necessary condition" for Russian society that helped, like the novels upon which they are based, "to wake the nation from a lethargic, Stalinist slumber." Anton Zlatopol′skii, the producer of RTR's version of *The First Circle,* echoed these views, stating that he "considers the creation and transmission of such projects the most important function of state television," claiming, with apparently no irony, that all citizens of Russia should watch his production.[32]

The reappearance of the banned novel as a television serial, as Elena Prokhorova has argued, can be seen as a patriotic endeavor, one that reifies the role of Great Russian Literature for the television generation. Bulgakov, Pasternak, and Solzhenitsyn, in other words, "coexist in the media space as signs of national conciliation and imperial revival. Their works have been canonized, and the writers themselves—tortured, humiliated, or killed by the state—have been instated into the pantheon of Great Russian Literature."[33] Prokhorova sees a sinister element to this patriotic culture, one that bolstered Putin's regime by conflating past crimes with the current Communist Party. Sergei Kaznacheev sees *First Circle* similarly, as part of the continued upheaval of Russian nationhood, where heroes become villains—and villains heroes—through historical hindsight. In his view, Russian patriotism constantly changes like a weather vane, changing alongside political winds—governments taught Russians not to love Nicholas II and now the government says to love him. Solzhenitsyn and his ilk were anti-Soviet, now they are pro-Russian patriots.[34]

Yet it may be possible to understand these continued returns of repressed stories in a less sinister framework, one that takes into account the sweeping, soothing music that accompanies cinematic images and the longer history of Pasternak in late Soviet and post-Soviet culture. Dmitrii Bykov's review in *Iskusstvo kino* notes that the series achieved something significant by revealing the inner turmoil of a single man and—like Pasternak—by not offering easy answers to questions about who we are and what meanings we should take from the past. He called the series the best of the last decade. Part of this accomplishment, as Bykov writes, comes from the music of Eduard Artem′ev, who "wrote an outstanding musical number, without yielding to the temptation of mass culture, without composing waltzes for Lara or memorial motifs for Pasternak's verses."[35] In other words, the new series represents a continuation of the confrontation with the past first started in 1986 or even 1956. Artem′ev's music adds the latest element to this memory work, allowing viewers a chance to mourn.

In her near hagiography of Artem′ev, Tat′iana Egorova writes,

> It is possible to go on forever about Eduard Artem′ev's music because it possesses a surprising quality that allows hope into the soul that suggests peace is attainable, and that reveals goodness. This in no way means that he does not know suffering and pain, heartfelt feelings, and tragic break ups. It simply means that the composer sincerely believes that the spiritual essence of man is in determining our origins and that all calamities, misfortunes and sorrows are nothing more than tests sent by God that he must endure honorably.[36]

For Egorova, Artem′ev's music had the same effect as Pasternak's prose: both allowed the consumer a chance to reflect on history and tragedy, and both allowed the reader and listener a chance to hope for a better future. Both could serve as a requiem for communism, not just as a patriotic prop.

Artem′ev would accept this sort of judgment, commenting to an interviewer that he thinks the music for the series "revealed something that is in all of us [*mne kazhetsia, muzyka poluchilas′, chto-to v nei est′ svoe*]."[37] Many viewers agreed: in an otherwise critical review of the series compared to the novel, "Andreas" commented, "I liked 100 percent of the music."[38] Another viewer who took part in an online forum that hashed through the series wrote, "I would like to mention that Eduard Artem′ev's music contains surprising beauty, which ideally completed the film."[39] One even wrote, "Artem′ev's music deserves its own award."[40] The venerable critic Valerii Kichin also had this to say about the series: "One of the film's masterpieces and one of the events of decade, I would submit, is Eduard Artem′ev's music: it contains the sort of unattainable harmony and beauty that also attracts the heroes of this history." It is, in

Kichin's account, nothing less than "a new 'Leningrad symphony,' [for] it transmits with cataclysmic feeling a tragic force." "Artem′ev's music," he concludes, "should be played in concerts and, I really hope that the film's producers will decide to release his soundtrack on a separate disc."[41] They did so.

What the series and those that also adopted banned books for the small screen may have accomplished is a way to cope not just with the trauma of the Soviet past but the more recent trauma of the 1990s. This *Zhivago,* in other words, is about "survival in times of trouble," whether in the 1920s or the 1990s.[42] Proshkin's Zhivago truly is the everyman Likhachev identified, for his choices speak to "similar experiences during the troubled decade after the fall of the Soviet Union." When Zhivago asks Komarovskii how he has managed to survive well into the Soviet era, he phrases his questions for the contemporary viewer: "How come neither famine, cold, nor bullets can destroy creatures like Komarovskii? Why are you always successful? Under the tsar, under the dictatorship of the proletariat, under the socialist utopia, *even if someone could imagine the most unimaginable government for Russia* [my emphasis]? Where is God then? Where is his punishing hand?" This *Zhivago* is not just about working through the Soviet past, but also the post-Soviet past.[43] Artem′ev's Russian soundscape offers a chance for viewers to deal with a host of issues, even those that have to do with poverty in the era of crony capitalism.

Apparently the voters for Russia's Golden Eagle awards agreed, for they awarded Artem′ev the prize for best music for a film (feature or television) for 2006. The series took the award for best serial but lost out to at the TEFIs to *First Circle.* Both Oleg Iankovskii and Chulpan Khamatova swept all the awards, as did Artem′ev. "Lara's Theme" had been vanquished. Zhivago arrived home again and with him, the Russia that had been lost.

PART TWO

The Price of War

A 2004 Moscow survey about the sources of pride in contemporary Russia found that "the country's most significant achievement" remained the victory over Nazi Germany in 1945. Second on the list was the postwar construction, followed by Russia's cultural heritage.[1]

That the victory placed first in the poll should surprise no one. A host of excellent studies have appeared in the two decades since communism's collapse that explore how the Soviet victory over Nazi Germany functioned as a powerful myth.[2] The myth changed over time and, while state driven, was not just a univocal top-down program. Film, as Denise Youngblood's recent work has clarified, played a major role in the ongoing construction of the Great Patriotic War myth.[3] The Soviet Victory was therefore not just "movie-made" by the state; individual filmmakers and individual filmgoers all had parts in shaping how the war got remembered.[4]

By 2005, television and feature-length films about the Great Patriotic War had exploded onto screens. The Great Patriotic War yet again served as the basis for Russian patriotic renewal, particularly during the sixtieth anniversary of the victory. That year also saw the release of Fedor Bondarchuk's Afghan War blockbuster and buddy movie *Ninth Company*. The Afghan War had largely been a source of forgetting, not remembering, since it ended. A few documentaries appeared in the late 1980s that focused on the war's impact on individual families and a couple of feature films appeared in the early 1990s. The Afghan War, as Denise Youngblood has written, "seemed a dead topic in Russian cinema" until Bondarchuk's blockbuster.[5] The success of it and of numerous films about the Great Patriotic War suggested that past wars could serve the cause of present patriotic sentiment and national renewal. Cinematic wars filled theaters and made money; they also offered myths of renewal that sought to inspire audiences to return to the perceived collective heroism displayed in past wars.

To assess the return of cinematic war narratives, *Iskusstvo kino* held a 2005 roundtable titled "The Price of War [*Tsena voiny*]." Motivated by the sixtieth anniversary celebrations, the roundtable contained some surprising statements. Daniil Dondurei, the editor, set the tone by noting the number of deaths the Soviet Union incurred and by calling into question the ultimate price the war brought—namely, an officially sanctioned victory myth that sustained the Soviet system. Leonid Radzikhovskii agreed, positing that even compared to the Russian soldiers of 1914, Soviet soldiers lacked "a higher, political patriotism" to the state. Instead, Radzikhovskii theorized that Soviet soldiers either responded to 1941 with a "pleasant [*priatnyi*]" patriotism (that is, no love for the Soviet state but a recognition that the Nazi system was far worse and therefore their land should be defended) or an "unpleasant" patriotism (that is, out of fear because of what their brutal state would do to them afterward). As he wrote, Soviet soldiers mostly had "no faith in Pushkin and the Kazan′ Mother of God but fear in Beria and the Gulag."[6] In this view, the price of war was steep, for the Victory should be understood as part of a fifty-year Civil War in Russia that began in 1905 and ended in 1953 with Stalin's death.[7] The Great Patriotic War, therefore, was another instance in which Russia experienced "the psychology of war and death."

Anatolii Vishnevskii took issue with some of Dondurei's and Radzikhovskii's views, but agreed that of the "two myths" that twentieth-century Russia had developed, the war myth had triumphed over the revolutionary one. All agreed that the "Great Patriotic War" warranted the first adjective because the cost in human lives, including those of Soviet Jews who had perished in the Holocaust, had been so high. All agreed that the Stalinist state had used patriotism to mask the war's human costs and to unify the population around a new myth. In the end,

Vishnevskii declared, "The slightly retouched picture of the glorious past can flatter our national pride. However, the exaggeration of our past successes makes it impossible to take the right lessons from it and therefore can lead to future defeat."[8]

New cinematic narratives of war provided another layer to the notion of the "Russia that we lost." The myth of victory proved malleable in the new Russia. Victory still mattered, but it was not a victory for the Soviet state as much as a victory for the Russian nation. The state had harmed its citizens, but they had nonetheless responded patriotically to the crises of 1941–45. This patriotic script could also be applied to other wars, making timeless defense of the motherland the essence of Russianness and a usable virtue for post-Soviet citizens searching for meaning. The price of war in the USSR had been high, yet the recognition of this price had changed tremendously.

The Soviet Union as a *shtrafbat:* Tverdokhlebov (Aleksei Serebriakov) at the end of the series.

SIX

Mirror of War

In May 1985, the Soviet film critic Lev Anninskii published a seminal article in *Iskusstvo kino.* Appearing just two months after Mikhail Gorbachev became general secretary, Anninskii's "Quiet Explosions [*Tikhie vzryvy*]," promised, as the subtitle suggested, to be a series of "polemical notes."[1] Published to coincide with the fortieth anniversary of Victory Day, Anninskii asserted that the war against Nazi Germany had now passed into memory, particularly because of Soviet cinematic representations. What appears on screen, he wrote, "is not what *was,* but what is remembered [his emphasis]." Because cinema had fostered this memory work, turning the war into a myth that could be used by the Soviet state, Anninskii urged artists to break away from previous cinematic explorations of the war and to "sing their own songs about the war." What was needed, according to Anninskii, was a series of "silent explosions" that could shake up the memories produced onscreen. Anninskii got his wish, but only in part, for the Gorbachev era brought a series of loud cultural eruptions. The call for "silent explosions" seemed quaint by December 1991, when a new era dawned.

Nearly twenty years later, Anninskii published an equally important article in the same journal. Titled "The Shtrafbat as a Mirror of the Great Patriotic," Anninskii posited that the 2004 blockbuster television series about a Soviet penal battalion (*shtrafbat*) used as cannon fodder in the war represented a new apex in wartime cinematic remembrances.

According to Anninskii, the sixty years' worth of accumulated opinions about the Great Patriotic War amount to "some kind of circular repentance in answer to the eternal Russian question Who is to blame?" From the perspective of 2004, the war had been waged on two fronts, for "it seems that the army fought not just against German invaders, but against its own supreme commander and against its organizational structures." He concluded: "The point at which our sins, our repentance, and our misfortunes cross—our roles in the theater of war—is the penal battalion."[2]

Anninskii's use of "theater" and his invocation of memory both point to the powerful ways that cultures of remembrance, as Alon Confino has argued, can shape a society and not just reflect the social world around it.[3] Anninskii is one of many critics who view the past as presented on screen as a performance, or a "theater of memory."[4] The remembrances offered up by Russian filmmakers since 2002 have disturbed the mythic narrative of what Russians call the Great Patriotic War. In this explosive role, movies offer a performance of the past and past memories. As a result, the films of the zero years have helped to reaffirm the war as an important event while simultaneously changing the way the war is viewed in Russian society.

Shtrafbat, an eleven-part series that began in September 2004 on the channel "Russia [*Rossiia*]" provides a clear case of how memories and myths of World War II have been reflected and distorted, yet also shaped contemporary remembrance of the war. The series dominated the ratings; generated a great deal of discussions in print, on television, and on chatrooms; and led to a "memory boom" of sorts, in which survivors of Stalin's penal battalions began to grant interviews and publish memoirs. Nikolai Dostal′'s television series, in other words, took a taboo subject and turned it into an act of cultural recall. Before 2004, the existence of penal battalions was hidden away, only mentioned peripherally in banned books such as Boris Pasternak's *Doctor Zhivago* and Vasilii Grossman's *Life and Fate* or in Vladimir Vysotskii's 1964 song "Penal Battalions [*Shtrafnye batalony*]." After the series aired, one could buy copies of the DVD at kiosks both legal and illegal, purchase Eduard Volodarskii's novel that he turned into the screenplay, read about the penal battalions in the most important Russian newspapers, watch debates on television about the significance of these battalions (as well as the series), or even buy books at any number of stores written by former battalion members such as Aleksandr Pyl′tsyn or new books that promised the "truth" about penal battalions. Because of a blockbuster television series, suddenly discussions of penal battalions appeared everywhere and Russians began to look into the mirror of war to judge what it reflected back at them.

THEATER PRODUCTION

Anninskii's views and the explosion of movies about the war make sense within the context of the perceived crisis of patriotism that many believed had set in during the 1990s. Karen Shakhnazarov, the head of Mosfil′m, played a vital role in the renewed interest of the war by developing the first major film about World War II for nearly fifteen years. Adapted from a 1947 novella and produced by Mosfil′m, *Star* (*Zvezda*) became a sensation when it appeared in 2002, setting the stage for the spate of films to come. The film followed the heroic exploits of a group of Soviet scouts sent behind German lines to glean information about the enemy. The scouts uncover plans for a surprise attack and radio the information back to headquarters just as the Nazis close in on them. All of the soldiers die. As Shakhnazarov later claimed, "it was obvious we needed such a film" in part to counter "the American films with their own evaluation of the war constantly thrust upon us."[5] Shakhnazarov's fear over societal forgetting neatly summarized two other widespread beliefs in post-Soviet Russia: the supposed need for a new sense of national identity and the fear that Western (particularly American) popular culture threatened Russian values.

Throughout the 1990s, numerous Russian political and cultural figures attempted to find a "usable past" that could serve as a means to build a revived sense of nationhood. President Vladimir Putin decided to foster a revived sense of nationhood around the one achievement many Russians could still remember with pride—the victory over Nazi Germany. On Victory Day 2000 (May 9), Putin declared memories of the war "will help our generation to build a strong and prosperous country."[6] Part of Putin's plan for utilizing memories of the war included his support for the August 2000 plan for the "Culture of Russia, 2001–2005." Proposed by Mikhail Shvydkoi, minister of culture and film, Putin agreed to fund 20 billion rubles for cultural products that would help to revive Russian patriotism.[7] When Shakhnazarov decided to produce a new version of *Star* (the novella had been adapted for a 1949 film of the same name), he received funding from this program. Although this governmental support later raised eyebrows, Shakhnazarov's beliefs in 2001 about the "need for such a film" fit neatly within a larger cultural context about the state of patriotism in Russia.

By the early years of Putin's presidency, fueled by oil money and a more stable currency, the Russian economy recovered, making it possible to make new wartime cinematic narratives. Shakhnazarov, the person most responsible for initiating the revived narratives, cited both the economic revival and the need to adapt Russian cinema in the wake of the 1990s cultural invasion as primary reasons for why he could make a war film again. As he put it, "films of this kind require pyrotechnics, and pyrotechnics are expensive," while a war film that appealed to younger audiences "needed what the Americans call 'action.'"[8] *Star*'s producer therefore believed he had "found the right balance between entertainment and seriousness" to make a patriotic appeal.

The challenge to find new cinematic heroes, combined with the perceived need to react to Hollywood films, established the basis for the production of post-Soviet war films such as *Star.* Not every director or producer agreed with Shakhnazarov's assessment of the war and how Russia's youth had forgotten it, but everyone who made a film about the war after 2002 did so out of an individual belief that Russia needed new narratives about the conflict. What followed can only be called an explosion of cinematic narratives about World War II. Including *Star,* sixteen feature films set during the war appeared between 2002 and 2006 alone.[9] *Star*'s success, along with that of the other films, also produced an upsurge of wartime dramas on the small screen—in 2004 and 2005 Russian television broadcast eight television serials set during the war, including the most popular series of 2004, *Penal Battalion.*[10] Films about the Great Patriotic War dominated the big and small screens throughout the zero years: the explosions that started in 2002 continued for the rest of the decade.[11]

THE THEATER PERFORMANCE: NEW NARRATIVES ONSCREEN

Shakhnazarov was correct in one respect—the Great Patriotic War is, quite simply, *the* major event of twentieth-century Russian history. The myth of the Great Patriotic War in the USSR offered a chance to perform the past—parades, rituals, and the harnessing of memories presented the past as something to be relived and reexperienced through its performances.[12] The mythic version of the victory as it developed in the USSR had a compelling storyline—when the beastly Nazis invaded, the Soviet people suffered at their hands, but guided by Stalin they responded patriotically and ultimately triumphed. Amir Weiner has written that this narrative of the war contained two basic components, what he terms "hierarchical heroism" and "universal suffering."[13] In the first case, individual Soviet nations were ranked according to their supposed heroic contributions to the victory, with the Russians having acted the most heroically and therefore contributing the most to the victory. The second part of the narrative included all Soviet citizens in a sense of collective suffering at the hands of the inhuman Nazis. This narrative myth and its performances over the years contained many truths within it, but a simple story of heroic hierarchy and universal suffering ensured that problematic aspects of the wartime experience such as collaboration and occupation were ignored or suppressed.[14]

Soviet films that dealt with the war played a starring role in the Great Patriotic War myth's performances from 1945 to 1985. Denise Youngblood has highlighted how films about the war served as an important means for Soviet citizens to remember the event and their roles within it. War films also served as a means of narrating history and as a source for political discourse.[15] Among the numerous films that dealt with the war, several stand out: *The Cranes Are Flying* (*Letiat zhuravlyi,* dir. M. Kalatazov, 1957), *Fate of a Man* (*Sud'by cheloveka,* dir. S. Bondarchuk, 1959), *Ballad of a Soldier* (*Ballada o soldate,* dir. G. Chukhrai, 1959), *Ivan's Childhood* (*Ivanovo detstvo,* dir. A. Tarkovsky, 1962), and (much later) *Come and See* (*Idi i smotri,* dir. E. Klimov, 1985) all offered complex visions of the conflict where individual heroism mattered, yet all helped to perpetuate the memory of Soviet suffering in the war. The heroes of *Cranes are Flying,*

Fate of a Man, and *Ballad of a Soldier*—Boris, Andrei, and Alyosha—serve as symbols of the Russian soldier's courage and humanity in the face of incredible suffering. In Tarkovsky's film, Ivan functions as a symbol of how the war brutalized Russian children, robbing them of their childhood. Similarly, Klimov's hellish depiction of wartime Belarus focuses upon the brutalization of Florya, a boy who witnesses atrocity after atrocity. Even in these complex films, the basic outline of the wartime narrative is upheld—Russians are the most heroic, Germans are inhuman, and every Soviet citizen suffered.

Shakhnazarov's reasoning for producing a new war film drew on this existing narrative—as he mentioned, for his generation the war "had no two opinions about it" and "the heaviest burden fell on our people."[16] In adapting a Soviet-era story for post-Soviet society, however, *Star* and the films that followed it disrupted the myth in two crucial respects. First, the new films have suggested that Soviet citizens did not all suffer equally. Instead, zero-year films frequently depict Soviet officials causing the suffering of individual citizens. Secondly, post-Soviet cinematic performances have cast Germans, depicted in Soviet films almost universally as beasts, as human beings who also suffered during the war. *Shtrafbat,* as Anninskii noted in his review, mirrored all of these cinematic revisions the clearest and—as the reaction to the series demonstrated—in the least flattering light. The conditions of the new Russia, however, and the concern that new narratives were needed—a concern that Anninskii had been advocating for nearly twenty years—produced a stunning array of blockbusters, art-house pictures, commercially viable, and critically successful productions about the war. All of these films modified the Soviet myth of the war, most of them in radical ways: stories about occupation, about Stalinist oppression, and about sympathetic Germans had no place in the Soviet war as myth—yet they suddenly formed the basis for post-Soviet plotlines.[17]

Nikolai Dostal′'s *Penal Battalion* took the revision of wartime narratives to its most radical point. Dostal′ decided to make the series in part because his father had fought in the war and been captured by Germans, but "miraculously did not fall from German hands into Soviet, although the fact of his captivity was negatively reflected in his postwar life."[18] Building on this personal experience and using a script authored by Eduard Volodarskii, *Penal Battalion* follows the fortunes of Vasilii Stepanovich Tverdokhlebov (played by Aleksei Serebriakov), a Red Army officer captured by Nazi troops. The series opens as Tverdokhlebov and other Red Army soldiers are treated like animals at feeding time by their Nazi captors. Each of the Red Army soldiers is given the chance to fight for Vlasov's Russian Liberation Army, a collaborationist brigade established by the Nazis. When Tverdokhlebov and a handful of others refuse this "choice," they are sentenced to death and shot by a firing squad made up of Russians who have accepted. Miraculously, Vasilii is only wounded and digs himself out of his grave. He rejoins the Red Army only to be arrested. Interrogated by the NKVD and suspected of being a spy or a saboteur, Vasilii is beaten and sent to the Gulag.

Meanwhile, the war has dragged on too long and the Soviet government needs more soldiers. Stalin passes his Order No. 227 that, among other provisions, creates penal battalions. When Tverdokhlebov is given another "choice," this time to "rehabilitate" himself by commanding one, he accepts. The series reminded viewers, as Alexander Prokhorov has written, that the order acted as "a way to channel GULAG prisoners into the butchery of war."[19] In the next scene we get a glimpse of his new charges, mostly criminals and a few political prisoners who are also given the opportunity to atone for their sins. Within twenty-five minutes of the opening episode, a whole series of taboo subjects about the war have been exploded: collaboration, torture, the Gulag, the seedier side of Stalinist society, unpatriotic beliefs, and the suffering of "ordinary" Russians such as Tverdokhlebov at the hands of Nazi and Soviet officials alike. When Tverdokhlebov asks his new charges to forget their pasts and fight for their motherland, he also reminds them of the deadly irony behind this seemingly simple patriotic charge—if they don't, they will be shot, a call to arms that the members of the penal battalion understand all too well. One member will later say, "That's Soviet power for you."

By the second episode, Tverdokhlebov's ragtag band of brothers receives orders to attack German positions and soak up the brunt of the frontline fighting. Their actions have no strategic significance and are ordered so that HQ can plan future actions by learning from their deaths. Many of the *shtrafniki* openly question the orders and why they should fight for Soviet power. Tverdokhlebov counters with a more timeless quality, to fight for their motherland, their native soil, not for Stalin: he tellingly shouts, "*Za rodinu* [For the motherland]!" as he goes over the top, a cry that is not followed by "*Za Stalina* [For Stalin]!" When some members of the penal battalion decide to take a step back and return to their positions, they are mowed down by Soviet machine guns of the *zagradotriadov* ("blocking units" established to enforce Stalin's Order No. 227). Behind the front, the Red Army general and his staff who order this brutal policy make no bones about what they think of the penal battalion soldiers—they are "enemies of the people" and "bastards"—or whose orders they are following to use them or shoot them—"Comrade Stalin's."

Over the course of the series, we see just how much violence has pervaded the lives of the penal battalion members. They fight to the death over card games and steal food from the regular troops at gunpoint. We also see just how much wartime violence continues to pervade their existence. In addition to their assignments, penal battalion soldiers are used as firing squads to execute fellow members. In between, Volodarskii and Dostal′ explore and explode virtually all the taboo subjects about Stalinism and the war that existed during the Soviet era. We see episodes of antisemitism among Red Army soldiers (one member of the penal battalion, Savelii Tsukerman, is Jewish); learn about political purges through a Trotskyite member of the battalion; hear about the destructive impact of Stalin's collectivization policy through the memories of Glymov, a self-described "kulak and thief"; witness the desperate straits of Soviet citizens under occupation who are victimized by their "liberators" (in one episode, a shtrafnik rapes a local girl who then hangs herself); eavesdrop on a flashback conversation between Tverdokhlebov and a friend whether or not all those arrested in the 1930s are really "enemies of the people" (including Marshal Tukhachevskii, who was shot as a spy in 1937); and listen to a collaborator in Vlasov's army talk about his service for the Nazis as patriotic. *Shtrafbat* is an explosion as Anninskii ordered, but one that tears open unhealed wounds and unspoken secrets in order to expose them completely.

Tverdokhlebov's experiences and beliefs are central to this painful story. Through flashbacks the viewer learns that the battalion commander was a patriotic Soviet citizen before he left for the front. When he refuses to join the Vlasov force, he does so out of the same Soviet spirit. Tverdokhlebov's beliefs slowly change as he encounters his fellow shtrafniki and comes to see them as human beings that have been brutalized by the Stalinist system. He appeals to them as Russian patriots, not Soviet comrades. Two episodes confirm this change in Tverdokhlebov's outlook. The first comes when he encounters a wounded Russian soldier who has fought for Vlasov's army. Tverdokhlebov recognizes him as one of the captured soldiers who agreed to join the Nazis and who therefore joined the firing squad that nearly killed him. Tverdokhlebov understands that the wounded soldier, Sazonov, fights for the same patriotic beliefs about homeland that the penal battalion members do. Instead of turning Sazonov over to the NKVD and certain torture, Tverdokhlebov gives him a pistol and allows the Vlasov man to shoot himself. This understanding, however, is not what Soviet officials want from their penal battalion commanders, and Tverdokhlebov is arrested for this action and for spreading "anti-Soviet propaganda" to his men. Once again Tverdokhlebov is imprisoned and tortured, then asked to sign a document that implicates individual penal battalion members. He refuses and viewers see the change that has come over the former Soviet patriot. He is no longer afraid of death, the only scare tactic left to his NKVD oppressors. He now believes in a Russian, not Soviet, sense of nationhood. He will defend his motherland, but not his government.

Tverdokhlebov's morals help to turn the group into a real fighting unit. Dostal′ has his characters fighting two sets of enemies throughout—the Nazis and the NKVD—but also indicates that these doubly victimized men were far from heroes. The only redeeming aspects of the wartime epoch are Tverdokhlebov's newfound Russian patriotism, his family, and the faith of the Orthodox priest, Father Mikhail, who joins the battalion in episode 7. Father Mikhail first warns the unit about approaching Germans and then fights in the shtrafbat during the ensuing skirmish. Afterwards, he provides a moral lesson to the members by reminding them they should fight for their fatherland because it is holy, but also informing them that the state they serve is unholy. In the last episode, Tverdokhlebov's disillusionment and Father Mikhail's faith provide the conclusion to the series. Asked to fight against overwhelming

Father Mikhail's blessing: Still from Nikolai Dostal′'s *Penal Battalion* (2004).

force and against Nazi tanks, the penal battalion receives a blessing from the priest. They fight bravely, but perish. Only Father Mikhail and Tverdokhlebov survive. In the midst of the battle, as Father Mikhail fires a machine gun, he sees the Virgin Mary. Afterward, he blesses each of the dead shtrafniki and asks that God take their souls, for they are "holy warriors who have defended the Russian land." He intones an abbreviated *panikhida,* or requiem, over their dead bodies. Aleksei Shelygin's musical score, which has provided a cathedral-like solemnity throughout the series, provides the appropriate sounds for this liturgy. Tverdokhlebov, meanwhile, sits among the corpses of his men—men that he has trained, listened to, and come to see as like-minded comrades. His wounded and angry face speaks not only to the sacrifices the unit has made, sacrifices that have helped to turn the tide of war, but also the sacrifices they have made for a government that up to the end treats them as criminals. He knows that his battalion has helped to bring victory, but also Victory to the Soviet system that has oppressed his men. As the solemn music plays, a list of the soldiers who served in the 1,049 penal battalions and died as cannon fodder brings the serial to an end, an appropriate requiem for the 422,700 men who died in the penal battalions during the war.[20]

THEATER CRITICS: REVIEWING *SHTRAFBAT*'S PERFORMANCE

The slew of films devoted to the war produced an even greater number of reviews, internet postings, and arguments. Films such as *Star* led some critics to charge that Shakhnazarov had pandered to Putin's government and came up with this formula: "Give us money for these necessary films and we will provide you with patriotism."[21] Shakhnazarov had made no bones about his aim to "make a direct hit on the soul" of audience members, particularly young people. The film's apparent success in doing just that led many professional critics to charge that the film continued Soviet-era practices of "guiding" audience members to reach ideological conclusions about the war. As the number of films about the war increased after 2002, the debate grew more and more vocal.

Penal Battalion acted, as Anninskii articulated, as a mirror of the war, allowing multiple reflections of its meanings to emerge depending on the perspective of the viewer who gazed at what was reflected. Anninskii's article was part of thirty pages *Iskusstvo kino* devoted to the series. Justifying this unprecedented coverage to one television series, the editors wrote that "among the cine- and tele-versions of the military theme one of the most significant is Nikolai Dostal''s eleven-part *Penal Battalion*. . . . [T]he film did not leave the many different types of spectators indifferent. The leader in the TV ratings, it served as an occasion for serious reflections, analytical articles, and recollections by historians, critics, participants, and eyewitnesses."[22] Leonid Radzikhovskii, whose review opened the coverage, alluded to the recent saturation of war films on small screens and referred to this usage of cinematic memories as "military games conducted according to market rules." Moreover, "the Great Patriotic War is a sacred concept for Russians [and] . . . is the only thing that we can agree as a nation that unites us all." To tackle a taboo of this sacred event, Radzikhovskii writes, is to ruffle nationhood's most important feathers. And yet, as he claims, to reveal some of the darker truths about the war such as the penal battalions is worthwhile, "not only for ratings, but to reveal the truth by chopping the last icon with an axe, to dismember and to kill the last [Soviet] people's myth," even if this cinematic bloodletting might offend living veterans of the war who have come to accept Soviet cinematic memories as their own.[23] Shocking ratings busters, in other words, can have important ramifications for historical understanding.

Shtrafbat performed well in the ratings game, but it also performed well in another sense. Exploding a taboo subject allowed historians and participants to discuss both the real and fictionalized penal battalions' role. This debate centered on whether or not the fictional tale first written by Volodarskii and later filmed by Dostal′ captured the history well enough or whether the artistic license taken within the series distorted the view of the war. Using Anninskii's metaphor, did the look into the mirror reflect a larger truth back or refract the truth?

Volodarskii clearly believed the former, for he claimed that the role of a screenwriter is similar to that of a detective, uncovering sometimes-uncomfortable truths by wrapping them in fiction. In an interview published in *Iskusstvo kino,* Volodarskii defines his work as one "obsessed by history," but "history with a fresh view," one where a subjective, personal view of the past dominates, what "its sense is for you, specifically you." It is hard to argue with Volodarskii's successes in these endeavors, for among the fifty scripts he has authored are masterpieces such as Aleksei German's banned 1971 *Trial on the Roads* (about a Russian POW who joins the partisans to prove his patriotism), Nikita Mikhalkov's 1974 Civil War period piece *At Home among Strangers, a Stranger at Home,* and German's similarly banned 1984 masterpiece *My Friend Ivan Lapshin* (a dark film about the Stalin years). In the 1970s, Volodarskii applied to the state and asked to make a film about the penal battalions, but the topic was deemed too explosive and the request denied. Thirty years later, he used "the memories that floated up to me" as the basis for his story. Growing up in Moscow, Volodarskii noticed that the number of veterans who lived on his street did not conform to the image of the Great Patriotic hero promoted in official discourse. Many, as the writer commented, were disabled, amputees, or drunks. Over beers, he "heard many stories of frontline soldiers, which, until now, lived inside me." Using these tales, he wrote the series rapidly and claimed, "My memory, thank the Lord, proved to be good." For him, working on a television series gave him the opportunity to do something that a single film cannot: "weave an historical fabric" through a "*kinoroman* [film-novel]."

As far as the message of his work on *Shtrafbat,* Volodarskii believes it is to work against two powerful strands of thought: the "destroyed Soviet ideology that is nevertheless still living" and the current "authority of money" that promotes "nihilism" and "addiction" among the young.[24] Confronting the past, even if painful, is for Volodarskii a way to rebuild Russian patriotism.

Given this view, offered so openly by the scriptwriter and echoed in the comments of Dostal′ (both men talked about their personal family histories as a reason for revising the history of the war), historians and veterans of the war took the series and its performance seriously. For the historian Boris Sokolov, author of *The Truth about the Great Patriotic War* and one of the proponents of the controversial thesis that the Soviet leadership provoked the war against Nazi Germany, the film reflected a "truer" portrait of the war in spite of its other inaccuracies.[25] Calling *Shtrafbat* "such an evil, terrible fairy tale about the war," Sokolov believes that the film serves a larger purpose in terms of how the Great Patriotic War had been memorialized, for "before they stuffed us with intensely propagandistic fairy tales [about it], but now we have terrible fairy tales." The specific truths captured in the film pale in comparison to the larger function performed by *Shtrafbat* in shattering previous propagandistic reflections. Among the inaccuracies Sokolov lists are Tverdokhlebov's leadership (as a former POW, he would not have led a penal battalion, a position that was given to a regular officer) and the fatalistic view that no soldiers could earn their way out of the penal battalions after proving their bravery under fire, seen in the series through the experiences of Private Tsukerman, who is wounded twice. Instead of being freed from punishment he is only returned to face combat again, and eventually perished at the end. For Sokolov, "This is pure fantasy, but, for the director it was important to show that not one of the penal battalion's members leaves alive, symbolically expressing the predestination of the battalion's heroes." Despite these and other faults, the series succeeds, according to Sokolov, for its revelation of the other side of Stalin's infamous Order No. 227. Moreover, *Shtrafbat* reveals "an entire miniature of Russia at war," for "the film correctly shows that the authorities considered the entire people as cannon fodder, and that victory was achieved by these people."[26]

By contrast, president of the Academy of Military Science and former Red Army general Makhmut Gareev, found much to dislike when peering into the penal battalion mirror. When asked by the newspaper *Nezavisimaia gazeta* about the series *Shtrafbat* and why it may be more harmful than good, Gareev replied bluntly, "It is necessary to ram into the heads of today's young people that Marshal Zhukov and Marshal Matrosov did not forge victory, but criminals did, and thus if we do not diminish the victory, then in a specific manner we minimize its value in the minds of the present generation." While he praises the performance of actors such as Serebriakov, Gareev criticizes the historical inaccuracies as a "clear sign" that "the entire series is impregnated with spite for our army, for the entire effort for which we warred, with hostility to our victory, our generals and our commanders, and with idealization of the German generals." Worse than the distortions onscreen, in Gareev's view, were the distortions offscreen. Gareev has heavy criticisms for the televised debates about the series that aired on Rossiia and other channels. Volodarskii appeared on most of these, but for historical commentaries most channels used (in Gareev's view) "the philologist" Boris Sokolov. Neither Vladimir Karpov, a writer who served in a penal battalion and became a Hero of the Soviet Union, nor Aleksandr Pyl′tsyn, who also served in one and survived to write a memoir about the experience, appeared on these televised discussions. Gareev summarizes his stance in stark language: "In one of his appearances President Putin spoke thus: 'We will protect the truth about this war and fight against any attempts to distort this truth, to humble and to insult the memory of those who fell, because history cannot be distorted.' But, apparently, this did not become a recommendation for those who, on the eve of the sixtieth anniversary of the victory, attempt to create translations and the books that distort the truth and defame the memory of those killed."[27]

Major Viacheslav Izmailov, the military affairs expert for *Novaia gazeta* (*New paper*), took a stance on *Shtrafbat* that went even further than Sokolov; one that the paper declared found "the truth in the falsities." For Izmailov, a veteran of the Afghan and Chechen campaigns, the series speaks not just to the past, but to the present. Despite some inconsistencies, the army man believes that Volodarskii and Dostal′ "show how different people all experience the overall misfortune of war."

As to the controversial assertion that *Shtrafbat* makes about the Soviet political and army leadership not caring about individual lives, Izmailov agrees with the view, citing the death of his uncle at the age of eighteen in 1945, the experiences of his father in the war, and his own experiences in Afghanistan, where he received commands to order soldiers to perform suicidal missions. However, for Izmailov, soldiers themselves tended to accept these orders without complaint, unlike the soldiers in the series: "Without any pressure our soldiers and our officers carry out the order, even at the price of their life. On the whole, they do not value their life." Izmailov sees this trait as carrying through Russian history to the present day, so much so that his interviewer asks if it is a "national trait" and if "all of Russia is a shtrafbat"—points that the major affirms: "Take Grozny. Terrible losses. A large brigade, eight thousand people, . . . are gathered . . . and thrown into the scorching heat. Is this not similar to a shtrafbat?" For Izmailov, the "truth" that emerges out of the many falsities screened in the television series is that the Russian army has always relied on sacrificial lambs, from Stalingrad to Grozny.[28]

Here the three commentators engaged in a classic debate about the relationship between film and history: does a fictionalized view of past events reflect larger truths or distort them by essentializing them too much? At stake in this debate is the most important myth of twentieth-century Russian history, the victory in the Great Patriotic War, and who can claim responsibility for this victory. *Shtrafbat* is clear about who owns the victory—average Russians, not the Party or the military leadership.

In addition to the debates that went on in the newspapers and on televised roundtables, *Shtrafbat* the series led to an increased awareness in the actual penal battalions. A topic that had previously been hidden suddenly became openly discussed. The popularity of the series helped sell Volodarskii's tie-in novel, complete with an image of Serebriakov as Tverdokhlebov on the cover. Former members of penal battalions found themselves on front pages. Sought after by major publishers, these hidden soldiers came out into the open, an extraordinary turn of events caused by the series.

The former shtrafnik who appeared the most in this role was Aleksandr Pyl′tsyn, whom Gareev mentioned in his tirade. Pyl′tsyn's story is indicative of how the memory of the penal battalion worked in Russia before the series appeared: he hid his membership in a unit for some time and found no official outlet to discuss his experiences before 2003. As he has claimed, this "wartime secret" meant that knowledge about the penal battalions was confined to "a mass of legends and fictions." The revival of interest in the war and its hidden aspects that came after *Star* led the St. Petersburg publisher Znanie to publish Pyl′tsyn's memoir, *Penalty Strike: Or How a Shtrafbat Officer Reached Berlin* (*Shtrafnoi udar, ili kak ofitserskii shtrafbat doshel do Berlina*) in 2003. It received a little interest, but the series turned it into a best seller, when Znanie issued a second edition. Suddenly Pyl′tsyn went from an unknown to a known veteran and Znanie could not keep up. The Moscow publisher Eksmo snapped up the rights to the memoir and issued it in 2007 under the name *The Truth about the Penal Battalions: How a Shtrafbat Officer Reached Berlin.* By that time, Pyl′tsyn's experiences had been translated into English under the title *Penalty Strike.*

When the series appeared, Pyl′tsyn's secret story became sought after. His memoir is an attempt to right what he sees as multiple misperceptions and historical wrongs done by Soviet forgetting and Dostal′′s cinematic remembering of the units. Above all, he sees two great faults with the series, beginning with the treatment of officers and Red Army officials. While Pyl′tsyn admitted that he felt wronged by the system because of his imprisonment and assignment to a penal battalion, he did not blame the Soviet system as a whole. Instead, he reserved his anger "mostly to those who served on military tribunals and prosecutors." Once in the "hell-fire of war," as Pyl′tsyn describes his harrowing front-line experiences (which included human minesweeping), however, "the fate of the penal battalion depended very much on the officers." Unlike the penal battalion soldiers from the series, Pyl′tsyn blamed those most directly responsible for his sentence and not the army command. Secondly, Pyl′tsyn did not think that the television series depicted the penal battalion soldiers accurately. In his mind, they were not criminals and shirkers: "I was convinced that the absolute majority of penal battalion soldiers, despite their fates, preserved a human feeling of military friendship and a true feeling of devotion to their native land. . . . I consider this to be heroism." While the units contained "cowards and deserters," "they were rare, and only emphasized the martial valor of the rest."[29] For Pyl'tsyn, shtrafniki remained Soviet patriots.

Pyl'tsyn's sudden prominence and popularity created a small genre of "truthful" accounts about the penal battalions. Eksmo—itself a post-Soviet sensation that began as a small press in 1991 and by 2005 published luminaries that ranged from Liudmila Ulitskaya to Darya Dontsova—alone put out *The Truth about the Penal Battalions* (Pyl'tsyn's memoir), *The Truth about the Penal Battalions 2, Penal Battalions and Red Army Atrocities, Penal Battalions on Both Sides of the Front,* and *The Whole Truth about the Penal Battalions* after the series aired.[30] Each came with a requisite introduction that mentioned the significance of the series in generating debate about the penal battalions and the necessity of correcting errors in the series. *Penal Battalions on Both Sides of the Front* gave a backhanded compliment to the series on its first page by stating that the penal battalions had become "military folklore" over the course of the USSR, and "if we believe contemporary television concoctions like the series *Shtrafbat,* then the impression is created as if World War II was won exclusively by penal battalion soldiers, driven on from behind by the *zagradotriadov*'s machine gun bursts."[31] Each mentioned Pyl'tsyn's memoir as a model, and two of them (*The Truth about the Penal Battalions 2* and *Penal Battalions on Both Sides of the Front*) featured other memories from survivors of the *shtrafbaty.* All of these books and others like them—for example, Aleksandr Belov's novel *Penal Battalion* from Olma Press and Andrei Vasil'chenko's *Hitler's Shtrafbat* from Iauza—appeared after 2005, when the series had aired. Dostal''s film, just as Anninskii predicted, served as a mirror of the war, allowing hidden reflections to become clearer through multiple glances.

The open debate *Shtrafbat* created had its most heated exchanges in internet chat rooms. The Afghan vet turned author and video game entrepreneur, Dmitrii Puchkov—better known in the gaming world as Goblin—felt particularly aggrieved at the history depicted on screen and established an online forum for discussing the "truth" about the battalions.[32] Goblin, in an introduction to his forum, stated plainly, "My reaction [to the series] is extremely negative." In particular, echoing Gareev and Pyl'tsyn, he did not care for the depiction of Red Army commanders, the hard fight to take Berlin, and even the NKVD's actions: "Volodarskii is not interested in them, he does not wish to examine them and to compare them." Instead, he wants to show a war "where we, the people, won not because of, but in spite of, the Party," a personal view of war that Goblin believes places Volodarskii "among a group of slanderers."[33] The vast majority of the people who posted on the forum agreed with Goblin's sentiments, praising him and stating, in the words of "Nikita" (the ninth to post), "This is not a film; it is shit." Nikita based this profound judgment on a fairly reliable source: Vladimir Karpov, a writer and former penal battalion member whose story had appeared in the press because of the popular series (the irony of this historical memory recovery was lost on Nikita). As for Goblin, his successful online debate and his anger over what he saw as historical misrepresentations on screen prepared him for what was to come, for when he saw Fedor Bondarchuk's 2005 blockbuster about the Afghan War, *Ninth Company* (a war in which Goblin took part), Goblin fought back, adopting the style of the *Shtrafbat* reaction: he made a video game and then a documentary film titled *The Truth about Ninth Company.* But that story is worthy of another chapter.

Not all of the online response to *Shtrafbat* was as negative as Goblin's forum. On ruskino.ru, viewers of the series engaged in serious debates about the significance of the units based on what the series had articulated, on whether or not the units represented a more just form of punishment than executions, and on whether or not the series captured the essence of the war's many dark truths. Online participants even quoted newspaper interviews with penal battalion survivors, critics who did not like the series, and critics like Daniil Dondurei, the editor of *Iskusstvo kino,* who viewed the series much like his colleague Anninskii had.[34] Other viewers proclaimed it "a strong film that forces us to think and rethink some moments from our history," or one that was "not your usual series, but an outstanding one." Many echoed the words of "Somnevaiushchiisia": "The war appears much more realistic than in Soviet heroic-patriotic films." A few labeled the series "disgusting" and claimed "just because they slung mud on the Soviet past it does not mean that they tell the truth completely."[35]

Dostal′ attributed *Penal Battalion*'s success to the honesty of its emotions and what he called "the awakening of and freeing from myths."[36]

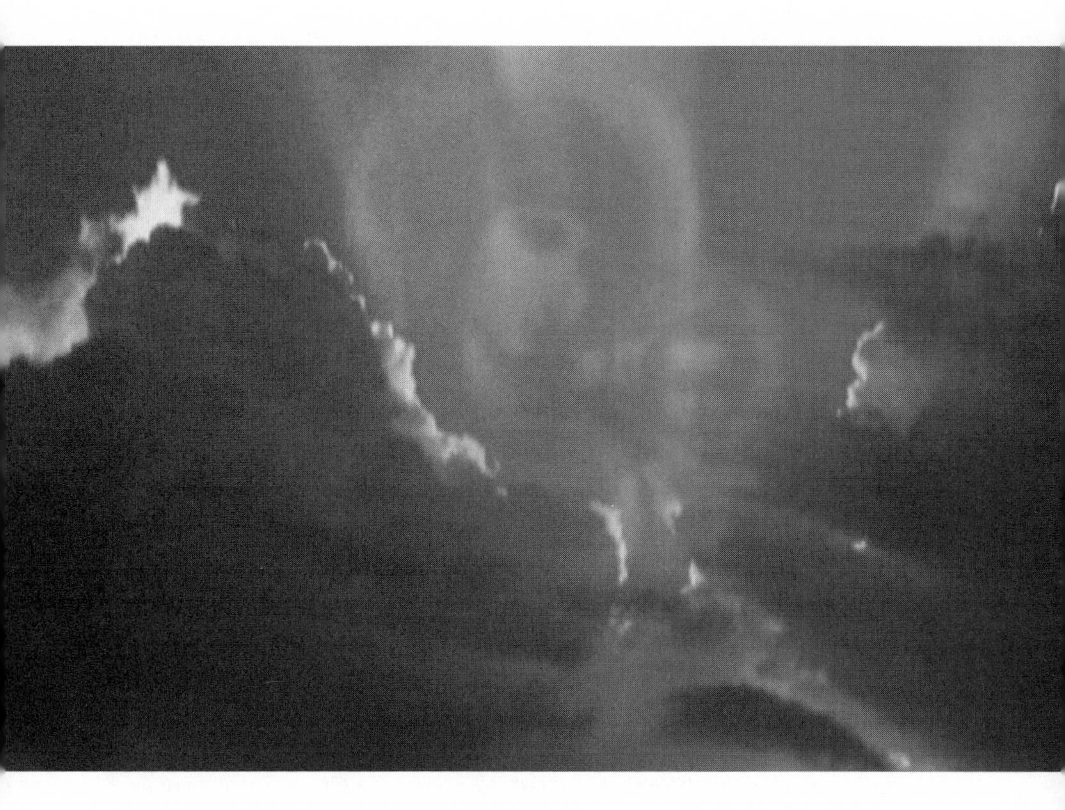

An Orthodox *shtrafbat*? Father Mikhail's vision.
Still from Nikolai Dostal′'s *Shtrafbat* (2004).

On a radio program where he took questions from viewers along with Serebriakov and Iurii Stepanov (who played Glymov, the "kulak and thief"), Dostal′ clarified his position on the film and its history: "There is historical truth and there is artistic truth," claiming that although the film has some "inaccuracies," it still reveals "the national character. . . . We showed the unknown pages of the war. Indeed, no one liked to recall the penal battalion soldiers. Their graves are nameless. The film wanted these people to be known and showed that they formed the building blocks for Victory's powerful foundations." For the director, "the further we leave myths behind, the greater the truth that will appear and people will know what war is." When asked to sum up what his film was about, Dostal′ answered succinctly: "It is about patriotism."[37]

Anninskii, the ever-perceptive critic, agreed with this claim in part, but also believed that some of the historical distortions, particularly the use of Father Mikhail, made the film "absolutely in the spirit of our age" and not 1944. For Anninskii, as revealing as the film is, it also has a troubling contemporary connection in the sense that the soldiers are all "sinners" who need to be redeemed by a priest to make them "an Orthodox shtrafbat." What this means, Anninskii suggests, is that "the entire world is a penal battalion, for all people are guilty [of sin]. Alas, in our new millennium the series confirms a Russian millennial view." In the end, "all are sacrificed. All fell on that last bridgehead . . . to pay the price for Russia in order to save Russia. The sounds of an Orthodox liturgy fill the field of corpses. My heart beats in unison to the requiem."[38] Anninskii's view that *Shtrafbat* suggests all of Russia needs to be redeemed through religion because of their Soviet sins predates the debates that would wage about Pavel Lungin's 2006 film, *The Island* (*Ostrov*), which featured a holy fool at an unnamed monastery in Russia's far north who had taken to religion in order to atone for his role in killing a fellow Soviet soldier during the war. Blessed by Patriarch Aleksei II, *The Island* left many critics feeling uncomfortable about the way history seemed to be manipulated to fit with the revival of the Orthodox Church and its open attempts to marry religion with patriotism in Putin's Russia.[39] Anninskii believed that *Shtrafbat* beat a similar message into the hearts of viewers.

Regardless of where one fell in the debates about *Shtrafbat,* it is hard to overestimate the impact that the series had on viewers. A 2005 poll conducted by the Moscow-based Public Opinion Foundation suggested that Russian audiences decoded the messages of World War II films in fascinating yet complex ways. Out of the 1,500 respondents from 44 regions in Russia, 69 percent stated that they had seen a recent film about the war. Nearly 1 in 5 (19 percent) replied that they had encountered "recent TV programs, movies, books, or articles that changed or enlarged their views about the Great Patriotic War." Over half considered new war films "more trustworthy" than Soviet movies (24 percent believed that Soviet movies were more truthful). Among the specific changes in views, respondents cited "the irresponsibility of our military officers," "real stories about penal battalions," and "too many people killed for nothing." In 2004, pollsters found that 27 percent of the 1,500 respondents claimed their views of the war had changed because of recent films. At the same time, respondents differed sharply over the quality of recent films—24 percent believed that newer films were better, 27 percent found Soviet films better, and 31 percent "found it difficult to discuss the issue."[40] The raw emotions onscreen and the reawakening of narratives freed from Soviet control certainly contributed to a widespread discussion about the war and its contemporary significance. As Anninskii wrote, the penal battalions stood at the center of this discussion.

BASTARDS, STALIN TESTS, AND REMEMBRANCE IN RUSSIA

Aleksandr Atanesian's 2006 film *Bastards* (*Svolochi*) took the revision of Soviet wartime narratives one step further. *Bastards* focused upon teenage orphans who subsisted in Soviet cities as criminals. The young men have lost their childhoods because of Stalinist state violence and are already hardened criminals by the time the war breaks out. They are further bastardized by Soviet wartime officials and by the Stalinist law that viewed teenage criminals as adults. Captured by the NKVD as the war rages, the young men are sent to a prison in Kazakhstan to train and to prepare to serve their country. The film focuses upon the two officers who try to coax the young men out of their hardened shells. *Bastards* spared nothing in its examination of the Stalinist state and the practices it engendered. Many of the "bastards" of the film have witnessed the deaths of their parents in purges and all have lost their humanity as a result of life on the streets. They kill without remorse, steal, and resist attempts to humanize them. In the end, their "reward" is to be sent on a suicide mission to take out a German base. Most of the boys are shot as they parachute to the ground. All but two perish. When a German officer glances at the dead bodies of the children who have failed in their mission, he curses the kind of system that would use children as cannon fodder. In short, it is *Penal Battalion* with kids.

Appearing less than five months after Dostal′'s television series debuted, *Bastards* prompted fiery exchanges about whether the events captured on film were accurate. Critics of the film charged the director with falsifying the historical record and with undermining Russian patriotism. When the film premiered, the Russian FSB (the successor to the KGB) released a report that stated they had failed to find any documents in Russian and Kazakh archives that confirmed the existence of the "children's diversionary schools" depicted in the film. The FSB did report, however, that they possessed documents that proved Nazi Germany had used children in operations.[41] The director, Aleksandr Atanesian, and the author of the work on which *Bastards* was based, Mikhail Kunin, both received a great deal of criticism. The greatest vitriol, however, was saved for Mikhail Shvydkoi, the minister of culture. The Moscow City Duma grilled Putin's film guru before a special session, asking him to explain the "scandal" brewing over *Bastards,* a vociferous debate that sounded a lot like the one that had waged over *Shtrafbat.* Shvydkoi hit back at his critics, stating, "Artists have the right to invention," and even countering that "opinion polls show that it carries out its patriotic mission." Members of the Moscow Duma responded by asking whether it was "patriotic" to allocate seven hundred thousand dollars of state funds to a film that featured Nazi officers discussing the "Soviet atrocity" of using children for suicide missions. Eventually, Atanesian admitted at the Moscow premiere that the story was fictional. The debate and Shvydkoi's comments were splashed across newspaper headlines, some quoting the cultural minister ironically: "*Bastards* is patriotic all the same!"[42]

Once again, Russian viewers looked into the mirror of wartime memories and found different reflections. Anninskii's metaphor can be interpreted as a means for understanding history as an encounter, a moment when the past becomes personal, a face-to-face viewing of what history tells us. Much as Omer Bartov has seen the meanings of the Holocaust as a hall of mirrors, "wherein repeated images, seen from different angles, provide a prism though which we can distill a clearer understanding of the origins, nature, and impact of the atrocity,"[43] so, too, can we view the reactions to *Shtrafbat* and other cinematic revisions of the Soviet war narrative. The significance of the Great Patriotic War is such that everyone in Russia periodically looks in the mirror to see how the event is currently reflected or refracted, depending on the position in which the viewer stands and their reaction to what they see.[44] Russian glances in this mirror are not that unusual, for the war continues to serve as a worldwide impetus for many to check out themselves and the state of their nations—Germans have wrestled with the legacies of guilt, the French have tried to understand Vichy, Poles have wrestled with their dual roles as victims and victimizers, and most Japanese have embraced defeat while forgetting Nanjing, just to name a few examples of this global process.[45]

And yet the cinematic explosions in post-Soviet Russia, while fitting within this soul searching, are rather unusual. Given the status of the war within Soviet culture and the unassailable facts that the Soviet Union bore the brunt of the fighting, that Soviet casualties accounted for nearly half of all the losses in the war, and that the identity crisis that swept Russia in the 1990s sought a new patriotic focal point, it is not surprising that filmmakers and politicians tried to use the war as a unifying myth once again. What is surprising, and even optimistic, is the extent to which post-Soviet filmmakers and audiences embraced radical revisions of wartime narratives and extraordinary investigations into the behavior of ordinary Soviet citizens. *Shtrafbat* is one of many post-Soviet films that tackle hard truths and forbidden subjects about the war, an exploration of history that would be comparable to a Polish director making a film about Jedwabne and not just Katyń, a German filmmaker about Wehrmacht atrocities on the Eastern Front and not about German suffering in Dresden, or a Japanese director about Nanjing and not Hiroshima.

Even more extraordinary is the fact that *Shtrafbat* proved to be a market sensation. Not only did Dostal′'s film do well in the ratings game, it also cleaned up on sales, moving thirty thousand DVD sets in its first month of release in a market where pirated DVDs frequently do better than official ones.[46] The success of the television series spilled over into other media outlets, with major publishers putting out accounts of the penal battalions. Odd as it may seem, the darker sides of the Great Patriotic War sell in contemporary Russia. *Bastards* made $9.67 million and led the Russian box office for three weeks in a row (knocking *Day Watch* from its perch and outdueling Hollywood blockbusters such as *Underworld: Evolution* and *Big Momma's House 2*) even in the face of condemnations.[47]

Given this performance, it is hard to buy into the critical view that the uses of the Great Patriotic War on small and large screens amounts to a rebirth of Soviet ideology. Mark Lipovetsky, one of the primary advocates of this critical view, argues that "post sots" has taken over Russian culture in part because "the new generation of children has no memory of the socialist past, with their minds shaped predominantly by Western mass culture and video games."[48] Although he does not necessarily see the revival of socialist realist mythologies as an attempt to restore totalitarian politics, Lipovetsky despairs at how post-sots texts "do not try to expose the absurdity or violence hidden beneath Socialist Realist mythology" and ultimately gets rid of, "or at least cover[s] up, the disturbing trauma of the totalitarian past."[49] Among the traits of this uncritical, post-sots culture, Lipovetsky sees simple plots of good and evil as the first indication and cites *Star* as one the best examples of the "new socialist realism" dominating contemporary Russian culture. War films, in this view, revive Soviet myths and use memories to construct another form of patriotism.

While many Russian critics look in to the mirror of wartime remembrances and see Soviet uses of the war myth, many American scholars tend to look into a different mirror altogether. Sarah Mendelson and Theodore Gerber's influential 2006 *Foreign Affairs* article charged Russians today with "failing the Stalin test." Based on a series of poll questions that asked whether Russians would vote for Stalin if he were alive today (25 percent stated they would), Mendelson and Gerber claim that Russians today "do not view Stalin with the revulsion he deserves," a situation that Western leaders "have failed to respond to."[50] The stakes, as they see it, are high, for they expanded on their findings in a *Wilson Quarterly* piece published almost simultaneously: "Soviet Nostalgia: An Impediment to Democratization."[51] Mendelson and Gerber's article encapsulates a widely held belief in America today, one that regularly appears in newspapers and journals with even larger circulations than *Foreign Affairs*. This view—that Russians are not confronting their past "correctly"—gets to the heart of how historical memory tends to be popularly perceived. For Mendelson and Gerber, the fact that Russians hold "ambivalent" views on the questions they pose (without realizing it is ridiculous to ask whether anyone would vote for a dead dictator) indicates a "memory disorder" of sorts.[52] Too often, as Alon Confino has written in the German context, the central question in studies that explore the ways Germans have attempted to master their Nazi past "has been *whether* Germans came to terms with this past," and not *what* they remembered, *how* they did it, and *who* remembered it.[53] The view of the "Stalin test" falls into this trap, and though it may be an important issue, as an historical question it has severe limitations. The range of views presented in *Penal Battalion* and the range of reactions to the series alone question the narrow view that Russians are failing the test. Instead, they seem to be taking an essay exam and not the multiple choice one offered by Mendelson and Gerber, who even conclude that Russian youth receive the greatest amount of information about the Stalin era from television.[54] If *Shtrafbat* is one of the sources of this knowledge, then it is hard to be overly pessimistic about the ways young people are consuming their past.

Perhaps it is best to turn to Jay Winter's concept of films as "theaters of memory" to understand the importance of the contemporary Russian war film. Sites of memory such as films and television series "are spaces where those who were not there see the past not in terms of their own personal memories, but rather in terms of public representations of the memories of those who come before." These performances of the past offer a chance for individuals to "negotiate the distance between history and memory in their representations of war."[55] For audiences who still invested a great deal in the Soviet narrative of the war or for penal battalion veterans, the series challenged their memories and at times provoked charges of unpatriotic culture. Others, particularly among those too young to remember the Soviet era, viewed the series as "patriotic" because it allowed them to learn something new about the war and find a way to understand the victory over Nazi Germany. Taken together, the range of reviews to the films suggests that they serve as a "multi-tiered theater" where "the individual viewer of a film brings to that film personal memories and historical narratives." This "amalgam of reflections individuals take out of cinema is therefore complex and volatile."[56]

Viewing the reactions to *Shtrafbat* alone makes it difficult to peg the reflections into an all-encompassing conclusion. Far from a state-driven "Putinization" of Russian culture, a revitalized socialist realism, or a failure to confront the past, recent films about the war such as *Shtrafbat* allow for complex interpretations about the meanings of the war and its present-day uses. Perhaps Daniil Dondurei, Anninskii's colleague cited by several of the online respondents to the film, said it best: "The inherent task of an artist is to be subjective," but "with respect to historical events, it is necessary to be extremely careful." The writer and director of *Bastards,* for Dondurei, proved to be an example of too much subjectivity, for they "actually told untruths." On the other hand, as Dondurei claimed, cinema artists could perform an important function by uncovering complex histories about the violence of the Soviet era. He approvingly cited *Shtrafbat,* for this series showcased a side of the war where criminals fought alongside believers, but where "in the majority of the cases they died for their family and for their native land." Watching the series, Dondurei mused, could help former Soviet citizens and post-Soviet young people "learn to be patriots in their daily, ordinary lives."[57]

As for the people responsible for the remarkable confluence of memory, they continued to look into the mirrors of the past. Karen Shakhnazarov, who first funded *Star* and who believed that Russian cinema needed new wartime explorations, loaned out Mosfil′m materials and props to most of the films that followed, including *Shtrafbat.* The Soviet Jeeps and tanks seen in *Star* were the very same ones seen in *Penal Battalion* and again in series like *The Saboteur* (and some of these vehicles had first appeared in classics like *Ballad of a Soldier*). Dostal′ next filmed a series based on the life and writings of Varlam Shalamov, a Gulag survivor and author of the extraordinary *Kolyma Tales.* Titled *Lenin's Will* (*Zaveshchanie Lenina*) and written by Iurii Arabov (who had just adapted *Doctor Zhivago* for television), the series aired on Rossiia in 2007 and followed the seventeen years Shalamov spent in the camps. Like *Shtrafbat,* it was a ratings smash and it won awards, including the Golden Eagle for best television series of the year.[58] Before this explosion, Volodarskii launched one of his own by following a similar path. He adapted one of Shalamov's tales, "The Last Fight of Major Pugachev" (about a war hero who is sent to the Gulag as an enemy of the people) for a four-part 2005 NTV serial. Volodarskii also returned to the war and its mirrors in his script for the 2008 blockbuster, *We are from the Future* (*My iz budushchego*), which transports four contemporary

St. Petersburg slackers (one of whom plays Goblin's war games) back to the 1942 Leningrad front.

Anninskii, who contributed his part to the critical and cultural debates about the mirror of war, continued to lob silent explosions in his writings and even filmed a six-part documentary program on Silver Age poets for the "Culture" channel that aired in 2004. As for the state of television and its uses of the past, Anninskii had this to say in November 2007: "We have the television that we deserve. It reflects all of our faces in the mirror."[59] He sees two types of reflections from glancing into mirrors of the past: those that air all types of information that can be difficult to absorb and those that allow viewers to gain a sense of humanity's "spiritual essence." Certainly the mirror of wartime memories reflected in *Penal Battalion,* however painful this look may be, fall in the latter category.

The greatest sign that the penal battalion now was the center of post-Soviet Russian reflections about the Great Patriotic War, however, came four years after the release of the television series. Nikita Mikhalkov's massive and massively expensive epic *Burnt by the Sun 2: Exodus* allowed General Kotov (played by Mikhalkov) to survive his death in the Oscar-winning first film. How could he be imprisoned by the NKVD and shot, but survive? How could Kotov rise from the dead to serve his motherland in the cauldron of war? The answer is simple: he could be like Tverdokhlebov. For Kotov, as Mikhalkov revealed in 2007, survived his execution and joined a penal battalion.

Playing with the past: The special edition of *Ninth Company: The Video Game.*

SEVEN

Playing with History

Dmitrii Puchkov left Fedor Bondarchuk's 2005 blockbuster *Ninth Company* [*9 rota*] in a foul mood. The army vet and former MVD agent did not like the film; in his words, "while it was billed as 'based on real events,' it had no relation to reality."[1] Bondarchuk's history of the events of 1988 on Hill 3234, promoted under the slogan "they wanted only to be loved" was for Puchkov "filth" and "slander." In his words, *Ninth Company* was not the "truth" and therefore not "history."

Many veterans of the Afghan War felt similarly. Yet Puchkov became the most vocal critic of the film's use of history because he is not a run-of-the mill, grumpy ultra-nationalist. He is more widely known as "Goblin," the voice behind a series of pirated film dubbings and video game commentaries. To fight back, Goblin combined his interests in new media and released a video game, a website, and a documentary film—all of which were titled *The Truth about Ninth Company*. The film and its video game ignited a memory war, one in which Bondarchuk, a man who calls himself Goblin, filmgoers, gamers, and veterans engaged in verbal combat over the meanings of Russia's Vietnam. Together, all the participants played with the past, using the Afghan War to score patriotic points and to fire cyber attacks at their enemies.

The Truth About Ninth Company: Special edition of the game.

AFGHANISTAN IN RUSSIAN MEMORY: THE FIRST NINTH COMPANY

The story of the Ninth Company in many ways is the story of the entire Afghan War from the Soviet perspective. One of the first detachments to enter Afghanistan in 1979, the Ninth Company of the 345th Guards Airborne Regiment stayed in the country until the war's end. The company was asked to defend the highest point within Soviet-controlled territory in 1987 during the last major front of the conflict. Brainchild of the new Soviet commander, Lieutenant General Boris Gromov, the attack involved ten thousand Soviet troops and eight thousand Afghan troops against the mujahideen rebels. Operation Magistral attempted to open up the road between Gardez and Khost, which had been blocked by mujahideen troops. Gromov's plan proved to be a success. Launched on November 19, 1987, the offensive succeeded in capturing the treacherous Satukandav Pass, the main passage between the two cities. Soviet forces entered Khost on December 30.

One of the key areas that protected the mountainous pass between the Afghan cities was a mountain held by Soviet soldiers. Known as "Height 3234 [10,500 feet]," the remote location meant that its Soviet defenders lacked reliable communication with headquarters. The mujahideen attacked the position eleven times January 7–8, 1988. Radio communication often failed and reserve forces were initially unable to relieve the company. Once the attacks had been repelled, reserves arrived, although the Ninth Company suffered serious casualties: six dead and ten wounded out of thirty-nine soldiers.

When Franz Klintsevich, a reconnaissance chief attached to the Soviet forces, arrived to relieve the Ninth Company at Height 3234, he first saw a soldier bleeding heavily from shrapnel wounds to his chest and trachea. With scant medical supplies available, Klintsevich stuffed some wax paper into the wounds and attempted to get the soldier to breathe through his mouth. Klintsevich then got through to the company's commander, Colonel Valerii Vostrotin, and begged for relief. Initially Vostrotin refused, but some pilots managed to bring ammunition and carry away the dead and wounded. The wounded private, Anatolii Kuznetsov, died before relief arrived. Klintsevich stayed on at Height 3234 for two weeks after January 8, only to learn that the Soviet command had decided not to hold Khost because it stretched Soviet forces too thin. By the end of January 1988, the city had returned to mujahideen hands and the Soviet government had decided to withdraw. Operation Magistral was a success, but the war had been lost.

As Gregory Feifer has recently written, many veterans and participants in the final offensive saw it "as no more than a completely unnecessary demonstration of toughness to the rebels."[2] The offensive, made as the Soviet leadership had begun the process of withdrawal, "came to be a symbol of the futility of the entire war, not merely its last years."[3] Just a few weeks after the events on Height 3234, Mikhail Gorbachev announced that the hundred thousand Soviet soldiers left in Afghanistan would begin pulling out in May.

When Soviet troops arrived home, they were feted as heroes. As the Soviet system began to collapse, however, Afghan veterans became "just another group of victims."[4] In the chaotic, euphoric days of 1990–92, few Soviet citizens concerned themselves with the aftermath of the Afghan War. Increasingly, veterans began to take care of their own needs, forming societies such as the Committee of Internationalist Soldiers to assist with the difficulties brought by the return to civilian life. As Feifer has concluded, many veterans who formed these groups "came to believe that the war's worst damage to the Soviet Union wasn't the dead in Afghanistan, but the severe psychological damage suffered by those who returned."[5] The *Afgantsy* ["Afghans"], as veterans referred to each other, found the breakup of the Soviet Union particularly hard to deal with. The state forgot them and their experiences.

The largest support group to emerge as the system fell apart was the Russian Union of Afghanistan Veterans (RSVA). Founded in 1991, the RSVA initially dealt with the difficult transition veterans experienced in the 1990s and the trauma many still suffered from their wartime experiences. For the next decade, the society attempted to raise awareness about the war through educational programs, lobbying efforts, and memorials dedicated to Soviet soldiers. Both Klintsevich and Vostrotin joined the group, serving as important officers: Klintsevich even became the head of the organization in 1994. Their efforts rarely succeeded, for the war has tended to be forgotten entirely or remembered solely as a disaster fought by a bankrupt regime. Two contract killings of important Afghan vets led to lurid press reports about afganitsy as mafia men. By the end of the 1990s, Serguei Oushakine has argued, "the figure of the afganets was turned into a cliché standing for an uncontrolled, violent, mafia-connected man, tortured by his military past."[6] Instead, the reports of journalists such as Aleksandr Oleinik and Artem Borovik, who exposed the incompetence and corruption within the Soviet leadership, remained more influential in shaping how Russians remembered the Afghan war than the RSVA's activities.[7]

The forgetting only deepened once Boris Yeltsin and then Vladimir Putin launched their wars in Chechnya. Memories of the previous war now competed with the situation in the Caucasus. The Union of the Committees of Soldiers' Mothers (SKSMR), founded in 1988 by mothers of Afghan soldiers who wanted information about their missing sons, switched its focus to the victims of the new war. For the most part Russian society did the same. Even those who actively tried to increase awareness about the Afghan war had mixed views about its meanings. Aleksandr Liakhovskii, a Russian historian who has compiled the most extensive history of the war, published his work under the title *The Tragedy and Valor of the Afghan War.*[8] As he notes, most veterans and Russians have had a difficult time balancing the widely accepted view that the war was a tragedy with their personal pride in having served their country. Until, that is, Fedor Bondarchuk arrived on the scene.

FULL METAL RUSSIAN JACKET: BONDARCHUK'S GUILT AND THE SECOND NINTH COMPANY

Fedor Bondarchuk, son of film director Sergei, got his start directing music videos and commercials. After graduating from VGIK (the All-Russian State Institute for Cinema) in 1991, Bondarchuk founded Art Pictures with Stepan Mikhalkov, Nikita's son. The two made clips of rock and pop stars such as Boris Grebenshchikov, Alla Pugacheva, and Dva Samoleta throughout the 1990s. Bondarchuk also acted. He has played Prince Myshkin in the 2000 film *Down House,*[9] General Denikin in the 2004 television series *Death of the Empire,* a Nazi collaborator in 2005's *Our Own* [*Svoi*], and the bumbling Burchinskii in Boris Akunin's 2005 big-screen version of *The State Counsellor.*

Born in 1967, Bondarchuk comes from the last generation of Soviet men who saw action in Afghanistan. Although he served in the army at the age of eighteen, his famous father kept his son away from the front. Bondarchuk is fully aware that he escaped what many in his generation did not and this guilt serves as one of the motivating factors for his war movie. Bondarchuk believed that his film could act as a means of memory recovery: "During the Soviet Union there was no possibility to make such a film. And for a long time Russia didn't want such a film because Russia didn't want to remember these ten years of shame. It's an incredible success for a serious film and it shows the audience is ready to think."[10]

Bondarchuk also wanted to follow in his father's footsteps. Originally he hoped to make an updated version of *Fate of a Man,* Sergei Bondarchuk's 1959 masterpiece about a World War II veteran who tries to come to terms with his wartime losses. Iurii Korotkov, Bondarchuk's scriptwriter, stated that the two initially planned to make a film about the Chechen War and its effects on one soldier, but when they decided that they could not compare the Chechen War to the Great Patriotic War, they switched to Afghanistan. For Korotkov and Bondarchuk, the two wars are comparable because many Soviet soldiers volunteered for the Afghan War, young Soviet citizens had their adult consciences formed within it, and many still see it as the happiest time in their lives.[11]

Bondarchuk's onscreen Afghan War, based on Korotkov's script and coproduced by Stepan Mikhalkov, appeared when the director was thirty-eight, the same age at which his father made *Fate of a Man.* It was edited at Pinewood Shepperton Studios in England, the second-ever Russian film to use their famous sound facilities—after Sergei Bondarchuk's *Waterloo* (1970). Released on September 29, 2005, *9 rota* smashed box-office records, becoming the highest-grossing Russian film of all time, eventually earning $25.6 million.[12] It would go on to be the official Russian Academy Award submission and won both the Nika and Golden Eagle awards for best picture in 2005. STS, the television channel that coproduced the film, also produced a massive marketing campaign that saturated billboards, airwaves, and commercials with information about the Afghan War blockbuster.[13]

Bondarchuk's cinematic war follows the final days of the conflict and the events surrounding Hill 3234. His Afghan War follows a bunch of young recruits—Bondarchuk's peers—as they train in Central Asia before heading to Afghanistan. The director claims, "I didn't make a film about the Afghan War. I was making a film about the friendship, comradeship, and love of boys whose state I remember from being 18 in the army in 1985."[14] His film is about how young boys form a band of brothers because of the brutal treatment they receive first from their officers at boot camp and then because they witness the war's horrors.

Bondarchuk's Afghan War, in other words, is the Vietnam War, or at least the cinematic Vietnam War.

The first half of the film follows a group of volunteers and draftees from Krasnoiarsk through their boot camp experience in Uzbekistan. They are slowly dehumanized, starting with the shaving of their heads. They are given nicknames: Liutyi (fierce one), Chugun (iron), Vorobei (sparrow), Pinochet (given to a Chechen soldier because he looks foreign), and Gioconda (given to one soldier who was an art student). When they arrive in the Ferghana Valley, their drill sergeant, Dygalo, physically and mentally beats them down, telling them, "Here you're not smart, not stupid, not good, not bad, not artists, you're nobody! You're not even people—you're shit!" They are drilled physically and mentally, moving from being unfit for combat to a unit that easily conquers their grueling tasks. They also form a bond that has at its core the "friendship, comradeship, and love of boys" Bondarchuk desired. While these soldiers mouth the words that they are "Soviet paratroopers, [who are] the force, the beauty, and the pride of the armed forces," their real love is for each other, not for the Soviet Union. They openly fear for their lives and mock their officers. They bond by sneaking around with Snow White, the daughter of their commanding officer, who sleeps with everyone and whom they dub a "glorious, pure fallen woman" after they all engage in group sex with her.[15]

Russian and American reviewers immediately noted the similarity of the first half of *Ninth Company* to Vietnam films, particularly Stanley Kubrick's 1987 *Full Metal Jacket*.[16] It, too, opens with a shaving scene and it witnesses its grunts receiving nicknames (Joker, Pyle, Cowboy, and Snowball). It too has a veteran drill sergeant who dehumanizes the soldiers (R. Lee Ermey's Sergeant Hartman), telling them, "You are pukes! You are the lowest form of life on earth! You are not even human fucking beings! You're nothing but unorganized grabastic pieces of amphibian shit!" It, too, has its soldiers bond around love for each other, not love for the United States. Yet Kubrick's Vietnam War is irredeemable, its combatants cynical. The only two believers are Private Pyle and Sergeant Hartman, the latter because he believes in all of America's wars, the former because he becomes a killing machine. Of course, at the end of Kubrick's boot camp sequence, Pyle kills Hartman and then himself.

None of these moral uncertainties cloud Bondarchuk's version of war. Instead, the film suggests that the soldiers all make a sacrifice for the Russian nation in a patriotic act that produces a "victory." This triumph, as the final scenes elucidate, clearly is not won on the battlefield, but in the mind. The Afghan War therefore should be understood as a recent example of the supposedly timeless "Russian spirit" exhibited by all the historic defenders of the motherland. The war, its costs, and the reasons Soviet soldiers were in Afghanistan do not really matter. What does matter is that they acted heroically and served their homeland by making a stand against great odds.

The second half of the film furthers this heroic position by following the fortunes of the young heroes and loosely follows the exploits of the real Ninth Company. The new recruits are transported to Afghanistan with little understanding of why the war is raging around them. They are told by their commanding officer that they are there "to fulfill our international duty to help the people of Afghanistan and defeat the imperial aggressor." Yet Bondarchuk takes the action surrounding the attack on Height 3234 and plays with it to ratchet up the drama. The soldiers heroically defend the heights against overwhelming numbers, not in January 1988 but in January 1989. Thus, the battle for the Heights becomes the last action in the war, and the lack of communication from the center serves as a metaphor for how ordinary soldiers were cast aside by their leaders. In the end, only one of the heroes we have followed throughout—Liutyi—survives. When relief comes, he tells his commanding officer, "mission accomplished." His officer replies that the entire army is leaving. The next scene is set in February 1989 when the last Soviet troops leave Afghanistan. Liutyi comments, "We won our war, but we had no way of knowing that the country we fought for would vanish two years later." As Liutyi concludes, "We didn't know that in the chaos of the army's retreat, they'd simply forgotten us on those far-away heights. We left Afghanistan, the Ninth Company, and we were victorious." The final intertitles play with this sequence, stating, "The film is based on real events that took place on January 8, 1988, on the far-flung Heights 3234."[17] Bondarchuk dedicated the film to the memory of his father.

Bondarchuk's blockbuster may not have adhered entirely to the "true story" of the Ninth Company, but it spared no expense to capture other historical truths. At $9 million, it was the second-most-expensive Russian film ever made at the time it appeared after *The Barber of Siberia. Ninth Company* was shot over 150 days in eighteen locations spread between Moscow, Uzbekistan, and the Crimea, which stood in for Afghanistan. The war sequences used fifteen Ukrainian units employing thirty T-64-B tanks, ten MI-24 and MI-8 helicopters, and twenty-two AN and MiG fighter planes.[18] The effects were realistic enough that when Bondarchuk filmed a helicopter sequence near an official meeting at Foros between the Russian, Ukrainian, and Kazakh presidents, Kuchma's and Nazarbayev's security details warned their leaders of an impending attack (Putin had already departed). Bondarchuk had to pay a visit to the police afterwards and prove he had the proper permits for staging such a scene.

After he finished the edits, Bondarchuk held two preview screenings for two very select audiences. The first was with Putin and other luminaries. The Russian president invited the filmmakers and veterans to his residence to watch the film. Putin concluded that it was "a very good film," for it showed "everything as it is in life." Putin particularly praised the actors for work that "takes on the soul."[19] He expanded that "it is about time to stop all this political noise around the events that took place in Afghanistan. Clearly, these events should be . . . studied by politicians, historians, experts, militaries, and so on. But it is just as clear that those who fought in Afghanistan have nothing to be ashamed of."[20] The second, held at the Pushkin Theater a week before its wide release, was for the Russian Union of Afghanistan Veterans (RSVA). Among those present at the screening were the president of the RSVA, Franz Klintsevich, the former recon chief who acted as an official consultant to the film. Klintsevich now serves as a Duma deputy for United Russia and also attended the Putin screening. The other stars of the screening were three survivors of the events, Vladimir Shchigolev, Vladimir Veregin, and Valerii Vostrotin, who also acted as official consultants for the film. These veterans compared their ordeal to that of World War II penal battalions. For many veterans, Bondarchuk's film acted in a similar fashion to Dostal′'s television blockbuster, working to uncover memories. "Igor," an Afghan vet who attended the screening, commented afterward, "It will be possible to discuss this film, its merits, and its demerits for a while now." Another vet opined, "The film takes some artistic license, but I still took my sixteen-year-old son and made him watch it because it is the best movie about the Afghan War." Many agreed with one viewer's comment that if films such as Vladimir Bortko's 1990's *Afghanistan Fracture* contained "about 30 percent truth about the war," Bondarchuk's had "60 percent." As the RSVA website concluded, many veterans disagreed over the accuracy of Bondarchuk's war, but they agreed that it at least made audiences think about the conflict. For his contributions to this memory recovery, the RSVA gave Bondarchuk a special commendation, awarded by Vostrotin, also a Duma deputy for United Russia.[21]

The veterans association later organized five hundred free screenings of the film. At the Novosibirsk screening three thousand people showed up and afterward, Evgenii Iakovenko, an RSVA council member, stated, "The events are real. The film shows everything as it was." Children of Afghan vets at the screening commented, "Now we know why our fathers don't like to talk about the war."[22] Because of the success of these screenings, the organization now boasts on its home page, "[T]he most striking example of RSVA noncommercial collaboration with people in the cultural field came through the patriotic education of our citizens created through the film *Ninth Company*."[23]

The film's producers also created a website as part of their marketing campaign. Billed as a "military-patriotic forum," the site allowed audience members to follow up on the memory recovery first experienced by the Veterans' Association. Over forty-one thousand posts debated every angle of the film and every possible meaning one could take from Bondarchuk's history lesson.[24] Internet users could talk about the film's soundtrack, post photographs from the war, or argue about the accuracy of the history on screen.

Nikolai Peshkov, a colonel in the Russian army who served in Afghanistan and is now involved with the Society of Afghan Veterans, commented, "Bondarchuk has created something in the best tradition of American films about Vietnam." Peshkov saw the film on opening weekend and believed that the use of American cinematic tropes was a good decision: "We have a lot in common with our American friends. We were in a similar situation. I don't like to talk about defeat, but the execution of both wars was wrong. The soldiers were confused and at a loss, but they were pure in their souls. They died for their brothers like soldiers everywhere."[25] Reaction among Afghan vets like Peshkov was by and large positive. Most thought the film played loose with the facts, but ultimately concluded that Bondarchuk brought a larger truth about the war to the screen.

Critics also engaged in lengthy debate about Bondarchuk's artistic vision. Valerii Kichin saw the film's present-day meanings in a positive light: "For a Russian audience, the experience of the Afghan war is completely mixed up with our experience in the Chechen war, and that's why this is so timely and urgent. This film is about any war where people don't understand what they are dying for. The audience remembers Afghanistan, but they also see Chechnya."[26] Others saw things differently: Katia Barabash opined, "U.S. cinema makes these kinds of films so much better. We should leave it to them to give us *Saving Private Ryan.*"[27] Diliara Tasbulatova of *Itogi* wrote that Bondarchuk filmed a "forgotten company" but also "completely forgot about the sufferings of the other side—the Afghan people." Ultimately, the film paled in comparison to anti-war "masterpieces" like *Paths of Glory* and *Full Metal Jacket* because it "is not entirely free from the clichés of ideological thinking."[28]

On *Kinopoisk*'s website forum, the first person to post a response to the film was an Afghan vet who had been to one of the special screenings. "Zampolit" stated that he served in 1983 and that "its impressions on me are ambiguous. Too much negativity is shown and must this be so? Someone will object: this is the truth, this is how it really was."[29] "Kila1972," like Barabash, criticized the film by claiming it tries to be too much like *Saving Private Ryan* but ultimately "reminds me of an unpolished and somewhat stupid peasant who attempts to be an aristocrat." "Pitonch" stood up for the film on patriotic grounds: "The film is not a masterpiece, but it pleased me. . . . The battles are professionally set, beautifully filmed, and unpleasant. Compared to what you can see in Russia these days, *Ninth Company* is on a higher level."

Bondarchuk himself concluded that his film "is about the latest striving to find a hero of our time."[30] He explained,

> I wanted to shoot a major, large-scale film, and one about war, and, lastly, one that concerned my own generation. It begins in 1987 and ends in 1989, with the Soviet withdrawal from Afghanistan. Its heroes are my contemporaries. When

> the first Chechen war began, the whole world was talking about how conscript soldiers, fresh out of school, shouldn't be deployed in it. And no one remembered how our government had for ten years sent just such kids to Afghanistan, an absolutely alien country. They were lads whose views on life just weren't fully formed, so answering the question—"What am I doing here now with a weapon in my hand?"—proved very complicated. I wasn't interested in the political associations, but in the soldiers' motivations. As it later became clear, they had to ask themselves all the questions best known from Russian literature, from Raskolnikov through to Bolkonsky. Am I a frightened beast, or is right behind me? Who am I? Can I accomplish a mission for which I wasn't born—I didn't come into this world to leave it as a hero? The film isn't about how the country lost the war; it's about how those lads won their own internal battle. It goes on in all men. Each one of them has to decide for himself—what is love, what are treachery, comradeship, and heroism.[31]

What he desired, and in part what he accomplished, is what his father had done for the Great Patriotic War. He made a film that takes an event and uses it to offer a contemporary interpretation of its meanings. Bondarchuk's *Ninth Company* may be a Russian *Full Metal Jacket,* but it also turns the Afghan War into history, providing an answer to the search for meaning about that conflict.

PLAYING WITH THE PAST: GOBLIN'S THIRD NINTH COMPANY

Dmitrii Puchkov would have none of this. For Goblin, *Ninth Company* was not history at all because it did not adhere to factual truths about the war. Worse, in his view were the incorrect and anti-patriotic messages the film conveyed. Some Afghan vets echoed Goblin's gripes. "There are too many special effects that make the film look like Rambo,"[32] complained General Aleksandr Liakhovskii, the author of 2004's *The Tragedy and Valor of Afghanistan.* "The 9th Company shows the bravery of both soldiers and officers. But it is too simple. And it's historically distorted. There are too many populist tricks."[33]

Puchkov, like his adversary Bondarchuk, served in the army while the Afghan War waged but did not see frontline action. Like Bondarchuk, he got his start in the film business after the 1991 collapse. He is famous as the dubbed voice on a host of illegally transferred Hollywood films. Puchkov is a believer in translations that attempt to convey the meaning of the original into the second language, not the literal translations that tend to be the standard approach in Russian cinema. He has publicly condemned some editions for being too literal and even produced parodic versions of films for his company God's Spark (*Bozh′ia iskra*): *Shmatrix* (*Shmatritsa*) and *The Fellas and the Ring* (*Bratva i kol′tso*) are two of his most popular film parodies.

Puchkov's film parodies insert Soviet history into American cinematic narratives and in these adaptations Goblin plays games with the past. In *The Fellas and the Ring,* for example, Frodo Baggins becomes Fedor Sumkin, a Russian peasant everyman. He and Pendolf the wizard fight against a sorcerer, Sarumian—Tolkien's villain Saruman thus becomes Armenian. The sorcerer is aided by an army of pedophiles, convicts, and Nazis. The result of this sort of translation (keeping in mind Jackson's film is left as is, Goblin changes only the names and plot) is a "cynical adaptation" that turns communist culture and Hollywood culture into kitsch.[34] As Natalia Rulyova has described them, Puchkov's parodies are popular because they reflect "nostalgia for the past, the change of values from Soviet to post-Soviet, the new Russians and post-Soviet mafia, nationalist and ethnic issues (often treated in a xenophobic way), globalization and patriotism, westernization and domestication."[35] Puchkov's nostalgia is one rooted in "a need for the past in order to subvert it," for his adaptations routinely mock Soviet rhetoric and Soviet values.[36] He ultimately, to use Rulyova's argument, is a postmodern plagiarist, an artist who gets his viewers to laugh at crude jokes about the Soviet past.

Puchkov learned English in the 1980s by translating Led Zeppelin lyrics and by taking a two-year course at the Dzherzhinsky Police House of Culture. Afterward, he noticed that the glasnost′-era films were poorly dubbed: "The number of mistranslated phrases and obvious bloopers irritated me from the very beginning. And at that time I already wanted to make a translation thoroughly, in other words do it the way a good film deserves."[37] He got his start by dubbing 1993's *Carlito's Way,* starring Al Pacino, and has since gone on to dub hundreds of films. Because his initial work was illegal, he adopted the name "Goblin" after a 1990s *600 Seconds* television report that exposed police wrongdoing referred to the criminals as "goblins in militia overcoats [*gobliny v militseiskikh shineliakh*]." He started calling himself "Goblin" or "Senior Security Officer Goblin [*starshii operupolnomochennyi Goblin*]" after his rank in the MVD at the time.[38] In his film dubs, Goblin voices all the characters himself, yet he also believes that dubbing is not as good as subtitled versions in which you can hear the original language. Goblin has mostly become known for his take on the difficult transfer of American *mat* [swearing] to Russian *mat,* even citing as a particularly problematic example Sergeant Hartman's speech from *Full Metal Jacket.* Because profanity remains taboo in Russian film transfers, Goblin's versions of American films became much sought after in the ubiquitous kiosks that sold pirated films. Goblin's movies let loose with Russian obscenities: one kiosk owner in Moscow reported in 2002 that his work was "extremely fashionable" and that "people come by all day long asking if we have Goblin translations."[39]

While he was becoming known for his work on film, Puchkov was also garnering attention among the computer gaming community that blossomed in Russia in the 1990s. He began to publish well-received articles on *Quake,* a first-person shooter game that was particularly popular in Russia because of its multi-player format. Buoyed by the response to his writings on the game, Goblin started a personal website, "Goblin's Dead End [Tupichok Goblina]" that initially served as a forum for discussing *Quake.*[40] Later, the success of his fantasy-prisoner book *Dungeon Cleaners* which he made available on the site, led the video game company 1C to make a first-person shooter game based on it. The game introduced Russians to a Gulag planet where the worst criminals are sent and where players can fight for their freedom.[41]

Over the course of the late 1990s and early 2000s, therefore, Goblin became famous if not recognizable. The influx of cheap, pirated copies defined Russian cinema in the 1990s, and Dmitrii Puchkov became one of their champions. As video game culture developed in Russia, Goblin was also at its forefront. In both arenas he became known as an insightful commentator on military, action, fantasy, and gangster films and games.

When Bondarchuk released his film, Goblin immediately posted his views on his site. He liked the first half of the film, which he said was "high quality" and "recreated the atmosphere of those years." Puchkov noted that the film bears a strong resemblance to *Full Metal Jacket* and *Platoon* but thought this adaptation worked quite well. He liked the group sex scene, which in his view "added to the film's theme about love." When the film shifted to the Afghan war proper and the exploits on Height 3234, Puchkov praised the technical look of the film but thought the sounds of war were inferior to those heard in American war films. In sum, "From a technical point of view, the film *Ninth Company* came out not bad. It is no worse than an average Hollywood war film and this by itself is a serious breakthrough. It's not *Saving Private Ryan* or *Black Hawk Down*. But for domestic cinema, however you look at it, it's an unusual achievement."[42]

This achievement did not extend to the film's message, which Goblin labels "rubbish [*chush*′]." According to Puchkov, the Soviets won a military victory in Afghanistan and "Soviet servicemen showed themselves to be exceptionally competent professionals." As far as the general view that the war was a "bloody slaughter," a view he believes Bondarchuk's film upholds, Puchkov states it only "fills the brain with shit." To back up his statement, he claims that the Soviet army lost an average of only 1,668 men per year of the conflict,[43] but the post-Soviet army loses an average of 561 from suicides and hazing. He concludes, "The war was a bloody slaughter, but not for us." Goblin argues that Pakistan, Afghan rebels, and the United States provoked the Soviet Union; that the Soviet army acted successfully against this provocation; that "ideological idiots" ruled Afghanistan and required Soviet assistance; and that the Soviet army withdrew once the threat diminished: "There were no ideological tasks [for the USSR] in Afghanistan. We did not build kolkhozes there; we did not establish a Soviet regime. The army accomplished its tasks successfully and the rest . . . the rest does not concern the army." Bondarchuk, Puchkov wrote, fell into the usual trap of seeing the war as "immoral," "wild," and "senseless." Puchkov particularly hated the film's end, concluding that it was "completely magical" and not "what really happened." He compared the "defeat as victory" message in the film to that of *Shtrafbat:* "We have in our country a television series and a film made by people who are sincerely convinced that they made the factual truth. But what is more terrible is the fact that in our country an entire generation of idiots grew up piously believing that we lost here and everywhere. That soldiers who fought for their country all suffered from a bruised psyche. And that they all fought in vain for a country 'that ceased to exist two years later.'" To combat this message, Goblin calls on young people to watch the film but to see the "truth" about the Ninth Company as one where soldiers defended their Soviet motherland.[44]

What galled Goblin was the memory of the war solely as Russia's Vietnam and therefore a lesson in imperial overstretch. When asked about this version of the war and the parties responsible, Puchkov is vague about who is to blame: "They try to slander Soviet history from all sides today, Soviet exploits are silenced, the war in Afghanistan was only a mistake, Soviet soldiers killed children, and other gibberish that they say now. It is now only possible to report filth instead of facts about the USSR, including at the movies. I understand not everything was nice in the USSR, but why do we always have to lie? . . . I lived in the USSR and I was in the army and not everything was this way."[45]

Goblin did not just stop with his online posts and message board about *Ninth Company;* he also acted. His answer to Bondarchuk's war, the video game *The Truth about Ninth Company,* appeared on February 18, 2008. Andrei Kuzmin of KranX Productions led the game design, and Puchkov acted as "ideological spokesman" for what he saw as the ongoing memory damage caused by *Ninth Company:* "The historical memory of our people is being intentionally destroyed and replaced by completely idiotic stereotypes. Our game is our precise answer to the frantic lie apropos of our recent history. Our task is to show real events, real people. To show that our servicemen are first of all citizens of our country and professionals who competently carried out their stated tasks."[46] Much as Puchkov had consistently advocated preserving "the truth" of the original English language in his dubbings, so, too, did he demand strict incorporation of facts in his video game. The locales are not Crimean Mountains meant to suggest Chechnya as much as Afghanistan; they are computer-based visuals of Afghanistan taken from satellite maps. It uses survivors' memories from the Ninth Company defense of Height 3234 to enhance the game-playing experience and make it conform to the "truth" about what happened in 1988. All of these details, along with historical documents, memories written by veterans, maps, and photographs are part of *The Truth about Ninth Company.* The official website, www.pravdao9rote.ru, defines the product as a "docu-

Goblin's game: *The Truth About Ninth Company.*

mentary game." The deluxe version sold in stores even came with a Soviet soldier's canteen.

The Truth about Ninth Company allows players to become participants in seven specific episodes from the battle itself. They are asked to complete the same combat missions that veterans of the skirmish successfully did. The action begins on January 7, 1988, at 16:00. The player becomes Junior Sergeant Viacheslav Aleksandrov and is given his 12.7-caliber heavy machine gun. After the first grenade and rocket attack, which has killed the radioman (Corporal Andrei Fedotov), the player is asked to repulse the first mujahideen attack on the position. "Success" in the mission may bring an unexpected result—Aleksandrov covered the surprise attack and allowed his comrades to seek shelter, but died doing so. The virtual reward is Aleksandrov's posthumous one—a Hero of the Soviet Union medal. The remaining six episodes unfold over the course of that night, ending on January 8 at 03:00. Players try to prevent the mujahideen from concentrating in one position, call in artillery strikes, participate in sneak attacks on the enemy, destroy RPG operators, carry ammunition to Height 3234 comrades, and finally command the Ninth Company during the final mujahideen assault. As players inhabit each character, they literally take on their physical appearances and traits—the game's illustrators used 1988 photographs of the soldiers to render their likenesses. The creators also infused the war game with the actual sounds of RPGs and mines, the foreign voices of the enemy, and the cries for help from comrades. Finally, the game comes packed with facts: historical details and commentary by historians accompany players on their missions.

Goblin and his fellow gamers declared in an official press release that *The Truth about Ninth Company* was a "cooperative first-person gameplay." Players inhabit the bodies of real Soviet soldiers, but they also move from soldier to soldier performing missions that demonstrate how each relied on his comrades. As the press release claimed, "The sequential reincarnation of player first into one, then into another participant in the battle, will make it possible not only to feel and to be present at what is happening objectively, it will also clarify the pitiless logic of war, which does not pardon even minor errors."[47] *The Truth about Ninth Company* stresses the same theme of combat as *Ninth Company:* wartime comradeship. What is different, of course, is the way the game works. Filmgoers sit and eat popcorn while they contemplate the meanings of the past; gamers fire virtual weapons and kill virtual mujahideen.

Goblin's product can be viewed as one of many "intense first-person shooter" videogames that proliferate around the globe. Popular American World War II games such as the *Call of Duty,* the *Medal of Honor,* or the *Wolfenstein* series,[48] as well as individual Vietnam games such as EA's *Battlefield Vietnam,* sell millions of copies every year and send millions of players back to the past. As Zach Whalen and Laurie Taylor argue, these types of games "operate with a clear—and a clearly *mediated*—relationship to the past," one they view as nostalgic.[49] Video games reconstruct memory in similar ways to film, yet they go beyond an attempt to relive the past and instead offer players a chance to literally play with the past.

War games, as one scholar has posited, allow players a chance to impose what modern war lacks: rules.[50] In video games, weapons never jam, grenades always work, friendly fire never kills anyone, and the enemy is always clearly identified. The only real injury a player can receive while playing a war game is carpal tunnel syndrome. The result is that war games "do not so much attempt a representation of [war] as they attempt to domesticate the chaos of violent history into a simulacrum of other games in the genre."[51] Yet even in this regard war games have real significance: the U.S. Marine Corps uses a form of *Doom* for combat training, and the U.S. Army offers free downloads of first-person shooter games such as *America's Army* on its website.[52] Barracks in Iraq frequently had game rooms equipped with the latest Xbox combat games, army psychologists claim that playing video games can alleviate combat fatigue, and some soldiers even believe that the Navy Seal game *SOCOM* helps them understand what to expect in real combat.[53] War games may make history unreal, but they do so in a usable fashion, both for players wanting to believe they can commune with the past and for military officials who want potential soldiers to think war is a game.

The Truth about Ninth Company differs from its American counterparts. None of the major war game series mentioned above has players inhabit the personae of real veterans. Instead, Goblin's game comes packaged as a "docu-game" like *John Kerry's Silver Star Mission,* issued as the Swift Boat controversy heated up, or *JFK: Reloaded,* which allows gamers to be Lee Harvey Oswald and see just how hard it is to kill Kennedy. *The Truth about Ninth Company* represents something of a hybrid format, one where guns do not jam and war is not chaotic, yet also one where players are invited to play real characters from the past. It is not, therefore, entirely like the Great Patriotic War games that have proliferated in the zero years, such as *Tanks of the Second World War: T-34 against the Tiger* or *Heroes of War*—both also made by 1C. It is, as Puchkov makes clear, a patriotic play aimed at teenagers who have heard "nothing but slander about the Soviet Union." For him, the game's patriotism "is about the people, who honestly served their motherland and carried out their duty." Puchkov's patriotism, stressed in the game, is a timeless Russian one: "Respect for your country, for history, and for the readiness to serve one's country."[54]

This patriotic appeal got Goblin's game special promotion at the XII Worldwide Union of the Russian People's Congress in Moscow. Held on February 22, 2008, just as the game appeared, the Congress held a special session on "computer games as a new factor in education." Puchkov presented his game as the first docu-game in Russian history, explaining that it was created on the basis of meticulous research and a belief that the "truth" about the war should be widely known. The audience accepted Goblin's ideas about the war. Roman Silan′tev, the director of the forum, praised it for "not only reviving patriotism among young people, but also for providing objective knowledge in military science, history, and geography." "It may be," Silan′tev argued, "that this game will begin the process—first in a 'literary-play sphere'—of overcoming the myth about the fact that the war in Afghanistan was a crime. It not only was not a crime, in my view it was not a loss, but was a successfully realized operation, won with minimum losses."[55]

Others offered equally interesting insights into the meanings of Goblin's war game. The editors of the popular gaming site PlayGround.ru gushed that *The Truth about Ninth Company* created an engrossing journey into history and "created this enthusiasm not through cheap eulogies and spectacular effects, but through the detailed reconstruction of combat. . . . As a result, here we feel ourselves not as actors surveying the area in Bondarchuk's film, but as participants in a real exploit." Ultimately, the game deserved the tag "docu-game," for "we feel ourselves as people not by using a virtual automatic weapon to deliver nine grams in the [enemy's] heart, but as a real person: with his fate and history, with his letters to his family, with his photo of his wife and daughter."[56] Players who commented on the review compared Puchkov's version of the past to Bondarchuk's. Some, like "Mikha Molot," wrote that the game was a 10/10 but so, too, was the film. Others, like "Zlodey," admonished players "to visit Goblin's website," for there they will "find the truth" about why the film "spits on our soldiers' graves." To this player's mind, "such games are necessary for us." Still others went on lengthy rants about the game restoring honor to Russia and showing the West once again that the country has produced heroes who defend its soil, from Suvorov to Dmitrii Donskoi and even Ivan the Terrible.

Anatoly Subbotin, the head of the PR Department for 1C, believed that the game "was interesting first of all because it gave gamers an alternative view on the events described in the game. These events were mostly known from the movie by Bondarchuk. On the other hand the game offers quite a lot of information based on the memoirs of the participants. And the events in the game sometimes differ from the ones shown in the movie."[57] What is evident from the numerous players who posted on sites—including Goblin's—is that the video game acted not just as a nostalgic agent like most scholars believe, but as a patriotic exercise. Playing with the past, in other words, is more about asserting your Russianness in the present than feeling nostalgic about the past.

"IT'S OUR WAR AND NOT OUR WAR": PATRIOT GAMES

The film's producers fought back. Backed by the same companies who brought out Bondarchuk's film, the video game *9th Company: A War-Patriotic Strategy,* appeared on May 30, 2008. The packaging billed it as "the first tactical strategy game based on the Afghan War."[58] The game got much better marketing than Goblin's and also came with Bondarchuk's film, a patch with the Ninth Company insignia, a map of Height 3234, and two documentaries on the war and the film's soundtrack. The limited edition deluxe version came with a Soviet soldier's leather pack and compass that looks good with the canteen from *The Truth about Ninth Company.*

This game dissolves the separation between video games and cinema, for players essentially experience the Afghan War depicted by Bondarchuk. Its creators billed the game as being

> not a historical reconstruction. It is not "a game based on the film" in the classical sense. . . . It is the first tactical strategy dedicated to the Afghan War. The key word here is "tactical." . . . The player has at his disposal a large selection of tactical methods and weaponry. Use bombings and bombardments, cover the mujahideen with fire from the flanks, storm fortified areas and retain them until the approach of reinforcements. Like the soldiers of the Ninth Company, a player who fulfills combat missions assigned to him will do so with historically accurate combat technology. . . . This technology served as faith and as truth.[59]

The game follows this idea through the entire history of the Ninth Company's Afghanistan involvement, allowing gamers to play at the entire war. Players can learn the same sorts of lessons—that the war produced a band of brothers–like spirit—whether they take part in 1980 or 1988 simulations.

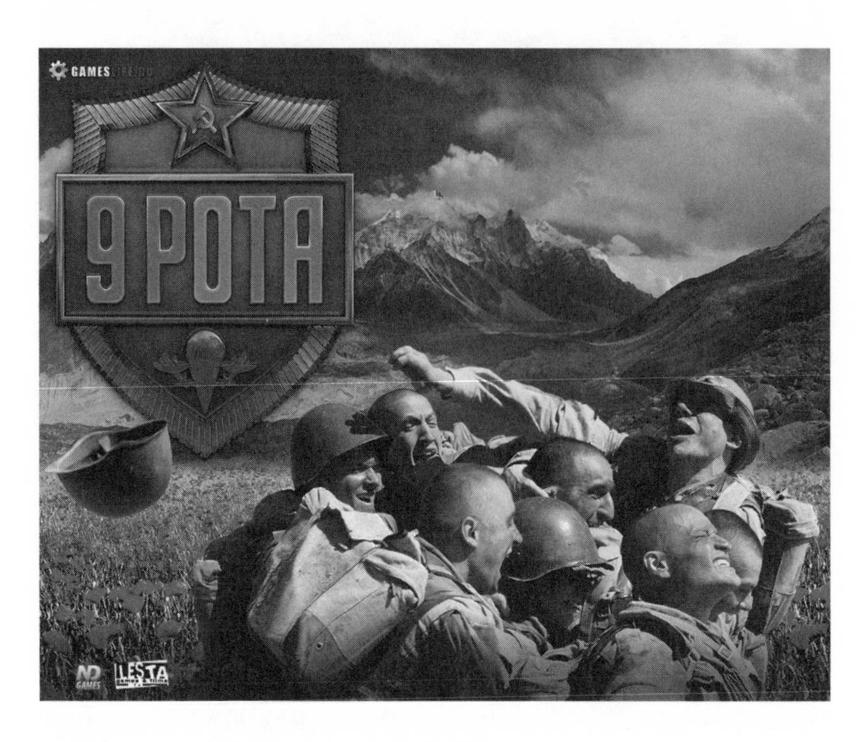

The film as game: *9th Company: A War-Patriotic Strategy.*

In its review, PlayGround.ru noted that that strategy and characters will be "familiar to the film's spectators."[60] Another game forum, 3dviewer.ru, stated, "The strategy leads to more strategy, complexities to more complexities, which has only one purpose—to encounter new difficulties in the next mission." Ultimately, the war was not fun at all, but "boring."[61] Most players agreed, rating the game lower than Goblin's. One quipped, "My sensation is that this game is just trying to duplicate the glory and money-making desire of Bondarchuk's film," posted one. Others posted the link to Goblin's site and implored gamers to read more about "the truth of Ninth Company," particularly the accounts by veterans.[62] Puchkov himself refused to discuss the game: "I did not look at it. It was based on the film. It is not interesting."[63]

In the game world, the film version of the war emerged triumphant. While Russians who saw both the blockbuster and encountered Goblin's truth believed in the latter's version, more Russians bought the game based on the film. Aleksandr Skakovskii, Lesta Production's PR manager, estimates that seventy thousand copies of the Bondarchuk-based game sold in the first three months alone. This success led foreign game companies to snap up the rights—Polish, Czech, Hungarian, Serbian, Croatian, Chinese, French, and English versions appeared by the end of 2009.[64] Skakovskii credits the film's popularity, the general interest in war games, and the fact that the game garnered a relatively tame rating on the Russian parental advisory labels for the game's appeal.

Goblin's company, 1C, also declared that their game "was very popular in Russia, especially among players who are interested in historically based games," yet could not release sales figures "because of the contract we have with the developer [i.e., Puchkov]."[65] Puchkov's small triumph "pleased him" and reaffirmed his decision to make a videogame aimed at teenagers so that they "would know history as it was in reality."[66] Fewer Russians purchased Goblin's game, but those who did liked it more than the Bondarchuk versions.

The gaming and film war over Afghanistan reveals, however, that the dominant version of the conflict remains Bondarchuk's. Goblin has not conceded defeat just yet and has sought other outlets for his views. He published *I Feel Bad for the State: Questions and Answers about the USSR* with the St. Petersburg publisher Krylov in 2008.[67] In it, he seeks to provide "truthful answers" to burning historical questions of today: "Was the Soviet Union essentially good or bad? How many people did Stalin kill and what should Russians think about him?"[68] Of course, Goblin also published *Manly Conversations about Life* the same year with the same publisher. It seeks "truthful answers" to burning issues such as "why Russians need pistols, how to clean up the gene pool, why you have to love your motherland, and whether or not you have to bribe fascist cops."[69]

Viacheslav Nekrasov, the spokesman for the Association of Afghan Veterans, summarized the *Ninth Company*'s impact best. "I have mixed feelings about this film. It's very dynamic and emotional. But Bondarchuk shows both our war and not our war. Some episodes remind us of how we felt at the time—saying goodbye to relatives and shooting a person. But too many of the details are wrong."[70] Goblin and his gamers mostly concurred. Even Puchkov, who strongly condemned the film's messages, still recommended that Russians should see it. Playing with the past on film and on your computer all started with Bondarchuk's truths about war. Regardless of what individual Russians thought about the final products, Bondarchuk ensured that a forgotten war has now been remembered and reimagined.

PART THREE

Back in the USSR

The Brezhnev era simultaneously served as the source of the greatest nostalgic longing and the most contested past in the zero years. Several polls indicated that many Russians would not mind living in late socialism again and certainly would rather return to the Brezhnev era than the Stalin era or the 1990s.[1] Leonid Parfenov's *Namedni* (*Not So Long Ago*) also proved a success because of its ability to capture Soviet politics, culture, and everyday life from 1961 to 2003. The project began as a TV series in 1997 that eventually ran forty-three episodes; Parfenov started publishing books based on the series in 2009. Responding to this apparent nostalgia, journalist Aleksandra Samarina posited that the Brezhnev era had become the new "Russia that we lost," a time when everyone seemed secure, when the Afghan war was still heroic, and when the welfare state seemingly worked. "If 'Dear Leonid Il′ich' announced his candidacy today for the presidential elections," Samarina opined, "he would easily surpass all the present candidates."[2]

Samarina might have added that contemporary Russians also remembered the Brezhnev era fondly because of its movies. The state began employing sociological surveys in the 1960s that gauged the relationship between media and consumer. Movies became more audience friendly as a result and the Brezhnev years saw some of the most beloved Soviet classics appear on screen: Leonid Gaidai's and El′dar Riazanov's comedies, melodramas such as *Moscow Does Not Believe in Tears,* and the action-adventure epic *Pirates of the Twentieth Century,* which became the highest-grossing domestic film in Soviet history when it came out in 1980.[3] The same could be said of Brezhnev-era television: one scholar has persuasively argued that 1970s hit series such as *Seventeen Moments of Spring* and *The Meeting Place Cannot be Changed* were anything but stagnant and helped to shape new values that did not just conform to the state's.[4] No wonder, then, that the Brezhnev era could be recalled with nostalgic fondness.

For its August 2008 issue, the St. Petersburg film journal *Seans* (*Performance*) devoted a major section to the phenomenon of nostalgia for the USSR. The special issue—titled (in English) "Back in the USSR"—featured fourteen articles from a host of famous Russians, ranging from historians to rock stars. An interview with Evgenii Anisimov, the historian of Petrine Russia, began the section. He declared, "In Russia state ideology is almost always built on that which claims to be our future—namely, our past."[5] As to the current uses of the past and nostalgia for the USSR, Anisimov declared that he was "an optimist" and that Russia's history has always proven to offer few lessons. Moreover, the appearance of "private property and globalization, in my view, makes a return to the past impossible."[6] Other contributors offered a range of ideas about why the Brezhnev period seemed so attractive in retrospect. Aleksei Zimin mused that it had something to do with the lost sensations of childhood that everyone feels nostalgic for but also for the lost sensations of "*sobornost´*" generated by living in a powerful empire.[7] The poet Timur Kibirov declared "nothing was more terrible than the Soviet state" and "hopes it will not be again." At the same time, he argues, "yet this was our life, and human life cannot all be garbage." Nostalgia for the Soviet past, as he views it, "cannot help but be dual." On the one hand, it involves recognition of "the regime's abominations." But on the other hand, it involves remembering good experiences, good songs, good movies, and a "Soviet civilization and so-called ideal Soviet man that were not entirely created by Stalin."[8]

Nostalgia for the Brezhnev era, at least for those who contributed to the special issue, was simply a normal feeling of remembering childhood and the past that had vanished, never to return. As Sergei Shnurov, the lead singer of the ska-punk group Leningrad, commented, "Everyone laughed derisively about Brezhnev. Ideology and the Party were no longer taken seriously.... But for me the Soviet Union was nevertheless my childhood and that cannot be anything but excellent."[9]

For filmmakers and audiences alike, cinematic explorations of the Brezhnev era represented a journey back to lost childhoods or a lost Russia. Returning to this time by watching it reappear on screen offered a host of symbols, images, and parts of material culture that could help to refashion a sense of belonging after 1991. Whether it was the Orthodox faith practiced secretly in Brezhnev's time or the group Kino's music, post-Soviet blockbusters repeatedly sent Russian audiences back to the future in an effort to recover past symbols of belonging and reforge a myth of a heroic age.[10]

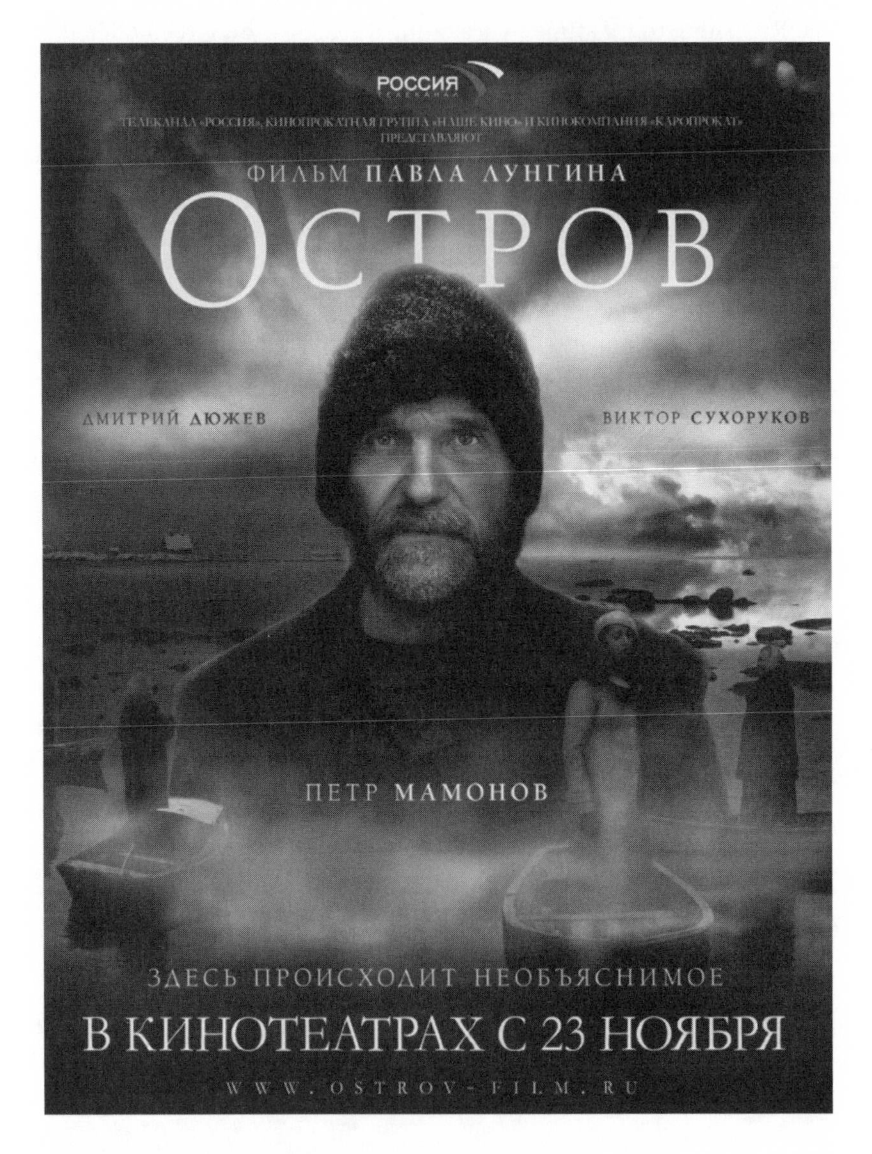

The blessed blockbuster? Poster for Pavel Lungin's *The Island* (2006).

EIGHT

The Blessed Blockbuster

Perhaps the most surprising success of the zero years was Pavel Lungin's art-house film turned national sensation, *The Island.* It opens in World War II, jumps to the Brezhnev era, and tells the story of how a Soviet citizen atones for a past misdeed by becoming a holy fool. The Patriarch of Russia, Aleksei II, officially blessed the film after more liberal members of the Church advised him to do so. For its supporters, *The Island* served as a spiritual guide to Russians looking for answers to tough metaphysical questions facing them. Father Vladimir Vigilianskii, press secretary for the Orthodox Church and a fan of the film, met with Lungin several times after shooting ended. According to Vigilianskii, *The Island* is not historically accurate; nevertheless, it offers "an artistic reality that captures real life and real issues."[1] After it received Aleksei II's blessing, Orthodox priests openly recommended it to their parishioners.

Many film experts thought the Orthodox Church, which has reasserted itself in post-Soviet Russia and openly calls for Orthodoxy to be a fundamental anchor of new Russian patriotism, had overstepped its bounds by entering the film world. The Patriarchy has advocated cooperation with the Russian state in several areas, including "spiritual, cultural, moral and patriotic education and formation."[2] On the concept of patriotism, the Church has this to say:

> The patriotism of the Orthodox Christian should be active. It is manifested when he defends his fatherland against an enemy, works for the good of the

> motherland, cares for nation's life through, among other things, participation in the affairs of government. The Christian is called to preserve and develop national culture and a national consciousness.[3]

The battle lines were drawn: on one side, the Church and the emerging Orthodox intelligentsia that backed its goals; and on the other, opponents of the Church who believe that Orthodoxy has stepped into the ideological role communism once held.[4] Pavel Lungin's *Island* sparked a debate about the relationships between the Church, popular culture, and the understanding of the past. It also attempted to present a Brezhnev-era USSR in which monks and Orthodox believers preserved a "lost Russia" that could be refound.

THE SOVIET HOLY FOOL: LUNGIN'S *ISLAND*

War, 1942. A desolate, foggy locale in northern Russia. Two Soviet sailors look out for Nazis. Suddenly, a Nazi ship appears out of the fog. The two are quickly taken captive after the subordinate reveals where his captain, Tikhon, has hidden from the Nazis. As a machine gunner is about to shoot them, the sailor begs for mercy. The Soviet captain spits on him and lights a cigarette to await his execution. A Nazi officer decides to play a macabre game instead. He asks the junior sailor to kill his commanding officer with a Luger, imploring him to "be a man." The Soviet sailor initially refuses, but when the Nazi officer twists his ear, he fires the pistol. The officer's body falls into the sea. The Nazis depart. The sailor laughs and cries tears of joy because he lives. Just then, the Nazis detonate a fuse that leaves the sailor unconscious. Later, he washes up on a desolate shore nearby. Monks from a nearby monastery take him in.

Monastery, 1976. The former sailor, named Anatolii, now lives near the monastery. He has spent the thirty years since his wartime action atoning for his sin. Although referred to as "Father Anatolii," he acts more like a holy fool and a spiritual healer than a reputable Orthodox monk.

We first see his role when a young woman comes to him asking for absolution. She is pregnant and wants to abort her baby. Anatolii replies, "You want a blessing for murder? . . . You are heading for hell and want to drag me, too?" He adds, "It was preordained you should have a baby," tells her to pray to God, and then to "get off my island." She flees.

Anatolii then prays before an icon. "O Lord, wash away our sins. Remember, O Lord, the soul of thy departed servant, the warrior Tikhon. Pardon him every sin and grant him the Kingdom of Heaven and the Fount of Everlasting Life. O Lord Jesus Christ, Son of God, have mercy on this sinner. O Lord, forsake me not. . . . Deliver my soul from the dungeon, O Lord, forsake me not. Have mercy upon me, Lord; blot out my transgressions. For I acknowledge my iniquity and my sin is ever before me."

The holy man has lived the life an ascetic in the decades after the war. He works as a coal stoker for the monastery's sole source of heat. He lives in a bare room next to the coal furnace. He spends most of his days gathering the coal to heat the small monastery. He lives at the margins of this holy community.

The monks often have tense relationships with Anatolii. Father Job, a young monk, becomes the butt of Anatolii's practical jokes, which are meant to remind the holy man about humility. Although Anatolii lives a spiritual life and seeks atonement for his sin, he also does not live according to the precepts of the church. Job, in a report to Father Filaret, the Superior, lists his transgressions:

> This is what in all honesty can no longer be tolerated. Firstly, Anatolii never washes his face and hands. Second, he is always late for work. Third, mainland folk are always coming to see him. Yesterday he showed up in church with a felt boot on one leg and a sock on the other and started singing through his nose. Father, the brethren are grumbling. On festive occasions he does come to church, but he doesn't pray, only mumbles . . .

Anatolii also does not know ritual, and often faces the wrong way while praying and commits other violations. Father Filaret inquires one day, "I've long wanted to ask you, prankster—why do you behave improperly during the service? You should pray in the prescribed way. If everyone starts praying in his own way, where will we be? What will be left of the Church?" Anatolii responds by asking about Father Filaret's boots, which he received from the Metropolitan, and his nice blanket, which he got on a pilgrimage to Athos. Anatolii burns the boots and sets the blanket adrift, stating, "Most sin resides in bishops' boot tops."

After his initial anger, Filaret tells Anatolii, "You've delivered me from things superficial and unnecessary. I thank you, brother." Anatolii asks why God has made him so saintly, lamenting that he "should be hanged for my sins." He then asks Tikhon for forgiveness, stating, "I'm suffering torments. I can't live and I can't die. . . . I've been carrying this sin for years. It never releases me, not even for one second. I know you forgave me. Pray that God takes this burden off my chest." Anatolii begins to prepare for his death and orders a coffin be made.

When one of the "mainland folk" comes to ask Anatolii to pray for her husband, who died in 1944, Anatolii pretends he is the servant of the "real" Father Anatolii and carries on a conversation with the widow behind a wall, playing the part of Father Anatolii and his subordinate. More significantly, he tells the woman that her husband was captured and is still alive in France. He concludes, "No requiem for the living," and tells her to go to France to see her ailing husband. She claims, "They will not let me go to a capitalist country," but Anatolii insists she must "go and do what was preordained."

Father Anatolii's next visitors are a woman and her young son, who has broken his leg and whose hip has become infected. She tells him, "We've seen all sorts of professors and surgeons," but "no one is able to help and his hip is rotting." Anatolii and the two pray together and the monk pronounces the boy healed. First, however, the two must stay overnight at the monastery and receive communion from Father Filaret in the morning. When the mother balks at the idea, citing her job, Anatolii explodes: "Do you think I'm playing games with you? What's more important, your son or your work?" When the woman tries to leave on the boat back to the mainland, Anatolii takes her child and says, "If you don't think about yourself, think about your boy. He'll be a cripple for life." They stay.

The last pilgrims to Anatolii are a Soviet admiral and his mentally ill daughter. Anatolii pronounces that the girl is possessed and performs an exorcism. He tells the girl, Nastia, to stay and receive communion. When the admiral resists, Anatolii tells him, "Don't be afraid, Admiral. No one is going to test your loyalty to the Party." The admiral replies he is not afraid, for he has known fear. The admiral is Tikhon. He was only wounded in the arm when Anatolii shot him. Father Anatolii asks if Tikhon can forgive him. The admiral replies that he did a long time ago. After the two depart, Anatolii climbs in his coffin and asks God to receive his sinful soul. He and Job forgive each other for their squabbles and agree to "let bygones be bygones." Job asks Anatolii how he should live. The old monk replies, "We are all sinners. Live the way you can. Just try not to sin too much." Anatolii dies. He has atoned.

THE PAST AS PARABLE

Produced by the "Russia" TV channel and Lungin's private studio, *The Island* had its premiere on June 27, 2006, at the Kinotavr Film Festival. Nashe Kino and Karo Theater coproduced it. *The Island* made its nationwide debut on November 23, and was billed with the slogan, "What occurs here cannot be explained." It made $2.5 million, a relatively modest amount, but also one that proved unexpected for what many initially believed was an art-house movie. *The Island* reunited Lungin with Petr Mamonov, the actor who had played a jazz saxophonist in Lungin's 1990 *Taxi Blues* and who played Anatolii. The film's significance rested more with the buzz it created than box office numbers, for *The Island* initiated a wave of press, television, and internet reports. Orthodox websites and major newspapers both reported that Lungin and Mamonov had gone through a spiritual transformation in the 1990s. Both men found the first post-Soviet decade to be one where they questioned their previous lives and previous work. Both decided that Orthodoxy represented the best path to spiritual renewal after seven decades of communism.

Lungin first gained notice with films that captured the corrosive effects of Soviet society. *Taxi Blues,* which won him a Best Director award at Cannes, dissected the relationship between an antisemitic communist cab driver and the Jewish saxophone player (played by Mamonov) who climbed into his cab one night. His follow-up, *Luna Park* (1992), explored the skinhead gangs that appeared after the collapse of communism. In both, Lungin tackled the issue of antisemitism in late Soviet and early post-Soviet society, laying bare the prejudices that fueled hatred and yet ultimately offering hopeful, cosmopolitan messages. In his more recent films, Lungin focused on the effects of the capitalist transition (in 2000's *The Wedding* and particularly in 2002's *Oligarch,* loosely based on Boris

Berezovskii's life) and then adapted Gogol's *Dead Souls* for the small screen. None of this career trajectory indicated he would make a film about monasticism and repentance.

But then he read Dmitrii Sobolev's script, which the thirty-two-year old wrote as his diploma from VGIK, where he worked with Iurii Arabov. According to Sobelev, he wrote about faith in the USSR because it seemed to him that "our entire culture—European and Russian—rests upon Christianity. In Russia even communism's arrival did not destroy Christianity's teaching, people considered good after the Revolution were good before the Revolution." For him, "history is filled with sin and atonement, and this is what I created."[5]

Lungin picked up Sobolev's script after his work on the TV series and could not put it down. In interviews he stated, "There came a time when I couldn't live without this script." It spoke to his religiosity and for him seemed to be a perfect vehicle for "the spiritual revival of Russian cinema."[6] His "ideological and spiritual Christianity" led him to agree to direct it.[7] Lungin saw the script as a chance to promote the Orthodox concept of *iurodstvo,* or "foolishness in Christ," to post-Soviet audiences in need of spiritual anchors. Holy Fools intentionally led strict ascetic lives, speak in riddles, and often engage in disruptive behavior to prove a point.[8] For Lungin, the idea of iurodstvo was one Russia needed to be reminded about, for

> our new world corrodes from within. If external danger threatened Soviet power, then today the threat comes from temptations, from small compromises, through tasty, cheerful consumption, which poisons us. Today it is difficult to stand firm. I know people who stood up to Soviet power but who proved to be powerless before the power of money. But people remain people, Russia remains Russia. Russia has always lived through ideas, the battle of ideas. She never became a supermarket in which people only go for consumption's sake.

Russia today, according to Lungin, needs to struggle with nineteenth-century ideas about sin, shame, and atonement: "A feeling of sin, a feeling of shame, a feeling of a sick conscience—these are normal feelings for a person." Lungin admits that "I do not have heavy sins, but I do have a feeling of guilt and pain." His film reveals this "normal state" and suggests "two simple truths: that God exists and that through shame and sin you become a man."[9]

Mamonov also felt these normal feelings. In the 1980s, he founded the rock group Zvuki Mu. Known for Mamonov's absurdist lyrics and dynamic stage presence, Zvuki Mu became a legendary band by the end of the decade, capturing the attention of Western luminaries such as Brian Eno, who produced their 1989 album. Mamonov first acted alongside fellow rock star Viktor Tsoi in Rashid Nugmanov's 1988 exploration of late Soviet drug culture, *The Needle,* before his star turn in Lungin's *Taxi Blues.* In the mid-1990s, however, Mamonov turned away from acting and music and moved into a small cottage in a village outside Moscow. Like the holy fool he plays on screen, Mamonov shunned attention yet cultivated the same quirky lifestyle that made him famous as a musician. When Lungin called him in 2005 about *The Island,* Mamonov reluctantly agreed to play Father Anatolii. He did so out of a belief that Russia needs to examine "the state of our soul." Russian cinema, in his opinion, needed topics that affected audience's "hearts and souls," to "work on the state of our souls. . . . This is what we tried to do in our cinema, in *The Island.*"[10]

The Russian Orthodox website Pravoslavie.ru proclaimed Lungin's and Mamonov's transformations as nothing less than miraculous. Igor′ Vinnichenko, who reviewed the film for the site, declared that Lungin had become like his hero, for he had been known for "his moderately postmodern views, servile attitudes to oligarchs, and [was] a convinced liberal."[11] Now he was a believer, and for Vinnichenko, Lungin's film could serve as a vita for how to live a holy life. "It is known that the best sermon for an Orthodox life is the personal behavior of Orthodox people, and in this sense [Lungin] opens great possibilities for cinematic creative activity." *The Island,* according to Vinnichenko, "attempts to look into the depths of faith, to present a new hero to the public, one who sought the Lord right to the end." He continues,

> Let us say right away that the plot of the film will cause numerous censures from the strict, Orthodox community. First of all, this censure will concern historical reality. In 1974 [*sic*] this monastery in the north could not exist, particularly with such a healing figure. . . . However, this film is a parable and does not pretend to be historically accurate. . . . And in this sense *The Island*'s value is difficult to overestimate. It is impossible to miss the keen sense of piety that accompanies the entire film and for which we longed so much. We hope that now the theme

> of Russian Orthodox spirituality will find its dignified place in national cinematography and that matters concerning spiritual development will finally become a priority for contemplation.[12]

Lungin's piety had transferred on screen, infusing the film with a sense of Orthodox spirituality. In a sense, as Vinnichenko commented about the film's hero, Lungin had become like Paul on the road to Damascus. After years of secular wandering, he had found God.

The most significant statement about the film came from none other than Patriarch Aleksei II, the head of the Russian Orthodox Church. Although he initially did not like the film, some of his younger and more media-savvy advisors (Father Vladimir Vigilianskii among them) persuaded the Patriarch that the film could serve as good PR for the Church.[13] Aleksei relented and gave the film his official blessing. In an interview with Elena Iakovleva that appeared in *Rossiiskaia gazeta,* the Patriarch declared, "The value of the film rests with the fact that its creators knew how to show the profound, sincere repentance of a person [*tsennost΄ fil΄ma v tom, chto ego sozdateli sumeli pokazat΄ glubokoe, iskrennee pokaianie cheloveka*]. It is difficult for me to determine what played the decisive role in the fact that the picture turned out to be so authentic and internally convincing. I think that the pure and sincere motivates of the film's authors were the necessary conditions that influenced the result."[14] The Patriarch also hoped that audience reception would be a key to the film's power: "Here the problems of a spiritual life and salvation are promoted to the foreground, and spectators, who came into contact with these problems for perhaps the first time, thought profoundly about them." As for what they thought about, the Patriarch elaborated, "[The film] even forced unbelievers to think about religion and about God, about sin and about repentance. This is the author's great achievement." He concluded, "I wish that the film *The Island* would introduce to Russian cinema a new, profound, religious view of the world and that films such as this one will become increasingly numerous."[15] Metropolitan Kirill, who would succeed Aleksei as Patriarch in January 2009, concurred, calling *The Island* "an event of enormous importance in our cultural life. For the first time the theme of faith was presented to contemporaries in such a talented and comprehensible way."[16]

The Patriarch certainly got his wish. His office expanded their public relations before and after Lungin's film appeared. The patriarchy created a cinema and television company, Orthodox Encyclopedia, which put out a number of documentary films. The goal, as Aleksei II stated, was "to increase the number of broadcasts, programs, and articles with spiritual and moral content on television, on radio, and in the press."[17] To make the goal possible, the Patriarch created the office of press secretary and appointed Father Vladimir Vigilianskii in 2005. Aleksei II also approved of the TV channel "Spas [Saved]," which broadcasts for sixteen hours a day on educational and spiritual matters. And before he blessed *The Island,* Aleksei II blessed the 2005 documentary *The Life of Saint Sergius,* a fifty-minute visual vita of Russia's most important monk, the founder of Trinity St. Sergius Lavra. Narrated by the venerable Soviet actor Viacheslav Tikhonov (best known for playing Stirlitz in the TV series *Seventeen Moments of Spring*), the blessed documentary focuses on the life of the saint and on his role in keeping "Russian national culture alive" during the Mongol invasions and occupation.

In the zero years, the Patriarchy became more media savvy, blessing a host of cultural parables that used the past to offer spiritual lessons for the present. As the Church proclaims, "the Church's educational, tutorial, and social missions compels it to maintain cooperation with the secular mass media," while "the Church also has its own media outlets, which are blessed by church authorities." Ultimately, "the information presented to the spectator, listener, and reader should be based not only on the firm commitment to truth, but also concern for the moral state of the individual and society."[18] Lungin's film was the most noticeable of these holy products, but far from the only one. The official blessing of the film, however, ensured that debates about its meanings would be extensive and intense.

The questions that fueled discussions about Lungin's film were simple yet complex: What did *The Island* mean? How, as Patriarch Aleksei II indicated, did Lungin's film "show the deep, sincere repentance of a man"? Did this repentance say anything about the Soviet past? What sort of "Russian national culture" did *The Island* present for audiences in need of a renewal? Answering these questions depended in large part upon the spectator's view of the contemporary Orthodox Church, particularly its patriotic role.

VIEWING *THE ISLAND*

NTV broadcast the following report after a November 2006 Voronezh screening:

> Pavel Lungin's *The Island* was shown in Voronezh with no empty seats. The local diocese leased the entire cinema hall. The clergymen, their followers, and seminary students sat in the theater seats.
>
> Before the screening everyone crossed themselves, including the spectators and even the movie technician....
>
> Voronezh priests gathered on Spartak Street to go into the "Spartak" cinema. As soon as all parishioners had arrived it was declared, "The Orthodox prelate recommended that they go into the film." On the request of the Metropolitan Sergius of Voronezhskiy and Borsioglebsk the local clergy booked the largest film auditorium in the region.
>
> A mass entry of priests into a cinema hall took place for the first time in the history of the Russian clergy. Fathers with their families, instructors and students of Voronezh seminary are intrigued: Father Sergius had invited them to Pavel Lungin's film *Ostrov*.
>
> The day before the first screening, the Metropolitan of Voronezh and Borisoglebsk gave an order to post an ad for the forthcoming premiere in all of the city's forty churches. Parishioners were astonished, for never before had films been advertised in church.
>
> One spectator: "If I saw this ad on television I probably would not have paid attention to it, but this announcement gave me greater trust in the film."
>
> Father Andrei, the diocese administrative secretary for Voronezh-Borisoglebsk: "His Holiness watched it; therefore we recommended it to the clergy and to laymen."
>
> The film screening began with a prayer. Some priests crossed themselves. The projectionist, Gena, was agitated because for the first time in the hall the spectators wore cassocks. Even more unusually, during the screening the spectators did not eat popcorn and did not drink cola.
>
> Gennadii Batishchev, the projectionist: "I approached this affair with a feeling of deep responsibility. Even here before the screening began I crossed myself as a believer because in our hall the entire clergy is located."
>
> Lungin's new film is about the daily life of an Orthodox brotherhood in a distant Russian village and attempts to explore the nature of faith. The lead actor Petr Mamonov came to Voronezh for the premiere and interacted with the spectators. Afterward he was pleasantly surprised that an additional screening was arranged; the clergy also requested a meeting with Mamonov.
>
> Petr Mamonov, the actor: "For me this means that our church is alive."

> The clergymen thanked Mamonov. By saying, "He played a monk so truthfully," they were asking whether he knew the prayers or had learned them specifically for the role.
>
> Petr Mamonov, the actor: "I did not study them, but I prayed. The struggle with sin is a very familiar one for me."
>
> For a long time the priests did not leave and instead shared impressions.
>
> His Holiness Sergius, the Metropolitan of Voronezh and Borisoglebsk: "It is a very timely film. Timely for our Russia and for the entire world."
>
> Archpriest Sergei Mozdor: "I crossed myself and said: 'Bless those people who created this film, Lord.'"
>
> The priests left, lamenting that it is a pity that such films are rarely made today. Now when will the entire diocese go to the cinema?[19]

NTV's report was one of many that discussed the tremendous support given to the film by the Orthodox hierarchy—once the Patriarch had blessed it, so his subordinates did the same, ensuring that theaters were filled with believers.

Lecture halls that discussed the film also filled up. One of the most crowded of these venues was the public hall at St. Tat′iana's Cathedral at Moscow State University, Vigilianskii's home church. Present at the December 17 roundtable were Lungin, Father Vladimir, and Archpriest Maksim Kozlov. Kozlov had been a vocal supporter of Mel Gibson's 2004 *The Passion of the Christ,* which opened in Russia during Holy Week. The film caused a great deal of debate among the very same people who would debate Lungin's film two years later.[20] The hall in 2006 was packed full of people who wanted to ask the director and the two churchmen about Lungin's film. Father Vladimir suggested that the film contains a truth about humanity that makes it more significant than the veracity of the film's historical details. Lungin agreed, stating, "*The Island*'s truth is covered not only through the truth of this real place, Kem′, actually in the White Sea, it's covered through the truth of personalities, through the fact that people live not just to prove a certain idea to themselves, but because they are living beings, with weaknesses, with cunningness, with meanness, all of which are within them, along with pride, which is clearly within Father Anatolii." The film, in other words, is about spirituality, but also about humanity. As for its inspiration, Lungin declared that he wanted to make a film about iurodstvo because "long ago I read Kliuchevskii's words that Muscovite Russia was an absolute autocracy with the exception of the Holy Fool. That is to say, that historically holy foolishness was also in Ivan the Terrible's Russia, it somehow permeates the spiritual nature of Russian martyrdom." His film, as he conceived it, was an updated parable about the life of Vasilii the Blessed (St. Basil). Holy fools and their spirituality could help contemporary Russians refind their national souls after communism.

All three—Lungin, Vigilianskii, and Kozlov—faced a wide range of questions from the audience. One audience member asked if the film could be seen as a contemporary update to *Crime and Punishment* (Lungin said no), another asked if a "cinematic prayer" that revealed the infallibility of the clergy was blasphemous (they all said no), while a third asked about the meanings of miracles in the film.[21] The question-and-answer session illustrated the popularity the film had achieved among Orthodox believers, but also the audience desire to discuss the meanings of the film. Was it like *Passion of the Christ,* as one asked (Lungin hadn't seen the film)? Was it about the past or the present? What was the spiritual message? What about the fact that the film had to make use of money and marketing? Lungin, Father Maksim, and Father Vladimir fielded these and other queries.

These sorts of accounts shaped all the discussions about the film's meanings. They heated up after Mamonov's Golden Eagle acceptance speech for best actor, when he called his former popularity "idolatry" and admonished "Russian wenches" to stop having abortions and "killing four million future Suvorovs and Pushkins." Mamonov went on to warn that Russians would all be speaking Chinese soon, then asked who would solve these problems: "Putin? Putin is weak [*khliupen′kii*]; he's an intelligence officer—what's he going to do? This is something we must do. The further matters go on, the sooner we'll be working for the Chinese. But they don't have God; here we'll be shown what to do." Many believed that Mamonov's speech was a sermon and therefore further proof that *The Island* did not minister, but preached.[22]

For detractors, the fact that provincial prelates encouraged their flock to see the film also signaled an aggressive Church patriotic project. Mark Lipovetsky, in one of the most critical reviews of the film, cites the NTV report and Pravoslavie.ru's review as signs of authoritarianism in present-day Russia: "To me, the very style of this authoritative blessing is reminiscent of the programmatic articles in *Pravda* from the years when most of *The Island* is set—the 1970s. . . . In this context, the first screening of *The Island* in the presence of clergy, a screening orchestrated by prayers, looks like a re-make of an 'all-Union premiere' of the newest propaganda film in the late Soviet Union."[23] Lipovetsky concludes that the film bolsters a new patriotism in which "piousness, apparently, plays the same role as a party card in Soviet times." He cites Mikhail Ryklin, author of the 2006 book *Swastika, Cross, Star,* for support. Ryklin argues that "the most ardent advocates of Soviet society have transformed nowadays into avid supporters of Russian Orthodox fundamentalism. . . . Thus, repression has changed its vector, but not its structure. More precisely, the vector has changed from the atheistic direction to the religious in order to keep intact the very right to repress."[24] Lipovetsky concludes, "[I]ts meaning is inseparable from the current cultural context in which the rhetoric of Russian Orthodoxy plays a repressive role. Lungin's new film justifies the repression stemming from Russian Orthodoxy by completely removing this very problem from sight, by making it not only irrelevant but also unmentionable."[25]

Lipovetsky's interpretation is indicative of the film's opponents, who also tended to see *The Island's* message as part of an official church campaign. Mikhail Iampolskii characterized the film as one that "generalizes guilt." "The state wants you to be guilty," he argues, "even if you did not commit a crime, for the only way to receive grace is to be guilty."[26] Evgeniia Vlasova, an Orthodox believer writing for *Ezhednevyi zhurnal,* dismissed *The Island* as "a weak, *lubok* film about a Christianity accepted by people without knowing anything about it." Regarding the "cult of the *starets*" and "the themes of holiness and iurodstvo," she also concludes that they are conveyed as if they were represented on the popular prints that flourished in nineteenth-century Russia: they come across as "miracle-working lubok Orthodoxy, probably for foreign consumption, for they judge Russians' skills by watching girls dancing in kokoshniks on television." In the end, though, Vlasova concludes, "Nevertheless, it is good that this film appeared. It is good that the contemporary spectator is prepared to go not only to *Wolfhound* and *Night Watch* and that he is capable of viewing serious themes on screen and reacting to them in a lively fashion."[27]

The fact that the film proved so popular provoked more debates. Several newspapers reported it was the only Russian film that year whose audience grew after its first week in release. *Vremia novosti* surveyed six prominent film critics for their take on the blessed blockbuster. Alla Bossart argued that Mamonov's character was the key, for Father Anatolii is "the embodiment of the great Russian belief in the magical resolution to the most terrible and blind questions." As proof, she writes, "I know people who left the cinema as if they had left a psychotherapist's office." Iurii Gladil′shchikov argues that the film appealed to the "newly converted politicos" and to those seeking absolution in the New Russia. For them "you can purchase *The Island* together with an icon even at the Trinity St. Sergius Monastery, where they are sold together." Kirill Razlogov took a similarly cynical view: "*The Island* appeared precisely at a time when several intersections came together that helped its success." He lists five: "the reformation of the Russian Federation as an Orthodox state and its state television as a channel that conducts official ideology; Pavel Lungin's aspiration to create a harmonious product after his exploration into the different degrees of chaos; Petr Mamonov's readiness to personify his spiritual transformation through fictitious means; the dissemination of mass mysticism (non-canonical religiosity) among the Russian population; and the useful PR campaign [*piar-kampanii*] by the country's influential second channel." To Razlogov, these tendencies mean that the product's artistic results "are a secondary question." What matters, as Svetlana Khokhriakova posited, was that the film helped to propagate "a myth capable of answering all expectations and doubts" about faith and about life.[28]

Tat′iana Moskvina-Iashchenko and Vita Ramm offered dissenting views. Moskvina wrote, "First of all, the film turned out to be unexpected for all of us." For audiences, the unexpected blockbuster provoked heated debates about the film's meanings, responses that ranged "from categorical rejection to complete enthusiasm": "These disputes flared up not only among secular viewers, but also among priests and the new generation of churchgoing people who appeared in the 1990s along with the restored cathedrals they helped rebuild. To listen to the arguments 'for' and 'against' the film is extremely interesting." To Moskvina, the film's importance rests in the fact that "it shone a light on the avid interest among film goers for true religious cinema: the film earnestly discusses mankind, the essence of life, about the paths to overcome internal crises through spiritual traditions . . . Neither *Harry Potter*'s occultism nor the similarly entertaining *Night Watch, Day Watch, The Swordbearer* [Filipp Iankovskii's fantasy blockbuster], nor *Wolfhound* caused such a lively audience response as the modest, but professionally precise film by Pavel Lungin and the excellent acting of Petr Mamonov, Viktor Sukhorukov, Dmitrii Diuzhev, and others." Ramm agreed, taking issue in part with the professor of theology Andrei Kuraev's view that *The Island* was successful because it offered a clear understanding of what holiness means. Instead, Ramm argues that the film's significance rests in the diversity of opinions about its meanings.[29]

Most viewers that posted responses to various online forums bore out Moskvina's and Ramm's conclusions. Kinopoisk.ru reviewers (eighteen thousand of them) scored the film 8/10. "Martino" wrote, "It's impossible to condemn, advertise, or criticize this film. You must see it. *The Island* is a small scrap of life in our soul, one that some cannot find and do not know that it's in them, while others know that it's a unique quality that we all need to uncover. . . . I asked a friend recently why did *The Island* not get the Oscar nomination [from our committee]; why did they give it to *Ninth Company*? He told me that they [Hollywood] wouldn't understand. How could they not understand its essence, that there is good in all of us?" "Boris 05" saw the film as part of a battle between good and evil, but one ultimately fought between "Russian Orthodoxy" and "Hollywood poison." "Urgh" agreed: "The film is saturated with our feelings, our shortcomings, and our worldview." Others posted that the film inspired them, made them discover their souls, or provoked complex emotions and deep thoughts.[30] Picking up on these threads, the journal *Seans* (*Performance*) posted a blog titled "*The Island* against *The Island*." Veronika Khlebnikova wrote a positive review of the film, and Stanislav Zel′venskii a negative one. Seven respondents posted their views: only one agreed with Zel′venskii. Those who sided with the positive review did so for various reasons: "Aleksei" called *The Island* "the most philosophical of recent Russian cinema," whereas "Polina" stated that even as an atheist, the film made her think about God and about sin. "Vera" replied, "Glory to God, I am not an atheist: I was a sinner, but not a mortal one. But sincere repentance gives you the possibility to live another life, just as it occurred with the film's hero."[31] *The Island*'s popularity extended to the small screen too: when the film aired on television for the first time, it drew 48 percent of viewers for that time slot.[32]

The film and its reception shone a light on the connections between memory and religion. In his *Confessions,* St. Augustine postulated one of the earliest treatises on memory and history. In book ten, Augustine muses on the concepts of memory, past sins, and reflection, concluding that confronting past sins allows an individual to move forward in the present. On the question of sin, confession, and what we should reveal to God about them, Augustine develops his idea of memory as a "spacious hall" that stores "as treasures the countless images that have been brought into them from all manner of things by the senses." Some of these treasures are easily relocated; others "require to be searched for longer, and then dragged out, as it were, from some hidden recess."[33] For Augustine, our individual "storehouses of memory," which include a host of things remembered and forgotten, makes us human. By plumbing the depths of this vast memory cave, we come closer to God. By confessing our sins of the past, we become better human beings.

Augustine's views help make sense of *The Island*'s significance. *The Island,* according to Father Vladimir Vigilianskii, was about artistic and metaphysical searches more than anything else. "The film is not historically accurate. The monastery depicted did not exist and if it had the Soviet government would not have let it operate so independently. Yet it is truthful. It is a good film about a religious person, about a man of faith who searches for answers to life's questions. Lungin's film is an artistic reality that captures real life and real issues. It therefore fits within a Russian artistic tradition that includes writers such as Tolstoy and Dostoevsky." Father Anatolii, in other words, plumbed the depths of his memory storehouse in order to reveal his past sins to God. When asked why the film was set in the Soviet era, despite its larger truths, Father Vladimir answered, "*The Island* presents characters who lived in the past but who for the most part now live in the present. It might serve as a source of repentance for sins committed in the past. It might help people who are critical of the church today see a metaphysical side to our views on faith and sin. There's a thoughtful, reflective part of the Russian character that was present even in the Soviet Union. Many people may need to be reminded of this."[34] The Soviet state, as Father Vladimir mused, attempted to take away an individual's ability to explore their memory storehouse, to reflect on sin, and to atone. Lungin's film blurred the past and the present as a means to have audiences think about the very issues St. Augustine raised centuries ago. The "heroic age" of Brezhnev contained a source of renewal in present-day Russia, but not because of its Soviet-era ideals. Instead, Brezhnev's Soviet Union could be retrofitted as a site of Russian spirituality.

Lungin's film served as a memory agent—a means to reflect even further on the past, on sin, and on the need for atonement. Vigilianskii spoke about the "necessity of such films": "Pavel Lungin told me about a screening he attended in Siberia. The theater was packed with young and old alike. All were entranced. The young people bought their Coca-Cola, their popcorn, their beer, but still stayed for the film and asked questions. They tend to see very bad American and very bad Russian films, too much mass culture."[35]

Maybe this is why Aleksei II blessed *The Island*—it is a good blockbuster meant to combat bad blockbusters. Perhaps, as Dmitrii Bykov wrote in *Iskusstvo kino,* the film itself is a miracle.[36]

Cinematic shock therapy: Poster for *Cargo 200.*

NINE

The Soviet Horror Show

Aleksei Balabanov knows how to court controversy. Best known for his cult-classic gangster film *Brother* (1997), Balabanov catapulted to iconic status with it and its sequel, *Brother 2* (2000), when the eponymous hero of the series, Danila Bagrov (played by the equally iconic Sergei Bodrov, Jr.) takes on American corporate gangsters who are holding a Russian hockey player for ransom. In between these two films, Balabanov made an art house attack on nostalgia for Silver Age St. Petersburg. His 1998 *Of Freaks and Men* is not the prerevolutionary lost Russia envisioned by Nikita Mikhalkov, but an unnerving and perverse place populated by sado-masochist pornographers. In his films of the 1990s, Balabanov advanced a vision of a dark and disturbed St. Petersburg that stood in the tradition of Dostoevsky and Gogol, a place where madness, murder, and mayhem are a product of the city itself—as a character from *Brother* puts it, "the city is a force."[1]

Brother 2's follow-up, *The War* (2002), offered a violent and vicious take on the Chechen War, one that drew the ire of critics and antiwar activists for its savage portrayals of Chechen warlords and imprisoned Russians. Much as *Brother* fit the chaotic and crime-ridden 1990s, *Brother 2* and *The War* offered early encapsulations of the aggressive nationalism promoted by President Vladimir Putin. By the time he made *Dead Man's Bluff* (2005), a dark comedy that poked fun at the *chernukha* of the 1990s and marketed "for those who survived the 1990s," Balabanov had seemingly become a perfect embodiment of the cultural changes unleashed by postcommunism. He always put his finger on the nation's pulse and always came up with the right cinematic diagnosis. When he released his tenth film, *It Doesn't Hurt,* in 2006, Balabanov returned to his preferred terrain of St. Petersburg, but this time captured a city undergoing renovation. It followed a group of young architects who dream big and build for the new rich. His turn toward melodrama and audience-friendly movies suggested a softer side of Balabanov and his filmmaking career.

This cinematic backstory makes *Cargo 200* all the more shocking and awesome. If it seemed that Balabanov's products were headed in a logical arc, from gangster cult classic to patriotic film, think again. *Cargo 200* is the bleakest, darkest, most repugnant, and yet most satisfying film made about late socialism. Although it only made $570,000 at the box office, it seemed to be everywhere and on everyone's lips in summer 2007. Despite Balabanov's stated opposition to the idea of Russian blockbusters (he likes American blockbusters because "that's what they do well"),[2] *Cargo 200* became one anyway, just as *Brother 2* and *Dead Man's Bluff* had before it (earning $1 million and $4 million, respectively). When it appeared at the Kinotavr Film Festival on June 14, 2007, the fireworks started. Before the film even began, representatives at the festival warned pregnant women to vacate the hall. Compared to the controversy that followed, however, this warning seemed tame. When the voting for the festival's grand prize was announced and Aleksei Popogrebskii's *Simple Things* beat Balabanov's film, many critics cried foul, issuing an unprecedented statement that claimed some of their colleagues had deliberately sabotaged the voting process because they hated *Cargo 200* so much.[3] Because of all the press, the film became a cultural phenomenon. It may not have earned much at the cinema halls, but it did a brisk business in the underground kiosks and video stores all over Russia, and when it aired on First Channel in April 2008 at midnight, it was the highest-rated program of the year.

The reason for all the fuss? *Cargo 200* presents the Soviet Union as nothing less than a horror show billed under the slogan "based on true events."

"A HORROR PARK OF THE SOVIET ERA"

Oleg Sul′kin's characterization of the film as a "horror park of the Soviet era" summed up *Cargo 200*'s content best. It follows the conventions of an American slasher movie, involving two young people who wander away from a disco into a rural hell. When a young man named Valera (Leonid Bichevin), who wears a CCCP shirt, gets out of his car to acquire homemade vodka at a creepy cabin lit only by a full moon and a bad outdoor light, he leaves a young woman, Angelika (Agniia Kuznetsova), alone. Stalked by a sinister-looking man while Valera and Aleksei, the moonshine maker (Aleksei Serebriakov) are passed out inside, Angelika attempts to escape with the help of the moonshiner's wife. The escape attempt fails and the man who has stalked her takes her prisoner, kills a Vietnamese worker who tries to help, rapes her with an empty bottle, and takes her to his apartment in the industrial wasteland of Leninsk. He then chains her to his bed and tells his drunk and deranged mother that he has brought a wife home. *Cargo 200* is, in a sense, a little *Psycho* mixed with *Halloween*.

Balabanov adds an element to his story that most American slasher films lack: history. For this tale is not just about gore, it is about the horror of the Soviet Union and the complete absence of morality within it. The horror film genre did not exist in the Soviet Union, where critics and filmmakers alike tended to dismiss it as "reactionary" and one that would not help to create a new society and new citizens.[4] Balabanov, therefore, takes a genre deemed unable to explain the Soviet system and uses it to do just that. After Angelika is chained to her captor's bed, we learn that her stalker is not just anyone, but Captain Zhurov (Aleksei Poluian), head of the local militia. Zhurov's sadism stems from his job, where he routinely uses his power to obtain what he wants. He frames Aleksei for the murder of his Vietnamese worker and oversees his execution. When Angelika claims that her fiancé serving in Afghanistan will come back and kill him, Zhurov learns that the paratrooper has been killed in action, manages to claim his lead-lined coffin (the name for these Afghan coffins is Gruz 200), opens it up, and deposits the remains on Angelika's bed. He then momentarily frees a criminal to rape Angelika in the same bed while he watches. After he kills the prisoner, he reads her letters from the dead fiancé that rots alongside her.

The unflinching violence and sadism that Zhurov employs has two roots. First, as a representative of the state, Zhurov embodies the moral decay of communism. He does what he does, Balabanov suggests, simply because he can. Second, the roots of Zhurov's evil stem from the time, when the Afghan war had gone on for five years and the numbers of Gruz 200 coffins had increased dramatically. It is an era, as one character states at the beginning of the film, when "everyone has begun to fidget." The long history of state violence employed by the Bolsheviks and their successors, Balabanov implies, has reached its logical if horrific apex in the form of Zhurov.

Yet Balabanov does not just stop there, for he damns all his characters for their lack of souls. The director himself has stated that the "clearly expressed hero is a negative."[5] Wrapped into the plot of Zhurov and Angelika is the story of a family that has sold its soul to the communist devil. We first meet Valera when he is with his girlfriend, the daughter of a Red Army officer. The officer's brother, Artem, a professor of scientific atheism at Leningrad State University, is visiting and is thanked for arranging for his niece's entry into the university. Before Valera departs for the club, Artem leaves for Leninsk, but his car breaks down on the way. He arrives at the same rundown home of Aleksei, a former zek before he was a local moonshiner. Aleksei desires to build a new City of the Sun in place of the communist hell he has experienced. Artem's story, therefore, is intertwined with that of the horror show involving Angelika and Zhurov, and it adds to the historical and moral judgment Balabanov delivers.

As Artem waits for Sunka, the Vietnamese man, to fix his car, he sits, drinks, and debates with Aleksei. The viewer is treated to a rundown of the Soviet experience, for both Aleskei—as a former Gulag inmate—and Artem—as a professor of atheism—are entirely Soviet creatures. Downing shots of homemade vodka, the zek asks his surprise guest about his work. "Just tell me, does God exist or not?" he asks. After Artem replies no, Aleksei asks if humans have souls. Again Artem says no, claiming that he "does not believe in the supernatural" but the material, and believes that morality is solely a product of religious and economic forces meant to dupe. When Artem confirms that he is not only a professor, but also a member of the Communist Party, Aleksei pounces: "All the evil comes from you, the communists. You want to replace God with your Party and your Lenin. . . . There's no God, so everything goes. You can kill millions." What has happened, in Balabanov's view (he was also the scriptwriter), is that communism deprived its citizens of souls and thereby created a real-life horror film.

Everyone in the film suffers from this horrific state. Aleksei went to a camp because he killed a man and eventually meets up with Zhurov, where the two broker a shadowy deal that helps explain why Aleksei accepts his fate. His wife, Tonya, suffers abuse from her husband and enables his alcoholic rages as well as his relationship with Zhurov. When she eventually has her revenge and shoots Zhurov in front of Angelika, however, she leaves the girl chained to the bed and ignores her pleas to be freed. Instead of helping her fellow citizen (and woman), Tonya simply kills and departs. For her part, Angelika (like many girls in horror films), is condemned for her loose morals, for although she has a fiancé who dies for the motherland, she goes to discos and picks up boys like Valera. Although her punishment is severe, she, too, pays for her sins. For his part, Valera is more interested in a good time and good music than anyone else—after he departs Aleksei's hut, he no longer concerns himself with Angelika's fate, seeking refuge in yet another club while still wearing his CCCP shirt. Finally, while Zhurov represents the moral evil at the heart of Soviet communism, Artem represents its heartless indifference. He knows that Aleksei has not killed the Vietnamese worker, but he refuses to testify at the ensuing trial because, as he tells Tonya as they sit at a bench beneath a banner proclaiming "Glory to the Communist Party!" "I am a Party member. If they find out about all this, I'll be in trouble, you see. They'll admonish me, or even fire me." This careerism and cowardice allows the violence of Zhurov and the state that employs it to flourish. *Cargo 200* is a horror film but also a dissection of two Soviet generations: those born in the Stalin era, such as Artem, who have learned to keep quiet and internalize their moral quandaries; and the last Soviet generation, exemplified by Valera and Angelika, who are concerned only with money and fun. Neither generation has any redeeming attributes, *Cargo 200* explains, for both have been compromised by the Soviet state's taking of their souls. By the end, Artem makes a journey to a church in order to atone for his sins, bringing a Dostoevskian closure to the disgusting and decrepit scenes onscreen.

Even the period soundtrack, which mostly features the Leningrad-based band Kino, does not emerge unscathed by Balabanov's criticism. Balabanov's musical soundscape of 1984 tends to highlight the distance between the gritty aspects of late Soviet life and the escapist nature of its popular culture, captured in the last song of the film, Kino's 1982 "Lots of Time but No Money [*Vremia est´ a deneg net*]." After hearing it, Valera and Artem's son emerge from the club and talk about a new moneymaking scheme. Buoyed by the music, Valera has forgotten the recent horror he witnessed. As Anthony Anemone has characterized it, "According to Balabanov, Soviet society circa 1984 was the poisonous wreck of an industrial civilization tottering on the verge of collapse from the sum of its political, social, and individual vices: a hopeless foreign war of choice bleeding the country dry, a terrorized and infantilized populace, rampant alcohol abuse among young and old, complete police lawlessness (*bespredel*), a geriatric and out of touch government, a dismal and hypocritical popular culture, an arrogant and cynical intelligentsia, a nihilistic younger generation, and the soul-crushing hopelessness of everyday life for the masses."[6] To convey this near complete bleakness, Balabanov shot his film in rundown apartments, amid the industrial decay of Leninsk, and in seedy clubs. His characters wear period clothes, hairstyles, and eyeglasses—all in an effort to convey the sense that Balabanov's 1984 is the real 1984, a "fact" suggested by the two intertitles that open and close the film: "This story is based on real events," and "These events occurred in the second half of 1984."

CULTURE SHOCK

Cargo 200's buzz had already hit fever pitch when Echo Moscow aired a segment devoted to the film on its program *Culture Shock*. Airing on June 16, 2007, the day the film hit cinema halls, host Kseniia Larina stated, "The film has in fact caused not just a storm of emotions, but simply improbable and incandescent emotions."[7] Joining her on the program to discuss these emotional responses were critics Andrei Plakhov, Iurii

Gladil′shchikov, and Vita Ramm as well as Sergei Sel′ianov, the film's producer. Larina set up the discussion by suggesting that the film's reception divided generations, much as the film itself focused upon generations: for those who remember 1984 well (or "the generation of Soviet people"), the film was a shock and a source of anger; for the younger generation ("those who know about the Soviet Union only from their parents' stories") the film was "a revelation," representing "an entirely different story than the one told to them by their parents and—apparently—at school." *Cargo 200,* in other words, served as a cinematic history lesson for the internet generation: Larina even admitted that she had formed her opinions after reading about the film in chat rooms.

For Sel′ianov, the producer, the fact that people were debating the film and having emotional responses to it was "completely outstanding." The more vociferous the debate, the better the film's ability to get people to talk about the past, and the more likely the film would make money. After discussing the Kinotavr controversy surrounding the film, Larina and her guests debated the messages and the ideology of the film. Gladil′shchikov answered that both were "very complex," for *Cargo 200* contains "a vast amount of components to discuss." Gladil′shchikov pointed to Valera's CCCP shirt and stated that this sartorial choice makes the character "maybe even more important" to an understanding of the film's ideology than the "maniac cop." No one, the critic reminded the audience, "walked around in 1984 with shirts that had 'CCCP' inscribed on them. Especially not in discos. They were not fashionable. The USSR was not popular among young people." The shirt appeared because of contemporary nostalgia for the USSR. Plakhov picked up the conversation and the significance of the CCCP shirt by stating that Valera is meant to be a time traveler of sorts, a "terminator from the future" to witness how decrepit the CCCP he waxes nostalgic about in the present really was. Ramm, by contrast, believed the messages of the film to be "very simplified . . . like a poster that says 'children, drink milk and you will be healthy'—there are no nuances here." For Ramm, the film hammers home the message that the USSR was morally unhealthy over and over again, "driving the last nail or wooden stake into the Soviet Union's coffin." The film, he said, "is simple cinema, which has a right to exist. Only I did not accept its content." Sel′ianov did not disagree with the idea that the visual and verbal codes of the film were "simple" ones, but took these to be a sign of strength.

The film's producer had to leave the interview to promote the film, but as he did, Larina made an astonishing remark, thanking Sel′ianov for this "event within our cultural world" and expresses the wish that "the film will live in its separate life and gather around it both worshippers and people who oppose it, but this is a crucial point. It seems to me to be a very crucial point in the history of our contemporary culture." Sel′ianov naturally agreed that the more people argue about the past, the better the health of the nation, stating, "One ought not to evaluate or pass judgment on the film immediately after seeing it. For it is a film that must be thought about for maybe ten minutes or a day or even a week. Everyone can think about it in their own way. And that's good."

To prove this point after Sel′ianov departed, Larina read internet postings about the film, commenting that the medium offered the freshest and most interesting space for her listeners to think about the film's meanings. She read three opinions. The first was from a young man:

> Well, brothers, I went yesterday to see the film *Cargo 200*. And this is what I want to say. I intended to go to the Kirpichi ["Bricks," a rock group] concert after the movie, but, after leaving the theater I understood that I did not want to go to that concert. I wanted to drink vodka. . . . I will not be able to speak about the film. Go yourselves and see it. But I warn you: it is dark and cruel. It is about everything: about the war in Afghanistan, about the Soviet Union, about love, about strong, close male friendships, and above all about the cruelty and stupidity of humankind.

The second came from a young woman:

> I saw Balabanov's *Cargo 200*. It's his best film. On the whole a masterpiece. I considered Balabanov to be a good director, but he proved himself above all to be a genius. I left the film numb, and wanted to cry or to drink.

The third was posted by another young man:

> The film is not a masterpiece, but attempts to be abstracted from its artistic value and seen as a documentary film about life such as it was, is, and, unfortunately, will be. . . . Many say that the reason to see this putrid reality is that for young people it is necessary to change their consciousness gained from films like *Shrek* and *Lord of the Rings*. And yet in their *No Country for Old Men* you have a masterpiece, while *Cargo 200* is shit. It is our *blin*, our country, no matter how

> disgusting it was we should realize this.... This is a film trap. You sit, you look, and only after an hour do you realize you have become a witness to a nightmare. I actually advise no one to see this film... Don't go.

Plakhov got the last word and provided a useful analysis of the response to *Cargo 200:*

> Naturally they all write differently. But I want to speak about the fact that undoubtedly this film is not for everyone. It is a film that some will consciously not want to see and a film that some will want to see and even they will be divided into supporters and detractors. In this sense the very strong reactions, which unite all viewers, are important.... I also want to speak about the fact that this film even exists... why there are such strong reactions, particularly for young people because for them this film is an absolute discovery, a new reality, a new country, which they did not know before. Not only because they did not live in 1984, but also because the contemporary reality surrounding them is glamorized by the completely banal and senseless commercial cinema, which is everywhere.... And by the way, an analog existed in Soviet reality.... The melodies and rhythms that constantly sounded on television on the whole led people to lose the sensation of reality.

Cargo 200, therefore, acts as shock therapy for those who have failed to remember their history, an electric shot to the brain that wards off the infection of banal commercialized and nostalgic pasts. Balabanov's film punctures two nostalgic balloons that had inflated by the time of its release: first, that the era of stagnation was not so bad after all and in fact would be a nice time to revisit,[8] and second, that Gorbachev unleashed all that was bad in post-Soviet Russia. *Cargo 200* posits that late socialism contained both the immorality of the Soviet system built by Lenin and Stalin and the predatory instincts of the New Russians.

"I AM RUSSIAN AND I LIKE MY COUNTRY VERY MUCH"

Balabanov, for his part, courted the controversy as only he could, having become something of an expert in the subject over the course of his career: when you make films that have gangster heroes, pornographers, African American pimps, and barbaric Chechens, it comes with the territory. One might think that making a movie about a deranged and decrepit Soviet citizenry, coming on the heels of films about tortured Russian troops in Chechnya, tortured Russian prostitutes in America, and tortured pornographic subjects in Silver Age St. Petersburg would not make you a committed nationalist, but think again; Balabanov is as nationalistic as they come.

Cargo 200 may employ the conventions of a horror film, but it is a horror that Balabanov claims he experienced. For five years (1983–87), while he worked in his hometown of Sverdlovsk (now Ekaterinburg) Balabanov collected stories about late socialism and the effects of the Afghan War. He also drew on his army service (1981–83), when he lived with a pilot who flew bodies to and from Afghanistan, including the lead-lined ones called Gruz 200. From these memories, Balabanov crafted a personal history but also one that spoke to two temporal issues. First, the look and feel of late socialism and the Brezhnev era: "The last Brezhnev was Chernenko [who appears on TV in the film] and then Gorbachev came," he claimed. "I wanted to make *Cargo 200* because I wanted to show the 'real life' of the time and what shaped our lives afterwards." Ultimately, Balabanov stated that he wanted to show the "bizarre country" that was the Soviet Union and "what it was like to live in such a place."[9] Moreover, he was "on the whole, a Soviet person. I was in the Pioneers, the Komsomol, and served in the army." He also was "born and grew up in a Soviet family. My mother was the director of an institute for health science and physiotherapy. Naturally, she was a member of the Party. My father [Oktiabrian Balabanov, named after the October Revolution] was editor-in-chief of the paper *Na smenu* [*For change*], the organ of the Sverdlovsk Komsomol."[10] For Balabanov, then, *Cargo 200* is autobiographical as well as a story of his generation: the scene in the film where the coffin carrying Angelika's fiancé is unloaded was shot in Pskov, at the very airfield where Balabanov worked during the war and where he personally saw the lead-lined coffins returning home and authorities attempting to cover up their numbers.[11]

Secondly, *Cargo 200* is a story for the post-Soviet generation. While careful not to overemphasize the role of mass culture, Balabanov believes that "young people today play video games and see blockbusters—they don't have time for literature."[12] If the onscreen story was about generational changes and the role they played in moral decline and collapse, so too was the offscreen story about generational changes from those who were still young in 1984 but had children by 2007. As Balabanov made clear, the target for his "truthful" film was the generation who lived in 1984 but had come to feel nostalgic for the Soviet era: "You know, it's interesting that people who lived in 1984 are less pleased by the film. Maybe they somehow associate themselves with the actions onscreen. . . . It's unpleasant for them." As far as the horror onscreen and whether or not it tests the boundaries of permissibility, Balabanov has equally sharp feelings: "Twice during prime time they showed the film where Hannibal Lecter opens a skull, fries the brain, and eats it. . . . This hypocritical perception does not please me."[13] Real horror, in other words, should take precedence over reel horror.

For Balabanov, *Cargo 200* is a patriotic film, however paradoxical that may seem. It is, as he muses, a film about how Russia transitioned from communism to capitalism and how some moralities transitioned within social and political ideas. As he has said, "I am Russian and I like my country very much."[14] His is a patriotism that does not reflect a particular political ideology, but rather a deep love for Russian culture and Russian suffering. In this view, *Cargo 200* is patriotic tough love, meant to reveal to audiences that conventional wisdom about the Brezhnev era is rose-colored.

Cargo 200 is either patriotic shock therapy or perhaps what the psychologists Bruce Ballon and Molyn Lezcz have called "cinematic neurosis."[15] As Ballon and Lezcz argue, horror films may induce neurosis in a fashion that most people believe they do—for instance, someone who watches too may slasher movies might commit murder. At the same time, horror films may also help to heal traumatic memories by bringing repressed violent tendencies to the surface. In their words, "the horror film [can be] a mechanism for helping [viewers] work through anxieties involving adolescent issues, such as separation from parents, achieving autonomy, and forming an adult identity."[16] Moreover, successful horror films tend to be embedded with cultural and autobiographical resonance: "Artists can, and often do, imbue their work with their own personal life experiences. In film, many sources contribute such elements, for example, the content of the screenplay, the process and skill with which an actor delivers material, the director's and cinematographer's skills, which heighten such material, and even the musical score. Films can therefore be powerful sources of embedded life-event narratives, and those narratives that resonate with a viewer's own life experiences will heighten identification with certain elements of a film."[17] Balabanov meant his film to help his viewers separate themselves from Soviet nostalgia and Soviet-era tendencies. *Cargo 200* allows audiences to deal with traumatic memories of the past and therefore achieve an adulthood of sorts. As Ballon and Lezcz posit, "It is possible to identify the representative elements of horror films in many ways, depending on the individual viewer. However, it is important to recognize that for a viewer dealing with issues of separation, loss, achieving autonomy, and forming identity, the cultural factors included in the story that such an individual identifies with, the easier the story could be incorporated into his or her identify formation. Life-narrative events can be embedded in a film's content in different ways, such as in symbols and characters. Individuals with current and/or similar life events may identify with such symbols or characters, as using representative symbols may be less anxiety provoking than dealing with the underlying subconscious issues they represent."[18] For anyone who lived during 1984 and saw *Cargo 200,* this view would make sense: What Russian viewer from this last Soviet generation was still not dealing with the loss, anxiety, and identity issues engendered by the end of communism? Strange as it may sound, *Cargo 200* may be therapeutic.

The film is also a story, however strange and horrific, of change, and of how, "by the end of the 1980s, the Soviet Union stopped being the Soviet Union—we began to be a capitalist country. Most people went from being communists to going to church. I was baptized in St. Petersburg, then my parents, then my children, which makes me both a communist and a believer."[19] It is hard to imagine a better statement about the contradictory ways patriotism has operated in Russia over the last twenty years, where it is possible to have been orthodox in more ways than one. This seeming contradiction, however, helps explain why Aleksei Balabanov can see himself as a patriot and his film *Cargo 200* as tough love for fellow Russians.

THE REEL 1984 VERSUS THE REAL 1984

Set in "the second half of 1984," the film's function as patriotic shock therapy not only wrestles with the nostalgia for the Brezhnev era, but also with the symbolic resonance of the year 1984. George Orwell looms over the film and films such as the German exploration of Stasi surveillance, *The Lives of Others* (*Das Leben des Anderen,* dir. Donnersmarck, 2006), which also was set in 1984 and also featured a voyeuristic, impotent policeman. What *Cargo 200* and *The Lives of Others* both suggested was that the "real" 1984 was far scarier than Orwell's dystopian nightmare, for nightmares could be found in everyday life.

Not surprisingly, one of the central debates that stemmed from the film concerned the veracity of the era recaptured onscreen. Given Balabanov's repeated interviews where he asserted that the film was autobiographical and "truthful," critics and viewers took up these claims. Was *Cargo 200,* in other words, the real 1984 or just a reel 1984? Unsurprisingly, Dmitrii Puchkov (Goblin) found the film distasteful. More surprisingly, Goblin was disappointed with what he saw as Balabanov's love for the USSR. After seeing it three times and preparing himself each time for its macabre scenes, Puchkov commented to the journal *Seans* (*Performance*) that the film was "a strange comedy about an abnormal policeman's love. It's said that Balabanov drove the final nails into the USSR's coffin. I don't know; personally I think he loves the USSR greatly and is just trying to convince himself otherwise."[20] The same journal devoted a special segment in its April 2008 issue to the question because of the buzz already gathering about Balabanov's film. One of the motivating factors for this coverage, as the editors admitted, was that they "consider Aleksei Balabanov's picture a true work of cinematic art" and feared that "it will not be advertised in the manner of other domestic blockbusters."[21] They need not have worried about the advertising. The journal's editors simply asked cultural figures to respond to the depiction of 1984 in *Cargo 200.*

Dmitrii Bykov, poet and TV personality, declared that the shot of Angelika in bed with her fiancé's corpse surrounded by flies as Aleksei's wife walks away and Zhurov's mother listens to *Vologda-Gda* on TV "serves as the absolute quintessence of Russian reality at the beginning of the 1980s." Anton Kostylev, a film critic, declared that the movie might help to bring about the end of the Soviet era, for it demonstrates "a perfect director's eye. . . . With its help he cuts open the spectator as an old tin of stew from the army store, letting out all the gloomy junk which has stayed there intact since 1984. And here we find out that although

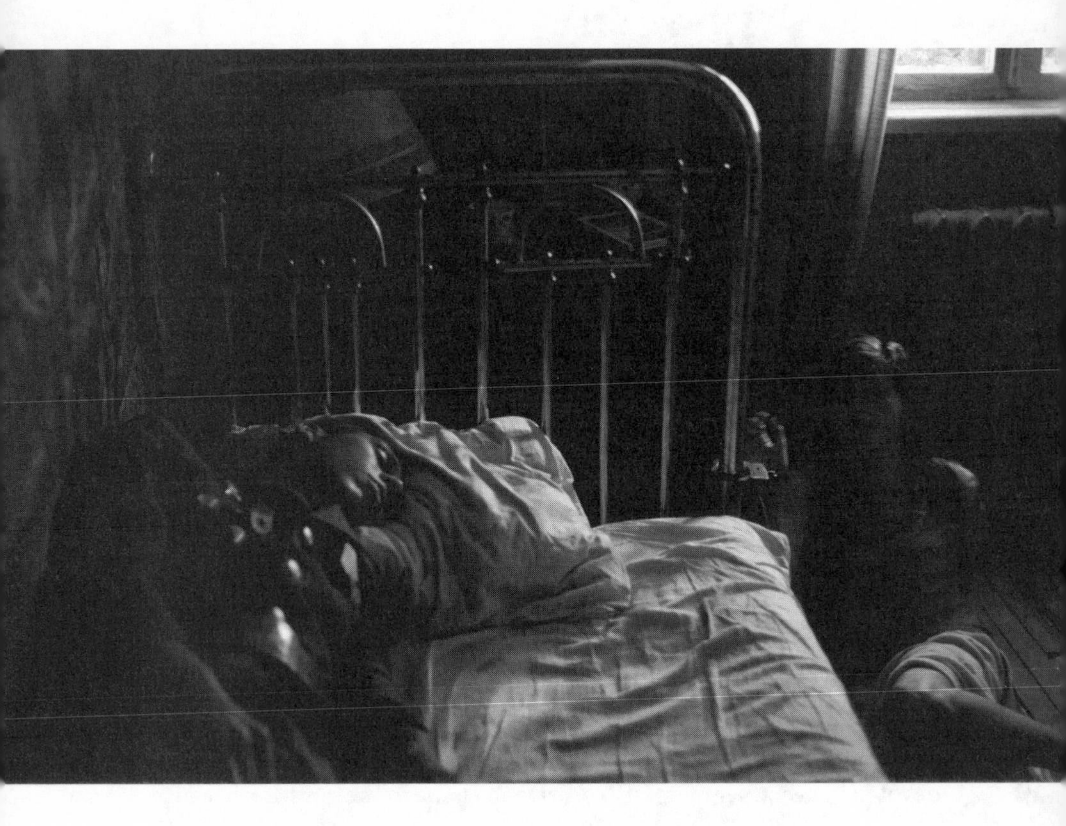

"The absolute quintessence of Russian reality at the beginning of the 1980s"? Angelika and her fiancé. Still from Aleksei Balabanov's *Cargo 200* (2007).

formally the film is about a decaying USSR on the verge of disintegration, the USSR is gone and the decay strangely remains."

Oleg Zintsov from *Vedomosti* connected the appeal to the historical and personal when he wrote, "A really brave artist had to articulate it: I am part of this time, this is my youth and in spite of all the dread shown there, to my own horror, I still love this time and nothing can change it; it is a disease, an obsession, a mania. In this sense *Cargo 200* is not only the most painful but also the most honest Russian film in many years. All that it asks of a spectator is to be honest in response." Konstantin Shavlovskii, who writes for *Seans,* had this to say: "Balabanov made his film not for those who understand but for those who remember. The rock concert in the legendary 'Saigon' and the provincial discotheque (girls in white socks and boys in T-shirts that read, 'Olympics-80'), the war in Afghanistan, kitchen table dissent, and the unrestrained police,—in one word, the polyphony of the 1980s, which is the flesh and blood of this film. A film that works like a time machine, *Cargo 200* makes you physically feel the time, smell its scent." Andrei Plakhov, president of FIPRESCI and participant in the radio debate cited above, declared, "The film reveals the deep personal ideological trauma, which Balabanov suffered as a serious artist who matured during the decline of the Soviet era . . . [where] the moral structure of society is more important than the social aspect." Vadim Rutkovskii, a journalist for GQ, opined that *Cargo 200* "is first and foremost an historical picture, a chronicle of the undeclared death of the USSR. A film which should be included in the compulsory school program if it was not for the age limit—as strict as it is absurd: you can die for your country at the age of eighteen but you can't see a film that harshly portrays that country."

Maria Kuvshinova, a critic who writes for *Izvestiia* and other major journals, had the most interesting review of Balabanov's 1984, one that fits into the generational revelation discussed on Echo Moscow (Kuvshinova was born in 1978). Her response is worth quoting in its entirety:

> I don't remember anything in film, literature, or art that would impose itself on man with such inevitable, unbearable heaviness. Balabanov's film knocks the ground from under your feet, deprives you of a point of reference, and once and for all strips you of all personal, religious, or social idealism. It's the most uncompromising and honest response to all that has happened and will happen in this country, and in general—in this world under this sky. The object of persistent social nostalgia—the Soviet Union—is presented here as a decomposed corpse, while the only healthy organism are the maggots in it, a statement to our contemporaries who have survived this era and modeled it on their new views. *Cargo 200* is incredibly harsh on the viewer; there's not a hint of purification. But everyone who has eyes should see it, because afterwards you have to find a new point of reference all by yourself, revaluing a great deal in your life and in the life of your country. *Cargo 200* is a film that makes you want to call your loved ones and just say you love them. No exaggeration, but for me it was the only way to get through this film.

Mikhail Trofimenkov offers the best summary of how critics tackled the issue of Balabanov's historical veracity: "Perhaps this film cannot be fully appreciated now but with time its weight and significance will grow. Because the brilliantly constructed plot conceals a host of metaphors that explain what happened to Russia in the mid-1980s and what is still happening here." Russian critics ultimately endorsed the film's take on history: in a poll conducted by *Seans,* nineteen of twenty-eight critics considered *Cargo 200* the best film of 2007, with the next–highest rated films (Kira Muratova's *Two in One* and Aleksandr Mindadze's *Soar*) each getting three votes. When asked what was the film story of the year, a year when Nikita Mikhalkov's *12* was short-listed for the Oscar, when Kira Muratova made another prize-winning film at the age of seventy, when debutants such as Aleksandr Mindadze made critically acclaimed films, and when Ingmar Bergman and Michelangelo Antonioni died, twenty out of fifty-two people questioned by the journal answered *Cargo 200* and its controversies.[22]

The journal then set up a blog for readers' responses. Although most agreed with the lofty sentiments expressed about Balabanov's "art," one respondent, "Evgeny," took issue with the 1984 offered onscreen: "From what kind of devilish circle did this haphazardly made film come from? From which era does this cheap horror reveal anything about a political regime? In 1984 the regime was shitty, but it's not an occasion to hang all its dead dogs and dead soldiers. Really in your entire shit-company there is not one person older than forty, who remember the time of chernukha . . . but not the USSR. . . . 1984 is not similar to 1937! And so the entire film lies in every scene. I hate the Soviet system, but Balabanov lies in every scene." To him, Balabanov's vision of late socialism was a sign that the director suffered from "an extreme and clear disorder." Balabanov, for his part, was typically direct about his view: "It's just a film about 1984 as I remember it, as I imagine and see it. I wanted to make a hard-hitting film about the end of the Soviet Union—and I made it."

The reaction to the film's vision of what 1984 was really like parallels the current scholarly debate about late socialism and its citizens. Historians, anthropologists, and political scientists have recently begun to tackle the complex question of the socialist subject: what defined the persona of *Homo sovieticus*? Were Soviet citizens liberal subjects who harbored thoughts of resistance and freedom? Or were they illiberal subjects, citizens who embodied at least in part the goals of the socialist system? One of the reasons why the debate over *Cargo 200* proved to be such a heated one rests with the fact that post-Soviet citizens are rethinking their roles and beliefs in the Soviet system. Like all subjects, post-

Soviet citizens are reconstituting themselves even as they are coming to terms with their participation in the past system. Recent scholarship, particularly by Russian-born but American-trained academics, suggests that Soviet citizens were illiberal subjects: in other words, for the most part they internalized the goals of the regime and sought to make themselves into communist citizens. Although most of this scholarly debate has focused on the Stalinist era, recent anthropological studies have started to explore "the last Soviet generation," as Alexei Yurchak calls the Brezhnev generation.

Yurchak's pathbreaking *Everything Was Forever, until It Was No More* bases its conclusions on a comment made by the musician Andrei Makarevich (the lead singer of Time Machine): "It had never even occurred to me that in the Soviet Union anything could ever change. Let alone that it could disappear. No one expected it. Neither children, nor adults. There was a complete impression that everything was forever."[23] Yurchak uses Makarevich's statements and those made by other former Soviet citizens to question the assumptions that socialism was "bad" and "immoral," that the collapse of the system was "predicated on this badness and immorality," and that Soviet citizens had no agency in the collapse because they so deeply subscribed to Soviet values because they were coerced or "had no means of reflecting upon them critically."[24] Yurchak, by contrast, seeks to move beyond the binary categories that tend to define the Soviet experience (state and people, resistance and oppression) to explore what he terms "the everyday realities" of late socialism—or "the crucial and seemingly paradoxical fact that, for great numbers of Soviet citizens, many of the fundamental values, ideals, and realities of socialist life (such as equality, community, selflessness, altruism, friendship, ethical relations, safety, education, work, creativity, and concern for the future) were of genuine importance, despite the fact that many of their everyday practices routinely transgressed, reinterpreted, or refused certain rules and norms represented in the official ideology of the state."[25] In short, Yurchak argues that "socialism" was not just a state-driven ideology, but an experience that mattered to Soviet citizens. It is this lived experience, he posits, that serves as the basis for post-Soviet nostalgia, for the values created under socialism continue to have meaning in contemporary Russia.

Yurchak's views of the last Soviet generation are exactly the same point of reference for Balabanov and his film. The director himself is a member of this generation (born in 1959, a year before Yurchak), but is also a Soviet citizen from the provinces, not Leningrad (like Yurchak). For Balabanov, the transgressions mattered more than the values. His view of Soviet citizens in many ways conforms to the views posited by scholars like Yurchak: Balabanov's own experiences and those that he creates in *Cargo 200* clearly demonstrate that Soviet citizens internalized the goals and values of the regime. At the same time, Balabanov's picture of Soviet reality and its lived experience is the negative of Yurchak's picture: both the system and its citizens lived in a horror show, not a web of negotiated practices where certain values still mattered. If Yurchak wants to "contemplate and rehumanize Soviet socialist life" by examining practices in his home city of Leningrad,[26] so does Balabanov, this time by focusing on the socialist backwoods, only to suggest that this contemplation of the past is one that should shock, not soothe.

The debate about 1984 was ultimately a debate about what defines the cultural representation of the past: is it enough to capture some sort of essence and "truth" about it or should filmmakers (and writers, artists, and others) attempt to employ strict accuracy and veracity in their adaptations of the past? Is a film about late socialism best captured in a biography of Brezhnev (such as Sergei Snezkin's 2005 miniseries)? A spy series about political intrigue (such as Rauf Kabaev's 2004 *Red Square*)? Or in a horror film about moral decay under communism? Should, in other words, history be subjective yet reveal something explosive, or should it attempt to be as objective as possible? Clearly critics and audiences would not agree about these issues just as historians have disagreed about this very topic since the nineteenth century. Regardless, *Cargo 200* accomplished what few other films in the post-Soviet era have: it got people talking about their own lived histories and their memories of them. Whether it was a shock or a salve, *Cargo 200* acted as therapy.

TELEVISION FINALES

Because Nashe Kino marketed the movie for audiences twenty-one and older, *Cargo 200* did not look like a likely candidate for a television airing.

Yet the buzz about the film, generated in large part because of its marketing as a horror show, eventually led Pervyi kanal to screen the film on its *Zakrytyi pokaz* program in April 2008. Because of its violent content, Balabanov's blockbuster aired after midnight. It also featured a roundtable discussion involving those "for" and those "against" the message onscreen—including Balabanov, Viktor Matizen (president of the Film Critics' Guild and "against"), and others. Not much in the way of new information or new argumentation was offered in the late-night screening, but the event proved that *Cargo 200* could still be a draw almost a year after it first hit screens. More significantly, it proved that Balabanov's brand of patriotism could still serve as the basis for a discussion about the meanings of the Soviet experience, the Brezhnev era, the state of morality in the USSR and in Putin's Russia, and the significance of film in provoking healthy debate. The horror show created by Balabanov could, in other words, still be shock therapy to help deal with the past.[27]

PART FOUR

Fantasy Pop History

In the middle of the decade, fantasy histories began to dominate box-office offerings. Animated films about Russian folk tales, epics about pre-Kyivan pasts, and even sci-fi blockbusters that reinterpreted Soviet history with the help of vampires profitably used the past in the zero years. Surveying the situation in January 2009, *Iskusstvo kino*'s Mikhail Morozov declared that Russian history was now "in the style of pop" and that it had successfully "simulated a new national idea."[1]

For Morozov, "The Name of Russia" competition that generated so much controversy throughout 2008 (namely because Stalin and Nicholas II held early leads) represented the last step in the decade-long attempt to "invent a national identity." Citing Benedict Anderson's influential view of nations as imagined communities and Geoffrey Hosking's argument that Russia has historically lacked a national identity because of its imperial one, Morozov believes that Putin's government had squared this circle by using mass culture to "rehabilitate and integrate" Soviet values alongside an invention of new national traditions such as the Day of National Unity. The process exploited so successfully by filmmakers, Morozov argues, began with Konstantin Ernst's 1995 television special *Old Songs about the Most Important,* which featured retro Soviet ditties sung by contemporary celebrities. The series "reconciled the spectator with the Soviet reality" because it avoided sharp angles about history and made it glamorous instead. The past, in short, had become pop history. The result is that Russia has become "a country conquered by simulation." Movies, television, and other forms of mass culture have "framed reality" as a "simulation," creating pop history, pop heroes from the past, pop religion, and therefore a simulated nation. "Today," he concludes, "the country lives . . . [as] a disoriented and atomized society."[2]

Certainly "The Name of Russia" competition that ran throughout 2008 generated a great deal of press and a lot of discussion about the uses of the past for present-day patriotic purposes. The competition, which was run by the Rossiia channel, the Institute of History in the Russian Academy of Sciences, and the Public Opinion Foundation, began in May 2008 with 500 potential names. Internet voting whittled the list down to 50 and then 12. The final 12 each received a show dedicated to them and various historians, politicians, celebrities, and journalists presented the pros and cons of each candidate. The final internet vote got nearly 3 million Russians to cast a ballot: in the end, Alexander Nevsky won with 524,575 votes; Petr Stolypin finished second with 523,766 votes; and Stalin third, with 519,071.[3]

The process became a means to debate not just history, but its uses. When the final episode, about Stalin, aired on October 19, the Russian Communist Party declared that a vote for the former Soviet leader was "a battle for Stalin." The KP website urged Russians to combat "the vulgarization of our country's past and the degradation of historical knowledge, particularly that related to understanding Soviet history" by voting for Stalin. Iurii Emel′ianov, who wrote the article, argued in part that the TV show had created a fantasy Stalin. "Instead of presenting to us an authentic Stalin," he wrote, "they palmed off a long scene from Mikhalkov's film sequel [*Burnt by the Sun 2*]."[4] Instead of using "real facts," Emel′ianov complained, the show had used fantastic blockbuster history.

On the opposite side of the political spectrum, the liberal *Novaia gazeta* railed against "The Name of Russia" competition for its cynical attempt to use "history and television to unite people around shared values." Slava Taroshchina, the television critic for the paper, tore into the "blockbuster 'Name of Russia'" for creating "a game" out of historical understanding. This game was ostensibly created for "patriotic purposes," but mostly "so that the patriotism . . . would without fail bring a high rating and a lot of money right here and now." As a result, Taroshchina argues, "history (or at least, its tele-version) is fitted within the needs of a business plan." She blames this state of affairs on Konstantin Ernst and Nikita Mikhalkov, who together have turned the past into profitable ventures by "rehabilitating" reds and whites alike. In the end, the show—and with it the new history on screen—has become "the combination of the un-combinable."[5]

For others, the competition—however flawed—represented something positive. Anatolii Baranov believed that the "tele-project had become a political event because referenda, except those initiated by the powers that be themselves, are de facto prohibited." The online voting and open discussions on and off the air gave Russians a chance to express themselves freely.[6] Others felt less sanguine about the overall meanings of the competition. Evgenii Lesin of *Nezavisimaia gazeta* believed that the final three represented a "Rus′ troika" of "Stalin, Stalin, and Stalin" because the list did not include "anyone who worked on behalf of Russia, for Russia, and for the glory of Russia." Nevsky, he argued, was a vote for the mythic Russian hero of the Stalinist 1930s, not the actual historical figure, whereas Stolypin is known for his repression of revolutionaries and "strong executive style." "He is better than Lavrentii Beriia or Maliuta Skuratov [Ivan the Terrible's infamous *oprichnik*], of course, but he could be ideally inserted into the Stalinist vertical line of power." And as for Stalin, Lesin wrote that he "simply destroyed people. Was that evil? Yes, it was. But it is a part of our history, a part which must not be forgotten and a sin that we must renounce."[7] The competition may have been free and open, Lesin acknowledged, but it revealed that Russians still admire authoritative figures, not "positive" ones such as Pushkin or Mendeleev.

"The Name of Russia" competition, Morozov concluded, "has made history into a sideshow booth [*balagan*]." For Morozov and critics who broadly subscribed to his conclusions, history had become a simulation, a fantasy pop past that could be used to create a new patriotism. In this reading, cinematic narratives about the past created an amalgam of new national myths—fantasy histories and pop histories presented tales of origin, ancestry, golden ages, and regeneration. Movies about

Prince Vladimir, pre-Kyivan pasts, the Time of Troubles, or alternative interpretations of the Soviet experience all attempted to provide myths about the Russian nation, its beginnings, its communal ties, its heroic values, and its sources of rebirth after 1991.[8]

For others, The Name of Russia competition represented a new Russia, one where—warts and all—the past could be debated freely. The past as pop show—whether it was animated, invented, or created for business purposes—could be interpreted as the basis for understanding a new Russia that had gotten over its past.

Animating the past: Andrei Riabovichev's sketch for *Prince Vladimir.* *Courtesy of Andrei Riabovichev.*

TEN

Animating the Past

The fact that animated films served as a blockbuster historical centerpiece in the new Russian cinematic showcase should come as no surprise. Russian animation has a long history and has engaged in a longstanding cultural dialogue with Hollywood animation. Disney itself has long been the source of mostly negative scholarly and cultural debates, particularly for its ability to shape national identity, gender roles, and childhood values.[1] In addition, the worldwide popularity of Disney films has led many critics to charge that they orientalize in a way that not only shapes childhood perceptions of evil, but also insults national sensitivities.[2]

The revival of Russian animation also provided a source of heated debate, particularly because the work of Andrei Riabovichev, the principal animator for the "first" post-Soviet animated film, *Prince Vladimir,* and his peers openly made use of Hollywood animated techniques at the expense of the "Soviet Russian tradition." At the same time, *Prince Vladimir* and the handful of other animated features that appeared in the zero years all used the past, particularly the Kyivan past, to articulate messages about history and nationhood needed for the present. The use of Vladimir and Russian bogatyrs as symbols of Russianness employed by post-Soviet animators were revived traditions: at the turn of the twentieth century, particularly after the 1905 Revolution, Russian rightists frequently used Vladimir and Russian medieval warriors as national icons.[3]

Vlad Strukov has perceptively concluded that these folkloric historical animations serve as "a 'Slavic epos,'" which he defines as "a cinematic form that may be loosely defined as a fantasy genre based on Slavic/Russian folklore as well as the creatively reworked or vigorously adapted history of early Russia."[4] Kyivan Rus′ and the history of the early Slavic peoples provided fertile territory for directors and animators to plow through: this past is so shrouded in myth that the "real Rus′" can be imagined or reimagined as the animator sees fit. As Strukov concludes, "the use of Slavic epos in both literature and film belongs to the ongoing Russian search for historical lineage and self-definition."[5] The mythic past of Prince Vladimir, as Riabovichev found out, is a virtual terra incognita. Not much historical truth is known about the Kyivan prince who Christianized Rus′ and what is known tends to be filtered through the lens of nineteenth-century Russian nationalists. As a powerful figure from the past who could be fitted for present-day cultural battles, Prince Vladimir is a perfect subject. His era and the folk tales created about it both serve as suitably "Russian" traditions for animated history.

ANIMATION IN THE USSR

Prince Vladimir made history in many respects, but in others it just resurrected the Soviet animation tradition. Soiuzmul′tfil′m, founded in 1936 to produce entertaining animation for Soviet children, produced more than 1500 films by the time of communism's collapse. In the words of David MacFadyen, "socialist animation . . . was a fundamentally emotional, not wordy, propagandistic enterprise."[6] Soviet cartoons presented a fun, inclusive world that could be temptingly read as an insidious attempt by the government to indoctrinate Soviet children very early on. At the same time this reading takes away the sheer enjoyment millions of Soviet citizens felt when watching a cartoon. Cheburashka, the furry creature animated by Roman Kachanov who came to the USSR in a crate of oranges in 1969, charmed audiences. He remains as beloved today as ever and even serves as the official Olympic mascot, facts that force anyone to reconsider the far-too-simplistic notion that Soviet animation was state propaganda.

What is undoubtedly true is that Soviet animation developed alongside, and often in response to, Western cartoons. Disney loomed large in the USSR and its worldwide popularity in part contributed to the 1936 foundation of Soiuzmul′tfil′m. Initially, Soviet animation mostly used rotoscoping, which involves animators tracing over live-action film movement frame by frame to produce their work (*Snow White and the Seven Dwarves, Who Framed Roger Rabbit?* and the video for a-ha's 1985 single "Take on Me" use this technique). The technique, known as éclair (*ekper*), was employed almost exclusively by animators, who considered the form best able to render a "Soviet-style" socialist realist cartoon. Worried about the entertainment value of 1950's *Cinderella,* Soviet journalists declared that animation's real magic was in the ability to covey a "national spirit" or "the correct personification of people and animals."[7] American children could see *Cinderella;* Soviet kids got to watch animated adaptations of Pushkin. Even after the death of Stalin, when Soviet animation employed techniques other than éclair—perhaps best seen in the enormously popular 1970s series *Just You Wait!* (*Nu, pogodi!*) or in the visionary work of Iurii Norshtein—the Soviet press proclaimed that their animation needed to combat the "emptiness" of *Yogi Bear* and *The Flintstones.* Soviet cartoons, by contrast, would contain "patriotism, a love of nature, friendship, comradeship, honesty, politeness, and neatness."[8]

By 1999 this tradition had all but died. Although President Yeltsin signed a decree on June 30 that pledged to resurrect the defunct Soiuzmul′tfil′m Studio, in reality the law attempted to reanimate a corpse. The studio still exists, but barely. Its 1990s story reads like the sort of fantastic tale the studio regularly put out over the course of its existence.

In 1989 the Soviet government declared that the studio, which had a staff of seven hundred working in its two branches (animation and puppets), would become a leased enterprise and therefore enter the marketplace. By the early 1990s, the Studio lost 90 percent of its staff. Worse was to come. Russian courts in 1991 transferred the puppet division, which had used the Church of the Savior on the Sands on the Arbat, back to the Orthodox Church (the church is famous as the background to Vasilii Polenov's 1878 painting *Moscow Backyard*). As the studio and the Soviet system crumbled together, chaos reigned among the animators, many of whom were literally thrown out of their workplace after the cathedral returned to the Church. In the early 1990s a Cossack squad even broke into the church and destroyed some of the "devilish puppets" within.[9]

From there the story gets even darker. In 1992 the director of Soiuzmul′tfil′m, Stanislav Rozhkov, signed an agreement with Films by Jove, a U.S. company run by Russian émigré actor Oleg Vidov and his wife, Joan Borsten. Rozhkov granted the American company rights to over five hundred Soiuzmul′tfil′m productions in return for 40 percent of profits. Films by Jove restored many of the studio's classics and released them on DVD. Soiuzmul′tfil′m received no money—Films by Jove consistently claimed they earned no net profits and the ten-year-lease agreement announced in 1989 expired in the meantime. Soiuzmul′tfil′m now has its own fund and has claimed ownership over all of its Soviet-era productions,[10] but its 1990s experience with early market capitalism continues to be a source of shame and anger. The oligarch Alisher Usmanov eventually bought back all of the Films by Jove restorations in September 2007, declaring them to be national treasures.[11]

But that gets a little ahead of the tale. In 1992, Sergei Skuliabin became director of the studio and turned it into part battlefield, part criminal enterprise.[12] Although legally elected, Skuliabin soon used his position to take over the entire studio and profit from it. His hired thugs beat up opponents and other animators when they were not looting the studios. Georgii Borodin, an animator at the Studio, described the Skuliabin regime in the following way:

> Artistic work at the studio became psychologically unbearable and impossible. No one had the guarantee that come morning, he would not find his cabinet broken open, and his worktable cleared. Similar cases became almost a regular occurrence during the years of occupation. Animators who worked in other studios refused to believe the tales about the working conditions at the stolen Soiuzmul′tfil′m. Imagine, for example, that you are the manager of one of the sections of the studio and you come to your work space and see several unidentified youths there engaged in packing away several large boxes with studio puppets to send them to an undisclosed location "at the command of Skuliabin." And when you, along with the director of the puppet department (who is, by the way, responsible for the safekeeping of these puppets) keep them from being

> stolen by hiding them in a studio room which is inaccessible to these men, you are officially charged with attempted robbery.[13]

Skuliabin also closed the studio for "fire inspections" in order to have his men loot materials, removed archival materials and equipment for "restoration" (they disappeared), and used the new company credit card for personal gain. Akop Kirakosian, the current director of the studio, appropriately described the Skuliabin era as "the time of the bandits." In 1997, the studio union voted Skuliabin out and Ernest Rakhimov in. Skuliabin's men beat Rakhimov with a pipe and fractured his skull. Luckily, he survived and oversaw Skuliabin's eventual removal. At the end of the decade, Skuliabin fled to America before the MVD, FSB, and Interpol caught him.[14] Needless to say, Soiuzmul´tfil´m did not make many animated films in the 1990s.

Yeltsin's 1999 decree ended this mess and made Soiuzmul´tfil´m into a state unitary enterprise. By 2006, the studio no longer employed animators but hired freelancers. The previous year, the studio released six shorts and Kirakosian talked about "getting out of the pit" caused by events of the 1990s.[15] Still, the events of the 1990s effectively killed Soiuzmul´tfil´m and its traditions. The resurrection of Russian animation had to come from other places. Moreover, it needed new techniques and new heroes.

PRINCE VLADIMIR UNITES POST-SOVIET RUSSIA

The story of *Prince Vladimir* could also stand in for the story of Russian cinema's revival. While Soiuzmul´tfil´m experienced its agonies, some animators saw other avenues for success. Once again Russia's past guided the way. Conceived in the 1990s, the film seemingly beat the economic odds and finally saw the light of day in February 2006, becoming the highest-grossing Russian animated film at that time (it trailed only *Madagascar* for the overall lead). Along the way the film explored history, used Hollywood-style animation techniques mixed with a "Russian" artistic touch, got blessed first by Dmitrii Likhachev and then by Patriarch Aleksei II, and was named by Vladimir Putin a "national film" during his first year in office. The film's website provides the account of the film's miraculous history:

> In 1997, the first steps were taken to create a film about the foundation of the ancient Russian state, one of the most complicated and mysterious periods of our history.
>
> What were those times like, what was Russia like in the tenth century, what kind of people lived in those immense spaces, what were the ceremonies, clothes, what was the atmosphere—these were the questions to answer. And the personality of Prince Vladimir was the most interesting thing. How did he manage to make his path from devastation to creation, to unite the people and to play a key role in history? The film is about his choice, his path, and about the feat in the name of a great goal.
>
> The same year, the characters and backgrounds were first designed and the literary scenario of *Prince Vladimir* was started. Initially, Andrei Dobrunov had to act both as a scriptwriter and a graphic designer. Then, the first group of graphic designers was formed who later on became the film's art directors.
>
> The project became interesting for many people. In particular, it was noted that the historical figure of Prince Vladimir had not yet been given proper attention both in feature films and in animation.
>
> In February 1999, the project was supported and completely approved of by D. S. Likhachev. The development of the theme was to a great extent assisted by V. L. Ianin, who has been continuously leading the archeological expedition in Novgorod the Great for many years.
>
> On December 16, 1998, the project was blessed by Patriarch of Moscow and All Russia Aleksei II—a first in the history of Russian animation.
>
> The film was launched into production in November 1999 at the Solnechny Dom Studio, which was specially organized for this project.
>
> In 2000, the project received official governmental support.
>
> On April 7, 2000, the first presentation of the Prince Vladimir was held in the Russian Cultural Fund.
>
> The same year, the project was given the status of a national film.[16]

The production of *Prince Vladimir* alone tells quite a story. The studio that produced it, Solnechny Dom, is the creation of Andrei Dobrunov, who had longed to make an animated film about the earliest episodes of Russian history. He founded the studio in 1999 without any real hopes. Over the next five years he received $5 million from a private investor and 120 artists who also believed in the revival of Russian animation. Along the way, Dobrunov played the political game very successfully, convincing a host of important figures that Russia needed animated history. Dmitrii Likhachev, venerable scholar of ancient Russian history and popularly perceived to be one of Russia's consciences, was the first to lend his approval (Likhachev had helped to oust Skuliabin from Soiuzmul′tfil′m). Valentin Ianin, an archeologist who has been working in Novgorod for decades, also did the same. Their support paved the way for Aleksei II to bless the film, which gave Dobrunov the opportunity to launch his studio. The support of so many big names helped Dobrunov to gather the funds necessary to make the film. "Persuading people was colossal work," he said. "I had to recruit people and went to Europe to meet our artists. Not everybody believed we'd get the financing."[17]

A key meeting in this process took place on April 7, 2000, when Dobrunov, Iurii Batanin (the film's original director; Iurii Kulakov would eventually take over), and several of the artists signed up for the film—Riabovichev among them—met with the Moscow Patriarchy. Bishop Bronnitskii Tikhon, the chairman of the Patriarchy's publishing house, met with the group and stressed that the film "should not contain violations of historical truth, theological principles, or Orthodox principles." Archpriest Artemii Vladimirov, present at the meeting, recounted how the film's creators had not given into temptation, explaining that they had met with a "Hollywood multiplexer" who wanted to do the film using animal characters for the historic figures. Father Artemii reported that "he was glad" when Dobrunov insisted on historical veracity, a move that led the Patriarch to grant his blessing. The meeting further confirmed that the film could act as an important historical agent. Likhachev's words provided further proof that the film would be an important one (he died in September 1999): "The film's concept, sketches and scenes from it show that at the present there is the complete possibility that through the means of an animated cartoon the events surrounding the baptism of Rus′ can be captivatingly and fully depicted without distorting historical truth. The value of this film cannot be overestimated." Dobrunov followed Likhachev's report with a statement that the film would allow children to "feel a little of the atmosphere of tenth- and eleventh-century Rus′."[18]

What about this atmosphere and how the filmmakers attempted to convey it onscreen? The website states the following:

> This film is about the ancient times, dating back as far as a thousand years—when the capital town Kyiv and wealthy Novgorod, strong Minsk and woody Murom, northern Ladoga and Tmutarakan at the Black Sea, and other many towns were parts of a united state: Kyivan Rus′. The Russians spoke the same language and the Russian land was riled by the princely family of the Riurikovich.

> We would like to tell you about Prince Vladimir Sviatoslavovich and praise his glorious doings and feats of arms. Some judge Prince Vladimir strictly for his proud temper and reproach him for his sins of youth and effeminacy. But, in the people's memory and in Russian epics he has remained as a wise and just ruler—Vladimir the Red Sun. The Prince was generous with entertainment. The people sang songs about his feasts, when the tables groaned with meals and drinks. And for the diseased and weak, the food was delivered all over the town by carts. The Prince stinted with nothing for his retinue; he asked for their advice regarding the state system, laws, campaigns, and accords. Vladimir established peace with the neighbors in the west and strengthened the defense against the combative Pechenegs in the south.
>
> And for the main deed of his life—the Christianization of Russia in 988—the Russian Orthodox Church named Prince Vladimir Saint in the rank of Apostle "for zeal in the Christian faith." However, nobody knows what this conversion into Christianity cost for Prince Vladimir Sviatoslavovich, who had been bred and matured in paganism, in terms of his thoughts and endeavor of soul. Against the background of the ever-present struggle between Russia and the Steppe, a saving transfiguration of the soul was going on inside Prince Vladimir's heart and mind.
>
> This is what the film is about.[19]

Prince Vladimir therefore attempts, in the schema established by Anthony D. Smith, to provide both a myth of Russian national origins (how Russia as a nation originated, developed, and fostered a national community) and a myth of regeneration (how to return to the previous ideals of nationhood in a time of crisis).[20]

As far as a plot, the film attempts to tell the tale of how Vladimir, prince of Novgorod, became the grand prince of Kyivan Rus′ and eventually united his realm by adopting Orthodoxy as the state religion in 988. Details of the historical Vladimir are sketchy at best; what we know tends to come from chronicles written by Orthodox monks at least one hundred years after Vladimir died. Historians agree about some facts. Vladimir was the third son of Sviatoslav, the grand prince of Kyivan Rus′. Prince Sviatoslav placed Vladimir on the throne of Novgorod, the oldest and northernmost city in the realm. When Sviatoslav died, a power struggle between three brothers—Oleg, Iaropolk, and Vladimir—ensued. After Iaropolk's forces killed Oleg, Vladimir fled to Scandinavia and gathered some forces. In peace talks with his brother, Vladimir ordered his assassination and became the grand prince in 980. To shore up his hold on the throne, Vladimir built a number of idols and temples dedicated to the gods most of his subjects worshipped.

The other event that Vladimir took part in was the adoption of Orthodoxy as the state religion. The chroniclers tend to present the story of Vladimir's personal conversion and the Christianization of Rus′ as a miraculous one where the prince sent missionaries to study the religions of the region. The group that traveled to Constantinople dazzled Vladimir's envoys so much that they "knew not whether they were in heaven or on earth." Accordingly, Vladimir converted to the "true faith," destroyed the idols around Kyiv, and built the Tithe Church in the center of his new palace complex on Starokievskaia Hill. Historians over the years have greeted this miraculous story with a great deal of skepticism. The holy Vladimir of the chroniclers, later canonized by the Orthodox Church, does not seem to be the same Vladimir who ruthlessly took power. Instead, most historians see Vladimir's conversion as a political tactic designed to ally Rus′ with the vast Byzantine Empire in order to protect his realm from raids by Pecheneg nomads and as a means to provide an ideology that would help him rule. When Vladimir married Anna, the daughter of the Byzantine Emperor, he sealed this alliance.[21]

Released with the slogan "It's your history," the film adapts Vladimir's story and introduces sorcerers to it. One of the central characters to the plot is Krivzha, formerly a student of Russian sages but whose thirst for personal power led him to choose evil. He betrays his people to the Pechenegs. In making these choices, Krivzha helps to bring discord to lands that formerly lived according to law. The chaos caused by the sorcerer explains Vladimir's actions. The Novgorod prince does not murder his brother; instead, Krivzha forges a letter from Iaropolk that enrages Vladimir. As Vladimir fights his brothers' forces, he learns of Krivzha's treachery, only for one of his warriors to kill Iaropolk on Krivzha's orders. Thus, the film absolves Prince Vladimir of his medieval power grab—the death of his brother came not because he was a fairly typical medieval ruler who wanted the Kyivan throne, but because a sorcerer tricked him and his men.

The sorcery as history also extends to the baptism of Russia. This part of the story is told through the eyes of Aleksha, a young boy enslaved by Krivzha after his family is killed by the Pechenegs. He eventually is freed by a Greek, baptized as an Orthodox Christian, and taken to Constantinople, which allows young Aleksha to be present when

Vladimir's envoys arrive and give the Emperor and Anna a flutelike instrument that will later cement her love for Vladimir. It is Aleksha, however, who becomes the true bearer of The Word to Russia. When the Greeks journey to Rus′, the Pechenegs attack them and kill Aleksha's rescuer. Before he dies, he saves Aleksha by putting him on a boat and sending him upriver to Vladimir's forces. He also gives the young boy a "holy book" that later will be used to persuade Vladimir to convert to Christianity. Krivzha attempts to persuade Vladimir's men that Aleksha is "*chuzhoi,*" or an "other," but they accept him as a "Russian." Aided by a good and noble holy man, Boian, Aleksha brings Christianity to Russia just as Vladimir defeats Krivzha and his Pecheneg forces. Krivzha's evil deeds "enabl[e] the filmmakers to present pre-Christian Rus as a harmonious paradise lost. Krivzha's desire for power over 'law' brings about a chaos crying out for Christianity."[22] Aleksha's grandfather and Boian also add to the mythmaking. The grandfather tells Aleksha about his trip to Constantinople as a member of Princess Ol′ga's retinue. When the young boy sees the city bathed in heavenly light, he sees what he has already pictured before in his head. As Jeremy Hicks argues, "the discovery of Christianity is shown to be less of a revelation of the unprecedented than a remembering of the familiar."[23] Rus′ as chronicled on screen had always been united, heavenly, and law abiding; only a sorcerer could disrupt this harmony. Boian, for his part, represents a transition between the worship of nature and the worship of the Christian God. At the end of the film, with Vladimir and Orthodoxy triumphant, Boian provides the epilogue: "all return." Pagan Rus′ and Christian Rus′ were populated by the same kind of "good and noble" people.

Voiced by Sergei Bezrukov, who played Fandorin in the first TV adaptation of *Azazel′,* Prince Vladimir is a serious, masculine, saintly hero for young people to emulate. Bezrukov claimed that "not to work on this film would have been a sin," for it is "a contemporary Orthodox project." He did not only see his work as that of a believer, he also saw it as the work of a patriot. "You will recall the films *Lion King* and *Beauty and the Beast,*" he told an interviewer. "Here we did not have this level of animated films. But we are not worse! Our Russia is by no means worse! Here, in this case, we can prove to everyone and to ourselves that we can work at the highest level, we can conform to European standards, to European levels, but with Russian themes."[24] The real patriot game, however, was for the kids: "We are already, honestly speaking, tired of American animated films, from the overabundance of American products. When our children play Pokémon, well, sure this is normal for anyone their age, but I wish they would play something of 'ours [*nashe*].' Now, . . . if they play as if [they were] Prince Vladimir this will be healthy! Our great Russian history now becomes made into animated films and very soon I hope it will be taken up in artistic films." Bezrukov concludes, "Such projects are particularly necessary now in order to raise our spirit to survive under any conditions. Particularly because of contemporary events that are so terrible and tragic, it is necessary that we come together so that our self-consciousness will be at the highest level. So that we will be not separate, but the opposite, we would all unite through our efforts to resist attacks, provocations, and acts of terror."[25] It is hard to imagine a better contemporary spin on Vladimir's mythic appeal to unity.

One particularly important means that animators used to recreate the past for the present was to draw familiar traditions, landscapes, and other customs. In this task, the film's animators both resurrected and retrofitted the past. The film opens with ancient cartoons of sorts, the illustrations from the Primary Chronicle, the source of information about the historical Vladimir. The animated backdrops of Slavic towns, which were created using 3-D animation techniques, look like the towns displayed on the illustrations. So, too, do the clothes. If these animations represent a form of resurrecting the historic look of the tenth century, the opening scenes also retrofit the past. Early in the film Vladimir celebrates Maslenitsa; the celebration could very well be from Mikhalkov's *Barber of Siberia*. Mead flows, *bubliki* are passed, and revelers eat blini and listen to folk music. Elsewhere the film introduces historical aspects of Kyivan Rus′: the *druzhina* (a prince's retinue), the *veche* (a town assembly, seen by some historians as the earliest Russian democratic institution), and the rule of "law" (later adapted into Iaroslav the Wise's famous eleventh-century *Russkaia pravda*). Dobrunov hired a host of consultants for the film, among them ethnomusicologist Sergei Starostin. Starostin included period instruments such as the *zhaleika* (a flute) to enhance the historical atmosphere of the film. As he claimed, his role was to "weave into the cloth of animation the earliest and most original musical genres preserved in Russian cultural traditions."[26] Other original songs featured vocals by Nikolai Rastorguev, the lead singer of Liube, and Natal′ia Kniazhinskaia, formerly the leader of the group Magic Pump (and later a writer for t.A.T.u.). In its music and in its use of history, *Prince Vladimir* fused the old and new, resurrecting and retrofitting the past as a means of animating values for the future.

ANDREI'S ANIMATION

The chief animator of the onscreen history was Andrei Riabovichev. Born in Apsheronsk, about two hours from the Black Sea, Riabovichev is a self-taught artist. At the age of sixteen, just before Gorbachev became first secretary, he enrolled in the Moscow State Forest University. He spent five years there interrupted in part so that he could do his army service. He graduated in 1991, just before the Soviet Union dissolved. Riabovichev, who had always loved artistic work and had a natural talent, "unexpectedly got into animation" that year as an "in-betweener" working at the Klassika studio.[27] He took a class in animation, was hooked, and became a character designer for the company. As a self-taught animator who first trained in post-Soviet Russia, Riabovichev drew on Soviet animation traditions, but just as significantly on Western models. The influx of Hollywood animated features and cartoons from across the planet (Japanese anime, popular art from the world of fantasy, and *Lilo and Stitch,* for example) gave Riabovichev a diverse palette from which to draw inspiration.

It was in his position as a new animation artist, in 1998, that Riabovichev met Andrei Dobrunov. The creator of *Prince Vladimir* had seen some of Riabovichev's work and asked him to do some sketches for a project on ancient Rus′. His initial work halted with the August 1998 ruble collapse. The following year, the two Andreis met and Dobrunov told Riabovichev that he had redesigned the project in order to tell the

Sketches for *Prince Vladimir. Courtesy of Andrei Riabovichev.*

tale of Prince Vladimir. "To be honest, I was not enthusiastic at first," Riabovichev recalled. "It seemed to me that this project was boring and that it would be better to make happier films, not historical cinema."[28] Nevertheless, Riabovichev agreed to draw characters for the film and in 2000 participated in the presentations to the Moscow Patriarchy. In the end, Riabovichev became converted to Dobrunov's mission to create the "most serious work of animation in the Russian market."[29]

In order to create the historical atmosphere necessary for the film, Riabovichev turned to Russian artistic classics. "When I worked on the film," he recounts, "I immersed myself in books about Russian artists like I never had done before in my life." He credits Mikhail Nesterov, Viktor Vasnetsov, Nikolai Roerich, Il′ia Repin, Vasilii Vereshchagin, Mikhail Vrubel′, Ivan Kramskoi, Vasilii Polenov, and Ivan Shishkin for inspiration. Later Riabovichev even created a blog devoted to their work and the work of other Russian artists.[30] In a sense, the look of old Kyiv looks a lot like their reimagined pasts: Vladimir uses a boat lifted from Roerich's 1901 *Guests from Overseas* and inhabits a landscape that looks like his sets for the opera *Prince Igor.* The landscapes captured on screen could be Shishkin's or Repin's. The battle scenes resemble Vasnetsov's famous bogatyrs while Boian bears a striking resemblance to a figure in Nesterov's *Visiting a Sorcerer* (1888). In short, Riabovichev's Rus′ resembles the imagined Golden Age painted by Russian artists of the nineteenth century.[31] Although the film's historical consultants vetted the drawings,[32] *Prince Vladimir* is as much a resurrection of that nationalist artistic vision as it is a resurrection of the tenth century.

Regardless, Andrei's animation revives a pre-Soviet artistic tradition and marries it with both Soviet-era and Western-style animation techniques. Riabovichev and the other animators who work for Solnechnyi Dom blended a host of styles and made animated features that explicitly adapt Hollywood conventions—no éclair is used. Whereas Riabovichev borrows from Russian painting and Western animation, Dobrunov is a graduate of the Kishinev Art Academy. Iurii Kulakov and Iurii Batanin both trained at Soiuzmul′tfil′m, and Grigorii Lozinskii, who did the landscapes and historical backdrops, graduated from the Moscow Architectural Institute around the time Riabovichev finished up at the Moscow State Forest University. Dobrunov, like his hero Prince Vladimir, united them all in an attempt to make a patriotic picture for contemporary children. As Riabovichev admits,

> I thought about the patriotic aspect of the film only after it appeared on screen. I heard that entire school classes went to see it, substituting their lessons for those of the film. This happened everywhere, both in Moscow and in distant villages. This speaks volumes about the film's patriotism. One girl even wrote me a letter, which stated that she walked around and cried in the rain for two hours after watching the film, and that for the first time she was proud that she was Russian. Patriotism in Russia today is increasing and our film is part of its rise. But patriotism is also a complex question and it is possible to say a great deal about it.[33]

Riabovichev's sentiments echo those of his boss. Dobrunov in particular wanted his film to speak to Russia's youth today, for "many lack an interest in their history." This state is an "unfortunate one," for Dobrunov believes the "patriotic education of our children" is essential for Russia's future.[34] Vladimir's story is an important step in this direction, for it "is about both spiritual and physical enlightenment."[35] Prince Vladimir gave up paganism and fratricidal fighting for Orthodoxy and unity, in other words, and Russians today could learn the same lessons.

ANIMATED HISTORY: VLADIMIR, MEL′NITSA, AND RESURRECTED PASTS

Prince Vladimir united Russians onscreen, but off screen he did not succeed in this effort. Writing for the online journal *Kinokadr,* Irina Kozel has some praise for the beautiful fairy tale world animated on screen but dismisses its "disastrous fantasy history" lesson. She reminds readers that initial trailers for the film proclaimed the film would be released around the time of the 2004 presidential elections and thought the "Vladimir" depicted onscreen was closer to Putin than to the prince of Kyiv. "Whoever wants to learn more about the historical truth," she concludes, should read works of history instead.[36] The online posters who commented on Kozel's views largely agreed with her: "It's a very beautiful and very empty cartoon" wrote the first. Dar′ia Pechorina of *Nashfilm* also praised the "splendid drawings" of Riabovichev and others, yet compared the scenes to a *lubok* and concluded that the "unfunny patriotic" cartoon paled in comparison to Hollywood features.[37] Respondents to her review disagreed sharply: for some it was "propaganda" and "deceitful" while others praised it as "teaching patriotism" and "love for your neighbor." *Time Out*'s reviewer, Dar′ia Serebrianaia, echoed the others, writing that *Prince Vladimir*'s "problem is not in how it is drawn . . . or in its historical improvisations," but in the "religious undercurrents" and its ultimate lack of humor.[38]

K. Tarkhanova summed up the sentiments of most critics: "Apparently, the secret of the Russian soul as manifested in the art of animation is in the complete absence of a sense of humor." Moreover, its claim to be a "national blockbuster" that was "different from others [Hollywood's]" is true because *Prince Vladimir* is "propaganda about spirituality and state power."[39] Apparently many Orthodox believers felt similarly: *Neskuchnyi sad,* an online "Orthodox life" journal (the literal translation of the title is "Not boring garden"), published an article about the historical Vladimir followed by its estimation of the film. In the end, Father Vasilii Sekachev, who wrote the piece, dismissed the attempt to depict Vladimir as a believer as "a fraud" and concluded "Russia's spiritual father must be shown differently and in a more complicated fashion."[40]

Despite its tepid reviews, *Prince Vladimir* proved that animated history could produce box-office returns. By 2008, animated history boomed.[41] The Solnechnyi Dom team released *Rolli and the Elf,* a fantasy set in Scandinavia, at the end of 2007.[42] Elsewhere, fairy-tale fantasy history mostly set in Vladimir's era dominated the new wave of Russian animated features. Valerii Ugarov, a former Soiuzmul′tfil′m director, completed two folkloric features before his death in 2007 (he also helmed the 2003 animated version of *The Nutcracker*). *Baba Ezhka and Co.* (2006) and *The New Adventures of Baba Ezhka* (2008) both reimagined Russian fairy tales by turning villains into heroes and vice versa. The eponymous heroine of both is the friendlier granddaughter of Baba Iaga.[43] In October 2008, *The Adventures of Alenushka and Yerioma* became the first-ever Russian 3-D animated film. It ups the ante of previous animated history by creating a musical comedy set to Russian fairy tales. It too is set in ancient Rus′ and it too uses this pseudohistorical setting to combat Dreamworks and Pixar creations.[44] Finally, Soiuzmul′tfill′m mounted a comeback of sorts and finished *Gofmaniada,* based on E. T. A. Hoffmann's tales and using only puppet animation with no special effects. The concept and art design is done by Mikhail Shemiakin; Kirakosian is the producer.

The St. Petersburg company Mel′nitsa, which was also founded in 1999, carried on patriotic work similar to that of Dobrunov's. Partnered with the STB studio, Mel′nitsa released its first animated feature on December 23, 2004. Titled *Alesha Popovich and Tugarin the Serpent,* the film made only $1.7 million back on its $4 million budget, but generated a great deal of press coverage that argued whether it was "Russian" enough (it featured a talking horse that drew comparisons to Eddie Murphy's donkey in *Shrek*). It became the first of the studio's "Three Bogatyrs" animated films, based on folk tales set in Vladimir's Rus′ and popularly imagined by Viktor Vasnetsov's 1898 painting *Bogatyrs.* Alesha (on the right in the painting) is best known for the folktale about his encounter with the monster Tugarin, the subject of this film. In the tale, Alesha attends a feast held by Prince Vladimir in Kyiv. When the monster Tugarin sits between Vladimir and his wife, Anna, Alesha provokes him into fighting a duel and defeats him. The film has Alesha spar with his foe again in ancient Rostov.[45] The second film in the series, *Dobrynia Nikitich and The Serpent Gorynych* follows the fortunes of the second medieval knight turned folk hero (on the left in the painting). It has the eponymous hero fight the dragon he is most famous for slaying in folk tales while also saving Prince Vladimir's niece from a kidnapper. Billed as a "heroic blockbuster," *Dobrynia Nikitich* premiered two weeks after *Prince Vladimir* and earned $3.5 million at the box office.[46] *Il′ia Muromets and the Nightingale Robber,* the last of the trilogy, provided an animated version of the most famous bogatyr of all (he is even canonized for his mythic defense of Vladimir's realm). The animated onscreen version instead valorizes Il′ia's "perseverance, good will and knowledge of popular customs rather than his physical strength."[47] By contrast, the film shows Prince Vladimir to be "a corrupt, short-sighted and manipulative ruler."[48] Opening on December 28, 2007, the tale of the epic hero shattered not only *Prince Vladimir*'s characterizations but also its box-office record; it earned $9.7 million.[49]

The trilogy combines Russian folk stories with a style of humor borrowed from Hollywood animation such as *Shrek* or Pixar films: the jokes are multi-layered and can be enjoyed by children and adults alike. *Il′ia Muromets,* for example, contains parodies of *The Matrix, Terminator,* and Russian gangster films such as *Bimmer.* The rhetoric surrounding Mel′nitsa's animated films echoed that surrounding *Prince Vladimir.* Konstantin Bronzit, the director of *Alesha* and a pupil of Soiuzmul′tfil′m's famous artist Fedor Khitruk, declared that his film was an antidote to the 1990s cultural chaos and one that provided a "national" focus for children in need of remembering Russian folklore.[50] While he admitted that Russian animation learns "like a child, through imitation," he did separate the difference between American and Russian animation by declaring that "they make money, we make cinema."[51] Bronzit's views may sound somewhat Soviet, but the Mel′nitsa brand nevertheless earned a lot of cash. The animation studio learned the Disney trick of promotional tie-ins to earn more than ticket sales: Teremok, the fast-food pancake stands, sold *Alesha* treats; and the Moscow publisher Egmont put out children's books related to the films. Bookstore chains and toy store chains in Russia sold all sorts of figurines, books, notebooks, and other products that bore the three bogatyrs on them.[52]

Reactions to the trilogy tended to be more positive than those to *Prince Vladimir* (users on *Kinopoisk* scored them 7.9, 7.8, and 7.6 vs. *Vladi-*

mir's 6.6). "Mikyno" posted that *Alesha* captured "the Russian soul" in a way Disney cartoons cannot, while "Zeke" wrote that "for domestic animation it is very good" and that "its humor will be intelligible only to Russians." Only "Fetti" saw it as "a Hollywood forgery" that used "simplistic American techniques" (yet still gave it a 6).[53] *Dobrynia Nikitich* produced similar reactions. "Vil" posted that while the film borrows heavily on Western animation ideas, this adaptation should not cause "pessimism" but be viewed as "a transition period where a foreign culture that we accepted in the 1990s becomes 'our own,' Russian." "The main thing," "Vil" concludes, "is that soon we will not only be enraptured with *Shrek* and *Ice Age, . . .* but with *Dobrynia Nikitin* and his love for our native land."[54] *Il´ia Muromets* posts on the site produced another revealing comment from a user, "UndeR," who spontaneously took his family to see the film while out strolling in Rostov-on-Don. For him, Muromets has "the same value for us as Superman in the USA" and is as significant as "Cheburashka." The film "astonished" him and "returns us to the times when there were no 3-D technologies." It caused "nostalgic feelings" and made him "hope that children today will grow up with such creations and not Superman and Batman." "Balmung" also praised what he saw as its use of "good old Soviet animation techniques that focused on education and not just entertainment."[55] The three bogatyrs, in other words, continued to do their patriotic duty and defend Russian soil from invaders.

Compared to recent Pixar features that depict a new, postfeminist model of masculinity,[56] post-Soviet Russian animated movies present a revived masculine alpha male hero. The three bogatyrs and particularly Prince Vladimir depict a fantastic and historical world in which stereotypes of patriarchy abound—the men have unquestioned authority, their physical strength is central to their identity, and their stoic heroism dominates their personality. As a collective message aimed primarily at children, the resurrected pasts depicted in recent Russian animation dovetail with contemporary concerns about the perceived crisis in masculinity. Judging by the heroes of recent animated history, Russians apparently really do need a man like Vladimir.

In an *Itogi* report, Larisa Maliukova commented that *Prince Vladimir* had started a new wave of Russian animated films. Although these films, she notes, revived a Soviet tradition, "they were also born in the chaotic 1990s," when "spectators had already forgotten about the existence [of animation]." With *Prince Vladimir* (which she calls average), however, a new tradition was born again. "Full-length films," she writes, "became the foundation on which our domestic multi-film industry is built anew." The problem with competing with Hollywood animators on their preferred turf, however, is in the quality. "Our directors dream about making films such as *Shrek* and *Ratatouille,* which are ingenious, emotional, spirited history," Maliukova concludes. "But on our screens appear sluggish and infantile films that are deprived of vivid characters and that have questionable taste. . . . Such as the pathos-inducing *Prince Vladimir.*"[57]

One important voice dissented. Fedor Khitruk, the legendary Soviet animator born in 1917, declared *Prince Vladimir* a return to form. For Khitruk, whose first work appeared in 1938 and perhaps best known for his Soviet adaptations of *Winnie-the-Pooh,* the new animated history successfully combated contemporary (read: American) television programs that "spoil both the tastes and psychology" of children. What Russia needs, according to him, is a return to the old ideals of Soviet animation; namely, "love for your native land." On this front and in terms of its adherence to "classical Soviet animation," Khitruk rates *Prince Vladimir* a triumph.[58]

Plus ça change . . .

Fantasy settings: Kusakova's Galirad.

ELEVEN

The Look of Fantasy

Billed as "the first Slavic fantasy film," Nikolai Lebedev's *Wolfhound* appeared in time for the 2006–07 winter holidays. Based on Mariia Semenova's best-selling novels, *Wolfhound* premiered on over six hundred screens (a new record at the time) and was blasted by some film critics for being a "fairy-tale for the twenty-first century" even as it won praise from some viewers, who called it "our answer to *Lord of the Rings.*" Unlike previous examples of blockbuster history, such as *Turkish Gambit* or *Ninth Company,* which fictionalized actual events from Russia's pasts to appeal to audiences, *Wolfhound* created a fictional past and packaged it as "Slavic history." Central to this attempt to make fantasy history "Russian" was Liudmila Kusakova's work. Kusakova, *Wolfhound's* set designer, had built 1905 Moscow for Karen Shakhnazarov. For Lebedev's film she built a different sort of set, one that turned fantasy history into a commentary on contemporary Russia.

To understand *Wolfhound's* significance, one first has to understand how the fantasy genre developed in Russia. Much like crime fiction had no place in a system in which no crime allegedly existed, fantasy proved anathema to the Soviet state that billed itself as the ultimate fantasy utopia (the folkloristic films of Aleksandr Ptushko that relied on Russian epics and fairy tales were exceptions because they captured the Russocentric element of postwar Soviet life). The genre of fantasy, as Richard Matthews has described it, is one that allows individuals to "enter worlds of infinite possibility" and "evokes wonder, mystery, or magic." Fantasy's function is to create "a sense of the possibility beyond the ordinary, material, rationally predictable world in which we live."[1] Fantasy usually invokes myth, fairy tales, folklore, and in doing so causes consumers to "hesitate" to allow for explanations beyond the ordinary.[2] The Soviet state clearly did not want this kind of hesitation, for the socialist experiment attempted to eliminate the need to dream of infinite possibilities.

As John Bushnell has written, Semenova "is a living embodiment of the genre's history in Russia."[3] Born to a family of scientists in 1958, Semenova graduated from the Leningrad Institute of Aviation Instrumentation in 1982. While a student, Semenova developed an interest in the Vikings and in the Norman invasions after reading a history of 1066. She began to think about writing a novel set in Northern Europe and finished a manuscript, *The Lame Blacksmith,* while still a student. It was also as a student that Semenova read Tolkien in the original English. Inspired by the conventions of the fantasy genre and by her interest in Nordic sagas, Semenova wrote stories and a novel set in ninth-century Russian lands. None of them were published because editors told her no one was interested in the Norman settlement of Rus′. Instead, they told her she should be writing about the fortieth anniversary of victory in the Great Patriotic War. With the advent of glasnost′, however, the climate for publishing fantasy changed. Semenova published her first work of Russian fantasy in 1989, a collection of stories set in pre-Kyivan times. Her first published novel, *Pelko and the Wolves,* appeared in 1992. That year she took a job with the publisher Severo-Zapad as a translator of fantasy novels. "From this point on," she writes, "the laws of the market economy began to influence my biography." As she immersed herself more and more into fantasy literature, she grew more and more agitated by the "pulp fiction" she translated, mostly about "dragons, elves, and goblins." Should Russians, she asked herself, essentially "eat the same Tolkien sandwich ten times" and thereby not consume "native fantasy"? In particular, Semenova claimed that "the ethnographer within me" was bothered by the lack of a "Russian" fantasy world.[4]

So she decided to become the first Russian fantasy writer. In 1995, Azbuka published *Wolfhound,* a novel set in the pre-Christian past. It

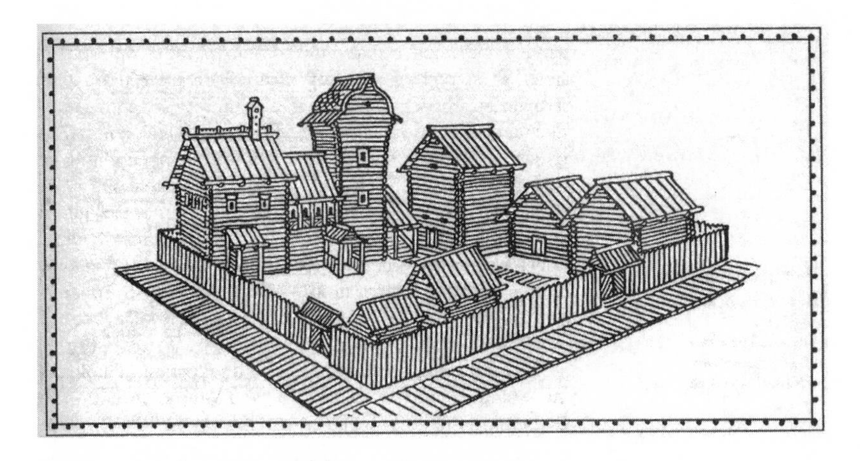

Real fantasy: Reconstruction of Novgorod buildings from Semenova's *My—Slaviane!* (1997).

became an overnight sensation, enjoying similar success to that of Boris Akunin and Sergei Luk′ianenko, the author of the *Watch* novels. By the end of 1997, Semenova had become an industry, having published novels named *Valkyrie, Swan Road, Two Kings, Vikings, Duel with a Dragon,* and a sequel to *Wolfhound.* In *Wolfhound,* Semenova stakes out the parameters of not only a Russian form of fantasy, but also an imaginary pre-Kyivan past, one in which her hero escapes from slavery, trains as a warrior, and fights for the oppressed. He eventually defends a princess in Galirad, a remarkably cosmopolitan trading city, and rescues her from nefarious plots. Her ethnographic interests also led her in 1997 to write and publish *We Are the Slavs!* (*My—Slaviane!*). In this work, Semenova compiled information about customs, living quarters, settlements, family life, laws, weaponry, decorations, and even cultural beliefs about "ours and theirs [*svoi i chuzhoi*]" that early Slavs shared in common. Her "historic" Slavs are remarkably similar to her fantasy Slavs: they tolerate religious diversity and non-Slavs ("others") who do not threaten their dwellings. Semenova's Slavs engage in international trade and build a remarkably sophisticated culture that rests on a firm legal basis.

Unsurprisingly, when the Russian economy recovered in the zero years, directors and studios jumped at the chance to transfer Semenova's world to the big screen. At its most basic level, the cinematic story of *Wolfhound* follows a hero who emerges in a society that needs one, and whose masculine virtues defeat the forces of evil that threaten stability. Set "in the times when gods lived among mortal men and men tried to be equal to gods in strength and power," *Wolfhound* tells the tale of the last survivor of the tribe of Gray Dogs after they are butchered by men led by Zhadoba and Maneater, followers of the goddess Moranna. As he watches his parents die, the young boy learns he will be sent as a slave to work in the mines, where "he'll rot alive." Instead, the boy survives, learns to fight, and eventually wins his freedom after killing his master. The hero (played by Aleksandr Bukharov) takes the name of his oppressor, Wolfhound, and attempts to enact revenge on his tribe's murderers. Wolfhound is joined in this quest by a bat named Torn Wing, a blind soothsayer named Tilorn (Andrei Rudenskii), and a young girl named Niilit (Evgeniia Sviridova). After a series of scrapes, they save Princess Elen′ of Galirad (Oksana Okinshina), a city suffering under a curse placed by followers of Moranna. Wolfhound also acquires a manuscript that Tilorn identifies as the mythic key to the Gates of Heaven, a potentially powerful weapon against Moranna's minions.

Wolfhound and his entourage head to Galirad, a Slavic fantasy village that literally lives under a black cloud. Although Wolfhound has rescued Galirad's Princess, the town is unwelcoming and split by internal fighting. Its residents accuse Wolfhound of being Zhadoba, the beast-like high priest of Moranna, have him arrested, and sentenced to death. Elen′ intervenes and frees him, recruiting him instead as a bodyguard. The primary action of the film follows Elen′, Wolfhound, and the Princess's retinue as they journey to meet Maneater's son, Lord Vinitar, to whom Elen′'s father has promised her in marriage—in order to lift the curse on his town. Wolfhound accompanies Elen′ to continue on his path toward revenge, for he has killed Maneater and wishes to find Zhadoba. In the course of their journey, which is filled with the strange encounters and action sequences one would expect from a fantasy blockbuster, Elen′ falls in love with Wolfhound. After one particularly harrowing experience, Elen′ explains that she holds the secret to Moranna's current imprisonment and then attempts to seduce her hero, telling him, "I want a son, not from the groom I've never seen, but from you, Wolfhound." Although his desire to repopulate his tribe is great, Wolfhound's personal honor is stronger and he resists Elen′'s pleas.

The attempt to marry off Elen′ is part of an elaborate plot that involves her brother, Prince Luchezar (Igor′ Petrenko). Luchezar is in cahoots with Zhadoba and together they want to wake the goddess Moranna from her slumber and ensure that she makes good on an old promise to enslave humanity and reward her priests. In order to bring about this hell on earth, they need the key to Heaven's Gate and a sacrifice, one who holds the secret to Moranna's earthly defeat. Luchezar is willing to supply his blood relative, Elen′, in return for the promise of power. While the entire traveling party is resting, Luchezar poisons Wolfhound and allows Zhadoba to attack, kidnapping Elen′. Having barely survived, Wolfhound disguises himself in time to prevent Elen′'s sacrifice. Luchezar, however, manages to use the key and open the path for Moranna's return. Faced with the possibility of a pagan judgment day, Wolfhound appeals to the Thunderstorm God in the name of the "good people" and receives a magic sword (which looks suspiciously like a Star Wars lightsaber) to defeat the forces of evil. With his triumph, Wolfhound also wins Elen′, for Vinitar gives her up to her true love.

Despite (or maybe because of) its contrived plot, *Wolfhound* cleaned up at the box office, grossing more than $17 million in its first two weeks, which more than covered its expensive $12 million price tag. Debuting as "the first film of the new year" on December 28, 2006, it eventually earned $20 million at the box office. Most Russian critics had a field day blasting its plot as one borrowed from *Lord of the Rings, Star Wars,* and *Conan the Barbarian,* but its billing as the "first Slavic fantasy" makes it an important film in Russian cinematic history. *Wolfhound* is the first major visual version of the homegrown fantasy genre discussed above. As John Bushnell has perceptively written, the boom in pre-Kyivan fantasy literature is distinctive because the era is "an empty vessel," for "so little is known about the East Slavs in the ninth century and earlier that there are scarcely any constraints on the imagination."[5] These "pre-histories" provide "what is entirely lacking in the historical record: a culture with complex political structures and a long written tradition."[6] What *Wolfhound* represents is an even more popular version of this fabulous history—Wolfhound himself is meant to be a timeless hero, providing contemporary audiences with both a historical lineage and a self-definition of Russianness from the pre-Kyivan past.

Several scenes from the film provide important elements to this fantastic usable history. After being released from near death in Galirad, Wolfhound encounters a public humiliation that threatens to become a lynching. A young man clutching a book is accused by a fat charlatan of loving "books that he calls holy." The charlatan and his hired mercenary aim to prove that the young captive's beliefs are hollow and that "words of false prophets won't protect him." Unless the young man, Evrikh (Artem Semakin), recants and "accepts the true gods—the Twin gods," he will remain a slave and meet his death. Wolfhound, after listening to this diatribe, intervenes and saves Evrikh. Arguing with the fat man about faith, Wolfhound asserts, "I believe in my gods and I don't offend other gods."

Another fantasy family value appears in one of the odder episodes as the group travels to meet Vinitar. They happen upon a backwoods tribe in the Land of the Kharuks. Led by Great Karil, mother of the Forest Berry Tribe, the townsmen and women are in the process of drowning an outsider for witchcraft. The witch's crime is that she cursed Karil's grandson with feebleness. As Wolfhound sees it, however, the "witch" helped to save the baby in childbirth, and although he initially vows not to intervene in local matters, his outrage at this injustice wins out and he saves the woman. Much like his decision later not to sleep with Elen′, Wolfhound's innate sense of justice proves correct, and the "witch" joins the retinue in its journey.

Part of the fantasy-as-usable-past element to the film also rests in the constant references to fate, particularly Wolfhound's. According to the strict social hierarchies that govern the fictional society, one's fate is determined by one's rank. A slave like Wolfhound, in other words, will always be a slave. Throughout the film, however, Wolfhound and those around him claim that it may be possible to "change one's fate." While encamping just before Elen′'s kidnapping, the woman Wolfhound rescued sings a *bylina* of a boy, born a slave, who frees himself from the Diamond Mountain mines by defeating the "fiercest slave master" to "regain his freedom." As the singer claims, her tale "tells that anyone can change his fate." She turns to Wolfhound and states, "This song was about you."

Wolfhound, whose exploits have thus become part of fantasy folklore, accomplishes this seemingly impossible feat again when he defeats Moranna. At the end, Tilorn exclaims, "Wolfhound! You changed destiny! Fate has no power over you. You make your own fortune!"

A make-believe Russian hero from an invented past who is cosmopolitan, religiously tolerant, morally upright, a defender of the downtrodden, a vanquisher of evil, and a masculine man of the people who can change his own destiny may seem unbelievable, but as far as expressing the desires of the society that produced this fable, an essential function of fantasy,[7] these attributes are hardly the worst imaginable. Leonid Butiakov's popular fantasy series presents a contrasting fantasy world. Butiakov followed on the heels of Sememova's success and published several fantasy novels in the 1990s. His hero, Vladigor, is a Slavic prince who fights evil with the help of more conventional fantasy elements—good sorcerers, magic trinkets, and a powerful sword. Vladigor's world is also a Russo-Slavic one, populated by people and gods that draw more explicitly on pre-Kyivan history (the gods are Perun, Dazhbog, and others from this historical period). More significantly, Vladigor's world is constantly surrounded by enemies and whose culture is under threat from within. His primary foe, Triglav, lives outside of the Slavic world. He fights with warriors that have Germanic and Turkic names. Triglav and his minions also attempt to destroy Vladigor's Union of Fraternal Principalities (an earlier version of what would become Kyivan Rus′) from within, by casting spells that corrupt language and by inciting non-Slavic minorities to clamor for equal rights. Butiakov's fantasy history not only retrofits pre-Kyivan history as a similar world to that imagined by postcommunist nationalists, it also offers thinly veiled references to the Soviet collapse. Even if a reader misses these references, as Bushnell notes, "we are [still] left with an explicitly Slavic world threatened from the West and South."[8] Wolfhound's world and worldview, by contrast, present a prehistory as a more tolerant present, one that does not replicate the wishes of contemporary Russian chauvinists.[9]

Nikolai Lebedev, the film's director, certainly sees *Wolfhound*'s significance as one that dissolves the distance between the pre-Kyivan past and the present. Nikita Mikhalkov targeted Lebedev's 1997 horror film *Snake Source* in his infamous montage presentation on the pernicious effects of *chernukha* during his May 1998 speech to the Russian Filmmakers' Union.[10] Mikhalkov called for dark films such as *Snake Source* to be replaced by films with "new positive heroes" that Russian audiences could relate to. Lebedev heeded the call, first in the form of his 2002 blockbuster, *Star,* which initiated the wave of World War II cinema, and then in *Wolfhound.* Although he admitted, "I never loved the fantasy genre, even as a kid," he saw an opportunity in Semenova's world: "History does interest me, and [*Wolfhound*] allowed me the possibility to design a new era, a new national hero who knows how to distinguish good from evil."[11] Lebedev argues that Semenova "wrote the novel by relying on national mythology" and could therefore serve as a good source of education for audiences. Apparently Lebedev took Mikhalkov's criticism to heart, stating that he turned to fantasy history because the success of TV shows such as *Brigade* and movies like *Bimmer* depressed him: "Why do I live in a society where the most desirable heroes are villains?" he asked.[12] The key to combat this cinematic disease, Lebedev clearly articulated, was the blockbuster, for only it could reach a mass audience.[13]

Lebedev's hero is meant to be an answer to the films that depressed him. Wolfhound represents a positive hero for the present that also inhabits a familiar landscape. *Wolfhound's* world is therefore built to be recognizably Russian. Semenova describes Galirad as an early version of Novgorod or Kyiv, a vital trade site where peoples from all over the world mingle. The town spawned phrases such as "all roads lead to Galirad" and "language is taken to Galirad."[14] On Galirad's streets walked "people of different countries and different beliefs." The city's significance also rests on its courts and rule of law, a necessary structure to keep peace in such a diverse locale.[15]

Filmed at an expensive outdoor set at Mosfil′m Studios and on location in Slovakia, *Wolfhound* the film attempted to make Semenova's pre-Kyivan Slavic world real. The centerpiece was the invented town of Galirad. Liudmila Kusakova's set fused wooden Russian architecture and peasant *izbas* to reinforce visually the outfitting of history that the film's story creates (the set is now part of the Mosfil′m tour, along with Kusakova's other imaginary Russia, the 1905 Moscow set). As media outlets reported, the wood used for the set came from ancient Russian cities such as Riazan′, Pskov, and Vologda. The result was that Kusakova oversaw "the building . . . of a new city. It literally grew not each day, but hour by hour. The construction, which astonished even the most experienced professionals by its scale and its careful execution, grew before the eyes of the oldest domestic movie studio's inhabitants. Timbered houses appeared one after the other, streets with planked pavements surrounded them, and squares paved by rounded wooden blocks made from tree trunks. Every day the high city walls appeared and made into reality Liudmila Kusakova's ideas. She created this fantastic city: Galirad."[16]

Kusakova commented about her role in creating the look of Russian fantasy,

> Fantasy arises from something. Since this is fantasy, it is possible to create a little temporal and stylistic mix, but it is most important that it looks nice, and that it is pleasant to film. I was attracted to the fact that these are old logs. But old logs have already been painted vividly. Therefore they must not be painted here. But drawings we have from recorded history also won't work here. This scenery harmonizes recorded and living history. The wood warms the soul.[17]

In a *Salon* piece, Iulia Sakharova praises *Wolfhound's* set for its "practical" and "artistic" sides. In the former case, the city, "built with wood from all over Russia," is carefully planned and "corresponds both to the logic of a drama and the fantasy genre." In the latter sense, Sakharova quotes Kusakova, who stated that she added a special gray tree color to her buildings in order to capture "the sensation of anxiety, of encroaching evil yet simultaneous, heroic enthusiasm."[18] Ultimately, though, Kusakova claims that "the spectator appreciates the art director only when he will not take note of it," advocating a view that the best possible set is "organic" to the film narrative.[19]

Kusakova's claims notwithstanding, *Wolfhound's* sets conform more to arguments put forth by C. S. Tashiro, one of the few scholars who studies set design. Moving beyond the taxonomy established by Charles and Mirella Affron that views sets on a scale from "denotation" (largely invisible) to "artifice" (highly visible and more significant for the film's impact), Tashiro argues that sets can even exceed the limits of narrative.[20] The set designer, as Tashiro reminds us, attempts to create the illusion of filming real objects. The task of the designer, in other words, is to take the fictional narrative provided by the screenwriter and filmed by the director and make it "real." In making the unreal real, set designers provide the "reality effect" of a film, a particularly crucial task for historical (and fantastical) films.[21] No one has accomplished this task better than Liudmila Kusakova. Her Soviet-era work includes sets for costume adaptations such as *Anna Karenina* (1967), *Tchaikovsky* (1969), and *Uncle Vanya* (1970). She has also served as Karen Shakhnazarov's set designer for *Zero City* (1988) and *The Tsar's Assassin* (1991), and built 1905 Moscow for *A Rider Called Death*. Kusakova's set designs, in other words, have provided the crucial look of history for a host of historical films.

In this sense, the locales of *Wolfhound* are not that fantastic, but they correspond to Myles Balfe's argument that "fantasy texts and landscapes . . . are located within, and inscribed by, particular social, geographical, and cultural discourses."[22] Lebedev has voiced this view as well, arguing that *Wolfhound* "is based on Slavic rites, traditions, and manners." According to him, it is both "the culture of the Slavic eighth century" and also "completely contemporary history" filled with "love, devotion, and treachery."[23] Kusakova's Galirad looks a lot like the Slavic villages and cities included in Semenova's quasi-ethnographic *We—Are the Slavs!* Semenova posits that wooden temples, streets with cut logs, and a particular "type" of wooden living space defined the dwelling places of pre-Christian Slavs.[24]

Kusakova thus made a fantasy world real and the fact that Mosfil′m now uses her two sets (1905 Moscow and Galirad) for other films and for tours affirms Tashiro's arguments. The fabulous history of Wolfhound is now part of the real history of Russian cinematic revival. And the fantasy sets of *Wolfhound* are now used for historical films—the next production to make use of Kusakova's creation was for a television series set in Ivan the Terrible's Moscow. Galirad, in other words, is just Kusakova's 1905 set four hundred years earlier. Both visualize a refound Russia.

GALIRAD'S MEANINGS AND FANTASY BLOCKBUSTERS

Critics mostly savaged the film. So too did audiences—nearly 2000 spectators rated the film on Kinopoisk, giving it on average 4.4/10.[25] Scores of spectators felt that the film did not hold up to the achievements of Peter Jackson's Tolkien adaptations. Many specifically criticized the set decorations, which had been reported in the press a great deal. "When I saw the city set, the houses, and the locks," "Anga" posted, "I felt I needed to cry." "I understand ancient society lived a severe life," she wrote, "but they could not live in the hovels they showed onscreen."[26] Other spectators found it "disgusting," "shameful," and "derivative." Most of the criticism centered on its ability to adapt Semenova's story or whether or not "fantasy" represented a "Russian" genre.

These kinds of criticisms also appeared in the press. Valerii Kichin lamented the fact that "fantasy" now gets applied to special effects–driven blockbusters such as *Star Wars* and *Lord of the Rings* and not to Soviet classics such as *Aeilta* (1924) and Tarkovsky's films. Instead, "the cataclysms space empires experienced coincided with the cataclysms the Soviet empire experienced," which meant that Soviet cultural products such as *Aeilta* gave way to new cultural forms and cultural definitions. "Fantasy," in other words, became a genre ascribed to visual effects and therefore became defined worldwide as Hollywood defined it. Kichin writes, "Hollywood blockbusters continued with the new special effects form and they contained ideas of universal human values, while Russian cinema was involved in an urgent search for a national idea. Hollywood fitted contemporary values to the future world, while Russian cinema failed to glance at the future and instead searched for meanings in the past." Kichin connects *Wolfhound* to films such as *The Island,* although this use of the past is "set in the pre-Christian roots of Slavdom" and told in the fashion of "a Russian epic." The problem with this "ancient Slavic form of contemporary patriotism," Kichin believes, is that it is made not according to the conventions established by Protazanov and Tarkovsky, but on Hollywood's terms. It is, he concludes, almost a Khrushchev-era attempt "to catch up and to overtake."[27]

Most critics more or less agreed with Kichin's view. Irina Liubarskaia, writing in *Iskusstvo kino,* titled her review "Spiritless [*dukh-less*]," an ironic combination of the Russian word "spirit" and the English ending "-less." For her, the film's attempt to catch up and overtake Hollywood conventions failed to allow for an appropriate amount of Russianness. Instead of offering ideas that relate to Russian fairy tales (she cites the Soviet films of Aleksandr Ptushko as an example), Lebedev chose to copy *Conan the Barbarian, Star Wars,* and other American fantasy films. She cites the Galirad set as a particular example of where the film went wrong, praising the revival of Russian cinematic set design and costume making as positive developments, but concluding that "with this patriotism they also went too far" by trying to make the film look and sound too Hollywood and not Russian enough.[28] The effect, she believes, could be negative, for the lack of a "Russian spirit" in the hero means that Danila Bagrov will continue to be the new Russian role model.[29]

Maria Kirillova wrote one of the few positive reviews of the film, and did so for three reasons: first, the film's "Slavic mythology" does more to capture the real "Russian soul" than most recent films and television serials; second, the film serves as a first entry into the new genre of "Slavic fantasy," a good sign but one where "only time will tell" its results; and third, the film's set—she calls Kusakova's creation a "miracle city [*chudo-gorod*]" that rivals her work for *A Rider Called Death*.[30] Diliara Tasbulatova, in an otherwise tepid review that pointed out Lebedev's narrative wanderings, also called Kusakova's sets and costumes "an inspired spectacle." In particular, Tasbulatova noted that Peter Jackson's films used computer effects almost exclusively; in contrast, Kusakova's creations are "alive," and Galirad serves to highlight the "boundless gloomy grandeur of the pre-Christian world recreated to instill great pride in the patriotically disposed spectators, whether they go to the cinema halls or Mos′film."[31] For Larisa Reznikova, the film was a "*skazka* [fairy tale] for the twenty-first century," an era "when mass cinema has begun to become oriented toward an audience of children and adolescents. Harry Potter and barefoot hobbits are the real heroes of our time." To watch the film one must watch dizzying special effects that the entire family can enjoy, but also one by which "you will be returned to your childhood" and reminded of how much the cinema from your childhood has changed.[32] For its defenders, *Wolfhound*'s significance was in its patriotic performance, one that gave birth to a new form of cinematic "native fantasy" and a new way to learn about fantastic history.

Yet the most crucial reviews came from the fantasy fan base that had emerged in post-Soviet Russia. The *Mir fantastiki* [Fantasy world] website covered the film extensively and promised readers it would explore all the angles in this attempt to "revive the glorious tradition of Soviet fantastic cinema."[33] Anton Karelin, who interviewed Nikolai Lebedev for the journal as part of its ongoing coverage, closed with the words he believed his readers felt: "Nikolai, from a person associated with *Mir fantastiki* and from all our readers we wish you success and inspiration! We all ache for and wait for your film."[34]

The aching and waiting ended in December 2006. In his review for the online site, Petr Tiulenev wavered between praise and damnation (Semenova's novel had become a bible of sorts for *Mir fantastiki* readers). Tiulenev's main problem with the film was that it veered too far from Semenova's Russian fantasy plot toward an adaptation of *Lord of the Rings.* Although he would have preferred a little more adherence to the original novel, Tiulenev understood why Lebedev did what he did: "to show that we also know how to make films no worse than Hollywood, even ones made in this case with a modest budget."[35] At the end of his review, he takes stock of the film's use of the novel. "Present" are "battle magic," "gods," "the spirit," and "the vengeance" of the novel; "absent" are several important personalities, "a logical plot," and "large-scale battles." Tiulenev awards the film 8/10 for entertainment value; 5/10 for plot; and 7/10 for atmosphere, direction, and acting.[36] Mikhail Popov, who reviewed the film for the journal as it was about to appear on DVD, mostly agreed with Tiulenev. "The film was briefly characterized [in a previous issue] as 'our answer to *Lord of the Rings,*'" he commented, "and the long-awaited 'Slavic fantasy' [therefore] proved to be not entirely Slavic but fortunately still fantasy."[37] He agreed that the film diverged too far from Semenova's text and was inferior to Peter Jackson's epic. At the same time, when he tackled the issue of whether or not fantasy lovers should buy the DVD, he wrote, "If you did not see it at the cinema, then there is only one answer: absolutely you must buy the film." The reason? "You can criticize *Wolfhound* as much as you want, but in this case you cannot forget that this film was the first large-scale Russian fantasy film."[38] For the reviewers on this site, in other words, *Wolfhound's* faults were far outweighed by its patriotic performance as "our" first fantasy epic.

Other fantasy fans debated the film along similar lines. On a Semenova fan site, registered users debated a host of topics, among them whether it is even possible to film a fantasy epic as complex as *Wolfhound.* Most believed the film flattened the philosophical elements the novel contained and most believed that you had to sacrifice philosophy for action. "Hawk [*Iastreb*]" agreed with a guest who posted that "literature cannot be filmed," but optimistically hoped that "the film will make viewers want to read the book."[39] Only in Sememova's textual world, in other words, could one truly find a "Russian" fantasy and not "Conan Wolfhound" (as one user posted). Participants in the "fantasy forum" set up on an unofficial *Wolfhound* (the novel) fan site were harsher. "Kirdzhava" wrote, "For the first time in my life after watching a film I wanted to shatter the box-office window and demand my money back. . . . They perverted the book." "Nilanel" remarked, "[I] waited two years for this film and after this wait I am so upset!" "Elva" was a little more conciliatory (and patriotic): "It pleased me; certainly it does not always go along with the book, but for the first Russian fantasy film experiment it was still very good."[40] For fans of Russian fantasy, the film offered a mixed bag. As the "first Russian fantasy epic," it could be defended on patriotic grounds. *Wolfhound* in this sense provided a "Russian/Slavic" look to fantasy history. As an adaptation of Semenova's more complex popular novels, however, most fantasy fans felt the film failed. In this view, the "real" Russian fantasy history was on the page, not onscreen.

In the film, Wolfhound's defense of "his" landscape is a defense of pluralistic values from domestic forces that want to unleash slavery, not from the threats posed by the evil West or East. The box office returns told a different story (in part). *Wolfhound* bested the competition, which included the Moscow-set comedy *Heat* [*Zhara*] and *Night at the Museum*.[41] *Heat* had also received heavy advertising that trumpeted the fact that the cast of this light comedy consisted of the same cast in from the previous year's big blockbuster, *Ninth Company* (Fedor Bondarchuk produced the film, which was also widely panned by critics). Some saw this "victory" of Russian cinema as a double-edged sword—domestic movies triumphed, but they weren't "Russian" enough: they lacked the "Russian spirit" or just were outputs of "the same blockbuster" production line that had released *Turkish Gambit* and *Ninth Company*. In the words of one of the harshest critics, Alena Solntseva, these films "are for them [spectators], only cheap, fast food, similar to a hamburger at McDonald's."[42]

Supporters, however, saw enough Russianness in the film. Aleksandr Bukharov, who played Wolfhound, stated that "we have a rich history, beginning in ancient Rus′, that can be filmed and we do not need to copy other histories. It seems to me that it's necessary to make historical and semi-historical films, to film our history, the history of our country." To tell these "necessary films" about "the Russian people," however, directors have to not only follow "the rules of fantasy" and to create "a Russian fantasy," it is also necessary to use the conventions of Hollywood blockbusters. Whether it succeeded, Bukharov muses, "Is for spectators to judge."[43] The judging will continue—a twelve-part television serial *Young Wolfhound,* starring Bukharov in the title role, appeared shortly afterward; more sequels are in store; and *Wolfhound* video games have since come out.[44] As a fantasy history blockbuster franchise that uses recognizably Russian sets, *Wolfhound* truly is a skazka for the twenty-first century.

Patriotic unicorns: Still from Vladimir Khotinenko's *1612* (2007).

TWELVE

The Business of Patriotism

The Renova Group is one of Russia's most successful businesses. Founded in 1990, by 2009 Renova was the largest private business group in Russia with twenty-five billion dollars in holdings.[1] The company owns and manages assets in metals, oil, mining, machine building, energy, telecommunications, and other industries. Renova also owns stakes in business across the world, from Switzerland's Sulzer AG to South Africa's Harmony Gold Mining.[2] Renova, by any economic indicator, is an unqualified success.

In its handbook for employees, Renova articulates a vision of selfhood that aims to transform communists into capitalists. Renova employees must not commit the business sins of insider trading or securities manipulation. They also have a social responsibility, for Renova "is committed to supporting economic, social, and cultural development of communities where it operates through creating jobs for resident population and charitable, cultural, and other initiatives." Moreover, Renova employees must comply with environmental requirements, "acknowledge internationally recognized human rights and freedoms as the highest values," "value the uniqueness of each member of its staff," maintain honesty and transparency in all business transactions, and not accept bribes.[3]

The policies and their attempts to build better businessmen through better social citizenship are the brainchild of Renova's chairman, Viktor

Vekselberg. He has also discovered that Russianness sells, and therefore much of Renova's cultural work involved the business of patriotism. Vekselberg expanded his patriotic portfolio in 2007 when he produced a film about the Polish invasion of Russia in 1610–1612. The film visualized the patriotic business strategy that Vekselberg had developed since communism's collapse. In doing so, *1612* collapsed the distance between the Time of Troubles of the seventeenth century and the Time of Troubles of the 1990s. Both were overcome, Vekselberg's project suggested, because Russian heroes and Russian virtues reasserted themselves.

BUSINESS STRATEGY AS PATRIOTIC PROJECT: RENOVA AND RUSSIA

Vekselberg's ideas about business structures and how his employees should behave serve as models for post-Soviet Russian behavior. According to the company's "Philosophy of Progress," Renova "is engaged in building active access to the global market; we strike up new alliances and partnerships with leading corporations while still remaining a Russia-based company." Vekselberg wants "Renova investments and major business assets to operate in Russia and to contribute to the development of technologies and industry in this country." "We invest," his website proclaims, "in social projects and participate in a Public Private Partnership while being an active charity contributor." Finally, Vekselberg stresses, "[O]ur corporate philosophy is based on business ethics and reliability principles; we are a results-oriented and resolute investor."[4] Doing business in the new Russia, in other words, is a patriotic effort that aims to build new citizens and a new Russian nation.

Born in 1957 in Drohobych, Ukraine, Vekselberg graduated from the Moscow Railway Transport Engineering Institute in 1979. He worked for a pump manufacturer until 1990, beginning as a technician but becoming a research manager. In 1988, as Gorbachev began loosening restrictions on businesses, Vekselberg founded NPO KomVek ("Vekselberg's Company"), a research and production company that cooperated with the Irkutsk Aluminum Plant. Two years later he founded Renova, a closed joint-stock company, with a college friend. He first gained wealth during the Yeltsin years and through the privatization of the aluminum industry in the early 1990s. Vekselberg's business expanded when he used his holdings in aluminum to become the co-owner and chairman of Tiumen Oil (TNK) in 1996. From that time onward, Vekselberg started to purchase shares of aluminum plants. His corporate management policies, combined with his savvy negotiations in the Russian stock market and the boom provided by petro-dollars, saw his personal stock rise with that of his business holdings: in 2001 the business newspaper *Vedomosti* rated Vekselberg the best businessman in the metals industry; the same year the Russian Association of Managers rated him the best manager in Russia. Two years later Vekselberg made the *Forbes* list, placing 147th with a personal fortune estimated at $2.5 billion. By 2007, his fortune had increased to $10.6 billion.[5] Vekselberg, *Forbes* declared, "is one oligarch that isn't afraid to get down and dirty," and "he is known for conducting Russia's first hostile takeover in 1994."[6] His approach is one based on acquisition or takeover—he has gathered oil and energy companies under his wing.[7] Vladimir Putin even hinted in 2005 that he considered appointing Vekselberg governor of Kamchatka, a reward for loyal business service and for strengthening the Russian state through patriotic purchases.[8]

Vekselberg personally fulfills his corporate mission. He has engaged in patriotic investments that are meant to restore some history and some pride within Russia. In 2004 Vekselberg bought nine Fabergé eggs from the Forbes family and "returned" them to Russia as part of his personal collection. Vekselberg negotiated the deal privately with the Forbes family and spent between $90–110 million for the eggs. In purchasing what he called "the most significant example of our cultural heritage outside Russia," Vekselberg preempted the public auction of the Fabergé collection that Sotheby's had planned for April 2004. After negotiating the purchase, Vekselberg declared that he "knew immediately that this was a once-in-a-lifetime chance to give back to my country one of its most revered treasures."[9]

Vekselberg also founded a business that aimed to return other treasures, naming it "Connection to Old Times [*Sviaz′ Vremen*]." The organization created programs that allow contemporary Russians—particularly urbanites—to get in touch with nature and with old ways of living. Primarily aimed at corporate clients, "Connection to Old Times" offers "unique opportunities for organizing corporate leisure rich with original play, entertainment, and excursions in the most picturesque corners of our country; namely, the Urals."[10] "Connection to Old Times," when not connecting businessmen to the Russian land, also continued Vekselberg's cultural repatriation work. Their first activity was the purchase of the Lowell bells from Harvard University and their return to Moscow's Danilov Monastery. The eighteen bells left Russia in 1929, when American philanthropist Charles Crane saved them from destruction by buying them from the Soviet government, which was then desperate for hard currency. Crane donated them to Harvard, where they rang at Lowell House from 1930 to 2007.[11] Billed by Danilov's website as "the return," the bells tolled again in Moscow on September 13, 2007. Patriarch Aleksei II, who had called on the bells and other holy artifacts to return to Russia, blessed them. Vekselberg took up the holy business of returning patriotic symbols to Russia and paid for the replicas that now hang in New England and for the costs of the bells' return trip and installation. He commented at the ceremony, "This is an important symbolic act" and "a small sign that Russia is returning to its roots and becoming great again."[12]

Vekselberg's business and patriotic efforts are meant to establish Russia as a "normal" country, one where the past can be safely relegated to the past and where Russians can come to terms with it. At the same time, his business and cultural strategies are part of the "commercialized nationalism" that has defined contemporary Russian business.[13] In a November 2008 interview conducted by Echo Moscow's Vitalii Dymarskii, Vekselberg stated that cultural-historical investments were "an integral part of our life and therefore are placed in the category of untouchable. We are obliged to support them independently of what else occurs around us." Vekselberg, speaking as the 2008 economic crisis worsened, stated he was "an optimist" because "many programs are mapping the level of the state's economic health." Far more important was the need to map out the state's cultural health in a time of crisis: culture "is a part of our ordinary life. We will not give up that which allows us to eat, to drink, to read, and to watch TV."[14]

Vekselberg's rise to prominence represents a perfect test case for understanding how economic growth, patriotic revival, and historical remembrance developed together in the zero years. Viktor Vekselberg is a new oligarch—a patriotic one. He has also waded into the business of blockbuster history, though his products in this sphere have fused fantasy with history.

UNICORNS AND WIZARDS: VEKSELBERG'S *1612*

Promoted with a *300*-style poster and a media campaign that branded it "patriotic cinema," Vladimir Khotinenko's 2007 film *1612* blurred the lines between present-day uses of the past and the political uses of cinema. Set during the Time of Troubles, *1612* is more about the 1990s than the seventeenth century and more about contemporary political concerns than adherence to historical accuracy. Coproduced by Nikita Mikhalkov's Studio Tri-te and Vekselberg's Renova Media, this cinematic Time of Troubles attempts to reclaim the past in a fashion similar to the reclamations of eggs and bells. Vekselberg himself contributed $4 million to the film. This time, though, the patriotic memory recovery employs unicorns and wizards.

The events that ultimately established the Romanov dynasty have provided fertile ground for artistic exploration. Between 1598 and 1613 the Muscovite state experienced political instability, a famine that killed nearly one-third of the population, a powerful uprising from within, a pretender to the throne who became Tsar Dmitrii, an invasion by the Polish and Swedish states that resulted in the occupation of Moscow and the near complete collapse of the state, and finally a resistance that first threw the Polish occupiers out and then elected a new dynasty for the realm. And that's just the highlights. Given all that happened in such a short time, it makes sense that afterward these events became known as the Time of Troubles, or *smutnoe vremia*.[15]

The Time of Troubles have captured the attention of political figures, priests, artists, and producers of folklore ever since. The events of 1612, the climatic point of the Time of Troubles when the Poles occupied Moscow and the legendary forces raised by Dmitrii Pozharskii and Kuzma Minin expelled them, provided rich story lines for writers and historians. This era appeals precisely because it is so difficult to explain and yet so decisive to the history of Russia. For Romanov propagandists, the Time of Troubles was a clear indication that God frowned on weak dynasties and illegitimate rulers such as Boris Godunov, who seized the throne in 1598 and who ruled during the 1601–1603 famine. After Napoléon's invasion of 1812, 1612 became the subject for a renewed retrofitting; in the words of Nikolai Karamzin, Godunov was a seventeenth-century Napoléon who suffered from "an immoderate, illicit thirst for power" and the true heroes of Russia were the patriotic butcher and prince from Nizhnii Novgorod, Minin and Pozharskii, or even mythic serfs like Ivan Susanin, who allegedly saved Mikhail Romanov and sacrificed himself for the future tsar. As Karamzin put it, "their [Minin and Pozharskii's] faith, their love of native customs, and hatred of alien rule engendered a general glorious uprising of the people."[16] During the Soviet era, the official story about the Time was made to fit with the Marxist viewpoint of history, where all the violence could be explained as an early form of class warfare. Accordingly, Glinka's 1836 patriotic opera *A Life for the Tsar* was renamed *Ivan Susanin* in order to stress the little man and not the oppressive autocracy; the chorus "Glory, glory, to our Russian tsar," became "Glory, glory to our Russian land."

These dominant narratives did not go unchallenged when they appeared. The popularity of the False Dmitrii lingered in Russian folklore, the social unrest and civil wars that dominated the Time of Troubles bubbled up again and again, poets like Pushkin and Lermontov challenged Karamzin's views, and operagoers in the Soviet Union did not soon forget that *Ivan Susanin* was a dressed-up version of the tsarist-era staging. In other words, the Time of Troubles and its part in Russian historical memories represented something of a memory overload, the meanings of which were constantly present and constantly contested. Perhaps the only thing that can be said definitively about the multitude of popular prints, songs, oral stories, novels, plays, poems, paintings, operas, and statues about 1612 (again only a few means by which memory was expressed) is that the only things missing from them were ghosts, wizards, and unicorns.

Thank goodness then for *1612,* which filled in these blank spots. This retrofitting has unicorns, a Tolkien-esque *starets,* and the ghost of a Spanish swordsman. Appearing as the cinematic component to the invented tradition that is National Unity Day—celebrated for the first time on November 4, 2005, and commemorating the day in 1612 on which Pozharskii's forces expelled the Poles from Moscow—Khotinenko's film acted as the centerpiece for a new narrative about the Time of Troubles for the new Russia. The appearance of a movie about 1612, given the short history of its memory work sketched above, is not much of a surprise. Nor is it surprising that the film was directed by Khotinenko, who has become a vocal Putin patriot, and coproduced by Nikita Mikhalkov, the quintessential contemporary cinematic patriot. Marketed as a new Russian patriotic blockbuster or a Russian historical fantasy, *1612* uses Russian historical memories and historical events it purportedly follows by not adhering to any sort of historical accuracy—violence is favored over chronology, Moscow is never occupied, Pozharskii appears only briefly, and a love story involving a slave and Boris Godunov's daughter dominates. It is James Cameron history with a Russian flavor.

What grabbed the attention of the Russian media and Russian film world was the seemingly Soviet-era attempt to use cinema to foster a sense of patriotism. As Denis Babichenko wrote in *Itogi,* "History should notice—as soon as Russian society searches for a national idea it always turns to the Time of Troubles." Babichenko, however, sees the 2007 search in fairly sinister terms: "present day ideologists are shaking the Time's tree in the hope of catching the matured fruit of a national idea." In particular, Babichenko believes that Vladislav Surkov, Putin's chief ideologue, ordered a film about 1612 so that the new National Unity Day would not only make sense, it would be seen as a day to celebrate Putin's achievements. Surkov pitched his film project to Putin, who naturally liked it. Then came the financiers. According to Babichenko, "A certain time back the businessman Viktor Vekselberg, who had already complained about the lack of a new state idea in an *Itogi* interview, decided to put four million dollars into the film project *1612*. This is already the oligarch's third 'pleasing to God [*bogougodnoe*]' act in the field of returning the true sources of spirituality lost after the Soviet Troubles." The first two involved the eggs and bells; Vekselberg was then to help create a "national brand [*natsional'nyi brend*]" of "kvas patriotism" for Vladimir Putin's government.[17]

The plot of this national brand involves a slave named Andrei (Petr Kislev) who once lived in Godunov's domains and who witnessed the murder of the tsar's wife and son by a Polish hetman (Michał Żebrowski) working for False Dmitrii. Andrei survives, but becomes a slave who enters Russia again in 1612 along with the Polish Army—led by the very same hetman. He manages to win his freedom and accompanies Alvar, a Spanish swordsman for hire, into his homeland. Andrei's real quest, however, is to consummate his desire for Godunov's daughter, Kseniia (Violetta Davydovskaia), who is now the Polish general's lover and intended wife. The real Kseniia Godunova, it is worth mentioning, first was forced by False Dmitrii to serve as his concubine and then became a nun at the Trinity St. Sergius Lavra during the events that the film covers. She was famous for her needlework, which still hangs at the monastery. Of course, sewing nuns do not really make historical blockbuster love stories, so in Khoteninko's history Kseniia is torn between two men, two countries, and two faiths. When Alvar dies in a skirmish against Russian partisans, Andrei assumes his identity with the help of Kostia (Artur Smol′ianinov), a Russified Tatar who has served the swordsman. Alvar's ghost visits Andrei every now and again to help him through tight spots. Because of this supernatural help, "the Spaniard" becomes an accepted part of the invading army who tries to woo Kseniia away from her Polish oppressor.

Andrei's desire, as the film reveals, stems from his glimpse of a naked Kseniia while he was still a young boy. Kseniia took pity on the brash boy, who was caught and whipped for his impudence, and gave him a wooden unicorn horn. Whenever Andrei finds himself in a tight spot—it is the Time of Troubles so tight spots abound, particularly when you are disguised as a Spaniard and invading your homeland with the Polish Army—he rubs the horn and viewers are treated to the appearance of a unicorn onscreen. Eventually, and predictably, Andrei, Kostia, and Kseniia manage to escape the clutches of the evil Polish hetman and help the Russians defend a nearby town from the Poles. A slave turned hero does not work very well in 1612, so Russian clergymen and boyars put their heads together, invent a genealogy for Andrei that includes a number of famous Russians and foreigners, and voilà! He becomes Mikhail Romanov, the new tsar of Russia. Kseniia, however, cannot become Tsarina Romanova because she has slept with the enemy and become a Catholic, but she does get the consolation prize of becoming a bride for Christ.

Forsaking her native religion for a Western one, the film posits, is the worst sin imaginable because it is a national one.

Where, it may be asked, is there room for a wizard? *1612* includes a subplot that implicates the Vatican in the Time and Troubles, for it involves an Italian monk sent to Russia by the Pope in order to learn about the barbarians as a means to convert them. While in Russia the monk becomes taken with the mystical nature of the land and its people, a view that Khotinenko drives home through the presence of a Gandalf-like starets (Valerii Zolotukhin) who has decided to stay up in a tree praying until the foreigners have left the country. The Italian is so impressed by the starets that he gives up his mission to become a wandering holy fool; he eventually returns to Rome muttering something along the lines that Russia is a riddle wrapped in an enigma. When the starets gets down at the exact time Andrei becomes Mikhail Romanov, the unicorn greets him. The ghost of Alvar's appearance at this point probably would have been over the top.

The film fits with its financier's cultural activities of connecting contemporary Russians to the past. Here it is history being returned, or perhaps patriotic fantasy packaged as the past and marketed to Russia's youth. Promoted by Khotinenko as an attempt to make the audience feel pride and a contemporary link with what happened four hundred years ago, *1612* is best read as the latest narrative in the long history of retrofitting these events—one in which the 1990s are a new Time of Troubles, another illegitimate Boris held power, and a weak state allowed a love for foreign goods to dominate the nation. "I . . . consider the seventeenth century an extremely important period in our history, without which you simply cannot understand Russia," Khotinenko declared in *Izvestiia*, "And now those times are really relevant. I am talking about the period after Perestroika. We lived in a Time of Troubles. Its duration even coincided with the one in the seventeenth century." The director was equally clear about the lessons to be learned from that Time: "the absence of lawful authority" caused the Troubles.[18] As concerns the state's bankrolling of the film, Khotinenko opined to his *Time Out* interviewer that artists as wide ranging as Andrei Rublev and Antoni Gaudi did work for governments: "and I see nothing bad in this." The varnishing of history onscreen also did not bother Khotinenko, for, as he claimed, "historical reality does not exist" when talking about the Time of Troubles.[19]

Critics cried foul on Khotinenko's views and the fact that a businessman such as Vekselberg bankrolled the project. Anton Dolin, a film critic for *Moskovskie novosti,* saw *1612* as a "public-service announcement" for the newly created National Unity Day. The film was released on November 1, three days before the third Unity Day. "The holiday had to be strengthened because it wasn't clear to people why they were supposed to love the president and the government," Dolin stated, "and this is why the holiday needed to be celebrated."[20] Vekselberg's ties to the Kremlin, Khotinenko's open nationalism, and Mikhalkov's hand in the film all spelled conspiracy to Dolin, a clear sign that the Kremlin had returned to using the past for present-day political purposes.

Even Andrei Panin, the star of *The Rider Named Death* and other recent Russian blockbusters, commented on *1612* during an *Izvestiia* interview about his film *Vanechka.* During the interview, Panin lamented the fact that cinema increasingly seemed to be serving state interests, and claimed this sort of *goszakaz* (state directive) was "destructive." When asked about what sort of film served this function, both Panin and his interviewer, Anna Fedin, mentioned *1612.* According to the actor, Khotinenko's film "is an action history, a view of combat, and beautifully shot. There have been many conversations about its patriotism, but truthfully I see nothing about this spirit in it."[21]

Polish critics also lambasted the anti-Polish overtones in the film. Anna Żebrowska, writing in *Gazeta Wyborcza,* quoted Putin's ideologue Vladislav Surkov, who stated, "We need a film now about how the Poles invaded Russia." For Żebrowska, Surkov's assertion that the country needed to be reminded of previous invasions from the West as a means of supporting a new National Unity Day represents a return to Soviet-era practices. She compared Surkov to Mikhail Suslov, the Khrushchev- and Brezhnev-era Kremlin ideologue.[22]

Khotinenko hit back. In an *Izvestiia* interview with Vita Ramm, the director dismissed widespread reports that he had received a goszakaz to make the film. According to him, he only received a phone call from Nikita Mikhalkov to helm a script by Arif Aliev (who had recently penned Sergei Bodrov's *Mongol*). Rumors that Surkov gave Mikhalkov

Kvas patriotism or goszakaz nationalism? The Poles burn Russia in *1612*.

the project because Putin wanted it and Vekselberg could finance it were, in Khotinenko's view, unfounded: "I discussed the film's goals with Nikita, the general producer. We looked at the material together, discussed it, and made some observations. But in this he was extremely delicate. We both thought as follows: *1612* should be made for a contemporary young audience and that the narration therefore must be captivating and humorous. There were no other tasks."[23] The film attempted to tell audiences that the Yeltsin era was a new Time of Troubles, but Khotinenko insisted it was not state propaganda.

His scriptwriter, Aliev, disagreed but defended the work nonetheless. Based on a historical novel Aliev had published earlier, *1612* had meanings important to Russians regardless of whether or not the Kremlin ordered it. According to Aliev, "we have a holiday on November 4 that is not exactly incomprehensible to the people but that is not yet rooted deeply in our historical consciousness." As for what the film script tells the people about their holiday, Aliev stated that 1612 "represents a time when there was no authority and when invaders, mercenaries, robbers, and gangs wandered Moscow's streets. And suddenly there occurred a wonderful revival of the Russian people." When pressed by his interviewer about a government order to make the film, Aliev replied, "Probably there was an order to produce it. But if you visit Luxor [Egypt] and get to the bottom of how ancient Egyptian architecture was built, you'll be astonished to discover the strict frameworks within which the architects created their buildings. All temples were created by government decrees. And yet they are rational, harmonious, and emotional. So the strict framework helped the artist. If there is not a framework at best you get the *Black Square*. This would be the death of audience-friendly cinema."[24]

State ordered or no, the more interesting aspect of this use of the past is that the film flopped at the box office. It not only earned the usual critical scorn heaped on all zero-year blockbusters,[25] it also earned back only $5.75 million of its $12 million budget. Claims that the film had been ordered by Putin and Surkov—a view widely reported in the press—kept young and old alike away from the multiplexes. As one online viewer noted, "Honestly, when I went to the cinema I hoped to see a contemporary historical-patriotic film, something like an adaptation of the novel *Russians in 1612*. Instead I got an amusing, colorful fairy tale. And it is nothing more."[26] Igor Dolutskii, historian of the Time of Troubles, commented, "[W]ith the help of culture you can create simplified versions of reality that are hugely beneficial to the government." In doing this, however, Dolutskii argues that film directors "have become representatives of the world's oldest profession."[27] It seems that certain retrofittings and returns of history work better than others and that in contemporary chronicles of the Time of Troubles unicorns, ghosts, and Gandalf are best left out.

PATRIOTIC CINEMA: VEKSELBERG INVESTS IN RUSSIANNESS

In 2005, as Khotinenko was starting his *1612* project, Vekselberg became involved with the new Foundation for the Support of Patriotic Cinema (FPPK). The foundation developed from three groups who wanted to promote patriotism in Russia: the National Military Foundation, a charitable foundation that supports veterans; the Combat Brotherhood, another veterans' group; and Iust-Ofis, a joint-stock company. The FPPK received the support of the Russian president, the Federal Agency of Culture and Cinematography, the State Duma, and the Federal Security Services of the Russian Federation. With this backing, the initial groups put together a board of trustees that now act as a lobbying group and as financial backers for their products. The trustees included Mikhail Shvydkoi, the head of the Federal Agency of Culture and Cinematography; Viacheslav Ushakov, the deputy director of the FSB; and Vladimir Pligin, the chairman of constitutional legislation and governmental restructuring in the Duma. The board of trustees also included Konstantin Ernst, head of Channel One, and even luminaries such as the actress Ekaterina Guseva. The real financial power in the foundation, however, lay with Vekselberg, who funded the foundation's first patriotic product.

The goals of the FPPK read similarly to Renova's cultural mission. The mission statement, articulated in the glossy handbook the foundation gives to anyone interested in helping with the patriotic business of making movies, is this:

> The Foundation for the Support of Patriotic Cinema is a non-profit organization founded on the basis of the founders' voluntary contributions. Its activity is aimed at cultural, educational, and other socially useful goals, specified in the Charter. The Foundation's main aims are the support of patriotic cinema and literature and the promotion of patriotic ideals.

In addition, the foundation produces its own movies; raises money for other films it deems "patriotic"; provides "assistance for promoting Russian patriotic movies in the Russian market"; organizes patriotic scriptwriting contests; and "assists with the development and realization of international, federal, and regional long-term programs on popularizing state symbols, attributes of Russian power, and other heraldic symbols of the state."

The FPPK's first patriotic product, financed by Vekselberg through his Renova Media holdings, was 2007's *The Apocalypse Code*. The state symbol or aspect of Russian power promoted in the film was the FSB. In it, a sexy FSB agent named Dar′ia (played by Anastasia Zavorotniuk), receives word from the Lubianka of a nefarious terrorist plot to ignite nuclear charges in four major cities—in Malaysia, France, Italy, and Norway. Dar′ia must sacrifice everything to go undercover, infiltrate the terrorist's plans, and save the world. The mission is personal, for the

The brand of patriotism: Logo of the Foundation for the Support of Patriotic Cinema (FPPK).

terrorists' leader, a French banker named Louis Devier, has murdered Dar′ia's lover. She succeeds.

Sergei Bazhenov, general director of the FPPK and the film's producer, declared in the film's press booklet that *Apocalypse Code* "deals with the newest scourge of humanity—international terrorism, a threat to security in Russia and worldwide. The action in the film, which cost $15 million to make, takes place in many parts of the world and we are hoping that audiences in about 50 countries will be able to see it." As for the film's larger aims, Bazhenov maps them onto the FPPK's goals: "We see as our mission the promotion of Russian film projects that foster a positive perception of Russia, bringing up young people in the spirit of patriotism, and cementing the paramount human moral and spiritual values." The organization, in short, seeks to reanimate national myths in order to rebuild a new nation.

Anastasia Zavorotniuk, the star, elaborated:

> In this film, I am a woman on a mission to save the world, risking her life, sacrificing her personal happiness. Someone might say these are just empty words, but that's not true. People like that really exist, but their identities are held in secret: such are the rules of the game. These people are looking out for us. A role like this is a dream come true for me. I got a taste of what it feels like to be a strong woman, and I loved it!

Vadim Shmelev, the film's director (he also helmed the 2006 terrorist film *Countdown*), opined,

> This film is about love, dignity, patriotic duty. Before they see *The Apocalypse Code* many people will downplay it as just another blockbuster with lots of shooting. But in fact, it's a serious and very powerful film that works on many levels. . . . We can make good films that don't need to be patronized. You know, many people will say a bad film is OK just because it's "Russian." In Russian movies, why does the main character always die in the end? And why is he always a nice guy but an alcoholic? And when a film aspires to be "serious," why does it always have to have Dostoevsky-style clichés? Our main character does not drink alcohol or betray others. It's a film where we win. . . . After hundreds of films where Americans save the world, one gets the impression that's all they ever do: they save the world over and over again, while Russians do nothing.[28]

To the minds of FPPK members, blockbusters should adapt Hollywood plots and endings to Russian situations. Fostering patriotism, in other words, is about sexy FSB agents who sacrifice themselves to save the world. It also helps not to drink.

Critics of all stripes savaged the film. *Time Out Moscow* gave it one star and stated that seeing it was like "surfing between television channels that are simultaneously showing unfunny state-controlled news; an unfunny, mediocre action movie from the early 1990s; and an unfunny parody about some 'James Bond in a Skirt.'"[29] Aleks Eksler, who runs a LiveJournal blog devoted to contemporary culture, declared the film a "comedy" and concluded, "On the whole, it is sad, girl. Earlier I was glad, when I watched this idiocy, but I'm not happy now. They throw crazy money into this 'patriotic cinema,' they advertise it in a manner as if they created a new *Lethal Weapon,* and then you watch this nightmare and are ashamed for the film crew." On a five-point scale, he gave the film a 4 for entertainment, 1 for acting, –14 for directing, and –384 for the script. As for the "patriotic" tag, Eksler wrote, "it was the opinion of some cretin."[30]

Some viewers disagreed, one of whom was "Fedot," who stated, "I will say nothing bad about the film. I liked it, it pleased me, was not badly filmed, had high-quality scenes, and the soundtrack was not pumped too loud."[31] Bazhenov set the stakes for success in the following fashion: "The viewer votes with his ruble. That's the most important thing, and we understand it. Today you can't force people into movie theaters."[32] The votes produced a mixed result. *Apocalypse Code* led the Russian box office for two weeks in a row, but only grossed $8 million, a little more than half of its $15 million budget. Still, much like Vekselberg's profligate payments for Fabergé eggs and church bells, the film represented an investment in patriotic culture that brought a lot of press for the Foundation and for Vekselberg's patriotic business. The FSB certainly liked the film, and awarded it their annual cultural award for best picture. Zavorotniuk won best actor.[33]

After their foray into contemporary Russian heroism, the foundation next produced four documentaries. Two—a three-part film about Iurii Andropov and a film about "the complex and dangerous work of the intelligence agencies"—focused on politics. The other two celebrates the lives of the ballet dancers Maris Liepa and Maya Plisetskaia.[34] The committee also green-lighted three new films slated to appear after 2012. All three are set in the past. The first, *Storm 333,* takes place during the Afghan War, and is "a story about honorable people, rare in our time, and about their notions of patriotism and sense of duty. It is a story not about one individual hero who saves the world, but an entire group of people united by one goal and single moral principle that allow them to do the impossible." It is, in other words, an anti–*Ninth Company* and anti–*Cargo 200* work. The second feature film is titled *Sevastopol.* Set during the Crimean War, the film is about "the unparalleled courage of Russian sailors, the madness of British aristocrats, the tenacity and courage of French soldiers, and the patriotic self-denial of the Greeks." The script tells this patriotic story through the romantic rivalry between a Russian officer and an English journalist over a St. Petersburg beauty. This rivalry "is witnessed and described by a young Russian officer who becomes a main character. His name is Leo Tolstoy." The final film, *The*

Priest [originally titled *The Pskov Mission*], is set during World War II, in occupied territories. It tells the story of Pskov Orthodox priests who, "under the conditions of German occupation, managed to preserve the unity of the Baltic canonical dioceses with the Russian Orthodox Church." Sergei Makovetskii played the Metropolitan Vilenskii, and Vladimir Khotinenko directed.[35] Released in 2009, the filmed garnered Khotinenko the Patriarchal Prize for Cinematography in 2010, which was awarded by Patriarch Kirill himself.

The foundation's work clearly follows Renova's business plan. The board meets several times a year to listen to project ideas and develop new plans. They choose one or two projects, of which one will be fully funded by the FPPK. The trustees also identify other projects to fund partially and then get to work obtaining financial backing for all the foundation's projects. Trustees lobby with Duma members and work with the Karo Film Company to get patriotic films screened in multiplexes. According to Natal′ia Markova, the FPPK's deputy general director, the turn to historical films is a necessary one, for, she says, "we want to produce historical films for young people—they need to understand their past in order to feel love for their motherland." As for what defines "patriotic" today in Russia, Markova mused, "Patriotic to me and to the foundation is not only about pride in our successful victories or pride in our special services, but a broad, simple notion: nature, sports, the past, everything that represents our country and something that can be good about it." She acknowledged that the search for what is "patriotic" and "national" is a difficult one: "Everything is mixed up now [2008]—our national football team is coached by a Dutchman [Guus Hiddink], our Eurovision Song Contest winner had his song written by Timbaland [Dima Bilan], and *Apocalypse Code* is an American-style action movie." Still, what is important, she says, is that "our Russian brains can win against international terrorism and our people can do something good for our country."[36]

Only time will tell if this patriotic investment produces concrete returns. Financially, neither *1612* nor *Apocalypse Code* have been clear successes. The business of patriotism, however, may have different criteria for evaluating what constitutes a good return. Iurii Pripachkin, chairman of Vekselberg's Renova Media, claimed in 2008 that *1612*

> was a good project and we're evaluating its outputs. We hope the bottom line for *1612* becomes clear by the New Year; then we'll decide if we want to stay in the movie business or not. We are hoping the movie will sell on DVD and will get some play outside Russia. We are currently working on a six-episode TV version. We are interested in the financial side of the project, but we also have a stake in learning how movies are made and how they generate returns on investment. Most recently, we've had to deal with the movie theater chain and learned a lot about how they work.[37]

Vekselberg's patriotic investments may pay off after all: E1 Entertainment bought the North American rights and released the DVD in April 2009.

New Year magic: Poster for *Irony of Fate 2* with striped Beeline cell phone ornament and photos from the first film.

THIRTEEN

The Production of the Past

Sergei Gurevich, a producer at Nikita Mikhalkov's Studio Tri-te, explained in 2008 the appearance of patriotic productions in the following way:

> We were all close to collapse—the film industry and the television industry. For a while our film *Barber of Siberia* stood alone against 1990s culture. Then the Russian television audience got fed up with Latin American soaps and other foreign productions. People didn't mind watching foreign films on TV in general, but Mexican passion every day only goes so far. Thanks to the leaders of our television networks—Konstantin Ernst first and foremost—investment began on domestic productions, on things that happen here in Russia. Studio Tri-te got involved right away, first with *The Requested Stop* [*Ostrovka potrebulia*] in 2000, which was produced by Ernst. Television, in other words, started this trend and it quickly became evident that there was an enormous demand for domestic themes. Film followed. Technologies had changed—the newer technologies and demand for domestic productions reinforced each other. The revival did not have much to do with the government. Mostly it was the intuition and good sense of network leaders. Ernst was the key—he loves movies and this love drives him.
>
> It's a coincidence that Putin and the revival happened at the same moment. No one has ever called us and said, "Do a patriotic film." . . . We are business oriented, not ideologically oriented. Right now, however, business points toward patriotism because of the mood in Russia. We respond to public demand for patriotism. For quite a long time people were deprived of anything to feel proud of. The news was bad, then worse, and then it was like living in Zanzibar or something, where nothing would ever get better. The low point was the ruble collapse, but it also gave us the point where we needed something positive.[1]

That "something positive" was the role Konstantin Ernst played in revitalizing Russian patriotism.

When the USSR collapsed, Channel One went through massive changes. It reached the largest number of television sets in the Union and served as the primary means through which Soviet information got disseminated. Its symbolic significance cannot be overstated: when hardliners attempted to wrest control of the crumbling union from Mikhail Gorbachev in August 1991, their primary aim was Channel One's Ostankino Tower.

The station became ORT (Obshchestvennoe Rossisskoe Televidenie, or Public Russian Television) through a November 30, 1994, presidential decree. Like the other formerly Soviet stations and new channels such as NTV, ORT in the 1990s took part in what Ellen Mickiewicz characterizes as a "battle ground, literally and figuratively, for those who would retain or gain political power." The story of post-Soviet television in the Yeltsin era, she writes, "Had moments of heroism and incompetence, tragedy and comic opera, war but almost never peace."[2] Konstantin Ernst emerged as the victor in these struggles; he became ORT General Director on September 6, 1999. Ernst oversaw the station's name change to Pervyi kanal, or First Channel, on September 1, 2002. In the eyes of his supporters, Ernst saved Russian television and even the Russian film industry. He has produced commercially successful programs, retaining stalwarts such as the news program *Vremia* while also introducing new fare such as *Poslednyi geroi* [*The last hero,* the Russian version of *Survivor*], and the popular American series *Lost* [*Ostat´sia v Zhivykh*]. His slick productions are seen by many as soulless propaganda for the zero years. Ernst has produced the past, turning Pervyi kanal into not only the television channel with the widest reception in the world's biggest country, but also into the most significant film production company.

Ernst started out as a biologist. Born in Moscow in 1961, he graduated from the biology department at Leningrad State University in 1983. Three years later, he defended his Ph.D. dissertation in biochemistry. In 1988, Ernst switched professions as jobs became more mobile during perestroika, later declaring that when he saw his future as the director of an institute, he "jumped off that train" because he "did not want to know his fate in advance."[3] He started to work for First Channel's news program *View* (*Vzgliad*). In 1991, he produced and wrote his first program for the station, *Matador.* He began to move up the corporate ladder as First Channel and then ORT experienced the ups and downs of the Yeltsin years. Ernst became the general producer of ORT in 1995 and its director general in September 1999.[4]

In the Yeltsin era, Ernst became known for his New Year's Eve magic. On December 31, 1995, he produced *Old Songs about the Most Important* (*Starye pesni o glavnom*) for ORT. The three-hour variety show featured contemporary pop stars singing 1950s hits. The show was a smash, and Ernst, with his co-author, Leonid Parfenov, produced additional New Year shows for 1996 and 1997. The first episode, which Serguei Oushakine has dubbed "the first major nostalgic eruption" of the post-Soviet era, used the plot and settings of the Stalinist musical *Cossacks of the Kuban* as its narrative center.[5] Subsequent episodes moved forward: the 1996 program contained 1960s songs and the following years had the hits of the Brezhnev era. As Oushakine has written, the three shows established "a major post-Soviet model for reframing and reappropriating the cultural repertoire of the past" by borrowing from past cultural products while separating them from their original contexts.[6] In doing this, Ernst discovered that the business of nostalgia could be profitable.

His success in producing the New Year programs led Ernst to produce feature films. He served as the senior producer for Aleksandr Rogozhkin's 1998 Chechen War drama, *Blockpost,* which won the Kinotavr prize for best film, and Denis Evstigneev's 1999 drama, *Mama,* which was based on a script by Arif Aliev and featured Eduard Artem′ev's music. When the ruble collapsed in August 1998 (after Ernst had agreed to produce these films), both Ernst and his employer faced a challenge. ORT could no longer afford the foreign-made soap operas and serials that made up the bulk of their non-news programming. Ernst and his fellow producers started to remaster Soviet series such as the 1973 super-series *The Eternal Call* (*Vechnyi zov*) as filler. More importantly, he began to order new Russian serials.

Ernst believes that the 1998 economic crisis meant in many ways that "cinema died" and needed to be reborn. Its revival could come only through "entertainment" and "marketing to a mass audience." "We work," he has declared, "in the business of population maintenance," for "television is the public's dining room."[7] In the lean years of 1998–99, the public needed some sustenance, and Ernst was there to provide it. Two of his first series, which both aired in 2000, set the tone for what was to follow. *Empire under Attack* (*Imperiia pod udarom*) first aired on New Year's Day of that year. Its 624 minutes followed the fortunes of tsarist agents attempting to save the empire from collapse. The series, as Ernst encapsulated it, "attempted to analyze a critical moment in our history, to say an important thing that the Okhrana [the tsarist secret police] was not entirely like the way Soviet textbooks wrote about it—these people also loved their native land and also envisioned its fate."[8] As one viewer commented, "the film made it finally possible to cleanse the communist, propagandistic shell from people's consciousness and to look at history from the point of view of a sober, normal, civilized person."[9] The second series saw Ernst team up with Nikita Mikhalkov and Studio Tri-te to produce the melodrama *The Requested Stop.* Directed by Dzhanik Faiziev, who had directed *Old Songs about the Most Important* and would go on to direct the Ernst-produced *Turkish Gambit,* the series proved popular enough that Ernst ordered a sequel, which aired in 2001.

From this beginning, when he learned how to make audience-friendly fare using domestic resources, Ernst launched an empire. He and his coworkers also learned how to make commercial cinema using Hollywood methods, a debt Ernst openly acknowledges. "We are eternally grateful to Hollywood," he claims, because "Hollywood [films] forced our lazy, fat Russian moviemakers to make films, to edit them, to make special effects, to talk in the language teenagers understand." "We are grateful," he concludes, "but now we will make our cinema ourselves."[10] His productions—nearly forty feature films or serials during the zero years alone—are some of the most popular and historically interesting films from the era. Ernst produced *Spetsnaz,* about Russian Special Forces in 2002 and again in 2003. He produced the first adaptation of Boris Akunin's work, *Azazel′,* which starred Sergei Bezrukov and which aired in 2002 on First Channel. He produced the Vladimir Khotinenko TV film 72 *Meters,* which put a patriotic spin on the Kursk tragedy of August 2000. His television serials in 2004–2005 alone include *Children of the Arbat, The Saboteur, Brezhnev,* Khotinenko's *Death of the Empire,* and

Esenin. The past proved to be fertile territory for Ernst and for Pervyi kanal, and he continued to retrofit the past profitably, serving up historical remembrances for hungry audiences. His productions retrofitted Soviet classics for post-Soviet audiences, explored the historical collapse of empires as tragic events, featured past and present-day detectives that could solve crimes, and explored Soviet history from Stalin to Brezhnev as "our national past."

Ernst's most dramatic move, however, may have been his September 2000 decision to remove Sergei Dorenko, the anchor and host of a popular television news program on ORT. Dorenko's program garnered 27 percent ratings for its timeslot, but by August 2000, the anchor drew Putin's ire for his outspoken criticism of the Kursk submarine disaster. Dorenko was also largely seen as "Berezovskii's man," a reference to the oligarch Boris Berezovskii, who at the time owned 49 percent of ORT's shares. Many commentators believed Berezovskii and Dorenko played a major part in elevating Putin from obscurity to state president in 1999–2000. Dorenko used his program to offer biting criticisms of Evgenii Primakov and Iurii Luzhkov, a policy that paved the way for Putin to win the March 2000 presidential elections with ease. Primakov and Luzhkov, who looked to be real contenders when Yeltsin resigned on New Year's Eve, 1999, did not even stand for election after the scathing reports. Putin won in the first round.

By fall 2000, both Berezovskii and Dorenko had fallen from official favor. In early September, after a meeting with Putin where he refused to declare his official support, Berezovskii gave up his ORT holdings. Less than a week later, Ernst fired Dorenko, stating, "[E]motional tension surrounding the situation threatens ORT's normal work." Dorenko fired back, declaring that the Ernst decision came from Putin himself. The popular presenter stated that he had met with the new president four times since September 1999 (when Putin became prime minister) and at their August 29, 2000, meeting Putin told Dorenko that he had broken all ties with Berezovskii. The new president asked the anchor for his unconditional support and Dorenko refused. Two weeks later, Ernst fired him. The news divided commentators. Evgenii Kiselev, the NTV anchor, declared, "[T]aking him off the air is undoubtedly an act of censorship, of government interference, against which we will always speak up."

Kiselev did not have much time left, for he was ousted in a boardroom coup in April 2001. As a result, NTV went from Russia's most significant independent channel to a state-owned one. Dorenko's critics charged that he had always been a mouthpiece for the unpopular Berezovskii. "It is better sooner than never," said Aleksei Pankin, editor of the *Sreda* media magazine. "It's too bad that it takes pressure from the Kremlin to get the right decision from [ORT] management."[11] Eventually Berezovskii's holdings transferred to three little-known companies (ORT-KB, Eberlink2002, and Rastrkom-2002), although most believe that they are managed by Roman Abramovich, Putin's most loyal oligarch.

The reshuffling of ORT and transformation into Pervyi kanal meant that Ernst had emerged as the real winner in the struggle over Soviet television holdings. This triumph came at the time when Ernst began to realize that the business of nostalgia could remake Russian cinema. His victory at ORT provided him with the opportunity to launch his productions. It also meant he could team up with Timur Bekmambetov to make the most popular films in Russian history.

DOZOR AS SYMPTOM

Ernst's desire to make not just audience-friendly television but to reanimate Russian cinema for the zero years found its fullest expression in the extraordinarily popular *Watch* movies: 2004's *Night Watch* and 2006's *Day Watch*. Both are based on the best-selling novels of the late 1990s by Sergei Luk′ianenko, a Ukrainian born in Kazakhstan. Timur Bekmambetov, an Uzbek also from Kazakhstan, directed both films and Ernst produced them. Bekmambetov first garnered attention for his extraordinary "Bank Imperial" historical commercials from 1992–97, which featured a cast of characters that included Napoléon, Tamerlane, Peter the Great, and Caesar—all in humorous episodes that had little to do with banking but a lot to do with retrofitting history.[12]

Night Watch, Bekmambetov's breakthrough blockbuster, follows the plot of the first novel in Luk′ianenko's trilogy. It opens with a battle between good and evil fought in Languedoc in 1342 (during the Hundred Years' War): as Gesser, the Lord of the Light, watches the slaughter, he appeals to Zavulon, the Lord of the Dark, for a truce. The two agree to establish boundaries in the age-old conflict—a Night Watch made up of the forces of the Light would ensure that the forces of Dark obeyed the truce, while a Day Watch would do the same for the forces of Light. The truce also acknowledged that "others" (vampires, witches, and other monsters) always live among us, and these others have the power to choose a side in the struggle between light and dark. After the opening scene, the film jumps first to August 19, 1992, one year exactly after the failed coup against Gorbachev that signaled the end of the USSR. Anton Gordetskii (Konstantin Khabenskii), desperate to win back his fiancée after she leaves him for a New Russian, seeks the help of a Muscovite witch. When the members of the Night Watch appear to put an end to the use of black magic, Anton discovers that he too is an "other." After this discovery, *Night Watch* leaps to the present and follows Anton and his fellow Night Watchmen in their attempts to find the "Great One," a boy with powers whose eventual choice between good and evil will signal the final triumph of one side—the Great One turns out to be the son Anton attempted to have aborted by the witch. They are guided in their quest by Gesser, who runs the Night Watch operation from the safety of the Moscow City Power Company, while Zavulon marshals his forces to oppose them. The culminating sequence of the film on top of a Moscow apartment rooftop, as David MacFadyen has argued, mixes a lightsaber fight from *Star Wars,* the special effects from *The Matrix,* Rembrandt's painting *Abraham and Isaac,* and notions of "evil as good and good as evil" borrowed from Dostoevsky and Bulgakov.[13]

A combination of slick special effects and a sophisticated marketing campaign made sure that *Night Watch* became a sensation. It shattered box-office records and, more importantly, bested the receipts from Western blockbusters such as *Lord of the Rings: The Return of the King* and *Spider-Man 2.* Its success generated a host of debates just as its clever use of stars and cultural icons made it both a cult film and a commercial one—the film features popular contemporary actors and Soviet-era stars in major and minor roles (in addition to Khabenskii, Aleksei Chadov plays Anton's young vampire neighbor Kostia, Vladimir Men′shov plays Gesser, and Valerii Zolotukhin plays Kostia's father), as well as pop stars such as Zhanna Friske and Gosha Kutsenko (a member of the girl group Blestiashchie and an MTV presenter turned actor, respectively). In the words of Nikita Mikhalkov at the premiere of the film at the Moscow International Film Festival: "[T]his is our answer to Tarantino."[14]

Night Watch soon took on a significance that far exceeded its plot. Bekmambetov himself provided one of the contexts for understanding the film when he stated upon its release that "cinema can be a catalyst of political processes."[15] Ernst's proclamation at the film's Pushkin Theater premiere that "this is our cinema, and whoever isn't with us is against us" filled in the political and cultural contexts for interpreting the film.[16] Russian audiences followed Ernst's lead and debated the film as either "ours" or "theirs." On one of the largest internet chat rooms devoted to debating the film, audience members disagreed about whether or not the commercialized, technologically savvy film could be classified as "Russian." For some, the film represented a "cheap version of *Lord of the Rings*" that "borrowed too much from American sentiments and Russian attempts to restructure cinema." Others took issue with Ernst and the marketing of the film, which declared that it was "Russia's first blockbuster" and had beaten American special effects at its own game. "Stan" posted a response online on July 1, 2004, that stated, "First Blockbuster? Special Effects at the level of American films? WHERE? In this pitiful and incomprehensible spectacle by the name of *Night Watch*? Ha!" "Dakota" similarly took issue with the proclamations about the film, for as she watched it she could only "see the smiling, great, and terrible Ernst (even thinking about him makes me disgusted)."[17]

Yet the overwhelming popular response to the film was to accept Ernst's vision. One viewer posted a reaction to the negative views above: "I do not love fantasy, but this film is cool." For him, the use of Moscow and its symbolic meanings makes the film "appear much better than any similar Hollywood one (especially because I live not far from the Sviblovo Metro [a setting used in the film])." "Gunzel" expressed a related view, stating that "in spite of the size and special effects it is clear that this is a RUSSIAN film. *Gorsvetovtsy* (*gorodskoi svet,* city light company workers) smoking in the halls, flea markets in the metros, even the simple act of scratching an eyebrow with an absurd grimace creates such an atmosphere!" Audience members debated the "national meanings" of the film and the onscreen others became symbols used to discuss the state of Russian culture, the mixing of "American-style" methods with "Russian philosophies" and the grandiose claims made by the moviemakers and its marketing campaign. The online response to *Night Watch* debated the film as either a sign of "victory" against "Hollywood" or a sign of "defeat" by caving into the moral decay offered by Western films. One viewer even mused that "vampire films about good and evil" are not "Russian," and if one wanted a national epic set in Moscow that discussed these issues, one should read *Master and Margarita.* Among audiences, *Night Watch* emerged as a hybrid of culture and a monster of sorts in its own right. For some, it represented a breakthrough, while others saw it as the creation of a monstrous Russian Hollywood.

One of the first reviews of *Night Watch* even generated discussions about anti-Semitism and racism in Russian political culture. The film critic Mikhail Zolotonov posited that *Night Watch* bears a strong resemblance to the antisemitic tracts *The Talmud and the Jews* (by I. K. Liutostanskii) and *Satan's Synagogues* (a 1909 screed by Stanislav Pshibyshevskii). These works respectively describe the ways in which a young antichrist will appear to "teach everyone to be good and human before all of humanity" and how children are supposedly used as sacrificial lambs in synagogues. With minor changes, these visions, Zolotonov argues, "are practically *Night Watch*'s program" and the film inadvertently reinforced antisemitic narratives in Russian culture.[18] Russian nationalists echoed (and eerily subscribed) to Zolotonov's views. Articles in the nationalist press and internet sites debated the "racial sense" of *Night Watch* and whether or not the film truly was "cinema for patriots." *Den′*, the ultra-nationalist daily, published an examination of "the racial sense of *Night Watch*" under the title "The Nation's Watch." Ultimately, the article concluded that the separation of "light" and "dark" into biologically determined categories may in fact be the way to interpret Bekmambetov's claim that "cinema can be a catalyst for political processes."[19]

If the film became a politically charged means to discuss contemporary Russian antisemitism and racism, so too did it become for some critics a deathblow for the Russian nation itself. The question of whether or not "patriots" could watch the film informed Vadim Nestorov's article titled "Vampires Will Ruin the Russians." Nestorov jokingly notes that Kazakhs have embraced Bekmambetov and Luk′ianenko as "their two

Stivens" (a reference to Spielberg and King), an acceptance that makes the claim of *Night Watch*'s Russianness laughable. He concludes that both the film and its debates about its alleged triumph of Russian cinema are "empty" and "poor" for the film ultimately is Hollywood-like and un-Russian. Because of the excessive tendency to discuss the nationalist implications of the film, the writer asserts, "Russian cinema [and by extension, Russia itself] loved itself to death."[20]

If the self-love did not lead to eventual disintegration of the Russian nation, in other pages the film's popularity prompted musings about the Russian soul. *Iskusstvo kino* ran an interview with Boris Polozhii, a Russian psychiatrist, to explain the phenomenal mass success of *Night Watch.* Polozhii agrees with the film's "apologists" who state, "finally we have a blockbuster that is not inferior to Hollywood." However, "as a specialist in psychiatry," he decisively states, "Such films do nothing good for the spiritual health of the nation [*takie fil´my nichego khoroshego dlia dushevnogo zdorov´ia natsii ne nesut*]." Polozhii particularly worries about the effects of the violence in *Night Watch* on children, "the basic audience of the film": "Already an entire generation has appeared that will grow up not on tales and folklore, but on cyborgs. Then we will be surprised why human life depreciates for this generation." Polozhii believes that the very reason that audiences responded to the film, the idea that it is spiritually "deep" because it does not offer an easy answer to the question of good and evil, is a particularly harmful message to send to young Russians. Moreover, he argues that fans of the film will apply its ideas of "light" and "dark" to social groups: "'dark' will be appointed to others—Caucasians, Jews, and blacks." In this psychological reading of how popular cinema creates and recreates mythologies, *Night Watch* as national epic is a potential catalyst for the monsters within all Russians. Polozhii suggests that Russians, who did not receive clear answers about good and evil under the "totalitarian ideology" of the twentieth century, will also not get clear answers in this century from mass cultural phenomena such as *Night Watch.*[21]

Polozhii had diagnosed a new Russian disease, a "sickness of the soul," that connected popular films to diseased beliefs within Russian society. In 2006, spurred by the continued popularity of *Night Watch* and its successor *Day Watch,* Russian intellectuals and cultural critics attempted to define the symptoms of this disease. In a collection of essays titled *Watch as Symptom (Dozor kak symptom)*, a wide range of writers debated the meanings of the film and its political significance. Just as the film broke barriers, so too did this publication—as Vladimir Kozlov noted, "books of this kind are rarely seen in Russia, not least because 'serious' writers tend to dismiss films like the *Dozors,* seeing them as purely commercial mass culture phenomena not worthy of any serious analysis."[22] However, the two editors of the volume claim that the films are an important part of "the intellectual life of Russia" and should be analyzed and understood by intellectuals.[23]

As far as the "symptoms" of the new disease first described by Polozhii, the contributors to *Watch as Symptom* offered a number of explanations. Irina Antanasievich, a folklorist and culturologist, argued that the main symptom of the film was "hunger."[24] For her, the film's mix of styles, genres, and ideas "completely corresponds to the culturological vinaigrette of post-Soviet Russia." Her prognosis for this cultural mixing is not good, for she argues that audiences will see the film not as a call to arms to delineate the meanings of good and evil, but only as a vampire movie. Ultimately, Antanasievich sees this reaction as further proof that political activism will not work in a contemporary Russia that loves culture such as *Night Watch* and concludes that idealists will "not be able to quench their hunger."[25] Konstantin Krylov, a young philosopher at Moscow State University, entitled his article "Investigating the Gloom [Razbiraia sumrak]." After thoroughly exploring the meanings of this fantasy nether region the forces of Light and Dark can enter into to and what he identifies as the seven layers necessary for evaluating it, Krylov concludes that "investigating the gloom completely pulls us to a political program," for it is in the gloom that one can escape evil and "do everything in a human manner."[26] The others on screen, in Krylov's view, provide political messages to viewers who might need to go "into the gloom," too. Extending Antanasievich's view, the anthropologist Elena Petrovskaia writes that *Night Watch* defines a number of cultural diseases and argues that "the vampire world is part of the 1990s emptiness—an era of a different experiment, this time a democratic one, and the complete loss of values."[27] This disease is one that originated in the first post-Soviet decade, when Luk′ianenko wrote his novel and one that manifests itself through symptoms such as "emptiness, trauma, and loss." Aleksandr Tarasov, a prominent sociologist, viewed the symptoms in a fashion similar to Polozhii's—for him, "there is no good and evil in the *Dozors,*" but "a competition between two *similar* forces—the Light (our special forces) and Dark (those who fight against our special forces)."[28] In other words, the meanings of *Night Watch* are a symptom of a larger disease, submission to governmental control—the ultimate message it sends to audience is "sit quietly and trust power."[29] In total, twenty-five intellectuals attempted to define the films and their meanings, and they found that the "diseases" *Night Watch* causes are all politically oriented ones, ranging from submissiveness to lingering political traumas inflicted by the Soviet era.

Bekmambetov's sequel, *Day Watch,* exploded onto screens as the "first movie" of 2006. It opens in Central Asia during the time of Tamerlane. The great conqueror is after the Chalk of Fate, which will allow its possessor to rewrite history. The film then jumps forward to the present and reintroduces viewers to the struggle between the Light Ones and the Dark Ones. Anton Gorodetsky (Khabensky) is framed by the Dark Ones for unlawful murders of members of their ranks and is pursued by both sides. At the same time, as Anton's son prepares for his birthday party hosted by Zavulon, his final choice between the two sides looms. He eventually chooses the Dark, plunging Moscow into an apocalyptic battle between the two sides, returning the city to the time of the Hundred Years' War or the time of Tamerlane's conquests. To prevent both the apocalypse and his son's choice from taking place, Anton uses the Chalk of Fate to rewrite history. He returns the city to 1992, the day he decided to approach the witch in *Night Watch.* This time, however, Anton rewrites his own fate too. This Moscow 1992 is sunny and happy.

Day Watch, like its predecessor, obliterated box office records. In one Moscow metro scene, Anton crashes through an ad for *Ninth Company,* then the highest-grossing Russian film of all time. *Day Watch* earned $32 million, $7 million more than Bondarchuk's blockbuster. Ernst's $4.2 million marketing budget for the film ensured that the trailer saturated the small screen (particularly Pervyi kanal) while posters flooded the streets of every major Russian city. Ernst used the full force of American film marketing for the *Watch* films, commenting: "Posters, trailers, teasers, billboards, and merchandising—there's practically not a single Russian dictionary equivalent for all the many and varied elements which go into the promo package of any major American film."[30] The film's marketing and message led to even more chatter about the film's messages. For some, the film bore a "national project" message where Ernst and Putin somehow conspired to get Russians to head to the movie theaters and see just how good they have it now. For others, Bekmambetov's claims that the films value "notions like responsibility, repentance, [and] penitence" meant that *Day Watch* allowed moviegoers to redo (or "just say no") to the Yeltsin era. For Ernst, the film offered more positive messages to become, as Anton does, "a human being." "To live for today," Ernst explains, "that's the basic slogan that Russia needs. And if we ourselves can learn to live for today, then we'll be able teach our audience to do this as well." To become human, as Ernst sees it, is to reconfigure present-day sensibilities. *Day Watch,* Ernst posits, seeks "to cure the 'Russian masochistic consciousness,' whose rejection of the ugly facts of life is a 'disgusting thing that has destroyed millions of lives.'" The film aims to "sell [audiences] certain behavioral codes that allow them to position themselves more precisely in reality." The *Watch* message, reinforced by Anton's use of the Chalk of Fate, attempts to rewrite the "overkill culture" of the 1990s, to get Russians to accentuate the positive and eliminate the negative.

The end result, as Thomas Campbell states, produces

> [an] allegory of the symbiosis of business and state power as well as that powerful organism's view of its "customers." [Ernst's and Bekmambetov's] project of myth/brand creation has a method and a message. Their method is employed to particularly totalizing effect in Day Watch's stunning finale—a montage of musical quotations and film-history citations that falsifies history by rendering it utterly unreadable; a utopian potpourri of post-imperial melancholy, revanchism, imperial restorationism, castrated shestidesiatnichestvo, and anti-American cinematic Americanism. . . . The message transmitted by all this cinematic muscle-baring is, however, much simpler and hardly veiled at all. The bad guys and the good guys are in cahoots, but don't worry. They want you to be happy—and forget about what they are up to (while remaining aware that they are the ones in charge).[31]

Night Watch and *Day Watch,* in other words, redraw both history and reality for the new Russia. With *Twilight Watch* originally set to be filmed in America and in English—proof of Bekmambetov's "triumph" over Hollywood cinema or his betrayal of "Russian" cinema, depending on your views—the next pairing of Ernst/Bekmambetov was seen by many as the "true" end to the trilogy. For this encore, Ernst and Bekmambetov used the Chalk of Fate to redraw the Brezhnev past for the present.

A COMMERCIAL FOR THE NEW RUSSIA

El′dar Riazanov's 1975 film *Irony of Fate* is unquestionably the most beloved Soviet film. When it debuted at 6:00 p.m. on January 1, 1976, one hundred million viewers watched it on Channel One. When it appeared on big screens later that year another twenty million viewers watched it. Since its first broadcast, it has aired every New Year's Eve, serving as a Soviet equivalent of *It's a Wonderful Life.*[32] Russian New Year would not be complete without *Irony of Fate.*

The plot is straightforward: on New Year's Eve, a young doctor named Zhenia Lukashin attends an annual gathering of friends at a Moscow *banya.* When Lukashin tells his friends he is planning to propose to his girlfriend that night, the boys break out vodka and begin to toast the otherwise tee totaling Zhenia. They end up so inebriated that they place Lukashin on a flight to Leningrad instead of his friend Pavlik. Without realizing that he is in another city, Lukahsin asks a cab driver at the airport to take him to his home at 3rd Builders Street, House 25, Apartment 12. The sameness of late-Soviet cities produces the biggest joke of the film, for Leningrad also has an apartment at that address. Zhenia's key even fits the lock. Passed out in the bed of what he believes to be his home, Zhenia is found by the apartment's resident, a beautiful woman named Nadia. Her boyfriend, Ippolit, is about to come over to propose to her. Over the course of the night, both Zhenia and Nadia realize that their relationships are not fulfilling. They fall in love but decide to part, believing that they cannot alter their fates. At the end, however, Nadia arrives in Zhenia's Moscow apartment, seemingly ready to live a happy life together.

The film's success affirmed Riazanov as the Soviet Union's most popular director: in a 1991 *Ekran* poll asking citizens to vote for the best director in Russian history, he received three times as many votes as the runner-up, Andrei Tarkovsky.[33] As Boris Minaev commented twenty years after the film's appearance,

> [A]ll came together because on top of [its] various layers there was TRUTH, an uncompromising, unspoken truth that knew no language in which it might be uttered. The truth that in a cheerless Soviet world you could still find cheer; you could be warm within the cold walls of new housing projects; in the midst of our awful Russian booze-ups, during our miserable New Year's celebrations, things could *still* be good. In what way? Why? Nowadays we can only guess.[34]

When the film airs today, one critic posited, every viewer "sighs nostalgically and then recalls his private experiences."[35]

At the very end, as Zhenia introduces Nadia to his mother and his friends, he asks them if they consider him fickle. The question implicitly asks whether or not Zhenia and Nadia will last. Lukashin's mother responds, "Let's wait and see [*Pozhivem, uvidim*]."

Thirty years later, Konstantin Ernst provided an answer to Lukashin's question. On New Year's Day, 2006, the day that *Day Watch* debuted, he announced that he would be writing and producing a sequel to Riazanov's classic. Eventually Bekmambetov signed on to direct and co-write the script. Just as Ernst had billed *Day Watch* as the "first film of 2006," he billed *Irony of Fate: Continuation* as the "first film" of 2008. Just as *Day Watch* broke box-office records, so, too, did its sequel of sorts: *Irony of Fate: Continuation* brought in $50 million. The remake of Riazanov also opens with a redrawing of the past: Zhenia and Nadia (the original actors appear in the sequel) did not marry after all. Nadia returned to Leningrad and married Ippolit. They had a daughter, Nadiusha (Elizaveta Boiarskaia). Zhenia had a son, Kostia (Konstantin Khabenskii), who also becomes a doctor. The film opens on New Year's Eve at the very same banya as in Riazanov's original, with Kostia joining his father's pals for their annual celebration. They tell the younger Lukashin about his father's adventures thirty years earlier and persuade young Kostia (who also does not drink) to down vodka shots to toast his dad. The friends pack Kostia off to St. Petersburg, where Nadiusha now lives at 3rd Builders Street. Her boyfriend, Iraklii (Sergei Bezrukov, the voice of Prince Vladimir) plans to propose to her at midnight. Kostia's arrival prevents the plan from being fulfilled. Kostia and Nadiusha naturally fall in love. Moreover, when Zhenia arrives in St. Petersburg to rescue his son, he meets up with Nadia again, fights with Ippolit again (Nadia and Ippolit are divorced), and falls in love again. At the end they both head back to Moscow, this time for real. As Arlene Forman concludes, "Bekmambetov's revisionist remake [one should add "Ernst's remake"] denies the possibility that intimacy, love and personal fulfillment could have existed in the Soviet era. His happy endings occur in the best of all possible worlds, the here-and-now. Even Putin is enlisted to convey the optimism of this Brave New Russia of abundance, vigor and youth."[36]

President Putin appears on a television, announcing the New Year on Pervyi kanal. The audience hears him declare, "These minutes always unite people of our large country because every one of us remembers the past, thinks about the future, and hopes for better." The film seemingly bears out Forman's comment that the new *Irony of Fate*'s message is to remind viewers that the Putin era is better than the Brezhnev era. Elena Iampol′skaia suggests in her review for *Izvestiia,* represents a "branding" for the New Russia. Iraklii works for Beeline Cell Phones and their products appear throughout the film, along with publicity for Nokia, Nestle, Aeroflot, Zolotaia Bochka beer, and Russian Standard vodka. Iampol′skaia argues that the first half of the film is a commercial for the cell phone company while the rest of the film brands "our life" around "cars, airplanes, mayonnaise, candy, chimes of Kremlin bells, and the new Russian national anthem."[37] The film, in other words, visually brands the zero years as prosperous and happy. She suggests that Ernst and Bekmambetov remake several other classic films (such as *Moscow Does Not Believe in Tears* and *Mimino*) in order to "update" them for Putin-era political considerations.

Iurii Bogomolov echoed some of Iampol′skaia's concerns. For him, *Irony of Fate Continuation* represented the two-pronged policy of the producer and his director. "Point 'A' is that they want people to return to the cinema," Bogomolov argued, while "point 'B' is to combine and draw together Russia's different generations" through a film everyone will like.[38] "Point 'B'," Bogomolov wrote, "appears to be particularly lofty and patriotic" and ultimately serves as an attempt to use television ads and movie attendance to unite Russians. For Bogomolov, the Ernst/Bekmambetov plan is "Stakhanovite" in its quest to best box office records with each new production and in its use of "propaganda" on the small screen to promote its products.[39] He concludes that the cinema business is just like politics: Pervyi kanal has no rivals just as "United Russia [Putin's political party]" has no rivals.[40]

Iampol′skaia also delves into the film's reception and finds it surprisingly positive among young and old alike. Surveying both her friends and internet chatrooms, she concludes that most viewers saw *Irony of Fate Continuation* not as great art like its predecessor, but as a suitable follow-up, a satisfactory addition to the New Year's film genre.[41] Although she remains unimpressed with the remake (she declares at the outset that to compare it to Riazanov is "dishonorable"), she does suggest that the new film represents twenty-first-century sensibilities. Watching *Irony of Fate: Continuation,* she writes, is an exercise in admitting "It is necessary to understand that the era of good old films is past." Riazanov's original, viewed through the lens of Ernst's remake, represents "another time, different sentiments."[42]

Many viewers, however, expressed extreme displeasure with the film and what they saw as Ernst's and Bekmambetov's shameless attempt to milk a film classic for cash. Because Ernst's project desired box-office returns above all else, critical filmgoers commented, *Irony of Fate: Continuation* lacked "soul." One viewer's post to *Kinopoisk* is worth quoting in its entirety:

AN OPEN LETTER TO TIMUR BEKMAMBETOV
(INSTEAD OF A REVIEW)

> You do not know me, Timur. I know you much better than I would like. I know you, because in your creations you reveal your soul to your viewers. And we, as spectators, receive a chance to glance into it, to see what is piled up and what swarms around in there.
>
> By the way, about the soul. Today is indeed Christmas, Timur. But it is usual on this important holiday for Orthodox people to show mercy to the sinful and to be occupied with self-reflection. His hands will not touch you, this is completely clear. Therefore, as a special favor to you, I will receive a lash in the hands. And why will I take your sins upon me? When you repent, your soul will be closer to God. However, it seems that you are not of the Orthodox faith . . .
>
> I saw your film, Timur. Timur, you do know that in Rus′ people created things that defiled the sacred? Do you understand that to ruin beauty is odious and loathsome? Please understand me; I love neither the Soviet Union nor Soviet films. But there are things that belong to Russian culture. Who gave you permission to mess with Russian culture?

I am sad: I saw Miagkov [the actor who plays Zhenia] and Shirvindt [the actor who plays Pavlik] in your film. Riazanov himself even appeared briefly [he appears, as he did in the original, as the passenger next to the drunk Lukashin]. Even if such people cannot give up the chance to dance on a masterpiece's corpse, then what is required from the others? For the old men, however, it is possible to make allowances—they must feed their families, give New Year gifts to grandchildren, and the salary given to elderly actors is miserly.

But here also is the millionaire Bezrukov, who captured everyone's fancy in the role of a district-metrosexual in the famous television-fairy tale.[[43]] They say that people like to have a finger in every pie. Indeed, did he already forget? Recently he promised to break his ties with television and film roles. He said, "I will play Jesus in *The Master and Margarita* for nothing and certainly not for all the tea in China [*ni za kovrizhki,* literally "not for all the honey cakes"]." . . . He promised to go into the theater. Forever. No lie. It frightened him, probably, that on the streets people will forget him. Or he calculated the salary paid to theater actors and cried a little (Do you know, Timur, how much an actor in the theater now earns? Seven thousand per month. Rubles, naturally).

But now, about Bezrukov. For me it is desirable to believe that he has deeply personal reasons to be in this film. Let us assume he secretly hates you, Timur, and he wanted to spoil your premiere with his mediocre acting. And bite off a little money in addition. Otherwise I cannot explain why he is so wooden and heartless in your film.

In general, Timur, did you take note? The greater the sparkles and colors, the less soul there is. The original *Irony* had no special effects. It was all based on acting and the spectator believed that living people were onscreen. But yesterday I looked at Khabenskii, at Boiarskaia, at Bezrukov, at Efremov [who plays Father Frost] and I was surprised. All these people studied at GITISakh and VGIK with great teachers. Why are they so impersonal and worthless? But then I thought perhaps it's not the actors who grew petty? Maybe there are such people that they play? Perhaps our society now has such impersonal, petty and hypocritical people? What say you?

But who is guilty, Timur? Who is guilty that we ceased to respect our parents? Do you not know, Timur, why Mikhail Efremov slandered his brilliant father in the latest interview with *Russian Newsweek*?[[44]] Allegedly, the father also believed cinema to be "hack work," therefore he does not reveal himself fully [as an actor] in cinema. Allegedly, theater is the most important thing for an actor. So let's then compare the father's film acting with his acting! Let's think a little—would the father begin to hold out on the public, would he begin to flaunt his alcoholism, would he begin to participate in such a vulgar show, would he begin to sell his face to any scoundrel for some kopecks?

Khabenskii also raves about the theater. "I came, as a youth, into the theater. As a young person I developed there." Well, then he wreaked havoc on the big screen! Who are you giving this to? Where it does hide, this great actor's gift, in what back streets? To whom, even if you don't go to the theater but to the cinema?

Recently much is said about the revival of Russian cinema. Our cinema, they say, already blooms like a magnificent flower. Yes, Timur, it blooms, but do not be deceived: this is not the smell of chamomile, but the usual nonsense. Moreover the major directors are no better than the other. I am not only referring to you; indeed the adolescent child Egorushka Konchalovsky, whose film *Konservy* caused prolonged nausea, and even our "*metry*" like Nikita Sergeevich Mikhalkov fell into the morass.

I understand, Timur, it's useless to appeal to yours and to Ernst's conscience. It's also useless to appeal to your mind. But let's think about the children. You know, a kindergarten stands next to my house; returning yesterday from the cinema, I thought about whether or not these girls and boys are really doomed to grow up watching SUCH films, SUCH telecasts and listening to THIS music? It mostly transported me—I was also a teenager during the post-Soviet era. I remember, for example, what NTV was in 2000–2002, and what it became after the loss of independence. Here you could think willy-nilly.

Certainly, Timur, the children and grandchildren of our television and cinema bosses will not grow up in Russia. They have long since been nursed in jolly old England, in America, or in France by the teachers of elite schools there.

This is the age-old dream of many people: to clean out the purses of Russian citizens and head to the hills. I heard that you will also move across the ocean and will make a film with Angelina Jolie. I pinch myself with the hope that your picture will come out. Then you will probably never return and you will allow us in Russia to breathe more freely. Only change your name so that the foreigners will understand your last name. Give yourself a pseudonym or leave to get married (and in California this is possible. I read their laws: there it is possible even for a little dog to take a wife. Not a state, but a paradise for *ushlepky* of all colors).

But nevertheless, Timur, tell us—why do you, along with Ernst, continue to consider us, the spectators, the ultimate morons? Yes, you again buttered up the critics. Now even respected, sensible journalists assert that commercial cinema must be "healthy," "slightly absurd," or "not taxing for the spectator." In a word, almost all are happy. Take note, these are the same critics who found faults in von Trier, Polansky, and in Kim Ki-duk. Confess, Timur, you are not von Trier, not Polansky and not Kim Ki-duk; there must be more faults in your work. But our press thankfully did not find them. Here is Russia's third misfortune after fools and roads—cowardly journalists.

But I, from the height of my twenty years of age, boldly assert that your film's script is written for thirteen-year-olds, it is uneven and ridiculous. Almost all my peers have the same opinion. If our parents, grandmas, and grandpas cling to another view, then it is only because Mr. Ernst's entertaining television washed out the remainder of their brains.

> Yes, Timur, it is painful and it is offensive to me that our great cinema and our great culture perish by a violent death and no one intervenes for them. Think about this. And maybe Ernst will think about it. And maybe your entire company, including the PR people and the sponsors.
>
> Bye-bye and Merry Christmas to you. Although perhaps you do not believe in God?[45]

As a window into the way a post-Soviet young person formulates a sense of self by thinking about blockbuster films, this post is an extreme but nevertheless revealing look. "Tony Cameron" suggests that films serve as an important means for self-evaluation. To be a patriotic Russian, his post reveals, is to believe in "Russian culture" but also to hate the Soviet Union. The response also equates Orthodoxy and ethnic Russianness with patriotism while remaining suspicious of any "foreign" (particularly American) elements within national culture (although it's fine to like foreign filmmakers and their craft). Ernst and Bekmambetov, "Tony Cameron" claims, have sucked the soul out of Russian culture, remaking it into light entertainment that will keep Russian children, parents, and grandparents from thinking for themselves in the years ahead.

Many professional critics and filmgoers alike viewed the film as the final part of the *Night Watch* trilogy, a reading shaped by the news that Bekmambetov had already finished *Wanted* (*Osobo opasen*), starring Angelina Jolie. "Ebel" posted that "we now have a sequential watch, a new-year WATCH, where all the ingredients are present: Bekmambetov, the seasoned Khabenskii, multimillion special effects, and a shallow plot." "Grou40" concluded that the remake "sincerely carries out 'Putin's plan.' Indeed, Konstantin Arkad'evich [Ernst] and his 'First Command' are the main spokesmen for this plan and here it is so." "Fedor79" agreed, calling the film "state cinema politics" and taking particular umbrage at the insertion of Putin's 2008 "PRESENT day speech" that called for Russians to stay the course in the last year of his presidency. "Kastaned" viewed the film solely as "an attempt to make a blockbuster, to tear cash away from the population by playing on their love for the Soviet film (and by the way this attempt was pretty successful, for around me at the cinema sat many people of the age, with respect, who are evidently far from cinema regulars)."[46]

Bekmambetov's and Ernst's trilogy suggests that Russians can rewrite their past. At the end of *Day Watch,* Anton opts to use the Chalk of Fate to stop Zavulon's apocalypse and return Russia to 1992. The film, as Boris Groys argues, "Is about the attempt to correct history." This urge does not say much about reality, he argues, but does speak volumes about "the psychology of people who live in this reality" and how "they cannot cope with it." Mikhail Ryklin expands on this: "The concealed code of the *Watch* films, as it seems to me, is in introducing an intermediate component between the loss of the USSR . . . and wild capitalism."[47] The films provide a means to understand both the collapse of everything that was forever until it was no more and the overkill of the 1990s. *Irony of Fate* provides a sequel to this search for meaning—here Khabenskii not only lives happily in contemporary Russia (he did not in *Day Watch*), he helps reunite Zhenia and Nadia. Zavulon is vanquished in this new, rewritten Russia: Viktor Verzhbitskii, who played the Day Watch leader in both films, appears as a clueless homeless man in *Irony of Fate Continuation.*[48] Ernst declared that he selected 1992 as the beginning and end of the two *Watch* films because it was "at that moment everything started and when a very promising model was not realized." Gaidar's reforms did not work for "objective reasons," but under Putin, Russia is witnessing "an attempt to put a brake on the incorrect motion." "The *Watch* films," Ernst concludes, "are about the history of Russian duality, about how brittle a Russian equilibrium is, for it is always disrupted because its construction is not perfect." "Russia," he goes on, "is not a Western country," and therefore the films do not have the Dark Others as pure evil and the Light Others as pure good. Instead, Russia constantly struggles with its identity, with good and bad within everyone, functioning as a cocktail of East and West.[49] The *Watch* films and *Irony of Fate Continuation* allow Russians to see this struggle onscreen, wrestle with it, and redraw their fates by turning back the clock.

NOSTALGIC CREATIONS

Ernst's projects, like Luk′ianenko's Chalk of Fate, rewrite the past for present-day consumption. They also tap into nostalgia, a word that many use when referring to Ernst's productions. As Svetlana Boym has defined it, "nostalgia is a longing for a home that no longer exists or has never existed." It has permeated the modern era, and "the nostalgic desires to obliterate history and turn it into private or collective mythology, to revisit time like space, refusing to surrender to the irreversibility of time that plagues the human condition."[50] In her largely sympathetic study of nostalgia, which Boym sees as particularly prevalent in post-Soviet Russia, she draws a distinction between "restorative" nostalgics and "reflective" nostalgics. The former want to rebuild the past by clinging to Golden Ages, while the former look to the past as past. As Boym defines them, "restorative nostalgia manifests itself in total reconstructions of monuments of the past, while reflective nostalgia lingers on ruins, the patina of time and history, in the dreams of another time and place."[51] Nikita Mikhalkov's œuvre is an example of the former, particularly his film *Barber of Siberia;*[52] Joseph Brodsky's works would be an example of the latter.[53]

Boym posits that communism's collapse unleashed a wave of restorative nostalgia in Russia. "The collective trauma of the past was hardly acknowledged at all," she argues, "or if it was, everyone was seen as an innocent victim or a cog in the system only following orders. The campaign for recovery of memory gave way to a new longing for the imaginary ahistorical past, the age of stability and normalcy."[54] One example she cites of the longing for the "old" in the 1990s is *Old Songs about the Most Important.*[55] In Boym's schema, Ernst's project is a restorative—and therefore a bad—form of nostalgia.

Following Boym, many Western and Russian critics have cynically viewed postcommunist nostalgia as "an impediment to democratization" or as dangerous kitsch that fails to engage in serious efforts to understand the USSR.[56] The Brezhnev era, *Irony of Fate*'s temporal setting, has polled particularly well in various publications that ask Russians to rate their past—by 2006, most Russians stated they would rather live in the present era than any other, but Brezhnev's Russia finished a respectable second.[57]

It is tempting to read Ernst's productions as tapping into and reinforcing nostalgia for the Brezhnev era. In addition to his *Old Songs about the Most Important* and *Irony of Fate: Continuation,* Ernst produced the television film *Brezhnev,* directed by Sergei Snezkin and from a script by Valentin Chernykh.[58] The four-part series covers Brezhnev's last year in office and attempts to present him as sickly and old, but far from the feeble leader who had lost touch with reality that Soviet anecdotes stress.[59] Airing in March 2005 on Pervyi kanal, just a week after Leonid Parfenov's documentary *The Face of Leonid Il′ich, Brezhnev* received good ratings that led *Itogi*'s Stanislav Odoevtsev to declare, "Konstantin Ernst and Anatolii Maksimov [the coproducer] have once more confirmed their unique producers' feelings."[60] Viewers liked Sergei Shakurov's performance as the general secretary and argued that the film showed Brezhnev "as he was": "his humaneness, kindness, and reasonable thinking" and not "the mumbling idiot that our humorists depicted him as." Another viewer wrote that "the twentieth century was incredibly hard on Russia," for it had to survive "two world wars, the Revolution, Stalin's reforms" and even the Khrushchev Thaw, when "people did not live so easily." By contrast, the Brezhnev years brought some "stability" and "the Soviet people for a time breathed more freely." The film, as this viewer noted, was "remarkable" for capturing "the reality of 1982."[61]

As a perfect encapsulation of Ernst's plan for patriotic productions, *Brezhnev* makes a strong case for viewing them as restorative nostalgia. The same could be said for the *Watch* films, which essentially return Anton to the Brezhnev era, and *Irony of Fate: Continuation,* which asks viewers to see present stability as even better than Brezhnev stability. In this conceptualization, Ernst's films essentially reemphasize the Brezhnev-era focus on accepting the status quo (a task Brezhnev-era films performed).[62] Bogomolov has made the case for Ernst's empire to be viewed thus. Pervyi kanal's "projects are accompanied by the congratulations, toasts, fireworks of self-glory, that cause you to recall the Communist Party of the Soviet Union's transparent decorations that read 'Glory to the CPSU!'"[63] Bogomolov notes that *Night Watch* appeared with a great deal of self-congratulatory adverts that "pushed its heroes, authors, scenes, and songs" and that "the very same occurs now with *Turkish Gambit.*" Pervyi kanal completed the process with *Brezhnev,* which Bogomolov labels a "bad anecdote" that masquerades as history. Ultimately, he concludes that *Brezhnev* "is not about Brezhnev" but is "an allegory of the life and death of the Soviet regime."[64] The original title of the series,

Brezhnev: Twilight of the Empire had to be shortened to just *Brezhnev* because Ernst planned to run Khotinenko's series *Death of the Empire* after Snezkin's. If one takes the 2000 serial *Empire under Attack, Brezhnev,* and *Death of the Empire* together, what Ernst produced is a nostalgic look at the death of empires. The USSR, in other words, should be seen as a nice, rational, humane old grandpa that died a natural death—just like the good old Russian Empire did.

Yet perhaps it is possible to read this nostalgic project differently. Peter Fritzsche, writing about the Napoleonic era, argues that Europeans understood the ruptures caused by wars and revolutions in profoundly important ways. "The past," he argues, "was conceived more and more as something bygone and lost, and also strange and mysterious, and although partially accessible, always remote."[65] Modern nostalgia, Fritzsche suggests (what he terms "the melancholy of history"), grew out of this period. In this periodization he agrees with Boym. However, Fritzsche's work suggests that it is not so easy to draw distinctions between "restorative" and "reflective" nostalgia. Instead, the fervor with which many Europeans researched, recovered, and consumed history after Napoléon was done with the knowledge that the past was past and could never be returned to. "Nostalgia," Fritzsche concludes, "calls for a return home, but it does so in conditions of homelessness and with the knowledge that home is lost and loss is what remains."[66]

Fritzsche's ideas transport nicely to the post-Soviet era. The rupture of 1991 provided an experience akin to the Napoleonic era. Russians today view the past, particularly the past as evoked by Ernst, as something to be looked upon and reflected upon but something that is irretrievable. As Serguei Oushakine has aptly characterized it, post-Soviet nostalgia "is an attempt to chronologically enclose, to 'complete' the past in order to correlate it with the present."[67] Leonid Parfenov phrased this feeling succinctly: "[W]e're nostalgic but we're not crazy."[68] Ernst's empire, in other words, is largely about retrofitting the past, allowing consumers to think nostalgically about history but also forcing them to recognize that they live in the present and that they cannot return to any golden eras. Viewed in this fashion, watching *Old Songs about the Most Important, Brezhnev,* and *Irony of Fate: Continuation* can been understood as evoking a host of nostalgias and a host of emotions, from wistful reminders of the past to an ironic capitalist consumption of the socialist past.[69]

Many Russian critics view Ernst as a creator of a nostalgic empire, a person who plays with the past in order to experiment on contemporary citizens. The author and critic Dmitrii Bykov believes that Ernst has remained in his original career of genetic engineer—instead of working on scientific experiments, however, he "has set up an immense experiment on reality."[70] "Ernst's aesthetics," Bykov writes, which first appeared in *Old Songs,* "soon became those of the state." It is Ernst's gift as a biologist, in other words, to first discover society's symptoms to treat. Aleksandr Sekatskii labels Ernst's work "a creation [*tvorchestvo*]" because it cannot be captured in words such as "architect" or "experience." For him, Ernst has created a fantasy world, an alternate, nostalgic, popular one for the masses. At the same time, Sekatskii writes, "It is necessary to give credit to Konstantin Ernst," for he "knew how to calculate all the details and competing interests in his audiences just as he succeeded earlier in accurately calculating the nostalgic musical score for *Old Songs about the Most Important.*"[71]

Ernst himself helped to define the zero years to his 2006 *Seans* (*Performance*) interviewer. When the film journalist commented that each decade of Russia's twentieth-century history can be explained in one word, he cited "terror" for the 1930s, "war" for the 1940s, "thaw" for the 1950s and 1960s, "stagnation" for the 1970s, and "perestroika" for the 1980s. "The 1990s," the journalist commented, "are known by two words: chaos and freedom." Ernst retorted, "It seems to me that the 1990s are a 'building block.'" How then would he characterize the zero years? "The time of chance," Ernst replied, "not for me, but for the entire country. . . . If we answer the calls [our country makes] correctly, then the zero years will become the time of realized chances. If we answer them incorrectly, then we will say that our chance was not realized."[72]

Whatever the outcome, Ernst took his chance and seized control of his fate in the zero years. Even the journal *Seans,* which has criticized "audience-friendly" "patriotic blockbusters," had two special additions to its end of the year publication for 2006. The journal first asked a host of film people what Ernst's fate would have been had he not become a producer and then asked the same people to come up with the "formula" for Ernst's success. Most stated he would have become a film producer even if he had used the Chalk of Fate himself (Roman Valubev suggested he would have been a gangster, Vladimir Khotinenko had him as a lepidopterist like Nabokov).[73] As to his formula, the respondents listed "talent," "creativity," "will power," "love for money," "a desire to be first," "romanticism plus pragmatism," "intuition," "ambition," and "a profound knowledge of the time."[74] The fact that the journal conceptualized its "*Seans* Asks" feature on Ernst's terms attests to just how successfully the producer extraordinaire has redrawn Russia. It seems Ernst is always capable of conjuring New Year magic.

Soiuz store, GUM, Moscow.

CONCLUSION

Packaging the Past

Our journey into blockbuster history began at the multiplex, which served as the initial locus for understanding film as a theater of historical remembrance. It ends at another new memory site that has appeared in post-Soviet Russia: the video store.

Video stores in the new Russia sell every film, game, and soundtrack mentioned in the previous chapters. The Soiuz chain, to pick one prominent example, operates 40 stores and 9 "hypermarkets" throughout Russia, while also distributing goods to 150 other shops. The company, founded in 1992, bills itself as one that "specializes in the production and realization of products related to the business category of intellectual entertainments."[1] Because of its nationwide reach, Soiuz also attempts to combat video piracy, which is traditionally high in Russia's provinces. The company also operates a music label, serves as an official distributor of foreign and domestic films, and even helps to produce DVD versions of films—Soiuz officially produced Aleksei Balabanov's *Cargo 200.* In short, a trip into the world of Soiuz is a trip into how much Russia has changed since 1991.

At a Soiuz shop or at the numerous video stores like it, the blockbuster history screened first in theaters is packaged and sold. The slick stores that populate Russian cities sell the latest Hollywood blockbusters but also now feature burgeoning sections devoted to "Russian cinema" or "Soviet classics." Because of the emergence of new Russian films and new shops to sell Russian films, distributors such as Nashe Kino (Our Cinema) have appeared. Sergei Selianov, Balabanov's producer, created the company in 2003 and devoted it to "advancing new Russian cinema."[2] Soiuz also sells the special edition DVDs of new blockbusters, Ruscico classics of Soviet and post-Soviet movies, and the new collections of Soviet classics packaged under the titles "our cinema," "our new serials," and "classics of Russian cinema." In other words, the past and patriotism, however they are packaged, sell well at Soiuz. Soiuz, Nashe Kino, and similar corporate structures parallel Karo's rise; collectively, they reinforce each other, making Russia's new patriotic cinema possible.

The meanings of the new Russian cinema and the stores that sell new products have been hotly debated throughout the zero years. Just as Soiuz customers buy a product, unwrap it, and interpret it in their own way, so too is it possible to unwrap several meanings for blockbuster history. Some critics have charged the state and the film industry with creating a "kvas patriotism" that goes down smoothly and keeps the population in line. Others have lamented what they view as the death of national cinema sacrificed at the altar of Hollywood-style commercialism. Still others have celebrated the revival of Russian national cinema. Let us unwrap some of these interpretations and see what they reveal.

KVAS PATRIOTISM

Every year, the editors of *Iskusstvo kino,* Russia's most influential film journal, hold a series of roundtable discussions about Russian cinema. Usually coinciding with the Moscow International Film Festival, these roundtables serve as a way to gauge the state of Russian film as seen through the eyes of important critics, academics, and directors. By January 2006, *Iskusstvo kino* had identified a singularly important trend developing within Russian cinema. The success of *Night Watch, Turkish Gambit, Ninth Company,* and of Russian films at various festivals had helped, the editors believed, to form a "new patriotism." *Iskusstvo kino* wanted to explore what this patriotism meant and how cinema had contributed to it. They gathered three sociologists (Daniil Dondurei, Tat′iana Kutkovets, and Dmitrii Oreshkin), one author (Denis Dragunskii), three directors (Vitalii Manskii, Aleksandr Mitta, and Nikita Mikhalkov), and three critics (Iurii Bogomolov, Viktor Matizen, and Kirill Razlogov). *Iskusstvo kino* posed four questions about patriotism to the panel:

> Do you believe that the attempt to unite society on a platform of patriotism is connected with a scarcity of ideas, a scarcity of social agreement, a scarcity of social prospects, and general civic passiveness?
>
> What mythologies, criteria, and formulas of patriotism exist today?
>
> What subjects, themes, and heroes does contemporary cinema propose as models?
>
> What and whose social expectations do the contemporary version of Russian patriotism answer?

Daniil Dondurei, the sociologist and editor of *Iskusstvo kino,* took the first stab. He located the new patriotic culture first in the public perception of what the 1990s meant: fifteen years after collapse, "entrepreneurs—on television, in the imagination, and therefore, also in life itself—are exclusively represented as bandits." Consequently, "in people's consciousness an entire ideological system has developed where labor, creativity, and activity are not values." Instead, a new patriotism has sprung up to fill the ideological void. While Dondurei did not view patriotism itself as evil, he lamented what he saw as the lack of "a peaceful understanding" of it, for he believed that Russian patriotism "besides sport, is associated only with war, with victims, and with violence." The result of this fixation on war remembrance as the basis for societal unity is that certain suppositions logically follow: namely, that "foreigners are terribly dangerous and that the most important thing is to protect our boundaries." Ultimately, Dondurei concludes, "the new patriotism . . . which is seen in films and in television programs . . . is connected with the restoration of socialist models" for "they tell us about the past as the present or on the future as arranged on the models of the past."[3] The "new" Russian patriotism is not so new after all.

Denis Dragunskii, the second to respond, took issue with Dondurei's negative, singular view of the new patriotism. For him, "the question about patriotism is very complex," for it is tied to individual love for and views of the native land. "Let us take the visual aspect of this love," he stated, "for some, this is an actual view of a little corner of the native land, for someone else it is Repin's painting *Ivan the Terrible Killing His*

Son, for another Levitan's picture *Above the Eternal Peace,* and for a third person even Glazunov's *Eternal Russia.*" For Dragunskii, a host of associations made up "Russian patriotism": individual aspects of this patriotism such as the works he listed "do not unite the majority of people, but some small groups," whereas the more general and abstract notion of "love for your country" unites everyone. The new Russian patriotism on screen thus encapsulates this process, potentially offering a range of views that symbolize "Russia."

The rest of the respondents followed this dichotomy. Iurii Bogomolov, while acknowledging that "patriotism is an instinct" that "man is born with," warned that Russian patriotism all too frequently gives way to xenophobia, for "when we search for 'ours,' immediately we imply 'not ours'" and "the search for the enemy of the people begins." Aleksandr Mitta believed that the very concept of patriotism "has been captured and compromised by our politicians" and instead proposed that Russians adopt "a more delicate formula—a feeling for the native land [*chuvstvo rodiny*]." This new formula should be connected to an environmental understanding of love for the land and the threats to it (he cites Lake Baikal's degeneration as an example). Tat′iana Kutkovets divided Russian patriotism into two components: "topographical and sacrificial patriotisms." The former, "patriotism of peace," is a "normal phenomenon" where a person loves his native land "isolated from the state." The latter is associated with war and the state and implicitly is abnormal.

Dmitrii Oreshkin picked up on this division to argue that Russian cinema may be creating a "liberal patriotism" in the broadest sense, one "that rests not on the demands of a corporation [either the government or a business]," but on "the interests and dreams of living people, on personality, on talent." Good literature and good cinema, the basis for a "liberal patriotism," is not tied to a particular political ideology, but to talent, "which always implies freedom." In this sense, Pushkin and Gogol, Nabokov and Bulgakov were liberal patriots, for they all wrote about their native land from different perspectives and in so doing "created expanding spaces . . . for cultural potential." For Oreshkin, the specific features of patriotism do not matter as much as the cultural conditions where patriotic ideas get created: "state patriotism is a mode of subtraction . . . where our general cultural space narrows," while liberal patriotism expands the cultural space. Although he sees some dangerous signs from Vladimir Putin, Oreshkin believed that the freedom represented by the internet meant that "the thinking spectator" will be able to create a liberal patriotism. Nikita Mikhalkov spoke not about freedom, but love, specifically the "intimate and strange love" for the motherland, one "you either have or you do not." Viktor Matizen declared himself a "cosmopolitan" and concluded that "all attempts to introduce conscious patriotic ideas into cinema do nothing but harm." Kirill Razlogov disagreed in part with all his fellow panelists, arguing that patriotism is "a deep psychological process," one that developed historically—today's patriotism developed out of Soviet definitions, whereas Soviet patriotism grew out of tsarist nationhood. For Razlogov, language served as the key to the psychological process: "All Russian speaking people will continue to be fed by the juices of Russian language culture regardless of whether we call this patriotism," a process he compared to England and France and termed "gastronomical orientation."

In sum, while all the *Iskusstvo kino* panelists agreed that Russian cinema had helped to fuel a "new patriotism" in the zero years, they all disagreed over the meanings of this development. Many observers argued that the patriotic blockbusters that dominated Russian screens appeared because the state wanted a form of "kvas patriotism," one that producers and government officials fermented together in order to unite Russians.[4] Others have explained the new "cinepatriotism [*kinopatriotika*]" as the product of a nationwide desire to understand the past and how it has impacted the present.[5] And that may be precisely the point: numerous newspaper articles, television roundtables, journal articles, and special reports noted that the zero years seemed to be dominated by a "new patriotism." Opinions divided over what defined this patriotism, whether it was a good or bad development, and whether or not it had worked. But these opinions matter less than the larger discussion, one where everyone agreed that a patriotic culture centered on Russia's pasts had dominated the decade. Patriotic cinema brought a renewal of sorts to the film industry and paved the way for stores such as Soiuz. On their shelves you could buy collector's editions of blockbuster history meant to appeal to your sense of patriotism. The new "kvas cinepatriotism" also paralleled, and helped to fuel, the rise of a new economic nationalism.[6]

Regardless of which side you took in the debate, one thing was certain—film critics and film goers now saw and debated something other than the *chernukha* culture of the 1990s.

THE DEATH OR RESURRECTION OF RUSSIAN CINEMA?

In 2008, Timur Bekmambetov became the first-ever Russian director to lead the worldwide box office when his film, *Wanted* (*Osobo opasen*), debuted in June. Much as opinions divided over the patriotic culture on show in theaters and elsewhere, so, too, did opinions diverge on what this development meant. For some, Russian cinema had successfully revived; for others, it had died, becoming just like Hollywood and losing whatever "national" flavor it once had. Bekmambetov's *Wanted* brought these views into sharp focus.

Filmed in English and starring Angelina Jolie, Bekmambetov's first Hollywood blockbuster for many commentators represented either the resurrection of Russian cinema or the final nail in its coffin. Based on a graphic novel by Mark Millar and J. G. Jones, *Wanted* tells the story of a timid office drone who gets caught up with the Fraternity, a group of assassins who have been operating for centuries. *Wanted* featured the dizzying special effects for which Bekmambetov had become famous, had a $75 million budget, earned nearly $35 million in its first weekend, and grossed $340 million worldwide. Universal Pictures, which produced the movie, allowed the director to make a special Russian version of the film. Sergei Luk′ianenko, the writer of *Night Watch,* penned the Russian translations for the dubbed version. Bekmambetov used CGI to make it appear as though the characters originally spoke in Russian. Several Russian actors, many of whom had worked in the *Watch* films, added the voice-overs. Danny Elfman even altered his theme song for the Russian audience to make it more "Russian" sounding.[7]

Most reviewers analyzed the cross-cultural nature of the film. Vita Ramm of *Izvestiia* declared, "Timur Bekmambetov's migration to Hollywood was, in my view, inevitable," for "he was the first of our directors to master international standards in the business of advertising."[8] Ramm continued, "First Channel, after deciding to create a Hollywood-style shop for the production of domestic blockbusters, called upon Bekmambetov for these projects."[9] Russian cinema, in other words, had become so Hollywood-like in its aims that it was logical for Bekmambetov to make a blockbuster in America. Bekmambetov even brought his "special talisman," Konstantin Khabenskii, with him to California to make the movie, and gave him a secondary role. Audiences predictably divided over their view of the film: one spectator who posted on *Kinopoisk* declared that "a high level of patriotism forces me to award the film 10/10" while another declared that the film was "a national disgrace."[10] *Wanted* led the domestic box office for two weeks straight, earning $14 million its first week and $12 million its second.[11]

Bekmambetov declared that his work in Hollywood represented a chance to "explore new worlds." When asked by an interviewer what he learned, he answered that his work destroyed "the stereotype of American cinema as a machine that devours a director's creative energy and forces him to make something against his will."[12] The same skills he employed in his Russian films still worked in his first American blockbuster; moreover, *Wanted* was special because it was the first time a Russian transfer had been made by the creators of the film, not a third party.[13] Bekmambetov's interviewers on Echo Moscow, however, openly wondered whether this distinction mattered at all. The film was a "commercial" one, not a film that "we could live on for thirty to forty years." It was fluff, in short, not "real Russian cinema."

At issue here was what one could call "Russian" cinema by the end of the decade and how much it differed from Hollywood cinema. Russian films, and not just historical epics, had started to resemble American blockbusters: before they appeared, PR campaigns promoted them, Russian film culture increasingly became driven by celebrities, action and special effects dominated what got screened, and both the heroes and plots of the new Russian blockbusters seemed alien to some. Russian philosopher and cultural critic Vitalii Kurennoi published *The Philosophy of Film,* a collection of his articles on film, with Novoe literaturnoe obozrenie in 2009. The book explored the new patriotic and mass cinema in Russia and argued in part that while American cinema is a combination of national and universal cultures, the new Russian cinema has abandoned the national aspects of Soviet cinema in favor of a product that only adapts "American tricks and pyrotechnics." As a result, "today there is no general perspective in domestic cinema," no single, unifying ideal that distinguishes it as "Russian." Instead, Kurennoi posits, Russian films contain a combination of old Soviet elements (particularly in war films), religious motifs, attempts to unite audiences around hatred for internal enemies such as the NKVD (he cites *Shtrafbat* as a primary example of this type), and even silly elements that serve no purpose (he cites the unicorn in *1612*).[14] In becoming more like American cinema, therefore, Russian cinema lost its national soul.

Ideas such as this one appeared across Russia media in the zero years, particularly when the new patriotic blockbusters appeared. Often lost in the laments that "Russian" cinema had died, sacrificed to the altar of commercial Hollywoodism (cries in the zero years that stretched back to the appearance of *Star* and that particularly grew louder after films such as *Night Watch* and *Turkish Gambit* appeared), was the big-picture perspective, one that acknowledged just what had transpired in the zero years. Seen as dead already by the end of the 1990s, Russian cinema resurrected itself in the next decade in part because of its attempt to harness Hollywood styles and effects to Russian histories and stories. After the depths to which it had sank in the 1990s, post-Soviet cinema had to develop from scratch a new (or renewed) cinematic field: from action films to sci-fi, full-length animated films to detective thrillers, horror films to historical epics. Russian film used Hollywood styles to remake national cinema: whether it was through special effects (some have interpreted Bekmambetov's films as ones that created a "new visual language"), the soundtrack (Artem′ev's explicit engagement with Jarre's score), cinematography (Andrei Zhegalov's work on films ranging from *The Cuckoo* to *The Island* that were meant to evoke Russian landscapes), or even the use of star power to promote films (the cast of *Ninth Company* that starred in the comedy *Heat*), the new Russian cinepatriotism developed out of a large spectrum of styles and genres that either did not exist in the Soviet Union, were marginalized, or were destroyed. The main "Russian" component to this new cinema consisted of the patriotic-historical content within and its ability to convince audiences that it contained a national flavor. Bekmambetov's effects on *Wanted,* to pick one example, used Russian computers and technologies, which prompted an *Izvestiia* interviewer to ask whether or not Russia had surpassed the West or whether or not Bekmambetov relied on domestic help out of a sense of patriotism.[15]

By decade's end, *Iskusstvo kino* could even report that the country had DCI auditoriums, 3-D cinemas, an ever-expanding number of multiplexes, and thriving markets for DVD rentals and purchasing. The driving force of these developments, the report noted, was the "blockbusterization [*blokbasterizatsiia*]" of the market.[16]

Some critics even acknowledged that the adoption of Hollywood-style effects and marketing could lead to improved Russian cinema. Dar′ia Goriacheva, reviewing Aleksei Uchitel′'s 2010 epic, *The Edge*—about a war veteran that heads to a position in a Siberian labor camp after 1945—declared that it represented "the most successful example in the history of the new Russian cinema to Russianize the form of the Hollywood blockbuster."[17] The film, she argued, successfully crossed genres and formats—it could be advertised as an art-house film or an audience-friendly one, an action movie and a historical epic. Its success, however, came because it had successfully created a new Russian blockbuster hero that did not just replicate Hollywood conventions. Goriacheva titled her article "The Peculiarities of the National Blockbuster."

GOSZAKAZ CULTURE?

The July 2008 report in the *Los Angeles Times* sounded ominous. It began with a mention of Russian Prime Minister Vladimir Putin's visit to the set of Nikita Mikhalkov's *Burnt by the Sun 2*. "Putin didn't direct the action," the reporter noted, but his presence "was a potent symbol of his government's expanding role in the country's film industry."[18] After a brief paragraph that reminded readers of Lenin's use of film, one that helped to bend audiences "to the will of the totalitarian state," the article went on to state that "now the Russian government is trying to revive the Soviet film tradition, helping to produce movies and miniseries that push the Kremlin's political views, vilify its critics, and glorify the military and intelligence services."[19]

The cinepatriotism of the zero years so closely matches the patriotism espoused by Vladimir Putin's government that the only possible relationship between the two, so critics charge, is that Putin is behind both. Vasilii Gerosin of *Novaia gazeta* opined, "Our patriotic movies are the subconscious of the Russian authorities," and characterized the movies as "a rehash of the old Soviet material with a little bit of Hollywood thrown in."[20] The problem with the movies themselves, Gerosin has argued, is that they have not come up with any original ideas. This failure stems in part from the government's "strictly utilitarian approach to patriotic films treating them as a machine that needs to be fed with fuel (money, advertising, etc.) and set moving in the right direction, and the rest will take care of itself." Ultimately, "patriotic cinema is above all unconvincing psychologically," for it shies away from the audience and "still prefers to dictate."[21] Post-Soviet Russian film, then, is still very Soviet.

Clearly this line of thinking attempts to explain the rise of a patriotic culture in the zero years to the rise of Vladimir Putin's brand of political authority. The two are linked, but not as much as the critics charge: the Russian state established a fund to help produce domestic movies, but did not issue a state decree (*goszakaz*) that mandated the content of film. Vladimir Putin was a nobody in 1998; he emerged on the scene and into public consciousness only in August 1999, when Boris Yeltsin plucked him from relative obscurity and named him prime minister. Yet the decisions reached by 1998 by people such as Leonid Ogorodnikov, Nikita Mikhalkov, Karen Shakhnazarov, and Boris Akunin served as the cultural preparation for the fixation on patriotism that became a hallmark of Putin's presidency. What Karo did first, creating a precedent that the rest of the people discussed in this book followed, was to offer a space for screening the past and with it the opportunity to commodify Russian history and Russian patriotism. The actors behind the production of blockbuster history offered up a brand for Russia, one that packaged the past for patriotic consumption. The development of a new cinepatriotism in no way determined the decisions Putin made, but it did create the conditions that made his presidency possible.[22] It may be that journalists and scholars have rushed to dub the zero years the "Putin era," reviving in the process notions that the Kremlin controls everything, including the cultural sphere.[23]

The topic of whether or not the state has tried to reassert control over national culture has been a hotly debated one. Two events in late 2008 and early 2009 added fuel to this fire and seemingly swayed the debate to Gerosin's side: Putin became the head of a new film panel in October 2008 and the Russian government created a Presidential Commission for the Prevention of Falsification of History to the Prejudice of Russia's Interests in May 2009. After Putin's appointment to head the new film panel, which led many to dub the prime minister the new "film tsar," the film critic Iurii Bogomolov opined that cinema had become "the most important art form again" and served "as the engine for building myths that the government sorely needs."[24] Viktor Yerofeyev declared that the government was creating "a new-old civilization, an Orthodox civilization" that "doesn't repress like the Soviets yet, but give them two years." Vladimir Sorokin weighed in and argued that "our future is becoming our past," for "we are returning to Ivan the Terrible's era" after Putin's initial attempts to bring culture into the governmental sphere.[25] The new law on historical falsification codified a debate that had taken place over "history standards" in Russian schools, a discussion that stemmed from Putin's attempt to stress happy history; as he told a 2007 conference of teachers, "we cannot allow ourselves to be saddled with guilt." When Putin's administration approved A. V. Filippov's *A Modern History of Russia* as the standard history for Russian schoolchildren, it seemed that both cinema and history had returned to Soviet practices. Writing in the *New Republic,* Leon Aron compared the new textbook to Stalin's infamous *Short Course.*[26]

And yet blockbuster history proved to be more unpredictable than any government attempts to curb it. The most talked about film of late 2008 and early 2009, as the developments above took place, was Valerii Todorovskii's *Stiliagi,* produced by the Soiuz chain, which also put out the soundtrack. Set in 1955 Moscow, the filmmakers openly borrowed Hollywood musical styles to present a story of the hipsters who appeared in the late 1940s and who dressed in outlandish clothes while openly admiring the swing music of the West.[27] Todorovskii's film takes a *West Side Story* approach to this historical subject: the hipsters square off against Komsomol members. The plot centers on a Komsomol member who becomes a hipster and adopts the name Mels (for "MarxEngelsLeninStalin"). Katia, the leader of the Komsomol, denounces Mels as "worse than an enemy": he is "a traitor." She leads her fellow communist youth in a song that denounces Mels, who "sold himself to our enemy for bright clothes" thereby "deserting your conscience and honor." At the end, however, it is Mels who has the last word. Although a fellow hipster has told him the West is not all it's cracked up to be, Mels remains defiant—it is his ability to express himself freely that matters more. As he sings, he walks down Gorky Street, which becomes present-day Tverskaia, packed full of punk rockers, skateboarders, hippies, and hip-hop artists. Stalinist non-conformists, in short, are essentially the same as contemporary non-conformists.

The fact that Vladimir Putin once told an Echo Moscow radio host that he was "worse than an enemy, but a traitor," made Todorovskii's comment that the film "wasn't about the 1950s, but is true for any time" all the more meaningful. He added that the message of freedom had particular relevance for contemporary young people, given the message of conformity proffered by the Putin youth group Nashi.[28] Todorovskii believes that *Stiliagi* can serve as a "third path" to reaching audiences in post-Soviet cinema: not a "patriotic blockbuster" that glorifies the past or an empty "celebrity comedy" such as *Heat,* but a film that is not a "retro nostalgia but a straight analogy" between past and present.[29]

The film's tone was not lost on either spectators or critics. It earned $17 million, losing its box-office duel with Fedor Bondarchuk's futuristic anti-Putin film *Inhabited Island,* but still earning more than its budget. *Stiliagi* won the Nika for best picture of 2008, a decided critical poke at Putin's new attempts to reign in the film industry. As Artemy Troitskii offered, "both *Stiliagi* and *Inhabited Island* are profoundly anti-state films and this is what makes them good. Freedom, reason, and honesty—these things are absolutely incompatible with the Russian state, at least in the way that I know it from the times of Ivan the Terrible to the times of Vladimir Putin."[30] Elena Iampol′skaia, writing in *Izvestiia,* commented that Rossiia channel, which produced the film, had enjoyed a banner year because it also sponsored and broadcast the "Name of Russia" contest where Alexander Nevsky emerged as winner after Stalin had led.[31]

Audience members chose their sides too in this battle over the meanings of history. It's worth quoting two at length. First, from "Personal Jesus,"

> I arrived home from work tired, hungry and bad-tempered, as is the case with anyone who has to work on a holiday. I wanted to revive my mood by watching a good new film. I recalled that *Stiliagi* had come out on DVD. Although promised by its advertisement to be a "holiday," it was definitely not. Instead it produced a range of negative emotions in me because of the deep offense it caused to the generation of our heroic grandfathers, who this "masterpiece" abused.

For "Personal Jesus," the film glorified America and American values at the expense of the "real" Russian people. Moreover, it used history to glorify the actions of "elite children" who tended to become *stiliagi,* a situation the tired viewer considered to be true today—the children of the elite acquire wealth and American habits while the rest of Russia tries to get by and remains patriotic. "Personal Jesus" gave the film a 0/10.

"Dentitov" took the opposite view, stating that he was "astonished by the large number of negative responses [online] to this remarkable film." The film does not abuse heroic grandfathers; instead it "represents accurately and worthily" a veteran, Mels's father (played by Sergei Garmash), who is "a real Russian peasant, who survived the war, and who raised two sons by himself that each have a personality." The film, in his view, was about opposing a totalitarian system; in his words "about being a patriot and loving jazz, too." Ultimately, the film is "a history about people who wanted freedom, joy, and happiness." He gave it a 10/10.[32]

The film that Prime Minister Putin visited in the *Los Angeles Times* report quoted above also serves as an important reminder against interpreting the cinepatriotism of the zero years as goszakaz culture. *Burnt by the Sun 2* opened in April 2010, just in time for the sixty-fifth anniversary of Victory Day. Billed in the massive marketing campaign as "the great film about the great war," Mikhalkov's epic contained many of the themes that had appeared in previous blockbuster history offerings: a tale of war, a religious fable, a masculine hero, a revision of wartime taboos all found space in the film. Yet just like *1612,* another movie that many viewed as having been ordered by the state, *Burnt by the Sun 2* flopped. The massive public relations campaign waged by Mikhalkov even before the film's premiere produced criticisms. Irina Liubarskaia entitled her review "Overtired [*Pereutomlenie*]" and commented that the film's tepid performance in the box office had to do with the "unprecedented PR campaign."[33] The campaign started, Liubarskaia notes, more than five years before the film's release, when trailers advertising the film screened at various film festivals. Mikhalkov bombarded the airwaves beginning in April: a Russian analytical center estimated that he appeared on television five times a day that month promoting the film. As a result of this PR overload, Liubarskaia writes, a "similarly pushy PR campaign operated against the film." Together, both campaigns ensured that "the mysteries of the film died together with its spin. Now it is only possible to go and be convinced of what you had already concluded about the film."[34]

Critics tended to expand on these parameters and, when the film only made $2.5 million of its $55 million budget back on opening weekend, they attempted to diagnose the reasons for the film's failure. Oleg Zolotarev believed that "the reasons it has flopped are psychological," for "Mikhalkov is no longer seen as a director but as a state bureaucrat."[35] Audiences by and large agreed: Mikhalkov, who had become widely viewed as a state director and who had loudly proclaimed his love for Putin's policies, turned people off. One respondent to *Argumenty i fakty*'s poll about the film stated that Mikhalkov wanted "the contemporary 'Pepsi generation' to feel the war's tragedy" and therefore pitched the film to them. For him, "every scene was full of absurdity." Another took issue even with the attempt to make a film for post-Soviet young people, declaring, "I saw the film and consider it complete ideological shit for those whom we call 'teenagers' or 'Generation Next.'" *Burnt by the Sun 2* is "not for normal young people, patriots of their country." In the paper's internet poll that asked whether or not viewers liked the film (1662 responded), 18 percent said no, 8 percent yes, 32 percent said they had not seen it but planned to go, and 42 percent said they had not seen it and would not on principle.[36]

In the end, *Burnt by the Sun 2* became defined by its failure. Mikhalkov had become too tainted by his association with Putin and his brand of patriotism. Iurii Gladil'shchikov, who was not invited to the premiere because of his earlier negative reviews (including his scathing critique of *Barber of Siberia*), concluded that the film had enough bad parts to make anyone angry, whether it was because of Kotov's "Freddy Krueger hand," its "brutal naturalism," its "propagation of Orthodoxy," or "the showing of Nadia Mikhalkova's breasts."[37] Mikhalkov's cinematic "classical authoritarianism," the brand he had first offered in *Barber of Siberia* and one built on conservative patriotism, no longer appealed.

What *Burnt's* failure and *Stiliagi's* success indicate is that blockbuster history—and with it, the economic nationalism and revived patriotic culture that dominated the zero years—is not so easily reducible as history produced by the state. Other actors were involved: in the end, a new, full-fledged national cinema was brought about by market forces and patriotic sensibilities. Putin himself may have grasped this combination: in December 2011, after announcing he would run for president again, he picked filmmaker Stanislav Govorukhin to run his campaign.

RUSSIAN CIVIL SOCIETY?

The interpretations of blockbuster history have not all been negative. The arguments over *Stiliagi's* meanings quoted above reflect several ongoing processes in post-Soviet Russia. Viewers "Personal Jesus" and "Dentitov" disagreed about the meanings of the past and what it tells us about the present; they also disagree about the meanings of patriotic culture in a fashion similar to the *Iskusstvo kino* panel. The fact that they could engage in this debate over cyberspace, after watching the film in a multiplex (*Stiliagi* had a lavish premiere at Karo's October Theater) or after purchasing it in a DVD store such as Soiuz demonstrates just how much the commercial landscape of Russia had changed. In this sense the debate over *Stiliagi*—and the debates over the meanings of the past and the meanings of the Russian blockbuster—reflect how the new market system itself should be viewed as an ongoing process, a struggle to define meanings.[38]

The ability to spar verbally in cyberspace helps to support Oreshkin's view of a "liberal patriotism" developing in Russia. In 2009, the Communist Party had 150,000 members. That year, social networking site odnoklassniki.ru had 20 million registered users. United Russia, Putin's Party, had 2 million members; Vkontakte.ru had 18 million registered users. What the 1990s and zero years witnessed, as these figures indicate, was the creation of new ways to communicate and new ways to shape Russianness. The specific words used ("Personal Jesus" and "Dentitov") do not matter as much as the fact that they used them in a public, open forum. While Putin curtailed the unprecedented freedom Russian media outlets enjoyed throughout the 1990s, the internet has continued to grow and continued to remain free from government interference. Holli Semetko and Natalya Krasnobodka have argued that the Internet helps to foster civic democracy in "transition countries" such as Russia and Ukraine,[39] a claim that points to the significance of the statistics listed above. Indeed, as a recent collection on media in Russia argues, "the biggest global challenge posed to Putin's media control campaign comes from the rapid spread of Internet usage." Moreover, even state-owned television stations such as Channel One feature internet forums that foster "surprisingly open discussion threads, often going back several years."[40]

Many scholars have started to interpret the Internet as the latest building block for constructing Russian civil society, a key aspect of post-Soviet Russian political debates. According to some scholars, Russia has never successfully developed a "public sphere" and therefore a civil society. This failure to create autonomous spaces outside of state control ensured that democracy failed in early-twentieth-century Russia and that Russia remained outside the "norm" for European development.[41] The same failure has led some scholars to claim that Putin's control over media, combined with the lack of widespread opposition to this media clampdown, will ensure democracy's continued failure.[42] For pessimists, the rise of blockbuster history and the internet chatter that accompanied it can be viewed in the framework of Russia's historic "unfinished civil society": patriotic films and the desire for happy history, in other words, helped to build Putin's managed authoritarianism by using "new patriotism" to return to Soviet models, as Dondurei claimed.

Others see the situation more optimistically. Joseph Bradley has urged scholars to understand the growth of civil society not in terms of what did not happen—what he terms "a story of essentialism"—but in terms of what did—namely, how "a lively, non-revolutionary civic life emerged" in prerevolutionary Russia.[43] If one takes the view that we should look for what did happen in Russia rather than what did not, then the "surprisingly open" internet debates that proliferate in Russian cyberspace may in fact be the impetus for the sort of "participatory culture," "civic engagement," and "citizen journalism" that Henry Jenkins has described as essential to understanding "YouTube culture."[44] Framed a different way, the rise of the Internet and the talk that took place on it proves that Russia is a "normal country" after all.[45]

NATIONHOOD AND REMEMBRANCE AFTER COMMUNISM

The pasts explored in Russian historical blockbusters appealed throughout the decade. In 2008 alone, Oleg Fomin's April film *Gentlemen Officers* returned to the "Russia we lost" and followed the fortunes of a group of White officers trying to save the autocracy after 1917. Andrei Maliukov's February release *We Are from the Future,* written by Eduard Volodarskii, and Marius Vaisberg's summer comedy *Hitler Kaput!* added to the ongoing memory work of war films. Karen Shakhnazarov set his February film *The Vanished Empire* in the era of late socialism, a choice many critics interpreted as the Mosfil′m director's response to *Cargo 200.* Fantasy films as diverse as Adel′ Al′-Khadad's *The Ancient Russians* [*Rusichi*] and Aleksandr Mel′nik's futuristic *Terra Nova* (from a script by Arif Aliev) used past and future to foster national myths of origin and regeneration. What to make of this cultural trend? Was it, as Dondurei suggested, a use of the past that essentially used socialist methods of mass control? Or was it, as Dragunskii articulated, a range of symbolic representations of Russianness?

Perhaps it is best to conclude and to rethink the *Iskusstvo kino* debate by returning to the Soiuz store. Inside we can envision the packaging of the past, and with it the commodification of historical remembrance, as a process that involves consumers unwrapping the DVD plastic and with it their own understanding of the product. The blockbuster cinepatriotism that defined the movies of the zero years might best be understood as part of the ongoing construction of Russian nationhood. In this sense, the choices available at the Soiuz store roughly correspond to an "à la carte menu" of nationhood, one in which "the present creates the past in its own image" and contemporary nation builders seek to offer a menu of symbols from the past in order to reconstitute the contemporary national community.[46] The packaging and unwrapping of the past that takes place when a spectator watches the latest historical blockbuster or buys its DVD represents the last phase in how historical films serve as a site of contestation, one that helps us understand the two processes of nationhood and remembrance. As Mette Mjort and Scott Mackenzie argue, films "do not simply represent or express the stable features of a national culture, but are themselves one of the loci of debates about a nation's governing principles, goals, heritage, and history."[47] Despite the fact that cinema tends to be transnational, particularly Hollywood blockbusters on screen at a Karo multiplex or on sale at a Soiuz store, Russian cinema today has acknowledged and co-opted this aspect of filmmaking and repackaged it as "ours." Historical reconstructions on screen, heroes from the past who serve as models for the present, and films that visualize the Russian landscape—in short, the topoi of blockbuster history—have served as the loci for debates about the meanings of the 1990s, the meanings of the Soviet experience, and the meanings of Russian history. Russian consumers can select from a full menu of nationhood offered up in recent historical films: Russianness can be represented and internalized as equating Siberian forests, tsarist officers, old traditions such as Maslenitsa, prerevolutionary Moscow, the heroic defense of the motherland, wintry landscapes, monasteries, church music, a vague but vital "Russian spirit," the tradition of the holy fool, nineteenth-century literature, the landscapes of the Far North, a special form of Russian suffering, Orthodoxy, an ancient history, nineteenth-century art, folklore, the izba, Slavic traditions, the Time of Troubles, the starets, New Year's nostalgia, the Brezhnev era, and the manliness and sober-minded patriotism embodied in the security forces. It is a rich menu of Russian national traditions both new and old.[48]

The process of ordering from the menu—one that begins with the production and screening of historical memory and ends with it consumed by spectators—has become a much more vocal, much more public process in the zero years. Russian blockbuster history gets promoted as a brand of new patriotism, but it also gets hotly debated and frequently contested. Russia today may live in a multi-historical condition where the past is omnipresent,[49] yet the debates about blockbusters suggest that audiences are finding important meanings from the past. The screening of the past that has dominated Russia's zero years has offered a menu of memories for Russians to select from. Filmmakers, film critics, and film spectators have often tried to locate a specific meaning to a given historical film or define precisely the patriotic culture blockbuster history has created. In doing so, they have all taken part in an ongoing attempt to redefine the Russian nation and with it, the ongoing process of historical remembrance.

Jay Winter has argued that the VCR represented "a new factor in the way history and memory [became] configured," for it expanded the archive of historical materials. The internet, as Winter argues, expanded this archive even more radically. This expansion brought with it more individual ways of thinking about the past while also allowing individuals more chances to record their conceptions about the past. In short, the VCR, DVD player, video camera, video game, and the internet have blended history and memory more than ever before. Winter argues that we should now analyze "historical remembrance" in order not to separate history from memory: it represents "a host of ways in which we try to give meaning to our violent past," while its practices and forms overlap with liturgical and family remembrances. As a specific example of historical remembrance, Winter states, "When we come together in public to exchange our reflections on the past stimulated by a film or a play or a novel or a visit to a museum, we enter this area between memory and history."[50] The near simultaneous introduction of the VCR, DVD player, internet, video game, and blockbuster format in Russia after 1991 ensured that historical remembrance radically changed. Films and the public debates about them in the zero years illustrate just how interrelated, contested, and significant history and memory are. The screening of the past and with it the production of both history and historical memory has opened up new avenues to think about and conceptualize the meanings of the past.

These individual activities collectively point to a an important conclusion: blockbuster history has provided an avenue out of the overkill culture of the 1990s while also offering up a menu of heroes and history for viewers to unwrap. The past has helped many Russians view the present in more positive ways: compared to the trauma of the Stalin era or the disruption of the 1990s, the 2000s seem stable. At the same time, the packaging of the past and the subsequent unwrapping of historical remembrance does not indicate that Russians desire a return to what was lost. Instead, these processes indicate that the memories screened in the movies serve as an important means for debating the past, understanding its multiple meanings, and for making the past history.[51] The new Russian patriotic cinema has helped to unmake the Soviet memory project. Blockbuster history has revisited controversial pasts and reinterpreted them, providing viewers with a chance to rethink what it means. The movies screened in Karo theaters and bought in Soiuz stores, in short, have not just made history, they have meaningfully interpreted it.

NOTES

1. INTRODUCTION

This introduction benefited from a lively discussion on December 4, 2009, at the Havighurst Center's work-in-progress series. I want to thank my colleagues Vitaly Chernetsky, Karen Dawisha, Josh First, Mila Ganeva, Gulnaz Sharafutdinova, and Ben Sutcliffe for their comments and critiques.

1. See the Karo Film website, www .karofilm.ru (accessed January 25, 2012).

2. Birgit Beumers, "Cinemarket, or the Russian Film Industry in 'Mission Possible,'" *Europe-Asia Studies* 51, no. 5 (1999): 871.

3. See Laura Holson and Steven Lee Myers, "The Russians Are Filming! The Russians Are Filming!" *New York Times*, July 16, 2006, www.nytimes.com/2006/07/16/business/yourmoney/16russia.html ?scp=2&sq=russian%20are%20filimg%20 the%20russians&st=cse.

4. "O kompanii/obshchaia informatssia," Karo Film website, www.karofilm.ru/about (accessed January 25, 2012).

5. Ibid.

6. Ibid.

7. Ibid.

8. "Multiplexing Russia: A Talk with Karo's Leonid Ogorodnikov," *Film Journal*, September 1, 2005, www.filmjournal .com/filmjournal/esearch/article_display .jsp?vnu_content_id=1001022020.

9. Holson and Myers, "The Russians Are Filming!"

10. Quoted in Amie Ferris-Rotman and Thomas Peter, "Russia Sees Revival in Film-Making," *New York Times*, June 3, 2008, www.nytimes.com/2008/06/03/technology/03iht-RUSfilm.4.13434938 .html.

11. Quoted in Boris Fishman, "Its Freedoms No Longer New, Russian Cinema Matures," *New York Times*, October 23, 2003, www.nytimes.com/2003/10/23/movies/its-freedoms-no-longer-new-russian-cinema-matures.html?scp=1&sq =russian%20cinema&st=cse.

12. Quoted in Nick Paton Walsh, "Russian Cinema Holds Out for a New Type of Hero," *The Guardian*, September 28, 2002, 19. See also Greg Dolgopolov, "Liquidating the Happy End of the Putin-era," *KinoKultura* 21 (July 2008), www .kinokultura.com/2008/21-dolgopolov .shtml.

13. Quoted in Holson and Myers, "The Russians Are Filming!"

14. Louis Menard has argued that "blockbusters today are commercials;

they're commercials for themselves." Contemporary American blockbusters specifically market themselves to capture foreign box office receipts; and, as Menard puts it, "foreign audiences aren't paying to hear an interesting conversation." See his "Gross Points," *New Yorker* 80, no. 45 (February 7, 2005): 82–87. Menard's views about the "emptiness" of Hollywood blockbusters and its aim to generate as much money as possible from foreign distribution was translated and included in the *Seans* roundtable on the Russian blockbuster cited below.

15. For more on these issues, see I. E. Kokarev, *Kino kak biznes i politika: sovremennaia kinoindustriia SShA i Rossii: uchebnoe posobie* (Moscow: Aspekt-Press, 2009).

16. Here I draw on the work of Jay Winter, *Remembering War: The Great War Between Memory and History in the Twentieth Century* (New Haven, Conn.: Yale University Press, 2006), 183–86.

17. Stephen Lovell, *The Soviet Union: A Very Short Introduction* (Oxford: Oxford University Press, 2009), 27.

18. This is the argument made by Evgeny Dobrenko in his *Stalinist Cinema and the Production of History: Museum of the Revolution* (New Haven, Conn.: Yale University Press, 2008).

19. Aleksandr Solzhenitsyn, *The Gulag Archipelago* (New York: Harper Perennial, 2007), 120.

20. I borrow the unmaking and remaking idea from Caroline Humphrey, *The Unmaking of Soviet Life: Everyday Economies After Socialism* (Ithaca, N.Y.: Cornell University Press, 2002).

21. The figures are from "Dark Blue World (2001): International Box Office Results," Box Office Mojo website, www.boxofficemojo.com/movies/?page=intl&id=darkblueworld.htm (accessed January 25, 2012). For more on postcommunist Czech historical films, see Peter Hames, "The Ironies of History: The Czech Experience," in Anikó Imre, ed., *East European Cinemas* (London: Routledge, 2005): 135–50.

22. See "Ballots and Box Office: Did Poland's President Exploit Katyn Tragedy?" *Spiegel,* October 5, 2007, www.spiegel.de/international/europe/0,1518,509645,00.html.

23. "Katyn (2009): International Box Office Results," Box Office Mojo website, www.boxofficemojo.com/movies/?page=intl&id=katyn.htm (accessed January 25, 2012). *Katyń* had a limited release in Russia and provoked some interesting responses. Some viewers who posted comments on the online forum *Kinopoisk* interpreted Wajda's film as anti-Russian; others viewed it as a necessary act of national atonement. See the discussion on "*Katyń,*" *Kinopoisk* website, www.kinopoisk.ru/level/1/film/270249 (accessed January 25, 2012).

24. I have tackled this subject in two articles that focus on Central Asian cinema: "The Gifts of History: Young Kazakh Cinema and the Past," *KinoKultura* 27 (January 2010), www.kinokultura.com/2010/27-norris.shtml; and "Landscapes of Loss: The Great Patriotic War in Central Asian Cinema," in Michael Rouland and Gulnara Abikeyeva, eds., *Central Asian Cinema* (London: I. B. Tauris, forthcoming, 2013). The topic of postcommunist cinema and the turn to the past could be the subject of another book; however, even to the casual observer the phenomenon of "blockbuster history" has dominated new national cinema narratives from Poland to Kazakhstan. For more on Polish cinema and its attempts to narrate the communist era, see Marek Haltof, *Polish National Cinema* (New York: Berghahn Books, 2002), chapters 8, 9, and 10. For a Ukrainian take, see the special issue of the Kyiv-based journal *Sho* from July-August 2011. Titled "Blokbasterko: U poshukakh natsional′noï kinoideï," the issue featured a cover image of a Na'vi character from James Cameron's *Avatar* wearing a traditional embroidered

Ukrainian shirt. See Iaroslav Pidgora-Gviazdovskii, "Blokbasterko, de ti?" *Sho* 7–8 (July–August 2011): 40–53. To get a sense for the range of films that have explored the past, see *KinoKultura*'s special issues, *KinoKultura* website, www.kinokultura.com/index.html (accessed January 25, 2012). For an insightful examination of postwar European memory and the "comparative victimhood" that defined former communist remembrance, see Tony Judt, "From the House of the Dead," the epilogue to his magisterial *Postwar: A History of Europe Since 1945* (New York: Penguin, 2005).

25. Olga Shevchenko, *Crisis and the Everyday in Postsocialist Moscow* (Bloomington: Indiana University Press, 2008).

26. "Afterword: Farewell to the Queue," in Vladimir Sorokin, *The Queue,* trans. Sally Laird (New York: New York Review of Books, 2008), 254.

27. Humphrey, *The Unmaking of Soviet Life,* xvii. I borrow the term "patriotism of despair" from Serguei Oushakine's examination of the state of Russian patriotism by the end of the 1990s. See Oushakine, *The Patriotism of Despair: Nation, War, and Loss in Russia* (Ithaca, N.Y.: Cornell University Press, 2009).

28. Anthony Anemone, "About Killers, Freaks, and Real Men: The Vigilante Hero of Aleksei Balabanov's Films," in Stephen M. Norris and Zara Torlone, eds., *Insiders and Outsiders in Russian Cinema* (Bloomington: Indiana University Press, 2008), 127–41, quotation on 130. See also the film's website, brat2.film.ru.

29. See N. Sirivlia, "Bratva," *Iskusstvo kino,* August 2000, kinoart.ru/2000/n8-article2.html.

30. Evgenii Gusiatinskii, "Brat zhil, brat zhiv, brat budet zhiv," *Iskusstvo kino,* March 2001, kinoart.ru/2001/n3-article7.html. See also Nancy Condee, *The Imperial Trace: Recent Russian Cinema* (Oxford: Oxford University Press, 2009), 229.

31. Gusiatinskii, "Brat zhil, brat zhiv, brat budet zhiv."

32. Ibid.

33. Ibid.

34. Tyler Cowen, *Creative Destruction: How Globalization is Changing the World's Cultures* (Princeton, N.J.: Princeton University Press, 2002), chapter 4. Joseph Schumpeter outlined his concept of "creative destruction" in chapter 7 of his *Capitalism, Socialism and Democracy* (New York: Harper, 1942). In it, Schumpeter outlines the evolutionary nature of capitalism and how the capitalist process always develops within specific social and natural environments. Moreover, Schumpeter argues that "the fundamental impulse that sets and keeps the capitalist engine in motion comes from the new consumers' goods, the new methods of production or transportation, the new markets, the new forms of industrial organization that capitalist enterprise creates" (82–83). These new mutations destroy old practices in what Schumpeter termed "Creative Destruction." Cowen adopts Schumpeter's views and uses them to explain the emerging global capitalism: rather than dismissing globalization as a homogenizing process, Cowen argues that it too creates new out of the old. In my thinking about economics, I am also indebted to Duncan Foley's lively work, *Adam's Fallacy: A Guide to Economic Theology* (Cambridge, Mass.: Harvard University Press, 2006). In it, Foley argues that the widespread belief, particularly among economists, that one can separate an economic sphere of life, one typically viewed as an arena of self-interest guided by objective laws, from social life, where the pursuit of self-interest is more complicated, is a fallacy. This separation between economics and politics, society, and culture, Foley asserts, is the foundation of modern political economy as a discipline. As he sees it—and I agree—

this division is a false one. Throughout the book, Foley foregrounds the leading thinkers of modern economic theory, starting with Adam Smith and ending with Schumpeter, against the politics, social concerns, and cultural issues they dealt with in their works.

35. For more on the reassertion of postsocialist national identities in the face of globalization, see Douglas Blum, *National Identity and Globalization: Youth, State, and Society in Post-Soviet Eurasia* (Cambridge: Cambridge University Press, 2007).

36. Humphrey, *The Unmaking of Soviet Life,* 63.

37. Stephen Lovell, *Destination in Doubt: Russia Since 1989* (London: Zed Books, 2006), 12. Lovell's book is the best historical account of postcommunist Russia. For another excellent history of the 1990s and the search for a new idea in that decade, see Robert Service, *Russia: Experiment with a People* (Cambridge, Mass.: Harvard University Press, 2003).

38. Jeremy Morris, "The Empire Strikes Back: Projections of National Identity in Contemporary Russian Advertising," *Russian Review* 64, no. 4 (October 2005): 643. Morris writes, "[U]nlike other countries, most of which have their share of 'buy home-grown' advertising, Russian products have become increasingly associated with propositions about Russian national identity in its broadest and most amorphous sense."

39. Lidiia Maslova, "Nezrimyi boi," *Seans* 23/24 (September 2005), seance.ru/n/23-24/filmyi-proekt-russkiy-blokbaster/nezrimyiy-boy.

40. Evgenii Maizel′, "Zhertva kachestva, vyigrysh tempa," *Seans* 23/24 (September 2005), seance.ru/n/23-24/filmyi-proekt-russkiy-blokbaster/zhertvakachestva-vyiigryish-tempa.

41. Larisa Iusipova, "Nashi poshli," *Seans* 23/24 (September 2005), seance.ru/n/23-24/filmyi-proekt-russkiy-blokbaster/nashi-poshli.

42. "Chto takoe russkii blokbaster?" *Seans* 23/24 (September 2005), seance.ru/category/n/23-24/filmyi-proekt-russkiy-blokbaster/seansu-otvechayut.

43. Ibid.

44. Ibid.

45. This debate is a long-running one in Soviet and Russian cinematic culture. It began in the 1920s, when Soviet audiences favored Hollywood movies over avant-garde cinema made by Sergei Eisenstein or Dziga Vertov. Soviet critics lamented what they saw as "petty bourgeois, stupid and dull" cinema while Stalin eventually championed "audience friendly" fare that fused Hollywood styles with Soviet content, most notably in the musical comedies of Grigorii Aleksandrov. For more on this initial discussion, see Denise Youngblood, *Movies for the Masses: Popular Cinema and Soviet Society in the 1920s* (Cambridge: Cambridge University Press, 1992); Peter Kenez, *Cinema and Soviet Society: From the Revolution to the Death of Stalin* (London: I. B. Tauris, 2001); and Birgit Beumers, *A History of Russian Cinema* (Oxford: Berg, 2009), chapter 2. The debate heated up again in the 1960s and 1970s, when the Brezhnev government commissioned a series of sociological studies that attempted to quantify what Soviet film spectators wanted to see onscreen. Film studios used the results to create 1970s and early 1980s blockbusters (the word "boevik" was used at the time) such as *Moscow Does Not Believe in Tears* (1979) and *Pirates of the Twentieth Century* (1980). Many critics and directors decried the new entertainment cinema that emerged in the 1970s. As Joshua First has argued, this 1970s development increasingly led Soviet studios to market their films and pay attention to box office returns. See his "From Spectator to 'Differentiated' Consumer: Film Audience Research in the Era of Developed

Socialism (1965–1980)." *Kritika* 9, no. 2 (Spring 2008): 317–44.

46. See Alexei Yurchak, *Everything Was Forever, until It Was No More: The Last Soviet Generation* (Princeton, N.J.: Princeton University Press, 2006), 205.

47. Here I am indebted to Richard Kuisel, *Seducing the French: The Dilemma of Americanization* (Berkeley: University of California Press, 1993); and Victoria de Grazia, *Irresistible Empire: America's Advance Through 20th Century Europe* (Cambridge, Mass.: Harvard University Press, 2005).

48. For more on television and its role in the new Russia, see David MacFadyen, *Russian Television Today: Primetime Drama and Comedy* (London: Routledge, 2008). MacFadyen explores the ways in which television series have dealt with recent history as a means of answering important questions such as "What really happened to us" and "Why?"

49. Condee, *The Imperial Trace*, 4.

50. The debate over Russian nationhood is a complex one that involves numerous scholars representing a number of disciplines. Condee's introduction is an excellent overview of one side of the debate and adapts the model advanced by Geoffrey Hosking, Ronald Grigor Suny, Boris Groys, Aleksandr Etkind, and others. This paradigm suggests that Russia has historically lacked a national identity (or nationhood) because the state focused its energies on fostering an imperial identity (first Russian, then Soviet). This argument is a powerfully suggestive one; however, Condee cites only scholars who support it. To take one rather elegant example from the scholars who argue against the "imperial identity over national identity" thesis, Simon Franklin and Emma Widdis have written, "[M]uch discussion of Russian identity is driven by the belief . . . that the question has an answer, that Russianness is a 'thing' to be located, described, and objectively described." Instead, they urge scholars to see Russian nationhood as "a field of cultural discourse," a "topic of continual argument, of conflicting claims, competing images, contradictory criteria." Collectively this discourse allows us to see Russianness as a collection of ideas, attitudes, images, and claims (and in that sense it resembles the rest of the world instead of being the source of a Russian *sonderweg* ["special path" in German; a reference to the contentious historical claim that Germany experienced a unique form of modernity that produced Nazism]). See Franklin and Widdis, *National Identity in Russian Culture* (Cambridge: Cambridge University Press, 2004), xii.

51. Condee, *The Imperial Trace*, 239.

52. For more on the multiple ways history is packed and consumed (and how popular audiences more and more frame the way the past gets understood through popular culture), see Jerome de Groot, *Consuming History: Historians and Heritage in Contemporary Popular Culture* (London: Routledge, 2009). My reading of Russian historical films was inspired in part by Naomi Greene's work on postwar French film, *Landscapes of Loss: The National Past in Postwar French Cinema* (Princeton, N.J.: Princeton University Press, 1999). Greene argues that films serve as an important "site of memory" (invoking Pierre Nora's famous conception). Every nation, she argues, creates images of its past that respond to contemporary modes of thought and feeling (3). Films "seem particularly well attuned to the slightest tremors of our collected psyche. They sense changing attitudes and moods more quickly than does the more private realm of literature or the more rarified world of academe" (5). Films help to screen yet also soften and repress the "most troubling zones of the national past" (6). Finally, cinema helps to shape political myths that are taken up by politi-

cians even while offering up "a certain idea of France" that can be appealing to audiences. It is, "an important site of national memory" (13).

53. My inspiration here is Anthony D. Smith's "Gastronomy or Geology? The Role of Nationalism in the Reconstruction of Nations," reprinted in his *Myths and Memories of the Nation* (Oxford: Oxford University Press, 1999): 163–86. Smith examines the debate over the origins of the nation by focusing on the gastronomical and geological metaphors that have accompanied both nation-building projects and scholarly attempts to understand them. "Is the nation," he asks, "a seamless whole or an à la carte menu? Is it an immemorial deposit that archeology has recovered and history explained, or a recent artifact that artists have created and media chefs purveyed to a bemused public?" (163). Smith finds both sides of the debate lacking (and I agree); however, in the case of post-Soviet Russia, the menu of nationhood and the metaphor of the nation as a sweet shop where the candy makers are the creators of blockbuster history and the consumers are the spectators picking and choosing which sweet (that is, symbol of Russianness) they most want is an apt characterization. Richard Stites has also argued that Russian national symbols have acted in a multivalent fashion over time and have collectively helped to build a sense of Russianness (a conclusion also reached by Franklin and Widdis). Michael Geisler, commenting on Stites's essay, argues that he "takes the sheer wealth and diversity of Russian national symbols as a cue to remind us of the importance of considering the *entire register of national symbols as a system of signification working in concert to maintain, stabilize, and reinforce the dominating constructions of collective memory* [his emphasis]" (xxxiii). See Michael E. Geisler, introduction, *National Symbols, Fractured Identities: Contesting the National Narrative* (Middlebury, Vt., and Hanover, N.H.: University Press of New England, 2005), xiii–xlii. Stites's essay is titled "Russian Symbols—Nation, People, Ideas" (101–17).

54. Here I follow the scholarship of Mark Bassin and Edyta Bojanowska. Both argue that national identity and imperial identity are inextricably linked in Russia. Russian nationhood is neither weak nor inarticulate; it has developed within an imperial framework. Bassin, *Imperial Visions: Nationalist Imagination and Geographical Expansion in the Russian Far East, 1840–1865* (Cambridge: Cambridge University Press, 1999); and Bojanowska, *Nikolai Gogol: Between Ukrainian and Russian Nationalism* (Cambridge, Mass.: Harvard University Press, 2007).

55. A 2006 poll carried out by the Moscow-based VTSIOM asked 3200 Russians what era they would choose to live in if they had the possibility: 39 percent stated they would choose to live in the present; 31 percent chose the Brezhnev era. See "Luchshe lidery: Brezhnev i Putin," VTSIOM web-site, April 25, 2007, www.rosbalt.ru/2007/04/25/294470.html.

PART 1. THE RUSSIA THAT WE LOST

1. See Walter Lacqueur, "1917: The Russia We Lost?" in his *The Dream That Failed: Reflections on the Soviet Union* (New York: Oxford University Press, 1994), for more on Govorukhin's film and the history it presents. Ol′denburg's book was published in two volumes in Belgrade and Munich between 1939 and 1949. It was translated into the four-volume English-language edition *Last Tsar: Nicholas II, His Reign, and His Russia* (Gulf Breeze, Fla.: Academic International Press, 1975–78).

2. Quoted in Anna Lawton, *Imagining Russia 2000: Film and Facts* (Washington, D.C.: New Academia Publishing, 2004), 64.

3. Frederick Corney examines this process in his brilliant *Telling October: Memory and the Making of the Bolshevik Revolution* (Ithaca, N.Y.: Cornell University Press, 2004), 10–11.

4. Ibid., 184.

5. Denise Youngblood, *Russian War Films: On the Cinema Front, 1914–2005* (Lawrence: University of Kansas Press, 2007), 17.

6. Ibid., 42.

7. See Daniel Peris, *Storming the Heavens: The Soviet League of the Militant Godless* (Ithaca, N.Y.: Cornell University Press, 1998); Glennys Young, *Power and the Sacred in Revolutionary Russia. Religious Activists in the Village* (University Park: Pennsylvania State University Press, 1997); William B. Husband, *"Godless Communists": Atheism and Society in Soviet Russia, 1917–1932* (DeKalb: Northern Illinois University Press, 2000); Richard Hernandez, "Sacred Sound and Sacred Substance: Church Bells and the Auditory Culture of Russian Villages during the Bolshevik *Velikii Perelom*," *American Historical Review* 109, no. 5 (December 2004): 1475–1504; and Robert Greene, *Bodies Like Bright Stars: Saints and Relics in Orthodox Russia* (DeKalb: Northern Illinois University Press, 2010).

8. Numerous articles throughout the 1990s and 2000s employed the phrase or a play on it to describe any number of national crises: *Moskovskii komsomelts* emblazoned a 1999 headline "The America That We Lost" in 1999 to discuss the end of the 1990s and its dreams. At the end of that same year, *Segodnia* could lament "The Ukraine That We Lost," *Izvestiia* "The Censorship That We Lost," and *Vremia MN* "The Money That We Lost" in article headlines that all used "kotorye my poteriali." Hundred of examples abound.

9. The articles were later issued in book form: Larisa Maliukova, ed., *90-e: kino, kotoroe my poteriali* (Moscow, Novaya gazeta/Zebra-E, 2007). For more on the cinema of the late socialist and early postsocialist period, see Andrew Horton and Michael Brashinsky, *The Zero Hour: Glasnost and Soviet Cinema in Transition* (Princeton, N.J.: Princeton University Press, 1992); Anna Lawton, *Kinoglasnost: Soviet Cinema in Our Time* (Cambridge: Cambridge University Press, 1992); Lawton, *Imagining Russia 2000;* Birgit Beumers, ed., *Russia on Reels: The Russian Idea in Post-Soviet Cinema* (London: I. B. Tauris, 1999); and George Faraday, *Revolt of the Filmmakers: The Struggle for Artistic Autonomy and the Fall of the Soviet Film Industry* (University Park: Pennsylania State University Press, 2000).

10. Anthony D. Smith argues that the "myth of national decline" and "myth of national regeneration" are two powerful tropes that form ethnic nationalism. "The Russia that We Lost" concept focused these ideas after 1991. See Smith, *Myths and Memories of the Nation* (Oxford: Oxford University Press, 1999): 67–68.

2. THE FIRST BLOCKBUSTER OF THE NEW NATION

This chapter updates material first published in my articles "Tsarist Russia, *Lubok* Style: Nikita Mikhalkov's *Barber of Siberia* (1999) and Post-Soviet National Identity," *The Historical Journal of Film, Radio and Television* 25, no. 1 (March 2005): 99–116; and "Family, Fatherland, and Faith: The Power of Nikita Mikhalkov's Celebrity," in Helena Goscilo and Vlad Strukov, eds., *Celebrity and Glamour in Contemporary Russia: Shocking Chic* (London: Routledge, 2010): 107–26.

1. See "Sistema koordinat Nikity Mikhalkova," Studio Tri-te website, www.trite.ru/mikhalkov.mhtml?PubID=131 (accessed March 28, 2008).

2. See the statistics compiled by Birgit Beumers on the *KinoKultura* website,

www.kinokultura.com/plus/prokat1.html (accessed January 26, 2012).

3. See Eliot Borenstein, *Overkill: Sex and Violence in Contemporary Russian Popular Culture* (Ithaca, N.Y.: Cornell University Press, 2007), 7–23; and Seth Graham, "Chernukha and Russian Film," *Studies in Slavic Cultures* 1 (2000): 9–27. "Broadly speaking," Borenstein writes, "chernukha is the pessimistic, naturalistic depiction of and obsession with bodily functions, sexuality (usually separate from love), and often sadistic violence, all against a backdrop of poverty, broken families, and unrelenting cynicism" (11). The trend emerged under Gorbachev and as part of glasnost′; chernukha dominated 1990s culture.

4. Nancy Condee, *The Imperial Trace: Recent Russian Cinema* (Oxford: Oxford University Press, 2009), 74.

5. Sergei Selianov, "Cinema and Life," in Birgit Beumers, ed., *Russia on Reels: The Russian Idea in Post-Soviet Cinema* (London: I. B. Tauris, 1999), 43–46.

6. Daniil Dondurei, "The State of National Cinema," in ibid., 46–50, quotation on 47.

7. Ibid., 48.

8. Ibid., 50.

9. Quoted in Anna Lawton, *Imagining Russia 2000: Film and Facts* (Washington, D.C.: New Academia Publishing, 2004), 28.

10. Ibid.

11. Birgit Beumers, *Nikita Mikhalkov: Between Nostalgia and Nationalism* (London: I. B. Tauris, 2005), 2.

12. Ibid., 1.

13. Sergei Gurevich, interview by Stephen M. Norris, July 14, 2008, Studio Tri-te, Moscow. The studio also served as the location base for *Russia House, K-19,* and *The Bourne Supremacy.* When I asked Gurevich about the depiction of Russians in these films, he answered, "They're just movies. What we learned was far more important than the way these films characterized Russians."

14. George Faraday, *Revolt of the Filmmakers: The Struggle for Artistic Autonomy and the Fall of the Soviet Film Industry* (University Park: Pennsylvania State University Press, 2000), 188–89.

15. Boris Yeltsin appreciated its anti-Stalinist message enough to have the film screened on state television the night before the 1996 elections, when Yeltsin feared he might lose to the Communist Party leader, Gennadii Ziuganov (see Faraday, *Revolt of the Filmmakers,* 190).

16. Leonid Pavliuchik, "Nikita Mikhalkov, utomlennyi kinoprokatom," *Izvestiia,* January 26, 1995. For more on the film, see Birgit Beumers, *Burnt by the Sun* (London: I. B. Tauris, 2000).

17. Nikita Mikhalkov, "The Function of a National Cinema," in Beumers, ed., *Russia on Reels,* 50–51.

18. Ibid., 51–52.

19. Ibid., 52.

20. Birgit Beumers makes this point in the only scholarly article that deals with the film, "*Sibirskii tsiriul′nik* (The Barber of Siberia)," in Jill Forbes and Sarah Street, ed., *European Cinema: An Introduction* (Houndmills, UK: Palgrave, 2000), 195–206. For a nice summary of the attempt to "redesign history" in post-Soviet Russia (although one that does not include film's role), see Catherine Merridale, "Redesigning History in Contemporary Russia," *Journal of Contemporary History* 38, no. 1 (2003): 13–28.

21. Pierre Sorlin, "How to Look at an 'Historical' Film," in Marcy Landy, ed., *The Historical Film: History and Memory in Media* (New Brunswick, N.J.: Rutgers University Press, 2001), 25.

22. Ibid., 36.

23. Ibid., 38.

24. Ibid., 38–39.

25. For more on this context, see Kathleen Smith, *Mythmaking in the New Rus-*

sia: Politics and Memory in the Yeltsin Era (Ithaca, N.Y.: Cornell University Press, 2002), chapter 6.

26. Denise Youngblood, "The Cosmopolitan and the Patriot: The Brothers Mikhalkov-Konchalovsky and Russian Cinema," *Historical Journal of Film, Radio and Television* 23, no. 1 (2003): 30; see also Beumers, *Nikita Mikhalkov.*

27. Quoted in Andrew Meier, "Riding to the Rescue: Can Nikita Mikhalkov Take the Reins of Russia?" *Time International,* March 8, 1999, 25.

28. Critics have pointed out numerous historical errors in the film. The terrorists who try to assassinate a tsarist official at the film's beginnings could not have existed in 1885, when Narodnaia volia had come to an end in 1883. The Maslenitsa festival would not have had fireworks or silver samovars in 1885. Russian elites spoke French and German, but not English, in Alexander III's Russia. The cadet ceremony was held after the young men finished two weeks of training—they arrived before the tsar sweaty and dirty, not cleaned and polished. The Grand Duke would not have had a telephone. And so on. See Nikita Sokolov, "Slav′sia, great Russia . . ." *Itogi* 10 (March 9, 1999): 48–49; Beumers, *Nikita Mikhalkov,* 118; and, most significantly, Aleksandr Kibovskii, *Sibirskii tsiriul′nik: pravda i vymysel kinoepopei* (Moscow: Eksprint, 2002). Kibovskii's seventy-six-page book, published through the historical-military journal *Tseikhgauz,* documents countless "problems associated with domestic cinema, particularly the lack of historical authenticity in films about Russia's past." Criticizing the actual history in *Barber,* however, seems beside the point: although Mikhalkov stated the film is "about Alexander III's Russia," he always accompanied this statement with one that said it is about "Russia as it should be."

29. For more on the connections between ideas about the "Russian soul" and post-Soviet culture, see the ever-reliable Svetlana Boym, "From the Russian Soul to Post-Communist Nostalgia," *Representations* 49 (1995): 133–66.

30. Quoted in Meier, "Riding to the Rescue."

31. For more on how Mikhalkov equates himself and his family with Russia, see Tat′iana Moskvina, "Ee zovut Rossiia, ee zovut Nikita," in *Pokhvala plokhomu shokoladu* (Moscow: Limbus, 2002): 152–65; and Stephen M. Norris, "Family, Fatherland, and Faith: The Power of Nikita Mikhalkov's Celebrity," in Helena Goscilo and Vlad Strukov, eds., *Celebrity and Glamour in Contemporary Russia: Shocking Chic* (London: Routledge, 2010).

32. Birgit Beumers concludes, "[I]n Mikhalkov's vision the whole of Russian society is transformed into one large family with a patriarch at its head" (200). Mikhalkov's depiction of family life as a model for Russian national identity mirrors many trends of nineteenth-century Russia. For more on this subject, see Alexander Martin, "The Family Model of Society and Russian National Identity in Sergei N. Glinka's *Russian Messenger," Slavic Review* 57, no. 1 (Spring 1998): 28–49.

33. For more on the importance of Christ the Savior Cathedral to Russian post-Soviet identity, see Andrew Genets, "The Life, Death, and Resurrection of the Cathedral of Christ the Savior, Moscow," *History Workshop Journal* 46 (1998): 63–95.

34. Richard Wortman, *Scenarios of Power: Myth and Ceremony in Russian Monarchy,* (Princeton, N.J.: Princeton University Press, 2000), 2:204–206.

35. The term comes from Eric Hobsbawm and Terence Ranger, eds., *The Invention of Tradition* (Cambridge: Cambridge University Press, 1983).

36. The holiday of Maslenitsa, with its religious overtones of asking for forgiveness, had been outlawed by the Soviet

regime. At the time of the film's debut it was undergoing a revival and since has become a regularly celebrated national holiday. In fact, in February 1999 I attended a Maslenitsa fair that was not nearly as much fun as the one in the film in front of the restored Christ the Savior Cathedral and right next to a giant poster advertising the film.

37. Quoted in Tom Whitehouse, "Film Aims to Rekindle Russia's Dying Pride," *The Guardian,* February 19, 1999, www.guardian.co.uk/Archive/Article/0,4273,3824382,00.html.

38. *Barber of Siberia* website, mikhalkov.comstar.ru (accessed March 22, 2008).

39. Beumers, "*Sibirskii,*" 197.

40. Kevin O'Flynn, "'Barber of Siberia' Captures Kremlin," *The Moscow Times,* February 23, 1999, 1.

41. Mikhalkov claimed the government gave him the money in return for the morale boost his film would provide. See the story by Patricia Daganskaia, "Two Brothers, at War and in Peace," *Los Angeles Times,* June 20, 1999, which focuses on Mikhalkov and his brother, the director Andrei Konchalovsky.

42. The incident was caught on camera (as was everything having to do with Mikhalkov and *Barber*) and broadcast on all the news channels in 1999.

43. Stephen Kotkin, "A Tsar Is Born," *New Republic,* April 5, 1999, 18.

44. Beumers, "*Sibirskii,*" 201.

45. Ibid., 197. One of the colognes made for the film was said to "contain the essence of Mikhalkov's moustache," and some television programs carried footage of perfume testers sniffing Mikhalkov's facial hair to get the smell right. See O'Flynn, "'Barber of Siberia' Captures Kremlin," 2.

46. Sorlin, "How to Look at an 'Historical' Film," 44–45.

47. Ibid., 45.

48. Quoted in Beumers, "*Sibirskii,*" 201. Maslova's reference to *Barber* as a "Russian souvenir" deliberately invoked Grigorii Aleksandrov's 1960 film *Russkii souvenir.* Given Aleksandrov's status as the creator of 1930s Stalinist musical comedies (which borrowed from Hollywood styles), Maslova's reference is doubly perceptive. I thank Serguei Oushakine for drawing my attention to Aleksandrov's film.

49. Sokolov, "Slav′ia, Great Russia," 48.

50. Tat′iana Moskvina, "Ne govori, chto molodost′ slubila," *Iskusstvo Kino,* June 1999, kinoart.ru/1999/n6-article4.html.

51. Ibid.

52. O'Flynn, "'Barber of Siberia' Captures Kremlin," 1.

53. Part of the forum on the film in *Seans* 17/18 (1999): 17–19.

54. Igor′ Zolotusskii, "Istoricheskii zhivopisets Mikhalkov," *Iskusstvo kino,* July 1999, kinoart.ru/1999/n7-article14.html; for more on Ivanov's painting and the initial reaction to it (which was indifference), see James Billington, *The Icon and the Axe: An Interpretative History of Russian Culture* (New York: Vintage, 1966), 341–46.

55. Zolotusskii, "Istoricheskii."

56. *Seans* 17/18 (1999): 17–19.

57. See the responses printed in Iurii Gladil′shchikov, "Pervyi blokbaster Rossiisskoi imperii," *Itogi* 10 (March 9, 1999): 42–47.

58. Ibid.

59. Anatolii Goluboevskii and Aleksandr Dmitrievskoi, "Mikhalkov kak narodnyi liubomets," *Itogi* 10 (March 9, 1999): 46.

60. Andrei Eshpai, "V poiskakh novogo zritelia," *Iskusstvo kino,* July 1999, kinoart.ru/1999/n7-article15.html.

61. See the responses at "Sibirskii tsiriul′nik," *Kinopoisk* website, www

.kinopoisk.ru/level/1/film/16445 (accessed January 26, 2012).

62. The level of criticism even surprised Mikhalkov. In an interview with *Seans* in May 1999, Mikhalkov asked, "[W]hy do you dislike me so much? Four hundred and twenty articles in two months. . . . At first I was shocked. . . . Then I thought: what's going on? What did I do to you, guys, to have you squawk that way?" Quoted in Lawton, *Imagining Russia 2000*, 92.

63. Gladil´shchikov, "Pervyi blokbaster Rossiiskoi imperii," 42.

64. Ibid., 43.

65. Ibid., 43, 45.

66. Ibid., 43–44.

67. Ibid., 45–46.

68. Ibid., 47.

69. Ibid., 43.

70. Kirill Razlogov, ". . . Il´ perechti 'Zhent´bu Figaro,'" *Iskusstvo kino*, June 1999, kinoart.ru/1999/n6-article3.html.

71. Quoted in Lawton, *Imagining Russia 2000*, 95.

72. Quoted in Tat´iana Moskvina, "La Grande Illusion," in Beumers, ed., *Russia on Reels*, 97.

73. Ibid.

74. See the National Academy of Motion Picture Arts and Sciences of Russia website, www.kinoacademy.ru/main.php (accessed January 26, 2012).

75. Dmitri Klimentov, "Calls for Rachmaninoff's Reburial in Russia, Lenin's Burial Follow the Ceremony of Moscow Reburial of the Leader of White Movement Anton Denikin," PRWeb, October 5, 2005, www.prweb.com/releases/2005/10/prweb293820.htm.

76. His comments are helpfully posted in "Nikita Mikhalkov: My pochemu-to ochen´ stesniaemsia slova 'russkii,'" Studio Tri-te website, www.trite.ru/mikhalkov.mhtml?PubID=117 (accessed January 26, 2012).

77. Quoted in Sophia Kishkovsky, "Echoes of Civil War in Reburial of Russian," *New York Times* October 3, 2005, www.nytimes.com/2005/10/03/world/europe/03iht-soviet.html.

78. See Mikhalkov's biography in "Biografiia," Studio Tri-te website, www.trite.ru/mikhalkov.mhtml?PubID=12 (accessed January 26, 2012).

79. The interview appears in "Sistema koordinat Nikity Mikhalkova," Studio Tri-te website, www.trite.ru/mikhalkov.mhtml?PubID=131 (accessed January 26, 2012).

80. Ibid.

81. Fiachra Gibbons, "Cannes Opener Meets Explosive Reception," *The Guardian*, May 13, 1999, www.guardian.co.uk/Archive/Article/0,4273,3864502,00.html.

82. Interview at the XXVII MIFF in "Kruglyi stol 'Nashestvie blokbasterov,'" Studio Tri-te website, www.trite.ru/mikhalkov.mhtml?PubID=94 (accessed January 26, 2012).

3. TERRORISM THEN AND NOW

This chapter was first presented at the University of Pennsylvania's Slavic Symposium, April 25, 2008. I thank Julia Verkholantsev for the invitation and Peter Holquist for his comments on the paper.

1. Birgit Beumers, ed., *Russia on Reels: The Russian Idea in Post-Soviet Cinema* (London: I. B. Tauris, 1999), 3.

2. Quoted in George Faraday, *The Revolt of the Filmmakers: The Struggle for Artistic Autonomy and the Fall of the Soviet Film Industry* (University Park: Pennsylvania State University Press, 2000), 115.

3. Sergei Anashkin, "Karen Shakhnazarov: ´Na 'Mosfil´me' situatsiia neopredelennosti . . . ,'' *Iskusstvo kino*, May 1999, kinoart.ru/1999/n5-article2.html.

4. Karen Shakhnazarov, interview by Stephen M. Norris, July 2, 2007, Mosfil´m Studio, Moscow.

5. Andrei Bandenko, "Kupanie blednogo konia," *Itogi*, November 11, 2003, www.itogi.ru/Paper2003.nsf/Article/

Itogi_2003_11_11_13_40 (accessed June 1, 2007).

6. "King of Terror Hits Moscow Cinema Screens," *Pravda,* April 29, 2004, newsfromrussia.com/science/2004/04/29/53706.html (accessed March 31, 2008).

7. Quoted in Anna Geifman, *Entangled in Terror: The Azef Affair and the Russian Revolution* (Wilmington, Del.: SR Books, 2000), 58.

8. On the memory of the Silver Age as an "age of anxiety," see Galina Rylkova, *The Archaeology of Anxiety: The Russian Silver Age and Its Legacy* (Pittsburgh, Pa.: University of Pittsburgh Press, 2007), particularly 1–22; the quotation about the Silver Age as an era when politics became a creative endeavor comes from Catherine Evtuhov, *The Cross and the Sickle: Sergei Bulgakov and the Fate of Russian Religious Philosophy, 1890–1920* (Ithaca, N.Y.: Cornell University Press, 1997), 10. For more on Voloshin and his circle (though one where Savinkov is absent), see Barbara Walker, *Maximilian Voloshin and the Russian Literary Circle* (Bloomington: Indiana University Press, 2005).

9. Ropshin's true identity was quickly found out in Russia and by the time of his second novel, many reviewers referred to the author as Savinkov. It was around this time that Savinkov admitted the novels were essentially autobiographical. See Daniel Beer, "The Morality of Terror: Contemporary Responses to Political Violence in Boris Savinkov's *The Pale Horse* (1909) and *What Never Happened* (1912)," *Slavonic and East European Journal* 85, no. 1 (January 2007): 25–46. By the time his sequel to *The Pale Horse* (*The Black Horse*) appeared in 1924, Savinkov had published his *Memoirs of a Terrorist* under his own name and confirmed that the line between fiction and memoir was very blurry indeed. Aside from the characters' names, the descriptions of the grand duke's assassination are similar.

10. Kaliaev carried out the successful attempt on the grand duke—see below.

11. Boris Savinkov, *Vsadnik po imeni smert′? Kon′ blednyi′ Kon′ voronoi* (St. Petersburg: Amfora, 2004), 147. This edition of Ropshin/Savinkov was timed to appear at the same time as the film and the cover was emblazoned with the film's poster.

12. Ibid., 94.

13. Ibid., 147.

14. Ibid., 131.

15. A. S. Izgoev, "Na perevale: Preodolenie terrora," *Russkaia mysl′,* January 1913, pt. 2, 108. Quoted in Beer, "The Morality of Terror," 25.

16. Quoted in Beer, "The Morality of Terror," 30.

17. Quoted in Beer, "The Morality of Terror," 34.

18. Quoted in Beer, "The Morality of Terror," 37.

19. Quoted in Beer, "The Morality of Terror," 40.

20. Anna Geifman, *Thou Shalt Kill: Revolutionary Terrorism in Russia, 1894–1917* (Princeton, N.J.: Princeton University Press, 1993), 21.

21. Dmitrii Merezhkovskii, quoted in introduction to V. Ropshin, *The Pale Horse,* trans. Z. Vengerova (Dublin and London: Maunsel and Co., 1917), v–ix, quotation on v–vi.

22. I was in Moscow in May 2004, two weeks after the film's release, and can attest to the marketing campaign for the film, the largest since Nikita Mikhalkov's 1999 blockbuster *The Barber of Siberia.* The premier also made national news headlines: see, for example, the coverage on First Channel for April 22, 2004, www.1tv.ru/news/n66180 (accessed March 31, 2008).

23. Robert Rosentone, *History on Film/Film on History* (London: Longman, 2006), 2. I thank Denise Youngblood for bringing this book to my attention.

24. Ibid., 8–9.

25. Ibid., 162.

26. Bandenko, "Kupanie blednogo konia."

27. "King of Terror Hits Moscow Cinema Screens."

28. Irina Potkina, "Moscow's Commercial Mosaic," in James L. West and Iurii A. Petrov, eds., *Merchant Moscow: Images of Russia's Vanished Bourgeoisie* (Princeton, N.J.: Princeton University Press, 1998), 37–44, quotation on 37.

29. Hayden White, "Historiography and Historiophoty," *American Historical Review* 93, no. 5 (December 1988): 1193–99, quotation on 1194.

30. The inaccuracies of Mikhalkov's Moscow are the subject of Nikita Sokolov, "Slav′sia, Great Russia," *Itogi* 10 (March 9, 1999): 48–49; and a series of articles that appeared in the military-historical journal *Tseikhgauz* collected and published as Aleksandr Kibovskii, *Sibirskii tsiriul′nik: pravda i vymysel kinoepopei* (Moscow: Eksprint, 2002).

31. Geifman, *Entangled in Terror,* 58.

32. Elena Monastireva-Ansdell, review of Karen Shakhnazarov, *A Rider Named Death, KinoKultura* 8 (April 2005), www.kinokultura.com/reviews/R4-05vsadnik.html.

33. Geifman, *Thou Shalt Kill,* 55.

34. See Monastireva-Ansdell, review of Karen Shakhnazarov, *A Rider Named Death,* for an excellent analysis of this sequence.

35. E-mail correspondence with Karen Shakhnazarov, March 27, 2008.

36. Karen Shakhnazarov, interview.

37. Ibid.

38. Alexander Yakovlev, *A Century of Violence in Soviet Russia,* trans. Anthony Austin (New Haven, Conn.: Yale University Press, 2002), 233.

39. Ibid., 234–35.

40. V. Buldakov, *Krasnaia smuta: priroda i posledstviia revoliutsionnogo nasiliia* (Moscow: Rosspen, 1997), 351.

41. O. V. Budnitskii, *Terrorizm v Rossiiskom osvoboditel′nom dvizhenii: ideologiia, etika, psikhologiia (vtoraia polovina XIX–nachalo XX v.)* (Moscow: Rosspen, 2000), 154–77.

42. Quoted in Anna Lawton, *Imagining Russia 2000: Film and Facts* (Washington, D.C.: New Academia Publishing, 2004), 65.

43. Geifman, *Thou Shalt Kill,* 167–72.

44. Geifman, *Thou Shalt Kill,* 7–8; Budnitskii, *Terrorizm,* 25.

45. Anna Geifman, review of Budnitskii, *Terrorizm v rossiiskom osvoboditelnom dvizhenii* in *Kritika* 3, no. 4 (Fall 2002): 739–45.

46. Peter Holquist, "Violent Russia, Deadly Marxism? Russia in the Epoch of Violence, 1905–1921," *Kritika* 4, no. 3 (Summer 2003): 627–52, quotation on 652.

47. Ibid., 485. This editor's introduction led off a series of article devoted to the theme of violence in Russian history. Much like the Russians who followed Izgoev's charge in 1913, the authors of the papers and the editors of *Kritika* reached no consensus about the nature of violence in Russia, the uniqueness or similarities of Russian violence, and the political nature of Russian violence (and they are all the stronger for not reaching any definitive answers).

48. Bandenko, "Kupanie blednogo konia."

49. "King of Terror Hits Moscow Cinema Screens."

50. See V. K. Vinogradov et al. eds., *Boris Savinkov v Lubianke: Dokumenty* (Moscow, 2001).

51. E-mail correspondence with Karen Shakhnazarov, March 27, 2008.

52. Bandenko, "Kupanie bladnogo konia."

53. Ibid.

54. Ibid.

55. Alexander Osipovich, "A Radical in Old Moscow," *Moscow Times,* February 6,

2004, themoscowtimes.com/arts_n_ideas/article/a-radical-in-old-moscow/365379.html.

56. Ibid.

57. Jay Winter, "Film and the Matrix of Memory," *American Historical Review* 106, no. 3 (June 2001): 857–58.

58. Ibid., 863.

59. See "Vsadnik po imenii smert′," *Kinopoisk* website, www.kinopoisk.ru/level/1/film/79928 (accessed April 11, 2008).

60. Irina Kozel, "Vsadnik, blednyi kak Smert′," *KinoKadr,* April 25, 2004, www.kinokadr.ru/articles/2004/04/25/vsadnik.shtml.

61. Lev Anninskii, "Vsadnik bez tsaria v golove?" *Iskusstvo kino,* May 2004, kinoart.ru/2004/n5-article9.html.

62. Valerii Kichin, "Bal oderzhimykh," *Rossiiskaia gazeta,* April 24, 2004, www.rg.ru/2004/04/24/vsadnik.html.

63. "King of Terror Hits Moscow Cinema Screens."

64. Ekaterina Barabash, "Kon′ bleklyi," *Nezavisimaia gazeta,* April 27, 2004, www.ng.ru/culture/2004-04-27/8_shahnazarov.html.

65. Monastireva-Ansdell, review of Karen Shakhnazarov, *A Rider Named Death.* Of course, Grand Duke Sergei Alexandrovich *did* look like Nicholas II, but for genetic reasons rather than insidious contemporary trickery—Sergei was Nicholas's uncle.

66. The forum is online at www.kino.ru/forum.php?id=1923#times (accessed March 19, 2008).

67. Rosenstone, *History on Film/Film on History,* 164.

68. Ibid.

69. Bandenko, "Kupanie blednogo konia."

70. Osipovich, "A Radical in Old Moscow."

71. See "Russia—CIS Box Office Index for 2004," Box Office Mojo website, www.boxofficemojo.com/intl/cis/?yr=2004¤cy=us&p=.htm (accessed March 31, 2008).

72. See David MacFadyen, review of Evgenii Lavrent′ev, *Countdown, KinoKultura* 10 (October 2005), www.kinokultura.com/reviews/R10-05lichnyinomer.html.

73. All of the productions that used the set paid tribute to Shakhnazarov and his "Old Moscow" (as the credits for *State Counsellor* and *Doctor Zhivago* called it).

74. "Russia—CIS Box Office Index for 2005," Box Office Mojo website, www.boxofficemojo.com/intl/cis (accessed March 20, 2008). *Statskii sovetnik* earned $2.9 million its opening weekend and eventually earned $7.5 million. See "Statskii sovetnik," *Kinopoisk* website, www.kinopoisk.ru/level/1/film/94111 (accessed April 11, 2008).

75. The first quotation is taken from "Statskii sovetnik: sledite za igoi," Pervyi kanal's documentary about the making of the film and included as part of the DVD extras to *Statskii sovetnik.* The second comments are direct quotations from Boris Akunin, *Statskii sovetnik* (Moscow: Zakharov, 2005), 176.

76. "Chto vy dumaete o Borise Akunine? 'Seansu' otvechaiut," *Seans* 23/24, seance.ru/category/n/23-24/strelyayte-v-pianista-akunin/seansu-otvechayut (accessed March 20, 2008).

77. Mieke Bal, Introduction to Mieke Bal, Jonathan Crewe, and Leo Spitzer, eds., *Acts of Memory: Cultural Recall in the Present* (Hanover, N.H.: University Press of New England, 1999), vii–xvii, quotation on vii.

78. "Chto takoe russkii blokbaster? 'Seansu' otvechaiut . . . ," *Seans* 23/24 (September 2005), seance.ru/category/n/23-24/filmyi-proekt-russkiy-blokbaster/seansu-otvechayut.

79. E-mail correspondence with Karen Shakhnazarov, March 27, 2008.

80. Bandenko, "Kupanie blednogo konia."

81. And it has been used in this way—I have visited the set three times now and the sign outside that lists the productions filmed on site has grown exponentially.

82. Bandenko, "Kupanie blednogo konia."

83. Perhaps the most significant film that used Mosfil′m's help was Paul Greengrass's *The Bourne Supremacy* (2005), which featured not only a spectacular car chase through Moscow, but also employed Oksana Akinshina as an actress playing the daughter of the murdered Russian politician Nevski. Akinshina had become well known by playing the title character in the 2002 Swedish film *Lilya 4-ever* and would be cast as Princess Helen in the 2007 Nikolai Lebedev blockbuster *Wolfhound,* which also used an expensive outdoor set created on Mosfil′m's grounds (built using state funds and the profits reaped from loaning out Mosfil′m to foreign filmmakers). Also in 2005, Roland Jaffe used Mosfil′m Studios to shoot his thriller *Captivity,* which is set entirely in New York. As some press reports claimed, Russia had beaten Hollywood again. See Tom Birchenough, "In the Picture," *Moscow Times,* July 8, 2005, www.themoscowtimes.com/printhttp://www.themoscowtimes.com/arts_n_ideas/article/in-the-picture/364530.html.

84. Iurii Gladil′shchikov, "Putevodnaia Zvezda: Novyi fil′m dolzhen vyrazit′ natsional′nuiu ideiu," *Izvestiia,* April 9, 2002, izvestia.ru/culture/article16885.

4. WARS AND GAMBITS

1. "Chto vy dumaete o Borise Akunine?" *Seans* 23/24 (September 2005), seance.ru/category/n/23-24/strelyayte-v-pianista-akunin/seansu-otvechayut (accessed January 27, 2012).

2. Ibid.

3. For more on Akunin's celebrity, see Brian James Baer and Nadezhda Korchagina, "Akunin's Secret and Fandorin's Luck: Postmodern Celebrity in Post-Soviet Russia," in Helena Goscilo and Vlad Strukov, eds., *Celebrity and Glamour in Contemporary Russia: Shocking Chic* (London: Routledge, 2011): 75–89.

4. Grigorii Chkhartishvili, interview by Stephen M. Norris, Moscow, July 13, 2008.

5. Ibid. Chkhartishvili's views correspond to those of his generation, explored best by Alexei Yurchak in *Everything Was Forever, until It Was No More: The Last Soviet Generation* (Princeton, N.J.: Princeton University Press, 2006).

6. Konstantine Klioutchkine, "Boris Akunin (Grigorii Shalovich Chkhartishvili)," in Marina Balina and Mark Lipovetsky, ed., *Russian Writers Since 1500* (Detroit, Mich.: Thompson Gale, 2004), 4.

7. For more on Skobelev, see Hans Rogger, "The Skobelev Phenomenon: The Hero and His Worship," *Oxford Slavonic Papers* 9 (1976): 46–78.

8. Boris Akunin, *The Turkish Gambit,* trans. Andrew Bromfield (New York: Random House, 2005), 177.

9. Ibid., 202.

10. Stanislav Govorukhin's 1992 documentary film, *The Russia That We Lost,* romanticized the Romanov Empire and since has become a symbol of post-Soviet nostalgia for the prerevolutionary past.

11. Boris Akunin, interview by Natal′ia Kochetkova, in "Shakh Gollivudu," *Izvestiia,* February 18, 2005, www.izvestia.ru/culture/article1232952. In the same interview, Akunin stated the film's audience was "exactly the same as *Night Watch*" with two new ingredients, "fans of costume cinema" and "non-filmgoers who read the novel." Egor Beroev, the actor who played Fandorin, recognized that *Night Watch* viewers might see *Gambit,* but attempted to draw a line between the two: "in *Gambit* we tell history, while in *Night Watch* it's not at all understand-

able how history happens." Secondly, for Beroev *Watch* is all about special effects while *Gambit* uses effects to enhance our understanding of history. See Beroev, interview by Anna Fedina, in "Egor Beroev: 'Esli ia sygraiu podonka, mne ne poveriat,'" *Izvestiia*, February 22, 2005, www.izvestia.ru/culture/article1252103.

12. Elena Prokhorova and Alexander Prokhorov, review of Dzhanik Faiziev, *Turkish Gambit*, in *KinoKultura* 10 (October 2005), www.kinokultura.com/reviews/R10-05gambit.html.

13. Boris Akunin, "My Russia is at a Crossroads," interview by Francesco Fantasia, May 2003. Published in Boris Akunin, *Sister Pelagia and the White Bulldog* (New York: Random House, 2006), 269–73, quotation on 271.

14. Ibid., 272.

15. Roman Arbitman, "Bumazhnyi oplot prianichnoi derzhavy," *Znamia* 7 (1999): 217–19.

16. Pavel Basinskii, "Shtil′ v stakane vody: Boris Akunin: pro et contra," *Literaturnaia gazeta* 21 (May 23–29, 2001), no. 5834, www.lgz.ru/archives/html_arch/lg212001/Literature/art6.htm.

17. See Tat′iana Blazhova, "'Gospodin nekhoroshii': B. Akunin i vokrug," *Literaturnaia gazeta* 7 (February 18–24, 2004), no. 5961, www.lgz.ru/archives/html_arch/lg072004/Tetrad/art11_1.htm.

18. Lev Pirogov, "Konets tsiaty," *Literaturnaia gazeta* 15 (April 11–17, 2001), no. 5830, www.lgz.ru/archives/html_arch/lg152001/Literature/art10.htm.

19. Elena D′iakova, "Boris Akunin kak uspeshnaia otrasl′ rossiiskoi promyshlennosti," *Novaia gazeta*, July 2, 2001, color.novayagazeta.ru/data/2001/45/34.html.

20. Boris Akunin, interview by Stephen M. Norris, July 13, 2008, Moscow.

21. Georgii Tsiplakov, "Evil Arising on the Road and the Tao of Erast Fandorin," *Russian Studies in Literature* 38, no. 3 (Summer 2002): 25–61, quotation on 48. The article appeared originally in Russian in *Novyi mir* 11 (2001): 159–81.

22. Ibid., 51–52.

23. Elena Baraban, "A Country Resembling Russia: The Use of History in Boris Akunin's Detective Novels," *Slavic and East European Journal* 48, no. 3 (2004): 396–420; Sofya Khagi, "Boris Akunin and Retro Mode in Contemporary Russia," *Toronto Slavic Quarterly* 13 (Summer 2005), www.utoronto.ca/tsq/13/khagi13.shtml.

24. Brian Baer, "Engendering Suspicion: Homosexual Panic in the Post-Soviet *Detektiv*," *Slavic Review* 64, no. 1 (2005): 24–42.

25. "Mat koroliam i vampiriam," *Izvestiia*, March 18, 2005, www.izvestia.ru/culture/article1409156.

26. See Sergei Varshavchik, "Turetskii gambit Stepashina," *Nezavisimaia gazeta*, June 30, 2005, www.ng.ru/politics/2005-06-30/1_stepashin.html.

27. "Mat koroliam i vampiriam."

28. Andrei Konchalovsky, "Pobeda rynka nad isskustvom: kak marketologi berut verkh nad tvortsami," *Rossisskaia gazeta*, February 9, 2005, www.rg.ru/2005/02/09/konchalovskiy.html.

29. Ibid.

30. Ibid.

31. Valerii Kichin, "Pobeg iz chernogo kvadrata: kak cozdat′ rynok, ne zhertvuia kul′turoi," *Rossisskaia gazeta*, March 16, 2005, www.rg.ru/2005/03/16/konchalovskij.html.

32. Ibid.

33. Ibid. Epstein has argued that the increased production of information has led mankind to fail increasingly in its ability to interpret it. In his words, "we are handicapped in the face of excessive data." The handicap is a natural result of what Epstein calls "the postmodern condition," which is open to everything but perceives everything superficially. He sees this condition as one akin to trauma and views Russia as a society particularly susceptible

to these symptoms. See Mikhail Epstein, "Between Humanity and Human Beings: Information Trauma and the Evolution of the Species," *Common Knowledge* 13, no. 1 (2007): 18–32.

34. The exact quotation is this: "Capital eschews no profit, or very small profit, just as Nature was formerly said to abhor a vacuum. With adequate profit, capital is very bold. A certain 10 percent will ensure its employment anywhere; 20 percent certain will produce eagerness; 50 percent, positive audacity; 100 percent will make it ready to trample on all human laws; 300 percent, and there is not a crime at which it will scruple, nor a risk it will not run, even to the chance of its owner being hanged. If turbulence and strife will bring a profit, it will freely encourage both. Smuggling and the slave-trade have amply proved all that is here stated."

35. Aleksandr Tolkachev, "Kinoshnyi lokhotron," *Rossisskaia gazeta*, March 29, 2005, www.rg.ru/2005/03/29/kino-loho tron.html.

36. Ibid.

37. Valerii Kichin, "Vmesto kino kazino v national′nom masshtabe," *Rossisskaia gazeta*, May 12, 2005, www.rg.ru/2005/05/12/abdrashitov.html.

38. Ibid.

39. The last article published in the paper that responded to this theme was penned by the poet Dmitrii Prigov. He did not mention *Turkish Gambit*, but essentially agreed with Abdrashitov's more nuanced view of culture and markets. For Prigov, contemporary culture is both "multicultural" and stratifies consumers much more rapidly than in the past—whereas father and sons broke over their respective cultures, Prigov now believes older and younger brothers do. At the same time, artists have a choice about how they position themselves and their creations within a market. See Dmitrii Prigov, "Pesn′ do vostrebovaniia: Rynok diktuet khudozhniku vybor pozitsii," *Rossiiskaia gazeta*, May 27, 2005, www.rg.ru/2005/05/27/prigov.html.

40. See the roundtable "Rossiiskoe kino: kak vernut′ den′gi? [Russian cinema: How can it recover its money?]," *Iskusstvo kino*, April 2005, kinoart.ru/2005/n4-article2.html; and the roundtable "Blokbaster: Perevod na russkii [Blockbuster transferred into Russian]," *Iskusstvo kino*, December 2005, kinoart.ru/2005/n12-article2.html. Both reference *Gambit* extensively.

41. Valerii Kichin, "Bomba osobovo naznacheniia," *Rossiiskaia gazeta*, April 21, 2005, www.rg.ru/2005/04/21/sovetnik.html.

42. Evegenii Maizel′, "Zhertva kachestva, vyigrysh tempa," *Seans* 23/24 (September 2005), seance.ru/n/23-24/filmyi-proekt-russkiy-blokbaster/zhertva-kachestva-vyiigryish-tempa.

43. Grigorii Chkhartishvili, interview.

44. Ibid.

45. Igor Shevelev, "Boris Akunin: 'I Belong to the Rhino Type,'" *New Times* (October 2005): 58–60.

46. Grigorii Chkhartishvili, interview. For more on Parfenov's sacking, see "Parfenonsense," *Kommersant*, June 4, 2004, www.kommersant.com/p480138/r_1/Parfenonsense.

47. Shevelev, "Boris Akunin."

48. Sergei Andreev, "Parfenov i Akunin forsirovali Dunai," *Komsomol′skaia pravda*, March 3, 2005, www.kp.ru/daily/23472.4/37396.

49. Parfenov and Ernst saw the documentary this way. See Susanna Al′perina, "Leonid Parfenov: Na Pervom kanale ia—rabkor," *Rossisskaia gazeta nedelia*, February 18, 2005, www.rg.ru/2005/02/18/parfenov.html. Parfenov would follow up the Russo-Turkish War documentary with films about Brezhnev, the Urals, and the Crimean War, all produced by Ernst for First Channel.

50. Grigorii Chkhartishvili, interview.

51. Ibid.

52. "Turetskii gambit," *Kinopoisk* website, www.kinopoisk.ru/level/1/film/40775 (accessed January 27, 2012).

53. Ibid. See also Dmitrii "Goblin" Puchkov's review stating that the villain as Russian represents "anti-Russian patriotic propaganda": "Kh/f Turetskii gambit," Tupichok Goblina website, kino.oper.ru/torture/read.php?t=1045689122 (accessed January 27, 2012).

54. Kira Lebedeva, "Sistema—prekrasnaia: No ne dlia nas," *Izvestiia,* February 4, 2009, www.izvestia.ru/spb/article3125067. Other uses of the film and its allusions were more comical. The food company Akmal′ko put out a sauce called "Turkish Gambit" that promised to taste like "the original spices of the East" and one that would work well on rice and meat. Zinaida Shumova, "S ekrana—na prilavki," *Izvestiia,* August 15, 2007, www.izvestia.ru/media/article3107235.

55. "Veteranam voiny ne nashlos′ dostoinogo mesta v teleefire," *Izvestiia,* May 18, 2005, www.izvestia.ru/tv/article1774471.

5. A REQUIEM FOR COMMUNISM

1. The entire soundtrack is available at "Edward Artemiev: Doctor Zhivago," World of Soundtrack website, October 24, 2008, worldofsoundtrack.blogspot.com/2008/10/edward-artemiev-doctor-zhivago.html.

2. Leontii Bukshtein, "Eduard Artem′ev: kak poluchaetsia, tak i sluchitsia," *Boss* 11 (2007), www.bossmag.ru/view.php?id=3071.

3. See David Burnand and Benedict Sarnaker, "The Articulation of National Identity Through Film Music," *National Identities* 1, no. 1 (1999): 7.

4. For more on this subject, see the introduction and essays in Daniel Goldmark, Lawrence Kramer, and Richard Leppert, eds., *Beyond the Soundtrack: Representing Music in Cinema* (Berkeley: University of California Press, 2007).

5. Caryl Flinn, "Strategies of Remembrance: Music and History in the New German Cinema," in James Buhler, Caryl Flinn, and David Neumeyer, eds., *Music and Cinema* (Hanover, N.H.: Wesleyan University Press, 2000), 118–41, quotation on 120.

6. Ibid., 128.

7. Annabel J. Cohen, "Film Music: Perspectives from Cognitive Psychology," in Buhler, Flinn, and Neumeyer, eds., *Music and Cinema,* 360–78, quotation on 361. See also Marilyn Boltz's work: "Musical Soundtracks as a Schematic Influence on the Cognitive Processing of Filmed Events," *Music Perception* 18, no. 4 (Summer 2001): 427–54; and "The Cognitive Processing of Film and Musical Soundtracks," *Memory and Cognition* 32, no. 7 (2004): 1194–1205.

8. "Eduard Artem′ev: ne mogu skazat′ sebe stop," *Zolotoe kol′tso* website, January 11, 2007, www.goldring.ru/index.php?option=com_content&task=view&id=84467&Itemid=3.

9. Interview with Artem′ev in 2003 included in the DVD extras for Ruscico's edition of Mikhalkov's *Unfinished Piece for Mechanical Piano.*

10. See Stephen Hutchings and Anat Vernitski, "Introduction: The *ekranizatsiia* in Russian Culture," in *Russian and Soviet Film Adaptations of Literature, 1900–2001: Screening the Word* (London: Routledge-Curzon, 2005), xiv–xxxii, quotation on xxii.

11. This Zhivago captures what André Bazin argued in 1948, namely that, adaptations could use cinematic techniques to create "equivalence in meaning" between the text and the film. Quoted in ibid., xv.

12. Iurii Arabov, "Stsenarii: Doktor Zhivago," *Iskusstvo kino,* December 2004, kinoart.ru/2004/n12-article6.html.

13. For a recent reexamination, see Denis Kozlov, "'I Have Not Read, But I Will Say': Soviet Literary Audiences and Changing Ideas of Social Membership, 1958–66," *Kritika* 7, no. 3 (2006): 557–97.

14. D. S. Likhachev, "Razmyshlennia nad romanon B. L. Pasternaka 'Doktor Zhivago,'" *Novyi mir* 1 (1988): 5–22.

15. S. P. Zalygin, "Istoriia i literature—iz odnoi kolybeli," *Voprosy istorii* 6 (1988): 61–63.

16. G. A. Belaia, "Dve modeli iskusstva," *Voprosy istorii* 6 (1988): 64–67, quotation on 67.

17. The roundtable appeared in *Voprosy literatury* 9 (1988): 54–130.

18. For more on how the series differs from Pasternak's novel, see Valentina L'vova, "Doktor Zhivago: Lish; syr'e dlia seriala?" *Komsomol'skaia Pravda* website, May 23, 2006, www.kp.ru/daily/23711/53328.

19. Pavel Basinskii, "Strashnee mistiki," *Rossiiskaia gazeta,* May 10, 2006, www.rg.ru/2006/05/10/arabov.html.

20. See Dmitrii Bykov's particularly effusive praise of the adaptation in "Proshkin sdelal Zhivago i nastoiashchago," *Izvestiia,* May 26, 2006, www.izvestia.ru/tv/article3093223.

21. See "Za kadrom: Men'shikov v 'Doktore Zhivago' 'travili' volkami," *Komsomol'skaia pravda,* May 25, 2006, www.kp.ru/daily/23712.3/53388.

22. Boris Pasternak, *Doctor Zhivago,* trans. John Bayley (New York: Pantheon, 1991), 362.

23. Eduard Artem'ev, interview by Margarita Katunian, "Muzyka: Iskusstvo rezonansa," Electroshock Records website, www.electroshock.ru/edward/interview/katunyan/index.html (accessed January 27, 2012).

24. Geoffrey Hosking, *The Awakening of the Soviet Union* (Cambridge, Mass.: Harvard University Press, 1990).

25. For more on this process among Soviet political leaders, see Paul Hollander's *Political Will and Personal Belief: The Decline and Fall of Soviet Communism* (New Haven, Conn.: Yale University Press, 1999), which explores the "political-psychological shifts from belief to disbelief and from the lust for power to a diminished will to power" among communist officials (viii). In many ways, the return of the repressed explored by Hosking represents a more popular version of this story.

26. See Vladislav Zubok, *Zhivago's Children: The Last Russian Intelligentsia* (Cambridge, Mass.: Harvard University Press, 2009).

27. See Anna Veligzhanina, "Rezhisser 'Doktora Zhivago' Aleksandr Proshkin: Serial pogubili reklamoi!" *Komsomol'skaia pravda,* May 24, 2006, www.kp.ru/daily/23712.3/53375; Valerii Kichin, "Eto tvoia rodina, Doktor Zhivago!" *Rossiiskaia gazeta,* March 17, 2006, www.rg.ru/2006/03/17/zhivago.html; and Valerii Kichin, "Nashestvie varvarov," *Rossiiskaia gazeta,* May 10, 2006, www.rg.ru/2006/05/10/zhivago.html. One viewer of the series commented in an online forum that potential viewers should skip the commercials and buy the DVD to enjoy it. See Vlada Grinevski, "Doktor Zhivago: glubina rezkosti," Nashfil'm website, www.nashfilm.ru/modernserials/353.html (accessed January 27, 2012).

28. Iurii Bogomolov, "Doktor Zhivago i my," *Iskusstvo kino,* June 2006, kinoart.ru/2006/n6-article3.html.

29. For more on the significance of this series, see Konstantin Klioutchkine, "'Fedor Mikhailovich Lucked Out with Vladimir Vladimirovich': *The Idiot* Television Series in the Context of Putin's Culture," *KinoKultura* 9 (July 2005), www.kinokultura.com/articles/jul05-klioutchkine.html.

30. El′ga Lindina, "Shestnadtsat′ let spustia," *Rossisskaia gazeta,* February 9, 2004, www.rg.ru/2004/02/09/eshpai.html.

31. Slava Taroshchina, "Pomnit′ o Staline," *Iskusstvo kino,* February 2005, kinoart.ru/2005/n2-article2.html.

32. See the interview by Nadezhda Stepanova of *Izvestiia* with the general director of the channel Rossiia in "Interv′iu," *V kruge pervom* official website, www.vkruge pervom.ru/content.html?id=301&cid=45 (accessed January 27, 2012).

33. See Elena Prokhorova, review of Gleb Panfilov, *The First Circle, KinoKultura* 15 (January 2007), www.kinokultura .com/2007/15r-vkruge.shtml.

34. Sergei Kaznacheev, "Zakliuchennye v limbe," *Literaturnaia gazeta* 6 (February 15–21, 2006), no. 6058, www .lgz.ru/archives/html_arch/lg062006/ Polosy/10_1.htm.

35. Dmitrii Bykov, ". . . a nas na svete net," *Iskusstvo kino,* June 2006, kinoart .ru/2006/n6-article2.html.

36. Tat′iana Egorova, *Vselennaia Eduarda Artem′eva* (Moscow, Vagrius, 2006), 180.

37. Bukshtein, "Eduard Artem′ev."

38. "Doktor Zhivago: Glubina rezkosti," Nashfil′m website, www.nashfilm.ru/ modernserials/353.html (accessed January 27, 2012).

39. "Doktor Zhivago (serial)," *Kinopoisk* website, www.kinopoisk.ru/level/1/film/ 89676/ord/date/#list (accessed January 27, 2012).

40. Ibid.

41. Valerii Kichin, "Nashestvie varvarov," *Rossiiskaia gazeta,* May 10, 2006, www.rg.ru/2006/05/10/zhivago.html.

42. Alexander Prokhorov, "The Third Time Is a Charm: Aleksandr Proshkin's *Doctor Zhivago* (2006) on Russia's Small Screen," *KinoKultura* 18 (October 2007), www.kinokultura.com/2007/18r-zhivago .shtml.

43. Ibid.

PART 2. THE PRICE OF WAR

1. M. K. Gorshkov and N. M. Davydova, "Istoricheskoe samosoznanie rossiian," *Monitoring obshchestvennogo mneniia* 1, no. 73 (2005): 17–24. The poll is cited in Stephen Lovell, *Destination in Doubt: Russia Since 1989* (London: Zed Books, 2006), 83.

2. These studies include Nina Tumarkin, *The Living and the Dead: The Rise and Fall of the Cult of World War II in Russia* (New York: Basic Books, 1995); E. S. Seniavskaia, "Heroic Symbols: The Reality and Mythology of War," *Russian Studies in History* 37 (Summer 1998): 61–87; Amir Weiner, *Making Sense of War: The Second World War and the Fate of the Bolshevik Revolution* (Princeton, N.J.: Princeton University Press, 2000); Thomas C. Wolfe, "Past as Present, Myth, or History? Discourses of Time and the Great Fatherland War," in Richard Ned Lebow, Wulf Kansteiner, and Claudio Fogu, eds., *The Politics of Memory in Postwar Europe* (Durham, N.C.: Duke University Press, 2006): 249–83; Lisa Kirschenbaum, *The Legacy of the Siege of Leningrad, 1941–1995: Myth, Memories, and Monuments* (New York: Cambridge University Press, 2006); and Mark Edele, *Soviet Veterans of the Second World War: A Popular Movement in an Authoritarian Society, 1941–1991* (Oxford University Press, 2008).

3. *Russian War Films: On the Cinema Front, 1914–2005* (Lawrence: University of Kansas Press, 2007).

4. I borrow the term "movie-made" from Eric Rentschler, who argues that Hitler's regime "can be seen as a sustained cinematic event" and that "the Third Reich was movie made." Rentschler, *The Ministry of Illusion: Nazi Cinema and Its Afterlife* (Cambridge, Mass.: Harvard University Press, 1996), 1. For an opposing view—one that treats Nazi cinema as entertainment and therefore not at as propaganda—see Linda Schulte-Sasse,

Entertaining the Third Reich: Illusions of Wholeness in Nazi Germany (Durham, N.C.: Duke University Press, 1996). My view on Soviet cinema as neither "movie-made" nor "univocal" is inspired by Scott Spector's article, "Was the Third Reich Movie-Made? Interdisciplinarity and the Reframing of 'Ideology,'" *American Historical Review* 106, no. 2 (April 2001): 460–84. See also Michael David-Fox, "Cultural Memory in the Century of Upheaval: Big Pictures and Snapshots," *Kritika* 2, no. 3 (Summer 2001): 601–13.

5. Youngblood, *Russian War Films,* 207.

6. "My za tsenoi ne postoim?" *Iskusstvo kino,* May 2005, kinoart.ru/2005/n5-article2.html.

7. Ibid.

8. Ibid.

6. MIRROR OF WAR

This chapter represents an updated version of my article "Guiding Stars: The Comet-Like Rise of the War Film in Putin's Russia: Recent World War II Films and Historical Memories," *Studies in Russian and Soviet Cinema* 2, no. 1 (February 2007): 163–89. I thank Birgit Beumers for allowing me to reprint portions of this article.

1. Lev Anninskii, "Tikhie vzryvy: Polemicheskie zametki," *Iskusstvo kino,* May 1985, 56–69.

2. Lev Anninskii, "Shtrafbat kak zerkalo Velikoi Otechestvennoi," *Iskusstvo kino,* November 2004, kinoart.ru/2004/n11-article2.html.

3. Alon Confino, *Germany as a Culture of Remembrance: Promises and Limits of Writing History* (Chapel Hill: University of North Carolina Press, 2006), 18–19.

4. Jay Winter, *Remembering War: The Great War Between Memory and History in the Twentieth Century* (New Haven, Conn.: Yale University Press, 2006), 183–86.

5. Karen Shakhnazarov, "Interv′iu s K. Shakhnazarovym," included as an extra on Ruscico DVD edition of *Zvezda* (2002).

6. Quoted in "Putin Hails Russian Military," BBC News website, May 9, 2000, news.bbc.co.uk/1/hi/world/europe/741415.stm.

7. Shvydkoi first gave an interview about the project that appeared in *Rossiiskaia gazeta,* September 9, 2000. For more on the document and its initial reaction, see Anna Lawton, *Before the Fall: Soviet Cinema in the Gorbachev Years* (Washington, D.C.: New Academia, 2002), 253.

8. "Interv′iu s K. Shakhnazarovym."

9. Aside from *Star,* the following films appeared between 2002 and 2006: *The Cuckoo* (*Kukushka,* dir. A. Rogozhkin, 2002); *Under the Sign of Taurus* (*V sozvezdii byka,* dir. P. Todorovskii, 2003); *Last Train* (*Poslednii poezd,* dir. A. German, Jr., 2003); *In June of '41* (*V iiune 41go,* dir. M. Ptashuk, 2004); *Our Own* (*Svoi,* dir. Dmitrii Meskhiev, 2004); *Unofficial Business* (*Nesluzhebnoe zadanie,* dir. V. Vorob′ev, 2004); *Red Sky, Black Snow* (*Krasnoe nebo, chernyi sneg,* dir. V. Ogorodnikov, 2005); *First After God* (*Pervyi posle Boga,* dir. V. Chiginskii, 2005); *A Time to Gather Stones* (*Vremia sobirat′ kamni,* dir. A. Karelin, 2005); *Polumgla* (*Polumgla,* dir. A. Antonov, 2005); *Secret Weapon* (*Sekretnoe oruzhie,* dir. V. Vorob′ev, 2006); *The Opposition* (*Protivostoianie,* dir. V. Vorob′ev, 2006); *Bastards* (*Svolochi,* dir. A. Atanesian, 2006); and *Transit* (*Peregon,* dir. A. Rogozhkin, 2006).

10. The serials, in order of their appearance, include *On the Nameless Height* (*Na bezymiannoi vysote,* dir. V. Nikiforov, 2004); *Penal Battalion* (*Shtrafbat,* dir. N. Dostal′, 2004); *The Red Choir* (*Krasnaia kapela,* dir. A. Aravin, 2004); *Saboteur* (*Diversant,* dir. A. Maliukov, 2004); *Cadets* (*Kursanty,* dir. A. Kavun, 2005); *Echelon* (*Eshelon,* dir. V. Arsenev, 2005);

The Last Battle of Major Pugachev (*Poslednyi boi maiora Pugacheva,* dir. V. Fat′ianov, 2005); and *Man of War* (*Chelovek voiny,* dir. A. Muradov, 2005).

11. Victory Day 2010, just to pick one important date, was celebrated with a host of films and serials, among them Nikita Mikhalkov's expensive sequel to *Burnt by the Sun,* the Belorussian-Russian blockbuster *The Brest Fortress, We are from the Future 2,* and Vera Glagoleva's art house film *One War.* On television, serials about the war included *Fog* (*Tuman*); *The Attempt* (*Pokushenie*); *The Vanished* (*Ischeznuvshie,* which first aired in 2009); and the end to the serial *The Saboteur* (*Diversant—konets voiny,* which first aired in 2007).

12. Thomas C. Wolfe, "Past as Present, Myth, or History? Discourses of Time and the Great Fatherland War," in Richard Ned Lebow, Wulf Kansteiner, and Claudio Fogu, eds., *The Politics of Memory in Postwar Europe* (Durham, N.C.: Duke University Press, 2006), 249–83, quotation on 267. See also Lisa Kirschenbaum's magnificent study of the remembrance of the Siege of Leningrad: *The Legacy of the Siege of Leningrad, 1941–1995: Myth, Memories, and Monuments* (New York: Cambridge University Press, 2006).

13. Amir Weiner, "When Memory Counts: War, Genocide, and Postwar Soviet Jewry," in Omer Bartov, Atina Grossmann, and Mary Nolan, eds., *Crimes of War: Guilt and Denial in the Twentieth Century* (New York: The New Press, 2002), 191–216, quotation on 192.

14. For more on this myth and its important functions within Soviet society, see Weiner's book, *Making Sense of War: The Second World War and the Fate of the Bolshevik Revolution* (Princeton, N.J.: Princeton University Press, 2000) and Nina Tumarkin, *The Living and the Dead: The Rise and Fall of the Cult of World War II in Russia* (New York: Basic Books, 1995). Given the Putin-era cultural landscape, it is fair to say that the cult did not fall as much as it took a break for the 1990s.

15. Denise Youngblood, *Russian War Films: On the Cinema Front, 1914–2005* (Lawrence: University of Kansas Press, 2006).

16. "Interv′iu s K. Shakhnazarovym."

17. For more on this issue and on the films that appeared between 2002 and 2006, see my article "Guiding Stars: The Comet-Like Rise of the War Film in Putin's Russia: Recent World War II Films and Historical Memories," *Studies in Russian and Soviet Cinema* 2, no. 1 (February 2007): 163–89.

18. Nikolai Dostal′, "Ikh prigovorili k podvigu," *Iskusstvo kino,* November 2004, kinoart.ru/2004/n11-article4.html.

19. Alexander Prokhorov, "The *Shtrafbat* Archipelago on Russia's Small Screen," *KinoKultura* 13 (July 2006), www.kinokultura.com/2006/13r-strafbat.shtml.

20. The statistic is reprinted in Vasily Grossman, *A Writer at War: A Soviet Journalist with the Red Army, 1941–1945,* ed. and trans. Antony Beever and Luba Vinogradova (New York: Vintage, 2005), 73n3. As a point of comparison, more Soviet citizens died in penal battalions than total number of Americans killed in World War II (the United States suffered 292,000 combat deaths and 110,000 other deaths).

21. Iurii Gladil′shchikov, "Putevodnaia Zvezda: Novyi fil′m dolzhen vyrazit′ natsional′nuiu ideiu," *Izvestiia,* April 9, 2002, izvestia.ru/culture/article16885. See also Sergei Varshavik, "'Zvezda' gosudarstvennogo patriotizma," *Nezavisimaia gazeta,* February 18, 2005, www.ng.ru/tv/2005-02-18/16_lebedev.html.

22. Leonid Radzikhovskii, "Molchanie—zoloto," *Iskusstvo kino,* November 2004, kinoart.ru/2004/n11-article1.html.

23. Ibid.

24. All quotations by Volodarskii are from the interview by Zhanna Vasil′eva, "V osnove dramaturgii lezhit detektiv," *Iskusstvo kino,* December 2004, kinoart.ru/2004/n12-article4.html.

25. See B. V. Sokolov, *Pravda o Velikoi Otechestvennoi voine (Sbornik statei)* (St. Petersburg: Aleteiia, 1999).

26. Boris Sokolov, "*Shtrafbat* glazami istorika," *Grani.ru* website, October 7, 2004, grani.ru/opinion/sokolov/m.77884.html.

27. Quoted in Oleg Elenskii, "Kakuiu 'pravdu' ishchut Shtrafbat i Kursanty?" *Nezavisimaia gazeta,* April 2, 2005, nvo.ng.ru/concepts/2005-02-04/1_gareev.html.

28. Larisa Maliukova, "Prigovorennye k podbigu, ili vsia Rossiia—Shtrafbat," *Novaya gazeta,* September 3, 2004, 2004.novayagazeta.ru/nomer/2004/72n/n72n-s19.shtml.

29. All quotations from Inna Rudenko, "Shtrafbat: kakim on byl ne v kino," *Komsomol′skaia pravda,* April 28, 2005, www.kp.ru/daily/23503.4/39382.

30. V. O. Daines and V. V. Abaturov, eds., *Pravda o shtrafbatakh 2* (Moscow: Eksmo, 2008); I. Pykhalov, A. Pyl′tsyn, A. Vasil′chenko, et al., *Shtrafbaty po obe storony fronta* (Moscow: Eksmo, 2007); I. Pykhalov et al., eds. *Vsia Pravda o shtrafbatakh* (Moscow: Eksmo, 2010).

31. Pykhalov et al., *Shtrafbaty po obe storony fronta,* 5.

32. See Puchkov's Wikipedia biography (surely a sign of his significance), ru.wikipedia.org/wiki/Пучков,_Дмитрий_Юрьевич (accessed January 30, 2012); and his official (Tupichok Goblina) website, oper.ru (accessed January 30, 2012).

33. "Pro serial shtrafbat," Tupichok Goblina website, December 17, 2004, oper.ru/news/read.php?t=1051601174.

34. "Shtrafbat," Ruskino website, ruskino.ru/mov/forum/537 (accessed January 30, 2012). See also the Orthodox Church forum at "Shtrafbat," Cirota website, www.cirota.ru/forum/view.php?subj=38521 (accessed January 30, 2012).

35. These responses are all taken from "Shtrafbat," Kinoexpert website, www.kinoexpert.ru/index.asp?comm=4&num=18413 (accessed January 3, 2007).

36. Dostal′, "Ikh prigovorili k podvigu."

37. "Sozdateli 'Shtrafbata': Nash fil′m—o patriotism," BBC *Russian,* October 30, 2004, news.bbc.co.uk/hi/russian/talking_point/newsid_3946000/3946233.stm.

38. Anninskii, "Shtrafbat kak zerkalo Velikoi Otechestvennoi."

39. See John Garrard and Carol Garrard, *Russian Orthodoxy Resurgent: Faith and Power in the New Russia* (Princeton, N.J.: Princeton University Press, 2008).

40. A. Petrova, "War Movies and the 60th Anniversary of Victory Day," a public opinion foundation poll, Public Opinion Foundation website, bd.english.fom.ru/report/map/eof051903 (accessed August 13, 2008).

41. The debate appeared in numerous newspapers—see *Komsomol′skaia Pravda*'s take at www.kp.ru/daily/2v013652/49495 (accessed May 5, 2006). See also the critical articles "'Svlolochi' Shvydkogo," *Pravda,* February 28, 2006, www.pravda.ru/culture/cinema/russiancinema/28-02-2006/77793-svolochi-0; and "'Svolochi,' eto zhe patriotichno!" *Pravda,* April 14, 2006, www.pravda.ru/culture/cinema/14-04-2006/81720-kino-0. See also Kirill Alekhin, "Vot svoloch′," *Ogonek,* www.ogonoik.com/4930/27 (accessed May 5, 2006); Elena Ardabatskaia, "Svolochi nashego vremeni," *Moskovskii komsomolets v Ufe,* www.mkufa.ru/index.php?cat=8&artid=2730 (accessed May 5, 2006); Larisa Maliukova, "Blagodariu FSB, ikh zavlenie rabotaet na interes k kartine 'Svolochi,'" *Novaia gazeta,* February 6, 2006, 2006.novayagazeta.ru/nomer/2006/08n/n08n-s20.shtml; Lidiia

Maslova, "Intermal′chiki," *Kommersant,* February 3, 2006, www.kommersant.ru/region/spb/page.htm?Id_doc=646291; and Andrei Shcherbakov and Stanislav Stremidlovskii, "Velikuiu Otechestvennuiu voinu vyigral 'Svolochi'?" *Rossiiskie vesti,* rosvesty.ru/1817/interes/?id=972 (accessed January 1, 2007).

42. Andrei Shcherbakov, "Svolochi, zhe patriotichno!" *Pravda,* April 14, 2006, www.pravda.ru/print/culture/cinema/81720-kino-0.

43. Omer Bartov, *Mirrors of Destruction: War, Genocide, and Modern Identity* (New York: Oxford University Press, 2000), 3.

44. Peter Burke's work is also particularly useful in this regard, for he sees the unreliability of images, which often act as "distorting mirrors," as an asset more than a liability. "Images," he writes, "are at once an essential and a treacherous source for historians of mentalities, concerned as they are with unspoken assumptions as much as with conscious attitudes." Yet these assumptions, these mentalities, are just as vital for the historians to glimpse out of the mirror. See Peter Burke, *Eyewitnessing: The Use of Images as Historical Evidence* (Ithaca, N.Y.: Cornell University Press, 2001), 31.

45. See Robert Moeller, *War Stories: The Search for a Usable Past in the Federal Republic of Germany* (Berkeley: University of California Press, 2001); Henry Rousso, *The Vichy Syndrome: History and Memory in France Since 1945* (Cambridge, Mass.: Harvard University Press, 1991); Robert Gildea, *Marianne in Chains: Daily Life in France in the Heart of France During the German Occupation* (New York: Picador, 2004); Tony Judt, *Postwar: A History of Europe Since 1945* (New York: Penguin, 2006); Jan Gross, *Neighbors: The Destruction of the Jewish Community in Jedwabne, Poland* (Princeton, N.J.: Princeton University Press, 2001); Antony Polonsky and Joanna Michlic, eds., *The Neighbors Respond: The Controversy over the Jedwabne Massacre in Poland* (Princeton, N.J.: Princeton University Press, 2003); and John Dower, *Embracing Defeat: Japan in the Wake of World War II* (New York: W. W. Norton, 2000).

46. Cited in Alexander Prokhorov, review of Nikolai Dostal′, *Penal Battalion, KinoKultura* 13 (July 2006), www.kinokultura.com/2006/13r-strafbat.shtml.

47. Stats from "Svolochi," *Kinopoisk* website, www.kinopoisk.ru/level/1/film/103414 (accessed January 30, 2012).

48. Mark Lipovetsky, "Post Sots: Transformations of Socialist Realism in the Popular Culture of the Recent Period," *Slavic and East European Journal* 48, no. 3 (2004): 356–57.

49. Ibid., 358–59.

50. Sarah Mendelson and Theodore Gerber, "Failing the Stalin Test," *Foreign Affairs* 85, no. 1 (January/February 2006): 2–8.

51. Sarah Mendelson and Theodore Gerber, "Soviet Nostalgia: An Impediment to Democratization," *Wilson Quarterly* 29, no. 1 (Winter 2006): 83–96.

52. See Maria Ferretti, "Memory Disorder: Russia and Stalinism," *Russian Politics and Law* 41, no. 6 (November/December 2003): 38–82. Anatoly Khazanov argues, "[T]he problem [in Russia] is not ignorance, but rather indifference, or an intentional desire to ignore the dark sides of the Soviet past." The result, as he sees it, is that "Russians feel neither guilt nor shame" about their past, a state of affairs that has led to "pseudo-democracy, pseudo-capitalism, pseudo-historicity, pseudo-remembrance, pseudo-democracy, pseudo-repentance." See his "Whom to Mourn and Whom to Forget? (Re)constructing Collective Memory in Contemporary Russia," *Totalitarian Movements and Political Religions* 9, no. 2 (June–September 2008): 293–310, quotations on 301, 308.

53. Confino, *Germany as a Culture of Remembrance,* 235. My emphasis.

54. For an expansion of these views, see my review of Andrei Kavun, *Cadets, KinoKultura* 14 (October 2006), www.kinokultura.com/2006/14r-cadets.shtml. See also Cathy Frierson's excellent rebuttal to Mendelson and Gerber, "An Open Call to Focus on Russia's Educated Young Adults," *Problems of Post-Communism* 54, no. 5 (September 2007): 3–18.

55. Winter, *Remembering War,* 2.

56. Ibid., 199–200.

57. Elena Novoseleva, "Lozh′, kino i svoboda," *Rossiskaia gazeta,* May 7, 2007, rg.ru/2007/05/07/dondurey.html.

58. For ratings, see "Prem′era sezona—'Zaveshchanie Lenina,'" *Kommersant,* June 15, 2007, www.kommersant.ru/doc/774596.

59. Ekaterina Kliuchnikova, "'My imeem televidenie, kotorye zasluzhbaem,'" *Vremia novostei,* November 19, 2007, www.tvkultura.ru/news.html?id=190436&cid=54.

7. PLAYING WITH HISTORY

This chapter benefited from the readings of my Miami colleagues at the Havighurst Center's work-in-progress series held on April 17, 2009. Brigid O'Keeffe, Karen Dawisha, Ben Sutcliffe, Dan Prior, and Vitaly Chernetsky all offered detailed comments and deserve particular thanks.

1. E-mail message from Dmitrii Puchkov, July 29, 2008.

2. Gregory Feifer, *The Great Gamble: The Soviet War in Afghanistan* (New York: Harper, 2009), 238.

3. Ibid.

4. Ibid., 258.

5. Ibid., 259.

6. Serguei Oushakine, *The Patriotism of Despair: Nation, War, and Loss in Russia* (Ithaca, N.Y.: Cornell University Press, 2009), 168.

7. See Borovik's *The Hidden War: A Russian Journalist's Account of the Soviet War in Afghanistan* (New York: Grove Press, 1990). Borovik became one of the faces of glasnost′-era journalism in Russia and in the United States, where he frequently appeared on *60 Minutes.* His account of the trauma of the war both for its soldiers and for Soviet society represents the dominant memory of the conflict. See also Svetlana Aleksievich's *Zinky Boys: Soviet Voices from a Forgotten War* (New York: W. W. Norton, 1992) for more on how the war had already been forgotten in Russia by 1992.

8. Aleksandr Liakhovskii, *Tragediia i doblest′ Afgana* (Moscow: Nord, 2004).

9. Roman Kachanov's film is a remake of Dostoevsky's *Idiot* set in contemporary Russia.

10. Quoted in Peter Finn, "From Bitter Memories, a Russian Blockbuster," *Washington Post,* October 20, 2005, www.washingtonpost.com/wp-dyn/content/article/2005/10/19/AR2005101902317.html.

11. Interview with Natal′ia Baladina, *Iskusstvo kino,* July 2005, kinoart.ru/2005/n7-article12.html. Dawn Seckler has written, "The validity of these claims is debatable. However, the following is undeniable: *Company 9* was conceived from these ideas." See Seckler, review of Fedor Bondarchuk, *Company 9, KinoKultura* 12 (April 2006), www.kinokultura.com/2006/12r-company9.shtml.

12. See the statistics in "9 rota," *Kinopoisk* website, www.kinopoisk.ru/level/1/film/84674 (accessed January 30, 2012).

13. The most memorable acknowledgment of this marketing campaign appeared in Timur Bekmambetov's 2006 blockbuster *Day Watch.* Anton Goredetsky, the hero of the film and its prequel, *Night Watch,* reenters Moscow from the Gloom by smashing through a metro poster for *9 rota. Day Watch* would go on

to smash Bondarchuk's box office record, topping out at $32 million.

14. Quoted in Sophia Kishkovsky, "From a Bitter War Defeat Comes Russia's Latest Blockbuster," *New York Times,* October 29, 2005, www.nytimes.com/2005/10/29/movies/MoviesFeatures/29inva.html.

15. Dawn Seckler describes the scene where all the boys have intercourse with Snow White as "truly a new low point for contemporary Russian cinema": "She is the Dostoevskiian whore with a heart of gold, who makes herself sexually available to all of the soldiers (first in rapid succession, then simultaneously) before they depart for battle. That is her sacrifice. Poetic as Bondarchuk's intentions may have been, the result is an offensive gang-bang scene presented as intimate, loving, respectful, and even transcendent." See Seckler, review of Fedor Bondarchuk, *Company 9*.

16. See Seckler, review of Fedor Bondarchuk, *Company 9;* Finn, "From Bitter Memories, a Russian Blockbuster"; review by Tat′iana Moskvina, *Iskusstvo kino,* November 2005, kinoart.ru/2005/n11-article8.html; and Diliara Tasbulatova, "Zabytaia rota," *Itogi,* September 26, 2005, www.itogi.ru/archive/2005/39/59635.html.

17. Curiously, the subtitles for the film change "1988" to "1989," although the original date remains in the intertitles.

18. For one scene that involved a soldier journeying into an Afghan village for some matches, Bondarchuk used an unlikely screen veteran: the donkey that carried Shurik across the Crimea in Leonid Gaidai's *Kidnapping, Caucasian Style.* It turned out that the donkey still lived in the Yalta Zoo.

19. Ol′ga Tropkina, "Pervyi kadr," *Rossiskaia gazeta,* November 9, 2005, www.rg.ru/2005/11/09/putin-bondarchuk.html.

20. Quoted in Oushakine, *The Patriotism of Despair,* 156.

21. All quotations are taken from "Veterany-afgantsy o fil′me F. Bondarchuka," RSVA website, www.rsva.ru/rus_guard/2005-11/rota.shtml (accessed January 30, 2012).

22. Ibid.

23. "Istoricheskaia spravka RSVA," RSVA website, www.rsva.ru/ARTICLES/50010008/200000008 (accessed January 30, 2012).

24. *9 rota* official website, 9rota.lacory.ru.

25. Quoted in Finn, "From Bitter Memories, A Russian Blockbuster."

26. Ibid.

27. Ibid.

28. Diliara Tasbulatova, "Zabytaia rota."

29. "9 rota," *Kinopoisk* website, www.kinopoisk.ru/level/1/film/84674 (accessed January 30, 2012).

30. Quoted in Kishkovsky, "From a Bitter War Defeat Comes Russia's Latest Blockbuster."

31. Quoted in the media guide on the *Ninth Company* website, www.9thcompany.com or 9rota.ru (accessed January 30, 2012).

32. Here Liakhovskii may have been referring to 1988's *Rambo III,* frequently shown on Russian television. In it, Rambo supplies the mujahideen with weapons. I thank Ben Sutcliffe for pointing out this link.

33. Quoted in Luke Harding, "It Shows Both Our War, and Not Our War," *Guardian,* February 2, 2007, www.guardian.co.uk/world/2007/feb/02/russia.

34. See Natalia Rulyova, "Piracy and Narrative Games": Dmitry Puchkov's Translations of *The Lord of the Rings,*" *Slavic and East European Journal* 49, no. 3 (Fall 2005): 625–38, and Theresa Sabonis-Chafee, "Communism as Kitsch: Soviet Symbols in Post-Soviet Society," in Adele

Marie Barker, ed., *Consuming Russia: Popular Culture, Sex, and Society Since Gorbachev* (Durham, N.C.: Duke University Press, 1999), 362–82.

35. Rulyova, "Piracy and Narrative Games," 628.

36. Ibid.

37. "Voprosy Gobliny pro perevody fil′mov," Tupichok Goblina website, June 14, 2003, oper.ru/torture/read.php?t=1045689061. This lengthy explanation is worth reading in its entirety for Puchkov's philosophies about literal translation, his theories on American curse words (the way he explains the many uses of "fuck" alone justifies reading the interview), and his digs at the "idiots" who often do translations for film.

38. See Anastasiia Belousova, "Dmitrii Puchkov (Goblin): 'Sutki dushil negodiaev, troe—otstrelival monstrov,'" *Segodnia,* July 1, 2008, www.segodnya.ua/interview/10050467.html. In this interview Puchkov states that he does not like to talk about his MVD work because he started working for the security service the same year he read Solzhenitsyn's *Gulag Archipelago* and learned of the crimes committed by his predecessors. He retired in 1998 to open a store in St. Petersburg.

39. Carl Schreck, "Goblin Makes Case against Demonizing Expletives," *St. Petersburg Times,* July 29, 2003, www.sptimes.ru/index.php?action_id=2&story_id=10583. See also Natalia Rulyova's two articles on Goblin's work: "*Anti-Bimmer:* Dmitrii Puchkov's Humorous Interpretation of *Bimmer,*" *KinoKultura* 9 (July 2005), www.kinokultura.com/reviews/R7-05antibumer.html; and "Piracy and Narrative Games." Puchkov is perhaps the clearest Russian example of what Henry Jenkins has defined as a "textual poacher," a person who takes a particular text or texts and transforms it, allowing us to observe the consumer's power in shaping the reception of that text. Jenkins develops most of his thesis around Trekkies and how they have shaped *Star Trek*'s significance, but Puchkov's activities certainly point to similar practices in Russia today. See Jenkins, *Textual Poachers: Television Fans and Participatory Culture* (New York: Routledge, 1992), as well as his follow-up work that deals with poaching and fandom in different arenas: *Fans, Bloggers, and Gamers: Exploring Participatory Culture* (New York: New York University Press, 2006).

40. He still maintains the Tupichok Goblina website, oper.ru (accessed January 30, 2012).

41. The company released a second game in 2008. See "Sanitarakh podzemelii 2," 1C website, sanitars2.ru (accessed January 30, 2012).

42. Dmitrii Puchkov, "Kh/F 9 rota," Tupichok Goblina website, September 28, 2005, kino.oper.ru/torture/read.php?t=1045689085.

43. Here Puchkov clearly sides with the official statistics of war dead. Unofficial estimates of Soviet soldiers killed in the war run as high as seventy-five thousand.

44. Puchkov, "Kh/F 9 rota."

45. E-mail message from Dmitrii Puchkov, July 29, 2008.

46. Quoted in "Pravda o deviatoi rote," *The Truth about Ninth Company* website, www.pravdao9rote.ru (accessed January 30, 2012).

47. "Pravda o deviatoi rote," 1C website, www.1c.ru/news/info.jsp?id=7884 (accessed January 30, 2012).

48. *Wolfenstein 3D,* released in 1992, is the granddaddy of first-person shooter games and is credited with popularizing the genre. Inspired by the 1980s game *Castle Wolfenstein,* it allows players to become a Polish soldier who hunts Nazis. The enemies are sometimes SS soldiers, and sometimes werewolves and other beasts. The series is still going strong and still

blazes new trails—*Wolfenstein* RPG became available as a mobile phone game in 2009.

49. Zach Whalen and Laurie Taylor, "Playing the Past: An Introduction," in *Playing the Past: History and Nostalgia in Video Games* (Nashville, Tenn.: Vanderbilt University Press, 2008), 1–18, quotation on 2.

50. James Campbell, "Just Less than Total War: Simulating World War II as Ludic Nostalgia," in Whalen and Talor, *Playing the Past,* 183–200, quotation on 185.

51. Ibid., 188.

52. Ibid., 192.

53. See "Troops Stationed in Iraq Turn to Gaming," MSNBC website, January 3, 2005, www.msnbc.msn.com/id/6780587.

54. E-mail message from Dmitrii Puchkov, July 29, 2008.

55. See "V ramkakh XII VRNS sostoialas′ prezentatsiia pervoi rossiiskoi documental′noi komp′iuternoi igry 'Pravda o deviatoi rote,'" Interfax website, February 22, 2008, www.interfax-religion.ru/?act=news&div=23011.

56. "Pravda o deviatoi rote," Playground website, February 22, 2008, www.playground.ru/articles/20253.

57. E-mail message from Anatoly Subbotin, March 20, 2009.

58. See *9th Company* game website, www.9rota-game.ru (accessed January 30, 2012).

59. "O igre," *9th Company* game website, www.9rota-game.ru/pages/game/about (accessed January 30, 2012).

60. "9 rota," Playground website, www.playground.ru/games/9th_company_roots_of_terror (accessed January 30, 2012).

61. "9 rota: skuchnaia slozhnost′," 3D News website, www.3dnews.ru/games/9_rota_skuchnaya_slozhnost (accessed January 30, 2012).

62. "9 rota," Playground website, news.playground.ru/16345/#comments (accessed January 30, 2012).

63. E-mail message from Dmitrii Puchkov, July 29, 2008.

64. E-mail message from Aleksandr Skakovskii, March 23, 2009. The UK version will be put out by Rewired, and the U.S. version by Strategy First.

65. E-mail message from Anatoly Subbotin, PR Director for 1C, March 20, 2009.

66. E-mail message from Dmitrii Puchkov, July 29, 2008.

67. The title of the book comes from one of the most popular Soviet films, 1969's *White Sun of the Desert* [*Beloe solntse pustyni*]. I thank Ben Sutcliffe and Vitaly Chernetsky for reminding me of this quotation.

68. "Seriia—knigi GOBLINa," Krylov website, www.vkrylov.ru/detail.php?seriaID=1244195653&bookID=259&type=2 (accessed January 30, 2012).

69. "Seriia—knigi GOBLINa," Krylov website, www.vkrylov.ru/detail.php?seriaID=1244195653&bookID=531&type=2 (accessed January 30, 2012). He has followed up these two books with *Notes of a Sanitation Worker about Cinema,* which expands on his translation views expounded on his website.

70. Quoted in Harding, "It Shows Both Our War, and Not Our War."

PART 3. BACK IN THE USSR

1. See the results of the 2006 poll in "Luchshie lidery: Brezhnev i Putin," VTSIOM website, April 25, 2007, www.rosbalt.ru/2007/04/25/294470.html.

2. Aleksandra Samarina, "Nostal′giia: preemnikam prosto povezlo, chto Brezhneva net," *Nezavisimaia gazeta,* December 19, 2006, www.ng.ru/ideas/2006-12-19/9_brezhnev.html.

3. See Joshua First, "From Spectator to 'Differentiated' Consumer: Film Audience Research in the Era of Developed Socialism (1965–80)," *Kritika* 9, no. 2 (Spring 2008): 317–44; and Kristin Roth-Ey, *Moscow Prime Time: How the Soviet Union Built*

the Media Empire that Lost the Cultural Cold War (Ithaca, N.Y.: Cornell University Press, 2011).

4. Elena Prokhorova, "Fragmented Mythologies: Soviet TV Mini-Series of the 1970s" (Ph.D. diss., University of Pittsburgh, 2003).

5. Evgenii Anisimov, "Istoriia Rossii menia nichemu ne nauchila," *Seans* 35/36 (2008), seance.ru/n/35-36/kino-otkrytogo-dejstvija/kino-otkryitogo-deystviya.

6. Ibid.

7. Aleksei Zimin, "Gruz utopii," *Seans* 35/36 (2008), seance.ru/n/35-36/vertigo-3536/gruz-utopii. Zakhar Prilepin expressed similar thoughts in his article "Vtoroe ubiistvo Sovetskoe Soiuza," *Seans* 35/36 (2008), seance.ru/n/35-36/vertigo-3536/vtoroe-ubiystvo-sovetskogo-soyuza. Prilepin lived in the provinces, and for him the Soviet Union was simply the way he experienced childhood; this past was murdered twice, first throughout the 1990s and again with 2000s retro-nostalgia for a Soviet Union that could not be restored.

8. Timur Kibirov, "Nostal′giia v gosudarstvennykh masshatbakh," *Seans* 35/36 (2008), seance.ru/n/35-36/vertigo-3536/timur-kibirov-nostalgiya-vgosudarst vennyih-masshtabah.

9. Sergei Shnurov, "SSSR—eto olympiiki, uzhe, kstati, nemodnye," *Seans* 35/36 (2008), seance.ru/n/35-36/vertigo-3536/sergey-shnurov-sssr-eto-olimpiyki-uzhe-kstati-nemodnyie. Shnurov's view of the 1990s and "democracy" in the 2000s runs throughout the article and informs his retrospective look at the 1970s.

10. Anthony D. Smith, *Myths and Memories of the Nation* (Oxford: Oxford University Press, 1999), 65–66. One central tenet of nationalist myths, as Smith defines them, is the "myth of the heroic age," which provides nationalists with a pristine era full of heroes, usable virtues, and glorious deeds.

8. THE BLESSED BLOCKBUSTER

1. Father Vladimir Vigilianskii, interview by Stephen M. Norris, July 12, 2008, Moscow.

2. See "Church and State" under "The Basis of the Social Concept," Moscow Patriarchy website, www.mospat.ru/index.php?mid=183 (accessed January 30, 2012).

3. "Osnovy sotsial′noi kontseptsii Russkoi Pravoslavnoi Tserkvi," Moscow Patriarchy website, www.mospat.ru/index.php?mid=182 (accessed January 30, 2012).

4. For more on the church after socialism, see Zoe Knox, *Russian Society and the Orthodox Church: Religion in Russia after Communism* (Routledge, 2005). Knox argues that the Church contributes to the emergence of a civil society in unofficial or informal ways while the Patriarchy obstructs it in its attempts to assert itself as the repository of Russianness. This view is also more or less reached by John Garrard and Carol Garrard in their contentious *Russian Orthodoxy Resurgent: Faith and Power in the New Russia* (Princeton, N.J.: Princeton University Press, 2008).

5. Elena Iakovleva, "'Ostrov' vezeniia," *Rossiskaia gazeta*, February 28, 2007, www.rg.ru/2007/02/28/sobolev.html.

6. Tat′iana Khoroshilova, "'Ostrov' Lungina: Chuvstvo bol′noi sovesti-normal′noe sostoianie cheloveka, schitaet izvestnyi rezhisser," *Rossisskaia gazeta*, December 21, 2006, www.rg.ru/2006/12/21/lungin.html.

7. Ibid.

8. The most famous Holy Fool in Russia, Vasilii (Basil) the Blessed, lived in the late fifteenth and early sixteenth centuries and is famous first for his rebuke of Ivan the Terrible and second for his Robin Hood–like thievery. He was canonized by the Church after his death and lent his name to the most famous Cathedral in Russia, St. Basil's.

9. Khoroshilova, "'Ostrov' Lungina."

10. Marina Leonidova, "Ot 'Zvuki Mu' do cheloveku-ostrovu," *Argumenty i Fakty Kaliningrad,* March 21, 2007, kaliningrad .aif.ru/issues/515.

11. Igor′ Vinnichenko, "Retsenziia na fil′m Pavla Lungina 'Ostrov,'" *Pravoslavnie,* September 5, 2006, www.pravoslavie.ru/ jurnal/060905150536.htm.

12. Ibid.

13. Father Vladimir Vigilianskii, interview. Vigilianskii also cited younger, more liberal monks at the Donskoi Monastery as particularly influential in persuading Aleksei II to bless the film.

14. Elena Iakovleva, "Dusha kak khristianka: Patriarkh Aleksei II o svobodnom slove i pokaianii geroev 'Ostrova,'" *Rossiiskaia gazeta,* January 19, 2007, www.rg.ru/ 2007/01/19/alexiy.html. The interview about *The Island* was reprinted in the newspaper on the eve of the 2007 Nika awards—Lungin's film won best picture, Lungin won best director, and Mamonov won best actor. The film also captured awards for best supporting actor (Viktor Sukhorukov), best cinematography, and best sound. See www.rg.ru/2007/01/26/ patriarh-ostrov.html (accessed January 30, 2012).

15. Ibid.

16. "Mitropolit Kirill vysoko otsenil fil′m 'Ostrov,' nazvav ego 'sobytiem ogromnoi vazhnosti,'" Religare website, April 20, 2007, www.religare.ru/article 40694.htm.

17. Iakovleva, "Dusha kak khristianka."

18. See the document "The Church and Mass Media," which spells out the official policy on the relationship with media, Patriarchy website, www.mospat.ru/index .php?mid=195 (accessed January 30, 2012).

19. See "V Voronezhe pri polnom anshlage proshel pokaz fil′ma 'Ostrov' Pavla Lungina," NTV website, November 16, 2006, news.ntv.ru/97895. An edited version of this report is quoted in Mark Lipovetsky's review of the film, "The Importance of Being Pious: Pavel Lungin's *The Island,*" *KinoKultura* 15 (January 2007), www.kinokultura.com/2007/15r-island.shtml.

20. Andrei Zolotov, Jr., "High Passion: Russian Audiences Embrace Gibson's 'Passion,'" *Moscow Times,* April 16–22, 2004, www.orthodoxytoday.org/articles4/ZolotovPassion.shtml.

21. "V domovom khrame MGU sostoialas′ vstrecha s regisserom fil′ma 'Ostrov' Pavlom Lunginym," St. Tat′iana's Cathedral website, December 19, 2006, www .st-tatiana.ru/text/30588.html.

22. The film won six awards, the most in the five years the awards had been handed out. The second most went to the TV series *Doctor Zhivago.* For reports of Mamonov's behavior, see Vadim Nestorov, "Zolotoi orel pomoinovo golubia," *Gazeta .ru,* January 29, 2007, www.gazeta.ru/ culture/2007/01/29/a_1308093.shtml; and "Na tseremonii 'Zolotogo orla' Petr Mamonov prochital otpoved′ svetskoi publike," News.ru website, January 29, 2007, www.newsru.com/cinema/29jan2007/ mamonov.html.

23. Lipovetsky, "The Importance of Being Pious."

24. Quoted in ibid. The original is Mikhail Ryklin, *Svastika, krest, zvezda* (Moscow: Logos, 2006), 174–75.

25. Ibid.

26. Mikhail Iampolskii, comments at the 2008 Pittsburgh Russian Film Symposium, May 6, 2008.

27. Evgeniia Vlasova, "Skhodila ia na 'Ostrov' (vzgliad pravoslavnogo cheloveka)" *Ezhednevnyi zhurnal,* January 10, 2007, www.ej.ru/?a=note&id=5811.

28. "'Ostrov' poiavilsia vovremia," *Vremia novosti,* January 25, 2007, www .vremya.ru/2007/12/10/170107.html.

29. Ibid.

30. "Ostrov," *Kinopoisk* website, www.kinopoisk.ru/level/1/film/257337

(accessed January 30, 2012). See also the review and comments on the religious site *Religiia kak naslazhdenie Boga* (religion as the enjoyment of God), where Orthodox believers argue about the film's messages: bridge.artsportal.ru/index.php?template=magazin_inner&id=236&magazine=12 (accessed January 30, 2012). Kino.ru online posts also praised the film: "Ostrov," www.kino.ru/forum.php?id=3015#times (accessed January 30, 2012).

31. "'Ostrov' protiv 'Ostrova,'" *Seans* website, seance.ru/blog/ostrov-vs-ostrov (accessed January 30, 2012).

32. "Pavel Lungin," Religare website, www.religare.ru/2_49480.html (accessed January 30, 2012).

33. Saint Augustine, *Confessions,* trans. Henry Chadwick (Oxford: Oxford University Press, 1998), 179–221.

34. Father Vladimir Vigilianskii, interview. One more sign of the film's cultural resonance: the writer Dmitrii Orekhov published *'Ostrov': Podlinnaia istoriia* [*The Island:* An authentic history] with the St. Petersburg publisher Amphora. In its 222 pages Orekhov discusses the cultural, religious, and historical bases that Sobolev's script taps into. Holy fools, northern monasteries, miracles, writers such as Leskov—all contributed, in Orekhov's view, to the "authenticity" of Lungin's film.

35. Father Vladimir Vigilianskii, interview.

36. Dmitrii Bykov, "Chudo ostrova," *Iskusstvo kino,* October 2006, 26–29.

9. THE SOVIET HORROR SHOW

The author wishes to thank Ian Christie for an informative discussion about *Cargo 200* while en route to Frank Lloyd Wright's Fallingwater in May 2008. I am sure Ian will disagree with my view of the film presented in this chapter, but our discussion helped me think about Balabanov's film more clearly than I had before. I also wish to thank Aleksei Balabanov for a memorable meeting on July 11, 2007.

1. See Anthony Anemone, "About Killers, Freaks, and Real Men: The Vigilante Hero of Aleksei Balabanov's Films," in Stephen M. Norris and Zara Torlone, eds., *Insiders and Outsiders in Russian Cinema* (Bloomington: Indiana University Press, 2008), 127–41.

2. Aleksei Balabanov, interview by Stephen M. Norris, July 11, 2007, Lenfilm Studios, St. Petersburg.

3. See the letter, "Otkrytoe pis′mo," and responses on the *Seans* website, www.seance.ru/blog/open-letter (accessed January 31, 2012).

4. Josephine Woll, "Exorcising the Devil: Russian Cinema and Horror," in Steven Jay Scheider and Tony Williams, eds., *Horror International* (Detroit, Mich.: Wayne State University Press, 2005), 341.

5. Quoted in "Aleksei Balabanov: 'Vsegda zhivem v Rossii,'" *Iskusstvo kino,* July 2007, kinoart.ru/2007/n7-article2.html.

6. Tony Anemone, review of Aleksei Balabanov, *Cargo 200, KinoKultura* 18 (October 2007), www.kinokultura.com/2007/18r-gruz.shtml.

7. All the quotations from the radio program are from the transcript that appeared on *Echo Moscow*'s website, www.echo.msk.ru/programs/kulshok/52541 (accessed January 31, 2012).

8. See the results of the 2006 poll in "Luchshie lidery: Brezhnev i Putin," VTSIOM website, April 25, 2007, www.rosbalt.ru/2007/04/25/294470.html; and Michael Schwirz, comp., "Russians Romanticize Brezhnev Era," *New York Times,* December 19, 2006, www.nytimes.com/2006/12/19/world/europe/19russiansumm.html?_r=1&partner=rssnyt&emc=rss&oref=slogin.

9. Information and quotations in this paragraph come from Aleksei Balabanov, interview.

10. See Larisa Maliukova, "'Gruz 200': Takogo kino eshche ne bylo," *Novaia gazeta,* June 21, 2007, www.novayagazeta.ru/data/2007/color23/09.html.

11. Ibid.

12. Aleskei Balabanov, interview. Balabanov's seventeen-year-old son was quick to interject at this point: "Dad, I play video games *and* read Dostoevsky."

13. Maliukova, "'Gruz 200.'"

14. Aleksei Balabanov, interview.

15. Bruce Ballon and Molyn Lezcz, "Horror Films: Tales to Master Terror or Shapers of Trauma?" *American Journal of Psychotherapy* 61, no. 2 (2007): 211–30. The film can also be seen as an "allegorical moment" in the way described by Adam Lowenstein: "a shocking collision of film, spectator, and history where registers of bodily space and historical time are distributed unevenly across the cinematic text, the film's audience, and the historical context." Horror films, as Lowenstein posits, may serve as a means to work through historical traumas. Adam Lowenstein, *Shocking Representation: Historical Trauma, National Cinema, and the Modern Horror Film* (New York: Columbia University Press, 2005), quotation on 2.

16. Ballon and Lezcz, "Horror Films," 216.

17. Ibid., 219.

18. Ibid., 228.

19. Aleksei Balabanov, interview.

20. Vasilii Stepanov and Konstantin Shavlovskii, eds., *Seans guide: Rossiiskie fil′my 2007 goda* (St. Petersburg: Seans, 2007), 68–69.

21. These and quotations that follow are from "1984," *Seans,* April 4, 2007, seance.ru/blog/year1984 (accessed February 1, 2012).

22. Liubov′ Arkus, Vasilii Stepanov, and Konstantin Shavlovskii, eds., *Seans guide: Rossiiskie fil′my 2007 goda* (St. Petersburg, Seans, 2008), 43–51, 281.

23. Alexei Yurchak, *Everything Was Forever, until It Was No More: The Last Soviet Generation* (Princeton, N.J.: Princeton University Press, 2006), 1.

24. Ibid., 5.

25. Ibid., 8.

26. Ibid., 10.

27. When the Tom Cruise film *Valkyrie* debuted in February 2009, Iurii Gladil′shchikov entitled his review "Kruz [Cruise] 200," *Stengazeta,* February 6, 2009, stengazeta.net/article.html?article=5813.

PART 4. FANTASY POP HISTORY

1. Mikhail Morozov, "Istoriia v stile 'pop,'" *Iskusstvo kino,* January 2009, kinoart.ru/2009/n1-article2.html.

2. Ibid.

3. The entire list of names and history of the competition is on the official Name of Russia website, www.nameofrussia.ru (accessed January 30, 2012).

4. Iurii Emel′ianov, "Proket 'Imia Rossiia': Boi za Stalina," KPRF website, October 21, 2008, kprf.ru/rus_soc/60572.html.

5. Slava Taroshchina, "Imiia Rossiia: kesarevo sechenie," *Novaia gazeta* 88 (November 27, 2008), novgaz.ru/data/2008/88/19.html.

6. Anatolii Baranov, "'Imiia Rossiia'—dazhe ne lozh′, a prosto melkoe zhul′nichestvo," Forum.msk.ru website, December 29, 2008, forum-msk.org/material/news/675766.html.

7. Evgenii Lesin, "Rus′-troika: Stalin, Stalin, i Stalin," *Nezavisimaia gazeta,* December 29, 2008, www.ng.ru/politics/2008-12-29/2_rusname.html?mthree=9.

8. Smith, *Myths and Memories of the Nation,* 62–70.

10. ANIMATING THE PAST

1. Henry Giroux, *The Mouse That Roared: Disney and the End of Innocence*

(Lanham, Md.: Roman and Littlefield, 1999), 10.

2. See Zan Jifang, "Panda Movie Raises Questions," *Beijing Review,* August 21, 2008, 42–43.

3. Oleg Minin, "Art and Politics in the Russian Satirical Press, 1905–1908" (Ph.D. diss., University of Southern California, 2008), 276–81.

4. Vlad Strukov, review of Vladimir Toropchin, *Il′ia Muromets and the Nightingale-Robber, KinoKultura* 22 (October 2008), www.kinokultura.com/2008/22r-muromets.shtml.

5. Ibid.

6. David MacFadyen, *Yellow Crocodiles and Blue Oranges: Russian Animated Film Since World War II* (Montreal: McGill-Queen's University Press, 2005), xii. See also Irina Margolina and Natal′ia Lozinskaia, eds., *Nashi mul′tifil′my* (Moscow: Interros, 2006), particularly Nikolai Izvolov's introduction, "Mul′tiplikatsionnoe kino v Rossii," 6–13.

7. Quoted in Margolina and Lozinskaia, eds., *Nashi mul′tifil′my,* 106.

8. Ibid., 108.

9. Il′ia Kriger, "Nu, pogodili," *Novaia gazeta,* April 6, 2006, 2006.novayagazeta.ru/nomer/2006/25n/n25n-s28.shtml.

10. See the Soiuzmul′tfil′m website, www.souzmult.ru.

11. Tatyana Gershkovich, "Cartoon Studio Back in Action," *The Moscow Times,* October 23, 2007, www.themoscowtimes.com/article/cartoon-studio-back-in-action/193474.html; "Cheburashka luchshe Faberzhe," *Vedomosti* website, www.vedomosti.ru/newspaper/article.shtml?2007/04/11/123914 (accessed January 31, 2012).

12. Kriger, "Nu, pogodili."

13. Borodin's quotation is from the website animators established to tell their story of Skuliabin's "occupation": "Proshchai, 'Soiuzmul′tfil′m!'" Animator.ru website, animator.ru/articles/article.phtml?id=28 (accessed January 31, 2012).

14. Vera Shchirova, "My otbili studiiu u banditov," *Novye izvestiia,* January 20, 2006, www.newizv.ru/news/2006-01-20/38731/; and "Proshchai, 'Soiuzmul′tfil′m!'"

15. Shchirova, "My otbili studiiu u banditov."

16. "O fil′me," *Kniaz′ Vladimir* official website, www.knyazvladimir.ru/about.asp (accessed January 31, 2012).

17. Anna Smolchenko, "Disney Looks to Reanimate Russian Cartoon Sector," *St. Petersburg Times,* May 2, 2006, www.sptimes.ru/index.php?actionid=2&story_id=17500.

18. "Prezentatsiia animatsionnogo fil′ma 'Kniaz′ Vladimir′ sostoialas′ v Rossiiskom fonde kul′tury," *Pravoslavie,* April 10, 2000, www.pravoslavie.ru/news/04_10/11.htm.

19. "Istoricheskaia osnova fil′ma," *Kniaz′ Vladimir* official website, www.knyazvladimir.ru/history.asp#dates (accessed January 31, 2012).

20. Anthony D. Smith, *Myths and Memories of the Nation* (Oxford: Oxford University Press, 1999), 62–70.

21. See Simon Franklin and Jonathan Shepard, *The Emergence of Rus, 750–1200* (London: Longman, 1996), 151–80. Franklin and Shepard depict Vladimir as a frequently cruel leader whose greatness lies in his savvy political decisions and his ability to depict himself as a legitimate ruler (serious accomplishments in the tenth century). See also Francis Butler, *The Enlightener of Rus′: The Image of Vladimir Sviatoslavich across the Centuries* (Bloomington, Ind.: Slavica, 2000).

22. Jeremy Hicks, review of Iurii Kulakov, *Prince Vladimir, KinoKultura* 16 (April 2007), www.kinokultura.com/2007/16r-vladimir.shtml.

23. Ibid.

24. "Sergei Bezrukov o proekte 'Kniaz′ Vladimir,'" *Kniaz′ Vladimir* of-

ficial website, www.knyazvladimir.ru/actors_bezrukov_interview_2.asp (accessed January 31, 2012).

25. Ibid.

26. "Muzyka," *Kniaz′ Vladimir* official website, www.knyazvladimir.ru/music.asp (accessed January 31, 2012).

27. Andrei Riabovichev Interview: Character Designer and Animator website, andrei-riabovitchev-interview.blogspot.com (accessed January 31, 2012).

28. E-mail message from Andrei Riabovichev, July 31, 2008.

29. Ibid.

30. Ibid. See Rusart blog, rusartilikeit.blogspot.com (accessed January 31, 2012).

31. As John McCannon has pointed out, Roerich's Russian landscapes were largely invented ones. See his article "In Search of Primeval Russia: Stylistic Evolution in the Landscapes of Nicholas Roerich, 1897–1914," *Ecumene* 7, no. 3 (2000): 271–97.

32. E-mail message from Andrei Riabovichev, July 31, 2008.

33. Ibid.

34. "Andrei Dobrunov," interview on *Kniaz′ Vladimir* official website, www.knyazvladimir.ru/studio_dobrunov_interview.asp (accessed January 31, 2012).

35. Ibid.

36. Irina Kozel, "V ogorode buzina, a v Kieve diad′ka," *Kinokadr,* February 26, 2006, www.kinokadr.ru/articles/2006/02/26/knyazvladimir.shtml.

37. Dar′ia Pechorina, "Kniaz′ Vladimir—v poiskakh zolotoi serdiny," Nashfil′m website, www.nashfilm.ru/multfilms/123.html (accessed January 31, 2012).

38. Dar′ia Serebrianaia, "Prince Vladimir," *Time Out,* February 15, 2006, www.timeout.ru/text/film/12671.

39. K. Tarkhanova, "Kniaz′ vtorogo plana," Film.ru website, February 20, 2006, www.film.ru/article.asp?id=4340.

40. Ierei Vasilii Sekachev, "'Zapiat′e' kniazia Vladimira," *Neskuchnyi sad* 22, no. 4 (2006), www.nsad.ru/index.php?issue=22§ion=4&article=466.

41. For more on the revival of animated shorts, see Larisa Maliukova, "The State of the Art: Russian Animation Today," *KinoKultura* 23 (January 2009), www.kinokultura.com/2009/23-maliukova.shtml.

42. See "Rolli i el′f," *Kinopoisk* website, www.kinopoisk.ru/level/1/film/265731 (accessed January 31, 2012).

43. See Jeremy Morris, review of Valerii Ugarov, *Babka Ezhka and Co.; and* Nikolai Titov and Oktiabrina Potapova: *The New Adventures of Babka Ezhka, KinoKultura* 23 (January 2009), www.kinokultura.com/2009/23r-babka.shtml.

44. See Lora Mjolsness, review of Georgii Gitis, *The Adventures of Alenushka and Yerioma, KinoKultura* 24 (April 2009), www.kinokultura.com/2009/24r-alenushka.shtml.

45. See the *3 Bogatyrs* website, 3bogatirya.ru (accessed January 31, 2012); and "O mul′tfil′me," *Alesha Popovich i Tugarin Zmei* official website, www.aleshapopovich.ru/About (accessed January 31, 2012).

46. See Ulrike Hartmann, review of Il′ia Maksimov, *Dobrynia Nikitich and the Serpent Gorynych, KinoKultura* 14 (October 2006), www.kinokultura.com/2006/14r-dobrynia.shtml.

47. Vlad Strukov, review of Vladimir Toropchin, *Il′ia Muromets and the Nightingale-Robber.*

48. Ibid.

49. "Il′ia Muromets i Solovei Razboinik," *Kinopoisk* website, www.kinopoisk.ru/level/1/film/252022 (accessed January 31, 2012).

50. See David MacFadyen, review of Konstantin Bronzit, *Alesha Popovich and Tugarin the Serpent, KinoKultura* 9 (July 2005), www.kinokultura.com/reviews/R7-05alesha.html.

51. Ibid.

52. S. Georgieva, *Il′ia Muromets i Solovei-Razvoinik* (Moscow: Egmont, 2008).

53. "Alesha Popovich i Tugarin Zmei," *Kinopoisk* website, www.kinopoisk.ru/level/1/film/81041 (accessed January 31, 2012).

54. "Dobrynia Nikitich i Zmei Gorynych," *Kinopoisk* website, www.kinopoisk.ru/level/1/film/147818 (accessed January 31, 2012).

55. " Il′ia Muromets i Solovei Razboinik."

56. See Ken Gillam and Shannon Wooden, "Post-Princess Models of Gender: The New Man in Disney/Pixar," *Journal of Popular Film and Television* 36, no. 1 (Spring 2008): 2–8.

57. Larisa Maliukova, "Narisiut—budut zhit," *Itogi,* March 11, 2008, www.itogi.ru/iskus/2008/11/4813.html.

58. "O fil′me," *Kniaz′ Vladimir* official website, www.knyazvladimir.ru/about_hitruk_interview.asp (accessed January 31, 2012). For more on Khitruk's work, see "Khitruk, Fedor Savel′evich," Animator.ru website, www.animator.ru/db/?p=show_person&pid=100 (accessed January 31, 2012).

11. THE LOOK OF FANTASY

Some commentary in this chapter first appeared in my review of Nikolai Lebedev, *Wolfhound, KinoKultura* 18 (October 2007), www.kinokultura.com/2007/18r-volkodav.shtml. I thank Birgit Beumers for granting permission to reprint it.

1. Richard Matthews, *Fantasy: The Liberation of Imagination* (London: Routledge, 2002), 1.

2. Tzvetan Todorov, *The Fantastic: A Structural Approach to a Literary Genre* (Ithaca, N.Y.: Cornell University Press, 1975).

3. John Bushnell, "Ante-Kiev in Fantasy and Fable," *The Slavic and East European Journal* 45, no. 2 (Summer 2001), 275–88, quotation on 275.

4. See Semenova's biography on her website, www.semenova.ru/bio.php (accessed January 31, 2012).

5. Bushnell, "Ante-Kiev in Fantasy and Fable," 275.

6. Ibid., 278.

7. See Rosemary Jackson, *Fantasy: The Literature of Subversion* (London: Routledge, 2003).

8. Bushnell, 277–78.

9. See Evgenii Gartsevich's interesting review of Russian fantasy novels, in which he divides the genre into "heroic" and "historical." Although all the writers who create Russian fantasy use both elements, Semenova's output can be viewed as a hybrid—"heroic" because they reclaim tales about Ilia Muromets, but "historical" in her use of pre-Christian ethnography. He places Iurii Nikitin's books in the "heroic" category and Butiakov's in the "historical." See Gartsevich, "Russkie derevenskie skazki, slavianskoe fentezi," *Mir Fantastiki,* December 27, 2005, www.mirf.ru/Articles/print689.html.

10. Nancy Condee, *The Imperial Trace: Recent Russian Cinema* (Oxford: Oxford University Press, 2009), 78.

11. Iunna Chuprinina, "Snimat′ po-chelovecheski," *Itogi,* February 8, 2005, www.itogi.ru/archive/2005/6/56877.html.

12. Ibid.

13. Ibid.

14. See "Galirad," Mariia Semenova website, www.semenova.ru/geography/galirad.php (accessed January 31, 2012).

15. Ibid.

16. "Natura," *Volkodav* (*Wolfhound*) official website, www.volkodaw.ru/lite/prod_notes/text_setting.html# (accessed January 31, 2012).

17. "Volkodav v Galirade," *Volkodav* (*Wolfhound*) unofficial website, volkodav.gondor.ru/text_vvg.php (accessed January 31, 2012).

18. Iulia Sakharova, "Volkodav," *Salon* 3, no. 92 (2005), www.salon.ru/article.plx?id=4176.

19. "Natura." See also "Vliublennyi Volkodav," *Moskovskii komsomolets,*

October 14, 2004, www.mk.ru/blogs/idmk/2004/10/14/mk-daily/40665.

20. See C. S. Tashiro, *Pretty Pictures: Production Design and the History Film* (Austin: University of Texas Press, 1999).

21. Ibid., 7. For an insightful examination of early Soviet set design, see Emma Widdis's "*Faktura:* Depth and Surface in Early Soviet Set Design," *Studies in Russian and Soviet Cinema* 3, no. 1 (2009): 5–32.

22. Myles Balfe, "Incredible Geographies? Orientalism and Genre Fantasy," *Social and Cultural Geographies* 5, no. 1 (March 2004): 75–76.

23. Tat´iana Khoroshilova, "Krestnyi otets 'Volkodava,'" *Rossiiskaia gazeta,* December 22, 2006, 16.

24. Maria Semenova, *My—Slaviane!* (St. Petersburg: Azbuka, 1997), 187–235.

25. "Volkodav," *Kinopoisk* website, www.kinopoisk.ru/level/1/film/81371 (accessed January 31, 2012).

26. Ibid.

27. Valerii Kichin, "Volkodav neletuchii," *Rossiiskaia gazeta,* December 26, 2006, 9.

28. Irina Liubarskaia, "Dukhless," *Iskusstvo kino,* January 2007, 40–44.

29. Ibid., 44. See also Lidiia Maslova, "Na strazhe poriadka i poskonnosti," *Kommersant,* December 14, 2006, www.kommersant.ru/doc.html?DocID=730071&IssueID=30277. Maslova laments that "Russian fantasy" gets a pathetic bat with a torn wing while Hollywood gets Batman.

30. Mariia Kirillova, "Otechestvennoe 'fentezi'—zhanr vostrebovannyi?" *Zvukovoe kino,* www.zvkino.ru/index.php/.1313 . . . . 0.0.0.html (accessed June 10, 2008).

31. Diliara Tasbulatova, "S volkami zhit´!" *Itogi,* December 25, 2006, 70–71.

32. Larisa Reznikova, "Skazka XXI veka," *Moskovskii komsomolets,* December 23, 2006, 7.

33. "Syn serykh psov: Nachalis´ s´´emki 'Volkodava,'" *Mir fantastiki,* www.mirf.ru/Articles/art381.htm (accessed January 31, 2012).

34. Anton Karelin, "'Fantezi snimat´ slozhno,'" *Mir fantastiki,* www.mirf.ru/Articles/print580.html (accessed January 31, 2012).

35. Petr Tiulenev, "Eshche odin pervyi blin," *Mir fantastiki,* www.mirf.ru/Reviews/review1487.htm (accessed January 31, 2012).

36. Ibid.

37. Mikhail Popov, "Volkodav," *Mir fantastiki,* www.mirf.ru/Reviews/review1593.htm (accessed January 31, 2012).

38. Ibid.

39. "Vse o kartine," Mariia Semenova website, semenova.ru/forum/index.php?showtopic=9 (accessed January 31, 2012).

40. "Volkodav," Fantasy Forum website, www.forum.gondor.ru/index.php?s=9ba514249a5b3397a5c62992a37f779c&showtopic=9575 (accessed January 31, 2012).

41. "Russia—CIS Box Office," Box Office Mojo website, www.boxofficemojo.com/intl/cis/?yr=2007&wk=1&p=htm (accessed January 31, 2012).

42. Alena Solntseva, "Blokbaster po-russki," *Vremia novostei,* January 15, 2007, 9. See also her earlier article "Tot samyi blokbaster: 'Volkodav´ pul´nut do Novogo goda," *Vremia novostei,* December 14, 2007, www.vremya.ru/print/167725.html.

43. Viktoriia Kataeva, "Akter Aleksandr Bukharov: 'Liudi na ulitsakh ne uznaiut vo mne Volkodava,'" *Novoe izvestiia,* February 16, 2007, 18.

44. See reviews of all of them on *Mir fantastiki,* www.mirf.ru.

12. THE BUSINESS OF PATRIOTISM

Some commentary in this chapter first appeared in my review of Vladimir Khotinenko, *1612: A Chronicle of the Time of Troubles, KinoKultura* 22 (October 2008), www.kinokultura.com/2008/

22r-1612.shtml. I thank Birgit Beumers for granting permission to reprint it.

1. "About Renova Group," Renova website, www.renova.ru/en/about (accessed January 31, 2012).

2. Goran Mijuk, "Renova Nears Sulzer Takeover," *Wall Street Journal,* April 9, 2009, online.wsj.com/article/SB123922908994602719.html; "Russia's Renova to Develop Gold, Uranium Deposits in Africa," RIA Novosti website, February 21, 2007, en.rian.ru/business/20070221/61072743.html.

3. *Code of Business Conduct of Renova Group of Companies,* available in Russian on the company's website, www.renova.ru; and in English on the Immamura website, www.immamura.com/immamura/renova_new/osnova-eng/080926_Code_of_Business_Conduct_eng.pdf (accessed January 31, 2012).

4. "Philosophy of Progress," Renova website, www.renova.ru/osnova-eng/index.html (accessed January 12, 2009).

5. "Vekselberg, Viktor," Lenta website, www.lenta.ru/lib/14160156 (accessed January 31, 2012).

6. Nadira Hira and Eugenia Levenson, "Russia's Billionaire Boys Club," *Fortune,* September 15, 2008, 96.

7. The best example of Vekselberg's approach can be seen in the TNK-BP merger spat that erupted in 2008 over joint shareholdings. Vekselberg controls part of TNK-BP through his AAR consortium (Alfa Group, Access, and Renova).

8. "Beyond Siberia: Russia and Its Regions," *Economist,* September 3, 2005, 45–46.

9. Carol Vogel, "Fabergé Collection Bought by Russian for a Return Home," February 5, 2004, www.nytimes.com/2004/02/05/us/faberge-collection-bought-by-russian-for-a-return-home.html.

10. "Kompaniia 'Viskonti; privetstvuet vas!" Viskonti website, www.tcip.ru/index.php?main=welcome (accessed February 26, 2009). The company has since updated their pages.

11. For an account of the Harvard bells, see Elif Batuman, "The Bells," *New Yorker* 85, no. 11 (April 27, 2009): 22–29.

12. John Varoli, "Harvard Returns Bell, Aided by Billionaire Vekselberg," Returning of St. Daniel's Bells website, www.danilovbells.com/news/publications/13.09.2007_15_58_0.html (accessed January 31, 2012).

13. Melissa Caldwell, "The Taste of Nationalism: Food Politics in Postsocialist Moscow," *Ethnos* 67, no. 3 (2002): 295–319, quotation on 297.

14. "Razvorot," Ekho Moskvy website, November 14, 2008, www.echo.msk.ru/programs/razvorot/553088-echo.

15. See Chester Dunning's *Russia's First Civil War: The Time of Troubles and the Founding of the Romanov Dynasty* (University Park: Pennsylvania State University Press, 2001).

16. Richard Pipes, *Karamzin's Memoir on Ancient and Modern Russia: A Translation and Analysis* (Ann Arbor: University of Michigan Press, 2005).

17. Denis Babichenko, "Razvitoi patriotism," *Itogi,* September 18, 2006, www.itogi.ru/archive/2006/38/36053.html. See also Babichenko's follow-up about Putin and the uses of the Time of Troubles, "Riurik nashego vremeni," *Itogi,* March 11, 2007, www.itogi.ru/archive/2007/45/12594.html.

18. Vita Ramm, "Kinorezhisser Vladimir Khotinenko: 'Ia ne poluchal goszakza snimat' pro to, kak liakhov gnali iz Kremlia'," *Izvestiia,* October 30, 2007, www.izvestia.ru/person/article3109867/index.html.

19. "'Istoricheskoi pravdy net': Interv'iu s Vladimirom Khotinenko," *Time Out Moscow,* www.timeout.ru/journal/feature/1779 (accessed January 31, 2012).

20. Quoted in Alexander Osipovich, "Un-Hollywood: In Russia, Films Promote the State," *Wall Street Journal,* January 9, 2008, online.wsj.com/public/article_print/SB119983168230075881.html. The original is at www.timeout.ru/text/film/85925 (accessed January 31, 2012).

21. Anna Fedin, "Akter Andrei Panin: 'Ia vor chelovecheskikh kachestv,'" *Izvestiia,* November 21, 2007, www.izvestia.ru/culture/article3110528.

22. Anna Żebrowska, "Taśmy Kremla: Smuta krzepi," *Gazeta Wyborcza,* October 31, 2006, wyborcza.pl/1,75480,3707451.html.

23. Vita Ramm, "Kinorezhisser Vladimir Khotinenko."

24. Valerii Kichin, "Vremia, kogda gosudarstva ne stalo," *Rossiiskaia gazeta,* November 2, 2007, www.rg.ru/2007/11/02/kino-1612.html.

25. Ivan Kulikov of *Gazeta* compared the film to a Leonid Gaidai slapstick comedy, and Aleksandr Kariaev entitled his review "Russian Trash." See Kulikov, "Khroniki Shurika," *Gazeta,* October 30, 2007, gazeta.ru/culture/2007/10/30/a_2276060.shtml; Kariaev, "Russkii tresh," *Nezavisimaia gazeta,* October 26, 2007, www.ng.ru/culture/2007-10-26/12_trash.html.

26. "1612," *Kinopoisk* website, www.kinopoisk.ru/level/1/film/277327 (accessed January 31, 2012).

27. Quoted in John Follet, "Kremlin-Funded Blockbuster Casts Putin in a Tsar Role," *Sunday Herald,* November 3, 2007, www.sundayherald.com/international/shinternational/display.var.1807806.0.0.php.

28. All quotations from Shmelev, Zavorotniuk, and Bazhenov are from the film's publicity booklet.

29. Quoted in Osipovich, "Un-Hollywood."

30. "Komediia 'Kod apokalipsisa,'" Exler website, www.exler.ru/films/29-10-2007.htm (accessed January 31, 2012).

31. See the posts on "Kod apokalipsisa," Kino-ru website, www.kino.ru/film.php?id=3310 (accessed January 31, 2012); and "Kod apokalipsisa," *Kinopoisk* website, www.kinopoisk.ru/level/1/film/257772 (accessed January 31, 2012).

32. Quoted in Osipovich, "Un-Hollywood."

33. Timofei Borisov, "Kod premii FSB," *Rossiiskaia gazeta,* December 18, 2007, www.rg.ru/2007/12/18/fsb.html.

34. "Kollekstionnye izdanniia Fonda," FPPK website, www.patriotfilm.ru/rus/gallery (accessed January 31, 2012).

35. See Anthony Anemone, review of Vladimir Khotinenko, *The Priest, KinoKultura* 30 (2010), www.kinokultura.com/2010/30r-pop-aa.shtml; and Seth Graham, review of Vladimir Khotinenko, *The Priest, KinoKultura* 30 (2010), www.kinokultura.com/2010/30r-pop-sg.shtml (accessed January 31, 2012).

36. Natal′ia Markova, interview by Stephen M. Norris, July 10, 2008, Moscow. I thank Ms. Markova for her hospitality and for providing me with Foundation press releases and copies of all the Foundation's films.

37. "We Plan Geographic Expansion Across Russia in 2008," *Izvestiia* interview with Iurii Pripachkin reprinted on Renova Media website, www.akado-group.ru/eng/group/press/smi/document137.html (accessed January 12, 2009).

13. THE PRODUCTION OF THE PAST

Some commentary in this chapter first appeared in my article "In the Gloom: The Political Lives of Undead Bodies in Timur Bekmambetov's *Night Watch,*" *KinoKultura* 16 (April 2007), www.kinokultura.com/2007/16-norris.shtml. I thank Birgit Beumers for granting permission to reprint it.

1. Sergei Gurevich, interview by Stephen M. Norris, July 14, 2008, Studio Tri-te, Moscow.

2. Ellen Mickiewicz, *Changing Channels: Television and the Struggle for Power in Russia* (Durham, N.C.: Duke University Press, 1999), xi.

3. "Sobesednik: Konstantin Ernst," interview in *Seans* 29/30 (December 2006), seance.ru/n/29-30/portret-konstantin-ernst/sobesednik-konstantin-ernst. For its end of the year issue, the journal contained an entire section devoted to Ernst, his work as a producer, and his successful "formula."

4. Ernst's official biography, Pervyi kanal website, www.1tv.ru/person/133 (accessed February 15, 2012).

5. Serguei Oushakine, "'We're Nostalgic But We're Not Crazy': Retrofitting the Past in Russia," *Russian Review* 66 (July 2007): 451–82, quotation on 454.

6. Ibid., 454–56. Tat′iana Moskvina commented in her review about Nikita Mikhalkov's *Barber of Siberia* that Mikhalkov had become "our old songs about the most important." See Moskvina, "Ne govori."

7. "Sobesednik: Konstantin Ernst."

8. Ibid.

9. "Imperiia pod udarom," *Kinopoisk* website, www.kinopoisk.ru/level/1/film/178563 (accessed January 31, 2012).

10. "Sobesednik: Konstantin Ernst." Ernst thanks Hollywood for jumpstarting domestic cinema, but also chastises what he sees as Hollywood's attempt to "conquer" Russia and "convert us."

11. The story of Dorenko's firing and the quotations above come from Andrei Zolotov, Jr., and Simon Saradzhyan, "Dorenko Program has Plug Pulled," *St. Petersburg Times,* September 12, 2000, www.sptimes.ru/index.php?action_id=2&story_id=12466.

12. My thanks go to Dave Schimmelpenninck for sending me a DVD with all the Bank Imperial commercials.

13. David MacFadyen, review of Timur Bekmambetov, *Night Watch, KinoKultura* 6 (October 2004), www.kinokultura.com/reviews/R104dozor.html.

14. Ibid.

15. Quoted in "Dozor natsii: Rasovyi smysl 'nochnogo dozora,'" *Den′,* July 14, 2004), www.dayudm.ru/lenta.php?id=8521.

16. "Zhazhda novoi kroi," *Iskusstvo kino,* December 2004, kinoart.ru/2004/n12-article2.html.

17. Here and below, the citations refer to responses on "Nochnoi dozor," Kino-ru website, www.kino.ru/forum.php?id=2008&offset=1020 (accessed January 31, 2012).

18. Mikhail Zolotonov, "Novye prikliucheniia neulovimykh," *Iskusstvo kino,* November 2004, kinoart.ru/2004/n11-article7.html.

19. "Dozor natsii."

20. Vadim Nestorov, "Upyri pogubiat russkikh," *Gazeta,* July 22, 2004, www.gazeta.ru/print/2004/07/22/oa_127866.shtml.

21. Boris Polozhii, "Dobro i zlo neotlichimy?" *Iskusstvo kino,* December 2004, kinoart.ru/2004/n12-article3.html.

22. Vladimir Kozlov, "Deep Thoughts on 'Dozor,'" *The Moscow Times,* December 15, 2006, context.themoscowtimes.com/stories/2006/12/15/101.html.

23. Boris Kupriianov and M. Surkov, eds., *Dozor kak simptom: Kul′turologicheskii sbornik* (Moscow: Falanster, 2006), 4.

24. Irina Antanasievich, "Golod," in ibid., 50–59, quotation on 58.

25. Ibid.

26. Konstantin Krylov, "Razbiraia sumrak," in Kupriianov and Surkov, eds., *Dozor kak symptom,* 119–49, quotation on 147.

27. Elena Petrovskaia, "Slezhka za vremenem," in Kupriianov and Surkov, eds., *Dozor kak symptom,* 256–76, quotation on 268.

28. Aleksandr Tarasov, "Anti-'matritsa': Vyberi siniuiu tabletku," in Kupriianov and Surkov, eds., *Dozor kak symptom,* 324–35, quotation on 333. Emphasis in original.

29. Ibid., 335.

30. "Zhazhda."

31. Thomas H. Campbell, "Five Theses About *Day Watch,*" *KinoKultura* 12 (April 2006), www.kinokultura.com/2006/12-campbell.shtml.

32. David MacFadyen, *The Sad Comedy of El´dar Riazanov: An Introduction to Russia's Most Popular Filmmaker* (Montreal: McGill-Queen's University Press, 2003), 5–6.

33. Ibid., 6.

34. Quoted in MacFadyen, *The Sad Comedy of El´dar Riazanov,* 6. The original is B. Minaev, "Kazhdyi raz pod Novyi god my otpravliaemsia v baniu . . . ," *Ogonek* 1 (January 1996): 66–67.

35. Quoted in MacFadyen, *The Sad Comedy of El´dar Riazanov,* 218. The original is "Raskhozhaia fraza 'Krasota spaset mir,'" *Knizhnoe obozrenie* 35 (August 29, 1995): 12.

36. Arlene Forman, review of Timur Bekmambetov, *The Irony of Fate: The Continuation, KinoKultura* 22 (October 2008), www.kinokultura.com/2008/22r-irony.shtml.

37. Elena Iampol´skaia, "'Ironiia sud´by: Prodolzhenie': S novym brendom," *Izvestiia,* December 24, 2007, www.izvestia.ru/culture/article3111577.

38. Iurii Bogomolov, "Ironiia sud´by Konstantina Ernsta," *Novaia gazeta,* January 28, 2008, www.novayagazeta.ru/data/2008/06/22.html.

39. Ibid.

40. Ibid.

41. For an insightful overview of the New Year film as genre, see Alyssa DeBlasio, "The New Year's Film as a Genre of Post-War Russian Cinema," *Studies in Russian and Soviet Cinema* 2, no. 1 (2008): 43–61.

42. Iampol´skaia, "Ironiia sud´by: Prodolzhenie."

43. The reference is to Bezrukov's role as the gangster Sasha Bely in the extraordinarily popular series *Brigada.*

44. Mikhail is the son of Oleg Efremov, the founder of the Contemporary Theater in Moscow.

45. "Ironiia sud´by Prodolxhenie," *Kinopoisk* website, www.kinopoisk.ru/level/1/film/276261 (accessed January 31, 2012).

46. Ibid.

47. "Dozor kak simptom," *Seans* 29/30 (December 2006), seance.ru/n/29-30/portret-konstantin-ernst/dozor-kak-simptom.

48. Verzhbitskii also played Aleksandr Kerenskii, another vanquished enemy, in *Admiral.*

49. "Sobesednik: Konstantin Ernst."

50. Svetlana Boym, *The Future of Nostalgia* (New York: Basic Books, 2001), xiii–xv.

51. Ibid., 41.

52. Ibid., 67–69.

53. Ibid., 285–308.

54. Ibid., 58.

55. Ibid., 65.

56. See Sarah Mendelson and Theodore Gerber, "Soviet Nostalgia: An Impediment to Russian Democratization," *The Washington Quarterly* 29, no. 1 (Winter 2005): 83–96; and Anson Rabinbach, "Soviet Kitsch," *Dissent* 51, no. 3 (Summer 2004): 26–29.

57. See Nabi Abdullaev, "Nostalgia Remains Strong for Brezhnev Era," *The Moscow Times,* December 15, 2006, www.themoscowtimes.com/news/article/nostalgia-remains-strong-for-brezhnev-era/200205.html.

58. Chernykh also published a novel based on his script that was also funded by Pervyi kanal and RedFish Books with the slogan "Watch the film and read the book." Chernykh, *Brezhnev:*

Sumerki imperii (St. Petersburg: RedFish, 2005).

59. The revision is not without parallel in academe: Edwin Bacon and Mark Sandle co-edited a volume that reconsiders Brezhnev and his era from a number of angles in an effort to add "many nuances which need drawing out" to the simplistic shorthand of "stagnation." See Bacon and Sandle, eds., *Brezhnev Reconsidered* (Basingstoke, UK: Palgrave Macmillan, 2002).

60. Stanislav Odoevtsev, "Ne v brov′, a v glaz," *Itogi,* April 5, 2005, www.itogi.ru/archive/2005/14/61540.html.

61. "Brezhnev," *Kinopoisk* website, www.kinopoisk.ru/level/1/film/250777 (accessed January 31, 2012).

62. See Lilya Kaganovsky, "The Cultural Logic of Late Socialism," *Studies in Russian and Soviet Cinema* 3, no. 2 (2009): 185–99.

63. Iurii Bogomolov, "Ukhodiat, ukhodiat . . . ," *Rossiskaia gazeta,* April 5, 2005, www.rg.ru/2005/04/05/a59425.html.

64. Ibid. See also his article "Ia sebia pod Brezhnevym chishchu," *Rossiskaia gazeta,* December 19, 2006, www.rg.ru/2006/12/19/brezhnev-stoletie.html.

65. Peter Fritzsche, *Stranded in the Present: Modern Time and the Melancholy of History* (Cambridge, Mass.: Harvard University Press, 2004), 5.

66. Ibid., 216.

67. Oushakine, "We're Nostalgic But We're Not Crazy," 455.

68. Quoted in ibid., 451.

69. See Maya Nadkarni and Olga Shevchenko, "The Politics of Nostalgia: A Case for Comparative Analysis of Post-socialist Practices, " *Ab Imperio* 2 (2004): 487–519.

70. Dmitrii Bykov, "Biolog," *Seans* 29/30 (December 2006), seance.ru/n/29-30/portret-konstantin-ernst. Aleksei Gusev also states that Ernst "became accustomed to performing experiments on living things" as a biologist and "now separates Pavlovian dogs on a national, mass scale." See Gusev, "Matador," in *Seans* 29/30 (December 2006), seance.ru/n/29-30/portret-konstantin-ernst/matador.

71. Aleksandr Sekatskii, "Zalozhnik," *Seans* 29/30 (December 2006), seance.ru/n/29-30/portret-konstantin-ernst/zalozhnik.

72. "Sobesednik: Konstantin Ernst."

73. "Sud′ba Ernsta," *Seans* 29/30 (December 2006), seance.ru/category/n/29-30/portret-konstantin-ernst/sudba-ernsta (accessed January 31, 2012).

74. "Formula Ernsta," *Seans* 29/30 (December 2006), seance.ru/category/n/29-30/portret-konstantin-ernst/formula-ernsta (accessed January 31, 2012).

14. CONCLUSION

1. See the Soiuz website, www.co.soyuz.ru/?left (accessed January 31, 2012).

2. "O kompanii," Nashe Kino website, www.nkino.ru/about.html (accessed January 31, 2012).

3. All quotations from the roundtable participants are from "V poiskakh smysla: novyi patriotism," *Iskusstvo kino,* January 2006, kinoart.ru/2006/n1-article2.html.

4. See, for example, Evgenii Maizel′, "Zhertva kachestva, vyigrysh tempa," *Seans* 23/24 (September 2005), seance.ru/n/23-24/filmyi-proekt-russkiy-blokbaster/zhertva-kachestva-vyiigryish-tempa.

5. Denis Dragunskii expanded on his *Iskusstvo kino* remarks in his article, "Patriotizm," *Chastnyi Korrespondent,* March 21, 2011, www.chaskor.ru/article/patriotizm_22679.

6. For more on economic nationalism, see Melissa Caldwell, "The Taste of Nationalism: Food Politics in Postsocialist Moscow," *Ethnos* 67, no. 3 (2002): 295–319.

7. These details are all from Ol′ga Bychkova and Matvei Ganapol′skii interview with Bekmambetov that aired on June 27, 2008, "Prem′era fil′ma 'Osobo opasen,'" Echo Moscow website, echo.msk.ru/programs/razvorot/523399-echo.phtml (accessed January 31, 2012).

8. Vita Ramm, "Bol′shoe kino dlia ofisnogo planktona," *Izvestiia*, July 1, 2008, www.izvestia.ru/culture/article3117978/index.html.

9. Ibid.

10. "Osobo opasen," *Kinopoisk* website, www.kinopoisk.ru/level/1/film/259876 (accessed January 31, 2012).

11. The figures are from "Russia—CIS Box Office Index," Box Office Mojo website, boxofficemojo.com/intl/cis/?yr=2008¤cy=us&p=.htm (accessed January 31, 2012).

12. Bychkova and Ganapol′skii, "Prem′era fil′ma 'Osobo opasen.'"

13. Ibid.

14. The quotations come from Kurennoi's interview with *Ogonek* when his book appeared (a sign of the sort of attention his thesis received), Andrei Arkhangel′skii, "'Zriteliu nuzhno ob′′iasniat,' za chto umiraiut geroi," *Ogonek* 10 (March 2011), www.kommersant.ru/Doc/1597233. The title of the interview comes from one of Kuprennoi's answers that American films have heroes die for a reason but Russian films do not. His book is titled *Filosofiia fil′ma: uprazhneniia v analize* (Moscow: Novoe literaturnoe obozrenie, 2009). In it, Kuprennoi argues that blockbusters can be viewed as a "system of knowledge" but that Russian blockbusters have yet to deliver a coherent knowledge system. His chapters on war cinema and the *Dozor* films fill in his argument that the new Russian cinema lacks some unifying idea.

15. Vasilii Molotov, "Kinorezhisser Timur Bekmambetov: 'Spetseffekty—vsego lish′ instrument v moikh rukakh,'" *Izvestiia*, February 26, 2008, www.izvestia.ru/news/333674.

16. Kseniia Leont′eva, "'Tsifra' presleduet artkhaus," *Iskusstvo kino*, June 2010, kinoart.ru/2010/n6-article14.html.

17. Dar′ia Goriacheva, "Osobennosti national′nogo blokbastera," *Gazeta*, September 23, 2010, www.gazeta.ru/culture/2010/09/23/a_3422191.shtml.

18. Mansur Mirovalev, "Soviet Agitprop? No, Russian Films," *Los Angeles Times*, July 1, 2008, articles.latimes.com/2008/jul/01/entertainment/et-russiafilm1.

19. Ibid.

20. Vasilii Gerosin, "Patriotic Movies in a Dead End," *Novaia gazeta*, August 12, 2011, en.novayagazeta.ru/data/2011/027/03.html.

21. Ibid.

22. Here I am influenced by Roger Chartier's *The Cultural Origins of the French Revolution* (Durham, N.C.: Duke University Press, 1991).

23. The scholarship on Putin and Putinism is already voluminous. Richard Sakwa's account of Putin, to my mind the best political approach to the popular president, stresses his personality, the dilemmas facing Russia in 1999, the practical nature of Putin's solutions, his charisma, and the way that Putin's life "reflected the lives of millions of his fellow citizens." Sakwa, *Putin: Russia's Choice* (London: Routledge, 2004). Helena Goscilo's wonderful "The Ultimate Celebrity: VVP as VIP *objet d'art*," in Goscilo and Vlad Strukov, eds., *Celebrity and Glamour in Contemporary Russia: Shocking Chic* (New York: Routledge, 2011), 29–55, examines the Putin phenomenon as part of a growing celebrity culture that has emerged in contemporary Russia. The two books by Andrei Kolesnikov (a correspondent for *Kommersant*) also tackle the Putin phenomenon as a reflection of societal desires: in them, Kolesnikov covers the banalities of modern leadership but also the

way Putin's charisma affected ordinary Russians. See *Ia Putina videl!* (I saw Putin! [Moscow: Eksmo, 2004]) and *Menia Putin videl!* (Putin saw me! [Moscow: Eksmo, 2004]). For more critical approaches on Putin's personality and his KGB past, see Anna Politkovskaya, *Putin's Russia: Life in a Failing Democracy* (New York: Henry Holt, 2007); Yuri Felshtinsky and Vladimir Pribylovsky, *The Corporation: Russia and the KGB in the Age of President Putin* (New York: Encounter Books, 2009); and Andrei Piontkovsky, *Another Look into Putin's Soul* (Washington, D.C.: Hudson Institute, 2006). Steve Levine calls Putin "an archetypal man from nowhere" who reflects Russian predispositions to authoritarianism in *Putin's Labyrinth: Spies, Murder, and the Dark Heart of the New Russia* (New York: Random House, 2009). Andrew Jack, another journalist working in Russia, describes Putin as a "man from nowhere" who is building "liberal authoritarianism" in *Inside Putin's Russia* (New York: Oxford University Press, 2004). Gordon Hahn provided Putinologists with two frameworks for understanding his Russia—"managed democracy" and "stealth authoritarianism"—in "Managed Democracy? Building Stealth Authoritarianism in St. Petersburg," *Demokratizatsiya* 12, no. 1 (Winter 2004): 195–231. Vladimir Shlapentokh has written scores about Putin's Russia, which he characterizes as a "feudal society" in *Contemporary Russia as a Feudal Society: A New Perspective on the Post-Soviet Era* (Basingstoke, UK: Palgrave, 2007). For two good accounts that examine patriotism and nationalism in the zero years as state projects, see Marlène Laruelle, *In the Name of the Nation: Nationalism and Politics in Contemporary Russia* (New York: Palgrave Macmillan, 2009); and Oxana Shevel, "Russian Nation-building from Yel′tsin to Putin: Ethnic, Civic, or Purposefully Ambiguous?" *Europe-Asia Studies* 63, no. 2 (March 2011): 179–202. All of these studies have much to recommend them—they cover the politics of the new Russia ably and offer important details about the nature of post-Soviet politics. At the same time, the tendency in all of them (and in virtually all of the Putinology literature) is to view the state in general and Putin in particular as the only important actor in Russian society, politics, and culture. In the case of blockbuster history and the patriotic culture it helped to create, a culture Putin and Medvedev certainly have made use of, the historical actors include producers, directors, writers, composers, critics, and audiences in addition to politicians and presidents.

24. Quoted in Robert Coalson, "Does Putin, Like Lenin, See Film as 'Most Important of the Arts'?" *Radio Free Europe,* December 20, 2008, www.rferl.org/content/Putin_To_Head_Film_Council/1361814.html.

25. Both quoted in Michael Kimmelman, "Putin's Last Realm to Conquer: Russian Culture," *New York Times,* December 1, 2007, www.nytimes.com/2007/12/01/arts/01abroad.html.

26. Leon Aron, "The Problematic Pages," *The New Republic,* September 24, 2008, 35–41. See also the forum in *Kritika* 10, no. 4 (2009): 35–41 about the new Filippov history book and its meanings.

27. For the historic stiliagi, see Mark Edele, "Strange Young Men in Stalin's Moscow: The Birth and Life of the Stiliagi, 1945–1953," *Jahrbücher für Geschichte Osteuropas* 50, no. 1 (2003): 37–61.

28. Quoted in Volha Isakava, review of Valerii Todorovskii, *Hipsters, KinoKultura* 25 (2009), www.kinokultura.com/2009/25r-stiliagi.shtml. For more on Putin-era youth groups as a "conservative vanguard" in the new Russia, see Ben Garza, "Conservative Vanguard? The Politics of New Russia's Youth," *Current History* (October 2006): 327–33.

29. Ian Levchenko, "Valerii Todorovskii: Nyzhna smelost′ nadet′ zelenye noski!" *Sobesednik,* December 23, 2008, www.sobesednik.ru/archive/sb/49_2008/stilyagi_49_2008/#.

30. Quoted in Mumin Shakirov, "Dissenting Blockbusters," *OpenDemocracy* website, www.opendemocracy.net/article/email/dissenting-blockbusters (accessed January 31, 2012).

31. Elena Iampol′skaia, "Ty za stiliag ili za komsomol′tsev?" *Izvestiia,* January 14, 2009, izvestia.ru/culture/article3124317/index.html.

32. Both reactions are posted online in "Stiliagi," *Kinopoisk* website, www.kinopoisk.ru/level/1/film/395690 (accessed January 31, 2012).

33. Irina Liubarskaia, "Pereutomlenie," *Itogi* 18 (May 3, 2010): 56.

34. Ibid.

35. Quoted in Luke Harding, "Nikita Mikhalkov's *Burnt by the Sun* 2 Becomes Russia's Most Expensive Flop," *The Guardian,* April 27, 2010, www.guardian.co.uk/world/2010/apr/27/nikita-mikhalkov-russia-war-film.

36. "Spasti komdiva Kotova!" *Argumenty i fakty,* May 5, 2010, 31.

37. Iurii Gladil′shchikov, "Utomlenie 'Utomlennymi solntsem,'" *Forbes.ru,* April 22, 2010, www.forbes.ru/blogpost/48738-utomlenie-utomlennymi-solntsem.

38. Jennifer Patico, *Consumption and Social Change in a Post-Soviet Middle Class* (Stanford, Calif.: Stanford University Press, 2008), 216.

39. Holli Semetko and Natalya Krasnoboka, "The Political Role of the Internet in Societies in Transition," *Party Politics* 9, no. 1 (January 2003): 77–104.

40. Birgit Beumers, Stephen Hutchings, and Natalia Rulyova, eds., *The Post-Soviet Russian Media: Conflicting Signals* (London: Routledge, 2009), 10. See also the articles by Igor Zassoursky and Vlad Strukov in this collection. For an opposing view, see Anikó Imre, *Identity Games: Globalization and the Transformation of Media Culture in the New Europe* (Cambridge, Mass.: MIT Press, 2009). Imre argues that the "fast colonization of virtually virginal postcommunist media and information technology markets by transnational corporations should make one very cautious about the democratizing potential of the Internet and other interactive digital technologies," and sees the infusion of European and American technologies in postcommunist societies as a "shift to spectacle culture" that introduces new "technologies of surveillance and control" in the form of consumerism and entertainment (3). To interpret this new "totalitarian" culture, Imre appropriates Western intellectual critiques (mostly French theorists) and uses them to critique postcommunist cultures. The irony is apparently lost on Imre: Western consumerism and technology brings a new totalitarianism; Western theory apparently brings liberation.

41. See Geoffrey Hosking, *Russia and the Russians: A History* (Cambridge, Mass.: Harvard University Press, 2003), 385, 400; and Samuel Kassow, "Russia's Unrealized Civil Society," in Edith Clowes, Samuel Kassow, and James West, eds., *Between Tsar and People: Educated Society and the Quest for Public Identity in Late Imperial Russia* (Princeton, N.J.: Princeton University Press, 1991), 367–72.

42. See Samuel Greene, "Shifting Media and the Failure of Political Communication in Russia," in Beumers et al., eds., *The Post Soviet Russian Media,* 56–70, quotation on 56.

43. Joseph Bradley, "Subjects into Citizens: Societies, Civil Society, and Autocracy in Tsarist Russia," *American Historical Review* 107, no. 4 (October 2002): 1094–1123. Bradley expanded his analysis in his recent monograph, *Voluntary Associations in Tsarist Russia: Science, Patriotism,*

and Civil Society (Cambridge, Mass.: Harvard University Press, 2009). For similar arguments, see also Murray Frame, *School for Citizens: Theatre and Civil Society in Imperial Russia* (New Haven, Conn.: Yale University Press, 2006); and Aaron J. Cohen, *Imagining the Unimaginable: World War, Modern Art, and the Politics of Public Culture in Russia, 1914–1917* (Lincoln: University of Nebraska Press, 2008).

44. Henry Jenkins, "Nine Propositions towards a Cultural Theory of YouTube," Henry Jenkins website, www.henryjenkins.org/2007/05/9_propositions_towards_a_cultu.html (accessed January 31, 2012).

45. See Andrei Shliefer and Daniel Treisman, "A Normal Country," *Foreign Affairs* 83, no. 2 (March/April 2004): 20–38; and Steven Rosefielde, "Russia: An Abnormal Country," *The European Journal of Comparative Economics* 2, no. 1 (June 2005): 3–16.

46. Anthony D. Smith, *Myths and Memories of the Nation* (Oxford: Oxford University Press, 1999), 180.

47. Mette Hjort and Scott Mackenzie, introduction, *Cinema and Nation* (London: Routledge, 2000), 1–18, quotation on 4.

48. It is also a menu, as Richard Stites has argued, that has always been varied. See his "Russian Symbols—Nation, People, Ideas," in Michael E. Geisler, ed., *National Symbols, Fractured Identities: Contesting the National Narrative* (Middlebury, Vt.: Middlebury College Press, 2005): 101–17. In his introduction to this edited volume, Michael Geisler notes that "the sheer wealth and diversity of Russian national symbols" is a "cue to remind us of the importance of considering the entire register of national symbols as a system of signification working in concert to maintain, stabilize, and reinforce the dominating constructions of collective memory" (xxxiii). The menu offered by contemporary Russian cinema does the same.

49. I adopt this term from Alexander Etkind, "Post-Soviet Hauntology: Cultural Memory of the Soviet Terror," *Constellations* 16, no. 1 (2009): 190.

50. Jay Winter, "Historical Remembrance in the Twenty-First Century," *Annals* AAPS 617 (May 2008): 6–13.

51. Here I am inspired by Alon Confino's concept of nationhood as a "culture of remembrance," one where a "product of collective negotiation and exchange between the many memories that exist in the nation" results. Nationhood and memory, Confino writes, "appear as modern sensibilities that give meaning to values and beliefs such as collective, selfhood, territoriality, and the past." Confino, *Germany as a Culture of Remembrance: Promises and Limits of Writing History* (Chapel Hill: University of North Carolina Press, 2006), 18.

INDEX

Page numbers in italics refer to illustrations.

STEPHEN M. NORRIS is Associate Professor of History at Miami University of Ohio. He is author of *A War of Images: Russian Popular Prints, Wartime Culture, and National Identity, 1812–1945;* and editor (with Helena Goscilo) of *Preserving Petersburg: History, Memory, Nostalgia* (IUP, 2008), (with Zara Torlone) of *Insiders and Outsiders in Russian Cinema* (IUP, 2008), and (with Willard Sunderland) of *Russia's People of Empire: Life Stories from Eurasia, 1500 to the Present* (IUP, 2012).